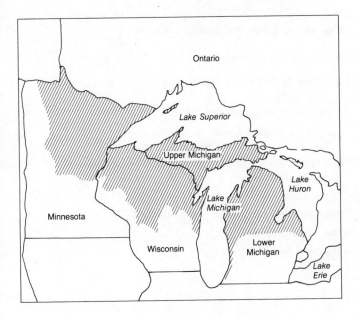

The Sierra Club Naturalist's Guides

The Deserts of the Southwest

The Middle Atlantic Coast:
  Cape Hatteras to Cape Cod

The North Atlantic Coast:
  Cape Cod to Newfoundland

The North Woods of Michigan, Wisconsin, Minnesota and
Southern Ontario

The Pacific Northwest

The Piedmont of Eastern North America

The Sierra Nevada

Southern New England

A Sierra Club Naturalist's Guide to

THE NORTH WOODS
of Michigan, Wisconsin, Minnesota
and Southern Ontario

by Glenda Daniel
and Jerry Sullivan

BOTANICAL DRAWINGS BY
CAROL LERNER

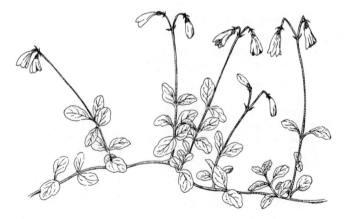

SIERRA CLUB BOOKS   *San Francisco*

For Eleanor

The Sierra Club, founded in 1892 by John Muir, has devoted
itself to the study and protection of the earth's scenic and
ecological resources—mountains, wetlands, woodlands, wild
shores and rivers, deserts and plains. The publishing program of
the Sierra Club offers books to the public as a nonprofit
educational service in the hope that they may enlarge the
public's understanding of the Club's basic concerns. The point of
view expressed in each book, however, does not necessarily
represent that of the Club. The Sierra Club has some fifty
chapters coast to coast, in Canada, Hawaii, and Alaska. For
information about how you may participate in its programs to
preserve wilderness and the quality of life, please address
inquiries to Sierra Club, 730 Polk Street, San Francisco, CA
94109.

Library of Congress Cataloging in Publication Data

Daniel, Glenda.
  A Sierra Club naturalist's guide to the North
Woods of Michigan, Wisconsin, and Minnesota.

  Bibliography: p.
  Includes index.
  1. Natural history—Michigan.   2. Natural history—
Wisconsin.   3. Natural history—Minnesota.
I. Sullivan, Jerry, 1938–   joint author.   II. Lerner,
Carol.   III. Sierra Club.   IV. Title.   V. Title: North
Woods.
QH105.M5D36   574.977   80-28742
ISBN 0-87156-248-0
ISBN 0-87156-277-4 (pbk.)

Book design by Ron Newcomer

Printed in the United States of America

10   9   8   7   6   5

TABLE OF CONTENTS

PART II / The Producers, 123

Introduction to the Plant Life of the North Woods, 123

Chapter 7—Plant Communities, 125

Characteristics of Communities, 126
Classifying Communities, 134

Chapter 8—A Guide to Plant Identification, 136

Plant Characteristics, 137
Equipment for Botanizing, 150

Chapter 9—Common Trees of the North Woods, 151

Key to the Common Trees, 151
Plant Descriptions, 154

Chapter 10—Ubiquitous Plants of the North Woods, 176

Key to the Ubiquitous Plants, 177
Plant Descriptions, 178

Chapter 11—The Pine Forest, 192

Pine Forest Communities, 193
Plants of the Pine Forest, 199
Succession in the Pine Forest, 200
A Human History of the Pine Woods, 204
Key to Common Plants of the Pine Forest, 210
Plant Descriptions, 212

Chapter 12—The Mixed-Hardwood Forest, 222

Characteristics of a Mesic Forest, 223
Trees of the Mixed-Hardwood Forest, 226
Typical Shrubs, 231
History of the Hardwoods, 231
Key to Common Plants of the Mixed-Hardwood Forest, 233
Plant Descriptions, 234

Chapter 13—The Boreal Forest, 241

Trees of the Boreal Forest, 243
Plants of the Understory, 245
Succession in the Boreal Forest, 246
Key to Common Plants of the Boreal Forest, 249
Plant Descriptions, 249

Chapter 14—The Second-Growth Forest, 255

Quaking Aspen, a Life History, 255

ACKNOWLEDGMENTS

SPECIAL THANKS are due to Professors E. Calvin Alexander and Alan Friedman of the University of Minnesota Department of Geology and to Dr. Mark Reshkin of Indiana University Northwest for reviewing chapters and suggesting new material in Part I; to Dr. Keith White of the University of Wisconsin, Green Bay, for performing a similar service in Part II; to Floyd Swink of the Morton Arboretum in Lisle, Illinois, for checking the accuracy of form and details in our taxonomic keys; to Dr. Wendel J. Johnson, associate professor of biology at the University of Wisconsin/Marinette, for reviewing Part III.

We would also like to express our appreciation to the University of Wisconsin, Superior, which made its resources available to us while we lived in the area. Special thanks go to the staffs of the library and the day-care center.

Diana Landau, project editor at Sierra Club Books, deserves special mention for her patience through the two years this book was in preparation.

INTRODUCTION

THE REGION Midwesterners call the North Woods is defined, as the name implies, by its vegetation, and especially by its forests. Plant geographers refer more precisely to a Great Lakes Forest and classify it as the western end of a belt of transition forest that extends from Minnesota east through southern Canada and northern New England to the Atlantic. A narrow tongue of this forest extends south on the high cool ridges of the Appalachians as far as Georgia.

South of this transition zone, the natural vegetation of most of the eastern United States is a forest of broad-leaved trees whose leaves are shed each autumn. To the north is the boreal forest dominated by evergreen conifers. In the transition zone, beech and sugar maple from the southern forest grow side by side with spruce and balsam fir from the north. The northern and southern species combine with trees such as red pine, white pine, and hemlock—whose ranges are centered in the transition belt—to create forest communities unlike those found anywhere else. Within the broad band of transition forest, small differences in composition justify separating the North Woods of the Lake States from those of New England.

The boundaries between different vegetation provinces such as the North Woods and the eastern deciduous forest to the south are called *ecotones.* In general, ecotones cannot be drawn as precisely as the borders that humans create, and this is especially true where no physiographic features such as mountain ranges or shorelines provide an abrupt demarcation.

Ecotones are usually more like zones than borders. If you were to start north from Ohio or Indiana and travel through Lower Michigan to the Straits of Mackinac at the northern tip of the peninsula, you would not make a sudden leap into the North Woods when you got to the line that represents the southern border on our map of the region, but you would notice a gradual change in the vegetation as you went. Trees and shrubs such as the hickories, sycamore, hackberry, flowering dogwood, and sassafras that were a prominent part of the woods farther south would become

1

1. The North Woods. Borders shown within states are county
lines for ease in referencing road maps. Many of the species discussed in this book are found north of the U. S.–Canada border;
boreal forest extends north as far as the tree line; hardwood forest
types are found mainly in eastern Canada.

steadily less common and more confined in their distribution. Instead of growing almost everywhere, they would
flourish only in sheltered areas such as south-facing slopes
and stream bottoms. Conifers such as hemlock and white
pine would become more common in forests dominated by
beech and sugar maple, and jack pine would begin to replace oak on sandy soils.

Similar kinds of changes occur in northeastern Minnesota where the Great Lakes forest gives way to boreal
forest.

In spite of their fuzziness, ecotones are quite real. In his
book, *Vegetation of Wisconsin*, John Curtis plotted the
ranges of a large number of plants. As the accompanying
map shows, a substantial number of species reach the limits
of their ranges in what Curtis called the *tension zone*, the
ecotone between northern and southern forests.

INTRODUCTION

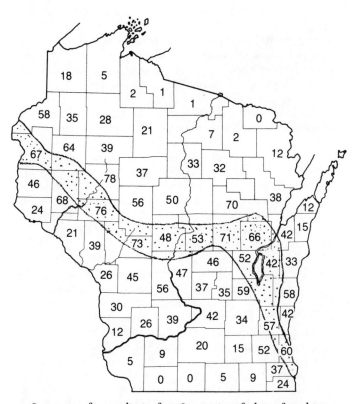

2. Summary of range limits for 182 species of plants found in Wisconsin. The figures in each county indicate the number of species attaining a range boundary there. The shaded band is the tension zone. Its exact location was determined from the densest concentration of individual range lines. (Reproduced by permission of Wisconsin University Press from *Vegetation of Wisconsin*, John T. Curtis, © 1959, 1971.)

The North Woods Landscape

The bedrock under the western end of our Great Lakes forest is some of the most ancient in North America, yet the landscape throughout the North Woods is quite young, the

Introduction

product of glaciers that receded less than 10,000 years ago. The glaciers created the lakes, more than 30,000 of them, ranging from Lake Superior, whose 21,000 square miles (54,000 square kilometers) of surface area make it the largest body of fresh water in the world, down to tiny ponds that dry up every August. The lakes are the most visible sign of an immature drainage system that in fact leaves much of the land undrained. Millions of acres of marshes, swamps, bogs, and other wetlands are another consequence of the glacier's rearrangement of the landscape.

In the eastern half of the North Woods—in Lower Michigan, the eastern Upper Peninsula, and eastern Wisconsin—where the bedrock of shale, sandstone, and limestone is soft and relatively easy to erode, glacial deposits that are sometimes hundreds of feet thick blanket the earth. Bedrock outcrops are scarce here, and the hills show the rounded, sinuous shapes that betray their origin in debris left by the ice.

In the western half of the region, the ice moved over the very old and very tough rock of the Canadian Shield, the ancient heart of North America. Bedrock is exposed at the surface much more often here, particularly in northeastern Minnesota and along the south shore of Lake Superior. Steep escarpments poke through the softer outlines of the glacial deposits. Indeed, in northeastern Minnesota, the main effect of the ice was to scour the land, scraping off surface deposits and softer rocks, leaving the angular ancient skeleton of the land exposed. Most of the lakes in this part of the region lie in basins scooped from the rock. Farther south, lakes are usually walled in by glacial debris.

Weather and Climate

The boundaries of the North Woods are set by climate. This is a region of cool summers and cold winters with deep snows. Near the Great Lakes, the harshness of this continental climate is ameliorated somewhat. Winter temperatures are not quite so bitterly cold, the growing season is longer, and the occasional hot days of summer are eased by lake breezes.

Human History

The sketchy archeological evidence indicates that people who lived by hunting big game moved into the North Woods practically on the heels of the retreating ice. When the French penetrated the Great Lakes in the 17th century, they found a small native population living by hunting, gathering, and some agriculture. The French and their successors in the fur trade established a few scattered settlements and trading posts, and their demand for pelts, particularly beaver, nearly eliminated some animals from the region.

Large-scale alteration of the primeval landscape did not begin until the loggers moved in during the 1830s. Over the next century, nearly all the North Woods was cut over at least once. Farmers moved onto the newly cleared land in some places. Mining for copper and iron began in the western Upper Peninsula of Michigan in the 1840s. Later, the enormously productive iron mines of northern Minnesota became the source of most of America's ore. Shipping ore and timber from ports on Lake Superior and northern Lake Michigan became a big business. With the settlement of the northern Great Plains, grain became another important commodity. Today, Duluth–Superior, at the western end of Lake Superior, is the largest grain shipping port in the world.

In time, the mines began to play out. Only one copper mine remains in operation in the Upper Peninsula. Only one of that state's three major iron ranges still produces ore. The loggers, who treated the woods like a mine, eventually ran out of virgin timber to cut. Some of the farmers remain, but many were forced out by poor soil and cold weather. In much of the North Woods, population levels are well below what they were 50 years ago.

Tourists began to come to the North Woods in the 19th century. In those days, they came by train to escape the heat of summer in Detroit, Milwaukee, and Chicago. They lived in rustic lodges and fished in the cool lakes. The automobile brought more of them. A few pioneering ski resorts drew people in the winter, and recently the development of snowmobiling and the discovery by Americans of cross-country skiing have brought thousands more. Today, many North Woods lakes are surrounded by summer cottages, and shoreline real estate is at a premium.

In spite of this development, millions of acres of the North Woods are still uninhabited. Land in public ownership—and therefore accessible to interested naturalists—totals about 12 million acres. (See Appendix A for a survey of public lands in the North Woods.) At the northern end of the region, along the border between Minnesota and Ontario, is the Boundary Waters Canoe Area Wilderness, the largest wilderness area in the United States outside of Alaska. Isle Royale National Park in Lake Superior and Porcupine Mountains Wilderness State Park in Upper Michigan are other large wilderness areas. Much of the Boundary Waters area and the Porkies is virgin timber.

How This Book Is Organized

Our goal in this book is to help you understand the land and the plants and animals that live on it, as well as the relationships among them. Ecologists divide ecosystems large and small into four parts: the physical environment, the producers, the consumers, and the decomposers. The physical environment includes the nonliving factors that affect the ecosystem, principally geology and climate. The producers are the green plants that, through photosynthesis, convert solar energy into simple sugars and thus provide energy to the system. The consumers are the animals that depend directly or indirectly for their sustenance on the plants. A specialized category of consumers, the decomposers, serve to break down the bodies of plants and animals, liberating water, minerals, and atmospheric gases so that they may cycle through the system again. Fungi are the most visible decomposers, but most of this vital work is done by microscopic creatures, particularly bacteria. Their cumulative effect is enormous—and essential—but since their individual workings are often obscure, we have not treated them in detail.

Our three-part structure—physical environment, producers, and consumers—provides a clear means of presenting the information, but it is important to remember that the interactions between the three are constant, intense, and varied. Minerals whose presence and abundance ultimately depend on geology are raw materials for soil building, but the soil itself is a joint production of geology, climate, vegetation, and animal life. Vegetation depends on climate, but it also modifies climate. The ground in a forest is sheltered from sun and wind and is consequently moister than bare ground and less subject to daily extremes in temperature. Given enough time, plants in the North Woods can even turn a lake into a forest and thus dramatically change the landscape.

Part I

Part I, "The Physical Environment," details the region's geologic history, describes the modern landscape of the North Woods, including its soils, and discusses climate.

The first two chapters concern the formation of bedrock. Chapter 1 focuses on northern Minnesota, northern Wisconsin, and the western half of Michigan's Upper Peninsula. It describes the volcanic eruptions, earthquakes, and mountain-building episodes which formed some of the oldest rocks on the continent there between 3 billion and 600 million years ago. In Chapter 2, the action shifts to the eastern half of the region and to Paleozoic times, when the first land plants and animals appeared. During that era, between 600 million and 220 million years ago, inland seas periodically covered most of Lower Michigan, the eastern half of the Upper Peninsula, and a narrow strip of land which borders Lake Michigan in Wisconsin. Deposits laid down in these ancient seas were compacted into sedimentary rock which now forms the bedrock of these areas.

In Chapter 3, we trace the advances and retreats of glaciers which occupied the region as recently as 10,000 years ago and describe features of the modern North Woods landscape which are legacies from those glaciers.

Chapter 4 tells what happened when the glaciers melted. In addition to chronicling the history of changing levels in each Great Lakes basin from 14,000 years ago to the present, this chapter also describes and tells where to see the dunes, wave-cut cliffs, and other shoreline features which helped scientists piece together the lakes' history.

Chapter 5 explains regional climate, the most critical factor in determining the vegetation of the North Woods and therefore the region's unique character. The chapter also contains a practical description of seasonal weather patterns.

Part II

Part II, "The Producers," begins (Chapter 7) with an introduction to the concept of plant communities. The exact nature of these groupings of species is in dispute among plant ecologists, but many of the processes that go on in them can be described. Among these is succession, the natural and continuous replacement of one kind of community by another. This chapter also introduces, very briefly, the common communities in the North Woods. Chapter 8 is a guide to plant identification. It is a primer on basic botanical terms and will familiarize novices with the characteristics used to identify plants in the field and to help them use the keys to identification in succeeding chapters.

Trees are a good place to start in identifying forest communities, so in Chapter 9 we describe the most common species in the region. Line drawings that concentrate on critical characteristics accompany the descriptions, and each description concludes with a list of the communities where the tree is usually found.

Chapter 10 describes a group of "ubiquitous" shrubs and herbs that grow in a broad range of circumstances throughout the region. These plants occur in many communities and help give the vegetation of the North Woods its recognizable character. It would be helpful to skim both this chapter and the preceding one before you use this book in the field.

Chapters 11 through 14 describe typical upland communities of the North Woods—the pine forests, the mixed-hardwood forests, boreal forests, and second-growth forests. Each chapter but the last includes keys and descriptions of common shrubs and herbs of these communities. The second-growth forest occurs in many situations in the North Woods following clear-cut logging or fire. We have

8   INTRODUCTION

given no key to the common shrubs and herbs of the second-growth forest because it has no "typical" plants of its own, with the possible exception of quaking aspen. The shrubs and herbs in second-growth stands are either among the ubiquitous plants of the North Woods or a reflection of the kind of plant community that occupied the site before logging or fire disturbed it.

Chapter 15 describes typical wetland communities and patterns of the North Woods plant succession in lakes and marshes, alder thickets, open bogs, bog forests, and swamp forests.

Part III

Part III, "The Consumers", is about the animals of the North Woods. The two chapters, *Animals of the Forest* and *Life in Northern Waters*, describe the habits of major species, grouping them not by taxonomic categories, i.e., birds, mammals, reptiles, and so on, but by ecological position as herbivores and carnivores and as dwellers on the ground, in the trees, or in water.

Public Lands

An appendix briefly describes some notable natural areas within the region and provides advice for those who would like to enjoy the millions of acres of public land that are open to use.

About Scientific Names

Scientists use a system of nomenclature for plants and animals developed by the Swedish naturalist, Linnaeus, in the 18th century. The system, called binomial nomenclature, uses two words to name each species. Dogs, for example, are *Canis familiaris*. The first word, which is always capitalized, is the genus, a group of closely related species. In this case, *Canis* includes dogs as well as wolves, coyotes, and jackals. The second word, which is usually not capitalized, is the species name. A third name may be added to these when subspecific groups—varieties or geographical races—need to be separated. Finally, an abbreviation of the name of the scientist who first described the species may be placed in parenthesis and added to the end of all this.

Scientific names are often daunting to beginners. It is much simpler to call a plant spreading dogbane than *Apocynum androsaemifolium*. However, scientific names offer a couple of important advantages, perhaps the most important being uniformity. A common, widespread species may have dozens of local names, while it will usually have only one scientific name. *Populus tremuloides*, one of the most common trees in North America, is quaking aspen over most of its range, but in the North Woods, the natives almost always call it popple.

We said that plants and animals "usually" have only one scientific name, and that qualifying adverb is needed because scientific names do vary. They may require alteration because older classifications have been found to be incorrect. Or they may differ because a group of creatures refuses to conform to our tidy system of classification. A few of the plants we describe in this book carry two scientific names because different authorities do not agree on how they should be classed.

Scientific names are also helpful in revealing relationships. Nothing in the words "dog," "coyote," and "wolf" gives any indication that the three animals are close relatives, but the genus name *Canis* shows it immediately.

The formal plant descriptions and the first mention of animal species in this book include both common and scientific names, but in the rest of the text we have used the most widespread common names in the interests of keeping things simple. However, as you use the book, it is worthwhile to make some effort to learn the scientific names of the plants and animals you identify. This is especially true if your interest in the North Woods carries you beyond this book and into the extensive scientific literature on the region.

A Note on Measurements

Metric equivalents are provided for all measurements used in this book. They are indicated in parentheses following the English units. The following conversions are applicable to the measurements in this book.

1 mile=1.67 kilometers (km)
1 kilometer=0.6 miles
1 foot=0.3 meters (m)
1 meter=3.28 feet
1 inch=2.5 centimeters (cm)
1 centimeter=0.4 inches
4 inches=10 centimeters or 1 decimeter (dm)

To convert degrees Fahrenheit (F) to degrees Celsius (C) or vice versa use the following equations:

$F = 9/5 \ C + 32$
$C = 5/9 \ (F - 32)$

PART I

The Physical Environment

Introduction to North Woods Geology and Landforms

THE NORTH WOODS extend over parts of two physiographic or geologic provinces. These provinces are defined by the nature of their bedrock. The Canadian Shield, roughly the western half of our area, contains some of the most ancient rocks on the continent. Its bedrock reveals a long, violent history of billions of years of volcanism, earthquakes, and mountain building. The Central Lowlands, roughly the eastern half, are underlain by bedrock formed from sediments deposited on the floors of ancient seas.

The Canadian Shield forms a broad circle around Hudson Bay and extends into the United States as the Superior Uplands in northeastern Minnesota, northwestern and north-central Wisconsin, and the western half of Michigan's Upper Peninsula. The Central Lowlands province includes most of the upper Midwest. That part of it that lies within the North Woods is called the Michigan Basin. The basin includes all of the Lower Peninsula of Michigan (which for convenience we will call simply "Lower Michigan"), the eastern Upper Peninsula of Michigan, and a narrow band along the eastern edge of Wisconsin.

13

The oldest rocks found to date on the Canadian Shield were formed more than 3 billion years ago. The youngest date from the beginning of Cambrian time, about 600 million years ago. The earliest complex creatures appear in the fossil record of the Cambrian period. The billions of years of the earth's history that precede this time are generally lumped together as the Precambrian.

Rock from Precambrian time underlies the Michigan Basin as well as the Canadian Shield, but in the basin, where it is overlain by Paleozoic rock, it is never exposed at the surface. During the Paleozoic, the era that began with the Cambrian period 600 million years ago and ended 220 million years ago, the older rocks of this low-lying area were covered by a series of shallow seas whose bottoms collected sediment that was compressed and solidified into rock strata with a combined maximum thickness of 14,000 feet (4200 meters).

Bedrock plays a major role in shaping any landscape. In the North Woods, the erosion-resistant rocks of the Canadian Shield have produced the rugged highlands along the north shore of Lake Superior, the knife ridges between Minnesota's border lakes, the stumps of the Penokee Mountains in northern Wisconsin, the Porcupine Mountains, and the ridges flanking the Keweenaw fault in Upper Michigan. In all of these areas, ancient Precambrian bedrock is exposed at the surface. The Paleozoic bedrock of the Michigan Basin reaches the surface much less often, but there are a few spectacular exposures. The rocks that form the cliffs of Upper Michigan's Pictured Rocks National Lakeshore are Cambrian sandstone laid down at the border between the Canadian Shield and the Michigan Basin. The cliffs along Green Bay, in Door County, Wisconsin, are dolomite—a kind of limestone rich in magnesium—formed from Paleozoic sediments.

The bedrock is very old, but most of the North Woods landscape was shaped by much more recent events in geologic time, the glaciers of the Pleistocene epoch, the Ice Age. The most recent glacial advance, the Wisconsin, melted from the upper Midwest less than 10,000 years ago. The lakes—including, of course, the Great Lakes—that are the region's main tourist attraction are a legacy of this glacier. The boulders that litter woods and fields are *glacial*

THE PHYSICAL ENVIRONMENT

erratics, fragments of bedrock picked up by the glacial ice and carried—sometimes for very long distances—before being deposited. Most of the hills in the North Woods are *moraines*, deposits of rock debris that form at the edges of ice lobes. A number of other distinctive glacial landforms are widespread.

The legacy of the glaciers continues to exert a powerful influence on the region. The distribution of the intermingled forest types whose sum is the North Woods is largely controlled by moisture and the physical nature of the soil. The young drainage system with its thousands of lakes and millions of acres of wetlands is a product of the glaciers, and the soils have developed on glacial deposits only slightly modified by time. Even the rigorous climate of the area is moderated by the Great Lakes.

The Structure of the Earth

Understanding the complex geological history of the North Woods requires some knowledge of the structure of the earth and the processes that are constantly at work changing its surface. The principle of *uniformitarianism*, a fundamental concept of modern geology, assumes that the present is the key to the past. If contemporary volcanoes produce lava that hardens into a particular kind of rock, we can surmise that ancient rocks of the same type had their origin in similar volcanoes.

The earth, from the center outward, can be divided into three distinct zones. The *core*, with a radius of about 2160 miles (3484 kilometers) is believed to be largely metallic iron, the outer part of it molten. The *mantle* is a dense, mostly solid layer that encloses the core. The uppermost layer of the mantle is a region of relatively lightweight brittle rocks ranging from 3 to 35 miles (5 to 56 kilometers) in thickness. This is the earth's *crust*.

Below the earth's surface at a distance variously estimated as 38 to 62 miles (61 to 100 kilometers) is a thick layer of plastic rock, the *asthenosphere* (astheno-, 'weak'). The *lithosphere* (litho-, 'stone'), the solid mantle and crust above this plastic layer, floats on the asthenosphere like a raft on a lake—or more accurately like a whole flotilla of rafts, for the crust appears to be broken up into a set of six major and several minor plates that either are moving or have moved in relation to each other.

Rock Types

The rocks that make up the bulk of these plates are igneous, that is they have formed from previously molten material. The general term for molten rock is *magma*. *Lava* is magma that has flowed out onto the earth's surface. Rocks formed from lava are called *extrusive* igneous rocks. Rocks formed from magma that solidified beneath the surface are called *intrusive* igneous rocks.

As magma cools, the minerals in it begin to build crystals, regular arrangements of atoms that form spontaneously as the elements in the rock change from liquid to solid. The slower the cooling, the larger the crystals. Extremely rapid cooling allows no time for crystal formation and produces an amorphous material like glass. Intrusive rocks, because

Table 1: Some Common Rock Types

Igneous Rocks		
Intrusives	*Extrusive equivalents*	*Metamorphic equivalents*
Granite	rhyolite	schist, gneiss
*Gabbro	*basalt	metadiabase, metagabbro, greenstone
*Diabase		
Sedimentary Rocks		
Clastic		
*Sandstone (higher quartz content)	quartzite	
Conglomerate		
*Shale	slate	
*Sandstone (lower quartz content)	schist	
Chemical		
Limestone, dolomite	marble	

*Heat and pressure of very high intensity can transform any of these parent rocks into schist or gneiss.

THE PHYSICAL ENVIRONMENT

they form within the earth, tend to cool more slowly—and therefore have larger crystals—than extrusive rocks formed from lava.

Rocks can also form from sediments deposited and then buried deeply enough for the weight of overlying materials to compact and cement them into rock. These *sedimentary rocks* generally erode more easily than the crystalline igneous rocks, although there are great differences in the comparative resistance of different sedimentary rocks.

Both igneous and sedimentary rocks can be extensively altered by heat and pressure. Where these forces are strong enough, they produce a change in molecular structure, rearranging the components and creating new minerals and a new crystal structure. This process is called *metamorphism,* and the new rocks produced are called *metamorphic.* All the world's rocks may be classified as igneous, sedimentary, or metamorphic.

Rocks of the Earth's Crust

The typical rock of the plates that underlie ocean basins is basalt. Basalt is an extrusive rock made up of crystals that generally do not become large enough to be seen with the naked eye. It is fine grained, dark, and rich in iron, magnesium, and calcium.

The typical rocks of the continents are broadly characterized as granitic. Granitic rocks are richer in silica than basalt—a fact that makes them flow less readily when they are molten. Granite is an intrusive rock whose coarse crystals are large enough to be seen with the naked eye (though there are also fine-grained extrusive rocks which are chemically granitic). Its high silica content is crystalized as quartz, a mineral that is extremely resistant to erosion.

Movements of the Earth's Crust

The seismically active areas of the earth, the places where volcanism, earthquakes, and mountain building are likely to occur, are along the borders of the floating plates of the crust. Where two plates are pulling away from each other, huge flows of basaltic lava pour out onto the surface.

This is happening today around Iceland in the mid-Atlantic. Just over one billion years ago, a widening rift in the earth poured out the magma that produced the rocks which now surround the western end of Lake Superior.

Where two plates carrying continents come together, the intense pressures push rocks up into folds that build mountains. Such a mountain-building episode, termed an *orogeny*, produced the Himalaya when the Indian plate and the Asian plate collided. More than 1.5 billion years ago, a similar collision produced a range of mountains as high as the Rockies that stretched from Minnesota across northern Wisconsin and Upper Michigan as far as New York.

When two plates of oceanic crust meet, one of them sinks under the other along a deep trench in the ocean floor. As it sinks, it melts, producing magma that rises back to the surface and begins to build volcanoes on the ocean bottom. Eventually, these may become high enough to create islands. The great arc of volcanic islands that fringe the Asian mainland from the Aleutians to the Philippines originated this way. It is likely that three billion years ago when the earliest events recorded in the rocks of the North Woods occurred, northeastern Minnesota, the western Upper Peninsula of Michigan, and northern Wisconsin were parts of an island arc fringing the mainland of the expanding North American continent.

CHAPTER ONE

The Superior Uplands

THE ROCKS of the western half of the North Woods—the Superior Uplands of the Canadian Shield—were formed during nearly three billion years of the earth's history, the time that ended with the Cambrian period and the appearance of complex creatures in the fossil record. Although they have been quiet now for more than 600 million years, these uplands were once the site of major geological events that helped build the continent. These events include at least two, and possibly three, major mountain-building episodes and enormous lava flows that built up deposits tens of thousands of feet thick. The most ancient rocks have been folded, shattered, and tipped on end, sometimes repeatedly. They have been invaded by magma, covered by sediments, and subjected to enough heat and pressure to produce metamorphism. The long, violent history written in the Precambrian rocks makes the process of piecing together the past very difficult. The older the rock, the more difficult the problem.

The Early Precambrian
(3.5 TO 2.7 BILLION YEARS AGO)

The earliest period we know about—geologists call it the Keewatin—was a time of volcanic activity when basaltic lavas flowed, many of them apparently hardening under water. The waters of that time also collected sediments that were eventually compressed into rock. Lava flows imply a surface to flow on, and eroded sediments imply a highland source nearby, but of these still older rocks we know nothing.

The Keewatin was followed by a mountain-building

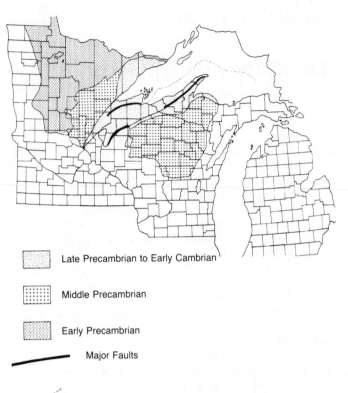

Late Precambrian to Early Cambrian

Middle Precambrian

Early Precambrian

——— Major Faults

‒‒‒ Axis of Superior Syncline

3. Generalized bedrock map of Superior Upland (adapted from U.S. National Atlas, 1970).

episode known as the Laurentian Orogeny. This was probably centered to the north of our area, because evidence for it here is very slight. Next, during a time of only slight volcanic activity called the Knife Lake period, the land subsided and shallow seas invaded much of the area, collecting sediments that later hardened into rock. The early Precambrian closed with an intensive mountain-building episode, the Algoman Orogeny, that involved massive folding of the crust, uplift, and emplacement of huge intrusive bodies of granitic rocks called *batholiths*. The intense heat and pressure associated with the Algoman Orogeny produced extensive metamorphism in all the existing rocks.

Keewatin Time

The oldest exposed rocks in our region, dating from Keewatin time over three billion years ago, are green-stones. They crop out in a series of belts generally trend-ing northeast–southwest that extend from northwestern Ontario into Minnesota. They are most widely exposed in our area in the Ely Greenstone formation in northeast-ern Minnesota, which crops out, among other places, within the town of Ely. (A *formation* is a body of rock large enough to be mapped and distinct from underlying and overlying strata. It is usually named after a town or other geographic feature near where it is exposed.)

Greenstone is basaltic lava whose color—which may range from gray–green to yellow–green—comes from the presence of the mineral chlorite. Chlorite is produced dur-ing metamorphic change, so we know that these rocks, which originally poured out from a volcanic source, were

Table 2: Early Precambrian on the Superior Upland

	Period	Events	Rocks
	Algoman	Major orogeny	Vermilion massif, Saganaga batholith, Giants Range, other igneous rocks; older rocks metamorphosed
2.7 billion years ago	Knife Lake	Shallow seas cover area; sedimentary deposits accumulate	graywackes, conglomerates
	Laurentian	Orogeny, probably centered north of our area; evidence here sketchy	Norway Lake Granite Gneiss, East Branch Arkose
3.5 billion years ago	Keewatin	Volcanism alternating with periods of deposition	Greenstones, graywackes, earliest iron formations

later buried deeply enough to experience the heat and pressure required for metamorphism, and then exposed again by erosion.

Ancient greenstones crop out in Upper Michigan too. Along U.S. 41 about 7 miles (11 kilometers) west of Marquette, road cuts reveal Keewatin-age basalts metamorphosed into a greenstone formation called the Mona schist. The rock was deposited in the billowy shapes that lavas create when they harden underwater. These *pillow structures* have been beveled flat by glacial ice, but the separate, ropy strands of lava can be seen quite clearly. Schists show a pronounced layering or foliation of minerals that is a product of metamorphism. It may indicate that the ancient basalts in Upper Michigan underwent a more intense metamorphism than those that became the greenstones of northern Minnesota. Pillow structures are common in Ely greenstone, too. They are an important part of the evidence that this area was an island arc in the early Precambrian.

Further evidence for the island arc idea is provided by the sedimentary rocks that in some places overlie the lavas and in some areas are interbedded with them. The most common sedimentary rocks in the greenstone belts are graywacke sandstones and siltstones, both indicators of an offshore environment.

Graywackes are made up of particles of various sizes usually arranged in thin beds. They are typically formed in offshore environments when currents carry sediments from close inshore and spread them out down the slope of the continental shelf, the portion of continental crust that lies below sea level. The big pieces fall first and as the lighter particles gradually settle, they form a thin stratum or layer above the layer of large pieces. Each episode will reproduce this stratigraphic pattern. The particles in these graywackes are fresh; they haven't been weathered by long exposure at the surface. This is characteristic of sediments from a highland that is undergoing the rapid erosion which must have been the rule in those ancient times. Simple life forms may have existed in the seas of three billion years ago, but there were no land plants to slow down the processes of erosion.

The iron formations are quite a different sort of sedimentary deposit. The oldest iron formations in the Superior Upland date from the early Precambrian and occur interbedded with greenstones. They apparently formed in shallow basins after a period of volcanism. The timing suggests that the materials came from volcanic activity. The iron would have been chemically precipitated out of the water in various forms—iron oxides, silicates, or sulfides—and deposited on the floor of the basin. The Soudan Iron formation west of Ely and another Lower Precambrian formation nearer the town have both been extensively mined.

Sedimentary rocks that form from precipitates in this way are called *chemical sedimentary rocks*. They include, besides iron, limestone and dolomite, chert, halite (rock salt), and gypsum. Sedimentary rocks like sandstone, siltstone, and mudstone, which form from solid particles—fragments of pre-existing rock—are called *clastic* sedimentary rocks.

The Laurentian Orogeny

The first mountain-building episode for which we have any record on the Canadian Shield was the Laurentian Orogeny. It occurred perhaps three billion years ago, mainly to the north of our area, near the heart of the ancient landmass in Ontario. There is slight and speculative evidence for rocks of Laurentian age in two locations in the Upper Peninsula of Michigan. One of these is on Sugarloaf Mountain north of Marquette and the other is at Norway Lake in Dickinson County. The Norway Lake rocks are a granite that has been metamorphosed into *gneiss*—a type of granite in which the minerals have been aligned in a series of bands—under extremely intense conditions. Other evidence for the Laurentian Orogeny comes from a rock called the East Branch arkose found near the Norway Lake granite gneiss and dated as slightly younger. Arkose is a sandstone that is rich in feldspar and quartz, minerals suggesting a granite highland as the source. What besides the Laurentian Orogeny could have created that highland?

The Knife Lake Period

Whether the Laurentian Orogeny intervened or not, the lava flows of Keewatin time gave way to a period of subsidence and deposition called the Knife Lake period. The name comes from an area along the border with Canada in Minnesota where unusually good examples of the rock are exposed. Graywacke is the most common rock type, but a variety of other sedimentary rocks are present. Graywacke, slate, and siltstone are often deposited in alternating layers. Most of the material in these sedimentary rocks is ultimately of volcanic origin, and interbeds of lava show that some volcanic activity continued through the period.

Another common rock type from the Knife Lake period is *conglomerate*, a sedimentary rock formed from large, rounded rock particles cemented together in a matrix of fine particles. A rock must consist mainly of particles more than 2 millimeters in diameter to qualify as a conglomerate; many conglomerates contain rocks of boulder size.

At Cache Bay at the western edge of Saganaga Lake in northeastern Minnesota, Knife Lake conglomerates overlie a huge intrusive formation called the Saganaga Batholith. The conglomerate is made of rocks weathered from the surface of the batholith. The rocks at Cache Bay were once used to support the theory that the Saganaga Batholith was created during the mysterious Laurentian Orogeny. The current interpretation is that the batholith was emplaced very early in the sequence of events called the Algoman Orogeny, which ended the early Precambrian. It must have solidified at a shallow depth and been unroofed quite quickly by erosion. The cycle of erosion in the Knife Lake period continued long enough to erode the batholith before the later events of the orogeny.

The batholith is formed of a medium- to coarse-grained gray granite. Quartz crystals clustered together on the rock form "eyes" one to two millimeters in diameter. It is the bedrock from Saganaga Lake south to Sea Gull Lake and southeast almost to Gunflint Lake. All these lakes are near the end of the Gunflint Trail, the road that goes northwest from Grand Marais to the Boundary Waters Canoe Area.

The Algoman Orogeny

The Knife Lake deposits and virtually all the other ancient rocks on the Canadian Shield were crumpled and metamorphosed during the complex deformation of the crust called the Algoman Orogeny, which marks the end of the early Precambrian. The Algoman events happened between 2.7 and 2.4 billion years ago and may have taken place within the relatively short geological time span of 50 to 100 million years.

Orogenies occur as a result of the movement of crustal plates. They may happen when a continent has moved over a plunging sea floor, as in the Andes, or when two continental plates collide. In any orogeny, compressional forces generated by the plate movement cause the bedrock to

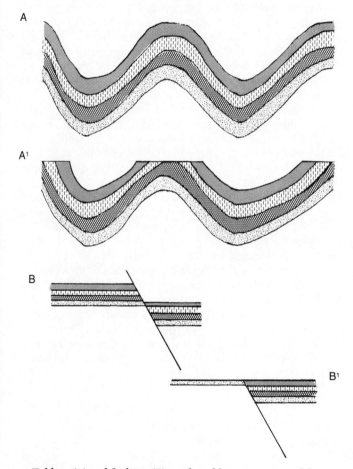

4. Folding (A) and faulting (B) produced by compressional forces during mountain building. Subsequent erosion (A¹) and (B¹) exposes rocks of different ages at surface.

bend into *folds* when events proceed slowly. If the pressure is strong enough and crustal movement is rapid, the rock will break, forming *faults* or cracks in the bedrock that may be hundreds of miles long. Subsequent vertical and horizontal movement along these faults places rocks of different ages and origins next to one another. Several faults of ancient origin are shown on our maps of the bedrock of the Canadian Shield (Figures 5 and 6).

Magma is often propelled upward during these periods of intense heat and pressure changes. Much of it cools slowly underground. We already mentioned the large intrusive bodies called batholiths. Tabular intrusive rocks that cut vertically across the layers of pre-existing rock are called *dikes*. If the new rock sheets are emplaced parallel to the older layers, they are called *sills*.

The Algoman Orogeny created mountains in northeastern Minnesota and in Upper Michigan. It also led to extensive folding and faulting of the older rocks and to the emplacement of huge batholiths. One such is the Vermilion Massif, which extends from just north of Ely northwest to about 20 miles (32 kilometers) from International Falls. It is 35 miles (55 kilometers) wide and 80 miles (130 kilometers) long. This huge mass of magma metamorphosed the rocks around it into migmatite, a composite created from the mixture of granite and the existing rock being intruded. Schist occurs at the boundaries of the Vermilion Massif but gradually gives way to a grayish pink granite toward the center.

The Giants Range, which survives as a low range of hills south of Ely, also originated as an Algoman intrusion.

Metamorphism, and perhaps mountain building, may have been more intense in Upper Michigan. The Algoman there altered existing rocks and lasted long enough for granites deposited early in the process to be metamorphosed into granite gneiss.

The Middle Precambrian

(2.6 TO 1.6 BILLION YEARS AGO)

This billion-year period of the region's history is called either Huronian or Animikean time. It begins with the ero-

THE PHYSICAL ENVIRONMENT

Table 3: Middle Precambrian on the Superior Upland

	Period	Events	Rocks
1.6 billion years ago	Late Huronian	Penokean Orogeny, major mountain-building episode forms range with Alpine peaks; centered in Wisconsin and Upper Michigan	Metamorphosed all older rocks; deposited granites, gabbros, other intrusives
2.6 billion years ago	Early and Middle Huronian	Subsidence of land and deposition of sediments; scattered volcanism	Major iron formations, limestones with earliest clear evidence of life

sion of the ridges uplifted during the Algoman, continues through a long period when much of the Superior Upland was under water, and ends with another mountain-building episode, the Penokean Orogeny.

The boundary between early and middle Precambrian is marked by an *unconformity* or gap in the rock record following the Algoman Orogeny. Such gaps indicate a period when erosion was occurring and there was no new deposition.

The earliest rocks from the middle Precambrian are conglomerates and sandstones that have since been metamorphosed into quartzite. At Sturgeon Falls near the town of Loretto in Dickinson County, Michigan, the Sturgeon River reveals a lower Precambrian gneiss, presumably metamorphosed during the Algoman Orogeny, then an unconformity, and then the Fern Creek formation, the basal conglomerate of the middle Precambrian. The Fern Creek formation has been metamorphosed into quartzite. Part of the formation is arkose, a sandstone that forms from sediments eroded from granite, probably indicating that the granites emplaced during the Algoman Orogeny were being eroded at this time.

Many of the deposits from early in the middle Precambrian are dolomites, a form of limestone rich in magnesium.

Dolomite is a chemical sediment, and its dominance suggests a stable continental shelf environment largely beyond the reach of clastic sediments washed in from the land.

The Huronian dolomites are the earliest unequivocal evidence of life in this region. Algal structures are found in the Randville, Bad River, and Kona dolomites in Michigan. The algae form domed structures of thin, rounded laminations rather like a stack of plates. There is an exposure of Kona dolomite along U.S. 41 about 3 miles (5 kilometers) southeast of Marquette. The rocks are at the end of a short trail at the east end of a large road cut.

Scattered volcanic and intrusive igneous activity occurred during the middle Precambrian. A belt of dikes across northeastern Minnesota from Baudette to Virginia and Tower dates from that time. The dikes are intrusive bodies of diabase, a variant of gabbro. Gabbro is the intrusive equivalent of the extrusive basalt. The same chemical mix at the same temperature will produce basalt if it cools at the surface and gabbro if it solidifies slowly underground. Gabbroic rocks are widespread in Minnesota, most of them produced during the last long eventful period of Precambrian time.

Huronian Iron Formations

The major iron deposits in Minnesota, Michigan, and Wisconsin were laid down as chemical sediments in the Animikean seas. Six major deposits date from this time: the Mesabi, Gunflint, and Cuyuna Ranges in Minnesota; and the Penokee–Gogebic, Marquette, and Menominee ranges in Wisconsin and Michigan.

The greatest of these ranges is the Mesabi, once the source of one-third of the world's iron ore. Mining opened there in 1890, and over the next 70 years, 2.8 billion tons of ore were shipped. Most of this ore was rich enough to go straight from mine to mill. Now, however, these natural ores are depleted and most of the current production is taconite, which has to be enriched, or *beneficiated*, before shipment.

The source of this ore is a body of ferruginous (iron-bearing) chert that averages 25 to 30 percent iron. The

Biwabik Iron formation, as it is called, is 120 miles (190 kilometers) long, 1/4 to 3 miles (0.4 to 5 kilometers) wide, and from 200 to 750 feet (75 to 225 meters) deep.

The creation of the Mesabi Range began early in Animikean time. A sea then covered Minnesota south of the Giants Range, and the Algoman granite from that batholith was eroded and transported into the waters. On a surface of eroded Lower Precambrian rocks, deposits built up parallel to the shore. These became lithified into sandstone that was later metamorphosed into the Pokegama Quartzite, the rock that underlies the Biwabik Iron formation. Then something happened at the edge of that ancient sea that cut off the supply of sediments from the land. It may have been a period of arid climate that cut down on erosion. Whatever it was, it allowed the clastic sediments of the Pokegama Quartzite to be replaced by the chemical sediments of the Biwabik Iron formation.

The iron is often found associated with chert, a very hard, tough rock formed when silicates precipitate out of water. Such precipitation can result from chemical reactions in the water, or it can result from the activities of living things. Geologists have identified structures formed by ancient algae and composed of red and white chert set in a matrix of jasper. It has been suggested that the iron itself is a precipitate produced by living things.

By late in Animikean time, clastic sediment again began to pile up offshore. A mixture of fine clays and silts along with fine-grained graywackes predominated. The transition from chemical to clastic sediments was gradual over most of the range. In some places there is even an almost iron-free layer of limestone or dolomite, chemical sediments, capping the iron formation. These capping sediments are collectively called the Virginia Formation.

The iron was deposited in various forms depending on the elements available to combine with it. Oxides are common in what was a nearshore environment. Sulfides formed in deep water under oxygen-poor conditions. Carbonates and silicates occur in intermediate situations. When subsequent uplift and erosion exposed iron formations at the surface during the Cretaceous period (135 to 60 million years ago), iron oxides were formed and many of the other minerals, such as the silicates, were leached out by rainwa-

The Superior Uplands   29

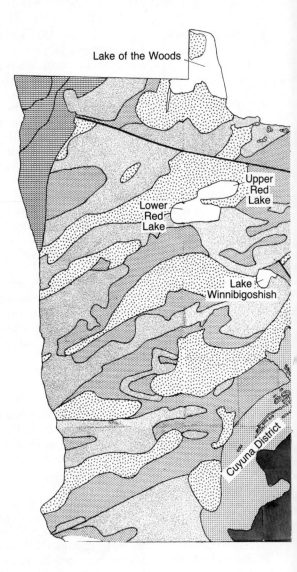

5. Bedrock of Minnesota (adapted from Minnesota Geological Survey, 1970).

THE PHYSICAL ENVIRONMENT

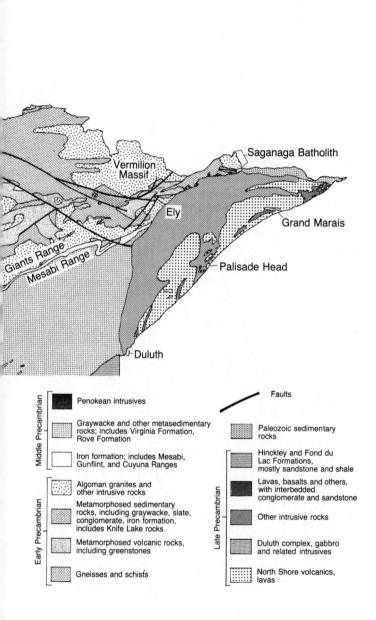

The Superior Uplands

31

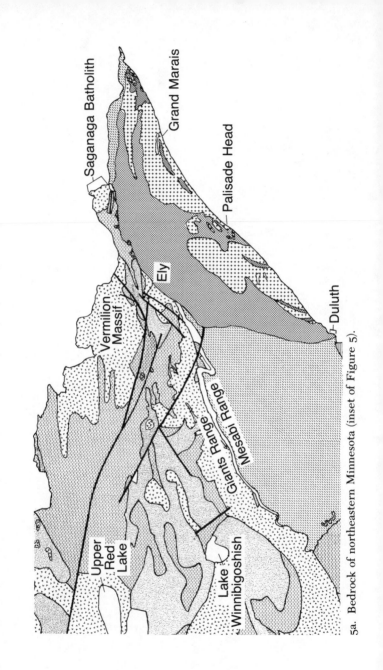

5a. Bedrock of northeastern Minnesota (inset of Figure 5).

Saganaga Batholith

Grand Marais

Palisade Head

Vermilion Massif

Ely

Duluth

Giants Range

Mesabi Range

Upper Red Lake

Lake Winnibigoshish

ter. The iron-rich residue of the leaching process formed the natural ore—also called direct shipping ore—of the iron ranges.

The Penokean Orogeny

The iron minerals in the Mesabi Range were also folded and possibly slightly metamorphosed by the Penokean Orogeny, although this event had much less effect on the Mesabi than on areas farther south. The Cuyuna district, west and north of Mille Lacs Lake in Minnesota, has a middle Precambrian iron formation that was apparently much more extensively folded by the Penokean. The folds trend east/northeast, indicating that the pressures causing the folding were coming generally from the north and south. However, none of the middle Precambrian rocks are exposed in this area. Everything we know about them comes from mines.

To the east, in northern Wisconsin and in Upper Michigan, the Penokean Orogeny was a major mountain-building event. Its peaks reached north into Ontario and as far east as New York. The Penokean also caused extensive metamorphism in all the older rocks in Upper Michigan: the middle Precambrian iron formations, the algal dolomites, the ancient greenstones. Extensive intrusions of granitic magma cut across the older rock; folding and faulting moved strata up and down by thousands of feet. Iron ores formed at the surface have been mined at depths of 4000 feet (1200 meters) in Upper Michigan.

The Penokean Range began to erode immediately, and today only a few remnants are left. These are the ridges of very hard, resistant rock that form the Penokee–Gogebic iron range. Iron formation and the associated quartzite and igneous intrusions of Penokean time form a chain of low but steep hills and ridges that runs from Lake Namekegon in Bayfield County, Wisconsin, to Lake Gogebic in Upper Michigan. The Penokee–Gogebic Range has been cut by a number of rivers that flow north into Lake Superior. From the Marengo River on the west to the Montreal River at the state line, there are several falls and rapids and a number of beautiful gorges.

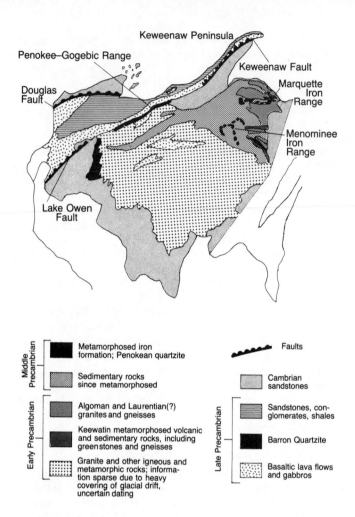

6. Bedrock of Wisconsin and Upper Michigan (adapted from Michigan Geological Survey, 1968; Wisconsin Geological Survey, 1971).

The other major iron ranges in Upper Michigan are similar. The extensive faulting of the Penokean Orogeny in this part of the world meant that deep mining has been required to get the iron out. On the Mesabi Range, the iron stayed near the surface—although the formation is surrounded by a number of faults—and the ore was accessible to strip mining. However, strip mining for the low-grade ore called taconite is now going on in the Marquette Range. There is currently no mining on the Penokee–Gogebic and Menominee ranges.

The Late Precambrian
(1.6 BILLION TO 600 MILLION YEARS AGO)

In the early Precambrian, if we have interpreted the evidence correctly, a young continent spreading south deposited lavas and sediments along an island arc. The Algoman Orogeny that closed this period left abundant traces in northeastern Minnesota. The middle Precambrian saw the accumulation of huge deposits of sediments in shallow seas on the continental shelf. The Penokean Orogeny that closed this period was concentrated in Upper Michigan and Wisconsin and left northern Minnesota largely untouched. The seismically active areas at the fringe of the continent were moving south.

The Superior Syncline

In the late Precambrian, the crust of this growing continent began to pull apart along a great arc from Lower Michigan through Lake Superior and then south and west as far as Kansas. Rifting like this occurs when two adjacent plates begin to pull apart under a continent. It is happening today under the great African Rift Valley that stretches from South Africa to the Red Sea. At the point of the ancient North American rift the continental crust actually thinned out. The surface layers bent downward in a deep fold called a *syncline*, and lava from the upper mantle began to pour out through the thin crust. The lava flows—apparently coming from fissures in the earth rather than from volcanoes—built up until at some places they totalled 50,000 feet (15,200 meters) in depth.

The record of the late Precambrian is written most clearly in the rocks around the western end of Lake

Table 4: Late Precambrian on the Superior Upland

	Period	Events	Rocks
600 million years ago	Late Keweenawan	Lava flows, intrusions gradually ending; streams carry sediments into Superior Syncline	Conglomerates, sandstones, shales
	Middle Keweenawan	Rifting begins along huge arc now partly under Lake Superior; enormous lava flows from rift; Porcupine Mountains uplifted	Basalts and intrusive equivalents; copper deposits form in Keweenaw Peninsula
1.6 billion years ago	Early Keweenawan	Erosion of Penokean Highlands	Sandstones and conglomerates, since metamorphosed

Superior. The lava flows and intrusions of the period originated from the axis of the syncline and flowed outward in
both directions, and the axis of the syncline is directly
below the lake here. The best exposures are on the
Keweenaw Peninsula in Upper Michigan, so geologists
have named the late Precambrian of the upper Great Lakes
the Keweenawan period.

The Superior syncline, the source of all the lava, is
clearly marked in the western half of modern Lake
Superior, but geophysical data indicate that it is much
larger than this relatively visible area. The force of gravity is
measurably greater than average under a narrow belt that
follows the whole arc of the rift from lower Michigan
through Lake Superior and then south and west to Kansas.
This is the Mid-Continent Gravity High, an effect that is
probably the result of the huge mass of the lavas and the
giant intrusive bodies emplaced during Keweenawan time.

The old crust sank steadily under the increasing weight
of these lava flows, although the surface of the earth over
the syncline probably remained at about the same level.
Apparently subsidence was balanced, more or less, by new

THE PHYSICAL ENVIRONMENT

flows. When eventually the lava flows ceased, the syncline continued to subside, and sedimentary rocks were deposited above the lavas, a process that continued into Cambrian time. In Lower Michigan, the old crust continued to subside through the Paleozoic (to 230 million years ago). The details of that story are given in Chapter 2.

Although these huge lava flows are the most striking evidence of the Keweenawan, they did not begin until about 300 million years after the period began. At the beginning of late Precambrian time, the highlands raised by the Penokean Orogeny were beginning to erode, and the earliest rocks of this time are basal conglomerates and sandstones which have since been metamorphosed to quartzite. One prominent deposit of rocks of this age is the Barron quartzite in northwestern Wisconsin.

Deposition continued through early Keweenawan time. Streams flowing north from the Penokean highlands deposited the sediment that became the Bessemer Quartzite north of the Penokee–Gogebic iron range. This gray-to-pink rock has a basal unit of conglomerate 10 feet (3 meters) thick in some places.

The first lava flows marked the beginning of the middle Keweenawan. They continued for hundreds of millions of years. Sometimes streams running from highlands on either side of the Superior syncline deposited thin layers of conglomerate or sandstone between the flows. As the syncline sank the layers of lava and sediment began to sag toward the middle. Today the rock strata along the Keweenaw Peninsula dip at an average angle of 40 degrees northwestward under Lake Superior. On the other side, the Keweenawan rocks of Isle Royale and neighboring Minnesota and Ontario dip southeast. A series of ridges running the length of the Keweenaw Peninsula mark the upturned edges of the separate layers of lava and sedimentary rock. The steep southeast side of each ridge follows the beveled edge of the deposit. The gentler northwest side follows the dip of the strata. Valleys form where the upturned ends of weaker strata are exposed; uplands form over stronger rocks. The peninsula has a low-lying shore area composed mainly of sedimentary rocks of the late Keweenawan. The earlier but more resistant lavas form the highland away from the shore.

Locally, the lake reaches over a resistant stratum and

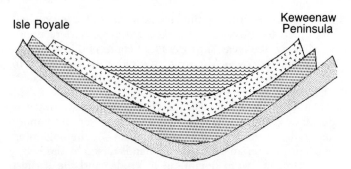

Isle Royale

Keweenaw
Peninsula

7. Diagram of bedrock of western Lake Superior. Rock strata dip
gently toward center of lake, producing shallow slopes. Steep
ridges mark ends of strata. On Isle Royale, steep ridges face
northwest; on Keweenaw Peninsula, they face southeast.

erodes the weaker rock behind it. Copper Harbor, Agate
Harbor, and Eagle Harbor were eroded in this way, and
Lake Fanny Hooe at Fort Wilkins State Park near the tip of
the peninsula had a similar origin.

Keweenawan Copper

The basalts that flowed out of the syncline often spread
out in thin layers that cooled so rapidly that bubbles of gas
were trapped in the solidified rock. Traces of the bubbles
remain as cavities—or *vesicles*—in the rock. Mineral deposits, perhaps carried dissolved in steam from groundwater, can often be found in the vesicles. Such deposits are
called *amygdules*, and the rock that contains them is called
amygdaloidal.

Most amygdules are quartz or chlorite or calcite, but
along the Keweenaw Peninsula some are pure metallic
copper. Other deposits of this *native copper* occupy cracks
in the rocks or openings in the conglomerates that formed
between flows. One mass of native copper in Keweenawan
deposits weighed over 500 tons, and a number of pieces
weighing 500 pounds have been found.

Since this copper is in metallic form, it can be worked
even without smelting. Indians of the Old Copper Culture
who lived here between 3000 and 1000 B.C. were the first
people to mine and work these deposits; and copper from

38   THE PHYSICAL ENVIRONMENT

Outer Copper Harbor Conglomerate
Middle Conglomerate
Lake Fanny Hooe
Lake Shore Traps (lava)
Lower Lake Shore Traps (lava)
Great Conglomerate

8. View northwest toward Copper Harbor on Michigan's Keweenaw Peninsula. Low areas such as Copper Harbor and the valley that contains Lake Fanny Hooe are underlain by lavas. High ground—including the reef that protects the harbor—have bedrock of more erosion-resistant conglomerates. Hills in the distance show a gentle slope northwest toward Lake Superior caused by dip in strata. Steeper slopes on southeast sides are the truncated edges of strata. *Larry Evans*.

9. Lake of the Clouds escarpment in Porcupine Mountains. The cliff is a Keweenawan amygdloidal basalt. *Photo by Robert Harrington, courtesy of Michigan Travel Commission.*

The Superior Uplands   39

the Keweenaw was widely traded throughout North America during that time. Mining native copper for smelting began in 1845 but stopped by the mid-1960s. By then some mines were down 6000 feet (1800 meters). Nearly all of the copper came from an area about 30 miles (50 kilometers) long between Painesdale and Eagle River. Copper also occurs here as a sulfide called chalcocite, and this mineral is currently being mined at the White Pine mine just east of the Porcupine Mountains.

Keweenawan Intrusive Bodies

On the Minnesota side of Lake Superior, the lava flows were similar, although they contained no significant copper deposits, at least none yet discovered.

In time the flows on the Minnesota side became so thick that new magma was prevented from reaching the surface. Huge intrusive bodies composed mainly of gabbro and its variants were emplaced near the base of this thickening volcanic pile. The largest of these intrusions, the Duluth Complex, is exposed for about 60 miles (95 kilometers) from Duluth northward. It extends to the Mesabi Range in the north and up the Superior shore almost to Canada. Further scattered exposures suggest that the whole body may be 160 miles (260 kilometers) long. Its underground thickness is estimated at about 10 miles (16 kilometers).

Gabbro is a dark, massive rock whose crystals are large enough to be seen with the naked eye. In the Duluth Complex its color generally lightens from the bottom to the top, and some red granitic rocks are found at the very top of the complex. The Misquah Hills in Cook County, Minnesota, are formed of this red rock. Anorthosite, which is green on fresh exposures and white where weathered, is another coarse-grained intrusive of the Duluth Complex. It forms Carlton Peak on the north shore in Cook County.

Diabase, with a crystal structure roughly intermediate between basalt and gabbro, is another common intrusive along the north shore. From Gunflint Lake along the Minnesota–Canada border east to Lake Superior, older slates of the Rove formation were intruded by dikes and sills of Keweenawan time. The strata are tipped 10 degrees south. In time the soft slate eroded, creating narrow river valleys separated by sawtooth ridges. More recently, the Ice Age glaciers scoured out the river valleys, creating long narrow lakes but leaving the steep diabase ridges standing between them.

Keweenawan intrusives and lava flows form much of the steep, rugged north shore of Lake Superior. A number of rivers flow into the lake from this highland, pouring over spectacular falls along the way. The falls often develop on rocks created by an accumulation of lavas from many separate flows. Vesicular zones at the top of each flow are relatively weak. Water can erode them away, undercutting the more solid base of the next higher flow.

One prominent extrusive feature here is Palisade Head. This huge mass, with its sheer cliff on the lakeside, formed from a flow of rhyolite. Chemically, rhyolite is granitic, but unlike most granites it reached the surface as lava rather than hardening deep underground. The rhyolite of the Palisade is *porphyritic*, that is, it contains a mixture of large crystals produced by slow cooling and finer crystals created by fast cooling. There are visible grains of quartz and feldspar in the reddish rock of the Palisade.

Intrusive bodies are scarce south of the Superior syncline in this time, though there is one centered in Mellen, Wisconsin, formed of gabbroic rocks changing to granite at the top.

A syncline is more than just a dip in the rock. On either "wing" of the axis, rock is folded upward into an *anticline*. Along one section of the anticline that bordered the Superior syncline to the south further uplift occurred, creating a dome-shaped anticlinal structure that may have had as much as 8000 feet (2400 meters) of local relief. This was the origin of the Porcupine Mountains of northern Michigan. The great escarpment that overlooks Lake of the Clouds in Porcupine Mountains Wilderness State Park is an amygdaloidal basalt, a Keweenawan lava flow.

By late in Keweenawan time, the lava flows had ceased and streams were once again carrying sediments from the neighboring highland into the lowland created by the Superior syncline. The first rocks laid down belong to the Oronto group, which is exposed on Isle Royale and in a belt extending along the Superior shore from the Keweenaw

Peninsula to northwest Wisconsin. Major members of this formation are, from oldest to youngest, the Copper Harbor Conglomerate, the Nonesuch Shale, and the Freda Sandstone. The sandstone is arkosic, suggesting erosion from granite; the shale contains the copper deposits mined at the White Pine mine. It also has organic compounds, microfossils, and crude oil. The Copper Harbor conglomerate marks the end of the Portage Lake lava flows, and its lower layers are interbedded with the lava.

Rocks of this group were deformed by pressures that compressed them from the southeast and northwest. The pressure may have been related to a mountain-building episode farther south. Since the deformation does not occur in rocks of the younger Bayfield group, we can date it as occurring in latest Precambrian. The Bayfield group was laid down at the end of the Precambrian or in earliest Cambrian time. These rocks, which underlie the Bayfield Peninsula and the Apostle Islands in Wisconsin, are described in Chapter 2.

The end of the Keweenawan also saw the beginning of the elevation of the St. Croix horst over the axis of the Superior syncline in northwestern Wisconsin and eastern Minnesota. A *horst* is a crustal block that is uplifted relative to the crust surrounding it. This horst was probably upthrust by forces in the mantle that balance the weight of the lithosphere on the asthenosphere. It is an answering upward shove after the huge downward push provided by the lava flows. The horst is outlined by a series of faults, and since most of the movement along those faults occurred in Paleozoic time, we have left their description until the next chapter.

On the Canadian Shield, late Precambrian or early Cambrian time held the last events recorded in the geologic record until the glaciers of the past 500,000 years. During the huge span of time from 600 million years ago until 500,000 years ago, this area was high enough to receive no sediments and stable enough to receive no igneous deposits. The Superior syncline filled with sediment that remained there until the recent glaciers scoured it out and created modern Lake Superior.

CHAPTER TWO

Under Inland Seas

WHEN THE PALEOZOIC ERA began about 600 million years ago, our region was already part of the stable interior of the North American continent. The upheavals that had characterized the area in previous times were now occurring elsewhere. Far to the east in what is now New England, the Green Mountains were forming. Before the era ended the Appalachians would rise.

Climates were warming and equalizing all over the world. Shallow seas rose and receded repeatedly, sometimes covering a third and sometimes two-thirds of what is now North America. Lower Michigan and the eastern Upper Peninsula were below sea level during most of the Paleozoic. Wisconsin and the western Upper Peninsula occupied slightly higher elevations, but they too were inundated periodically. Northeastern Minnesota, except the southeastern corner, was above water during at least the last half of the era. Paleozoic rock deposits in the North Woods include rock types such as sandstone, conglomerate, and shale that indicate beach or nearshore environments. Rocks of the era also include deep-water formations such as limestone and dolomite.

The Paleozoic is divided into seven periods based loosely on differences in environment reflected in the rock and fossil records of Western Europe. Table 5 summarizes the major events in the North Woods region during each period.

The Cambrian: Fossils and Fault Systems

When the earliest Paleozoic period—the Cambrian—began, remnants of the Penokean mountains still formed a

Table 5: The Paleozoic Era

Period	Began (millions of years ago)	Major Events in North Woods
Permian	280 ± 10	Dry uplands throughout region; erosion widespread.
Pennsylvanian	310 ± 10	Coal formation in river flood-plains, tidal swamps, northeastern Lower Michigan.
Mississippian	345 ± 10	Seas recede from Michigan Basin; land folded and uplifted.
Devonian	405 ± 10	Seas receded, land uplifted in Minnesota, Wisconsin, western U.P.; mud deposited in still-inundated Michigan Basin from erosion in Appalachians, Wisconsin highlands; continued coral reef formation.
Silurian	425 ± 10	Lower Michigan inundated; formation of Niagara escarpment, other coral reefs on Michigan Basin edge; outlets blocked by reefs caused slow evaporation, created salt-rich sediment.
Ordovician	500 ± 10	Rise of domes and arches in Wisconsin, western U.P., Minnesota; formation of Michigan Basin; spread of inland seas; explosion of plant and animal life.
Cambrian	600 ± 20	Erosion of Penokee mountains; first appearance of inland seas; first complex plant and animal life; continued sinking of Superior syncline and development of faults along its edge.

belt that extended from eastern Ontario across the central and southern Upper Peninsula and into northern Wisconsin. Streams flowing north from these mountains deposited the first Cambrian-age sediments on lowlands of the Superior basin.

In upper Michigan, rock that formed from these sediments is called Jacobsville sandstone and is visible along

Lake Superior bluffs at Presque Isle Point north of Marquette. The reddish color of this rock comes from the iron oxide it contains and was one of the most important clues to the origin of its parent material in the iron-rich Penokees.

In Wisconsin, this early Cambrian sandstone forms part of the Bayfield group and is exposed on the north-facing cliffs of the Apostle Islands National Lakeshore in Lake Superior. In northeastern Minnesota, rocks of the period are labeled Hinckley sandstone and the Fond du Lac formation.*

After Jacobsville time and before the late Cambrian, the western Upper Peninsula and adjacent areas in Wisconsin and Minnesota were slightly uplifted and tilted. We know this because the edges of strata in the Jacobsville sandstone are eroded and lie at an angle beneath overlying younger rock strata.

By the late Cambrian, rising seas had reached northern Michigan and Wisconsin and were lapping at the margins of the highlands from both north and south. Streams that continued to flow down mountain slopes now flowed into these seas, carrying with them eroded sediment from the Jacobsville sandstone and Precambrian rock to produce the Munising formation. The oldest member of this formation is Chapel Rock sandstone. The Chapel Rock for which the sandstone is named is a striking, wave-cut cliff on the south shore of Lake Superior in Pictured Rocks National Lakeshore. A large hole in the center was a cave entrance in early postglacial times when the water level was much higher than it is today. Sandstone deposited at the same time on the south side of what is today called the Northern Highlands in Wisconsin was named Mount Simon sandstone for a hill in Eau Claire where it is exposed.

During the late Cambrian, a sea rose over the top of the severely eroded Penokees, and sediment sources shifted to the east and northeast in Canada. Sediment deposited on

---

*A formation may include one or more rock or *lithologic* types. If it contains just one, that type will be included in the formation's name, as Jacobsville sandstone. If it includes two or more, the type will not be mentioned in the name. The Fond du Lac formation in Minnesota, for instance, consists of both sandstone and shale. Two or more formations typically associated with a particular geographic area form a *group*, such as the Bayfield group.

10. Miner's Castle, formed from Cambrian sandstone and shaped by the wave action of proglacial Lake Nipissing, at Pictured Rocks National Lakeshore near Munising, Michigan. The portion of the Munising Formation above the dark, horizontal striation near the waterline is Miner's Castle sandstone; the much smaller portion below is Chapel Rock sandstone. *Travel Bureau, Michigan Department of Commerce.*

top of the Chapel Rock sandstone at Pictured Rocks formed the second member of the Munising formation; it is called Miner's Castle sandstone. The Cambrian-age bluffs exposed as the Pictured Rocks turn inland and disappear beneath younger rock layers east of Au Sable Point and west of Munising; they crop out again at Tahquamenon Falls State Park in the eastern Upper Peninsula. The rock over which the Lower Falls tumble at Tahquamenon is Chapel Rock sandstone. The Upper Falls cut into the Miner's Castle sandstone. Other waterfalls in the Upper Peninsula which expose Cambrian age rocks—sometimes capped with Ordovician dolomite—include Laughing Whitefish Falls, Munising Falls, and Miner's Falls. The AuTrain Falls, on the AuTrain River near Munising, is located on the Ordovician-age AuTrain formation.

These Cambrian sandstones, which crop out today on or

near the south shore of Lake Superior, are the youngest rocks we have any record of that were deposited in the Superior syncline (see Chapter 1) and that contributed by their weight to its downward movement.

Fault Lines

Associated with the steeply northward-dipping south edge of this syncline is the Keweenaw fault, one of a series of faults which apparently began developing in late Keweenawan time and continued movement intermittently until the middle Cambrian.

The slow rise of the St. Croix horst along the synclinal axis created the fault system where this rising block of crust broke away from the surrounding rock.

11. This waterfall in Amnicon State Park, Douglas County, Wisconsin, tumbles over the Douglas Fault, formed in late Precambrian and early Cambrian times. *Wisconsin Department of Natural Resources.*

The Keweenaw fault runs under Lake Superior at the tip of the Keweenaw Peninsula. From there south it forms a high ridge down the center of the peninsula. It continues southwest at least as far as Lake Gogebic, and it may extend into Wisconsin and connect with the Lake Owen fault. The Keweenaw fault lifted Precambrian lava flows on the northwest side of the peninsula up over Cambrian Jacobsville sandstone on the southeast. Vertical movement along the fault may have been as much as 10,000 feet (3000 meters).

The Lake Owen fault, which may be an extension of the Keweenaw, can be traced from just east of Ashland southwest to Lake Owen in the Chequamegon National Forest north of Cable.

The Douglas fault forms an escarpment that rises above the glacial lake plain on the southwest shore of Lake Superior. Some of Wisconsin's highest waterfalls occur where streams cross this sudden drop in elevation on their way to Lake Superior. Big Manitou Falls is a 165-foot (50-meter) cascade in Pattison State Park on the Black River. Amnicon Falls on the Amnicon River drops 120 feet (35 meters) over the escarpment into a sandstone canyon in Amnicon Falls State Park. Both parks are located in Douglas County near Superior, Wisconsin.

The Isle Royale fault is exposed on the island of that name, now a national park, in Lake Superior.

In Minnesota, the Hastings fault continues southwest from the Lake Owen fault, and the Belle Plaine fault forms the southern edge of the horst.

First Records of Life

The first recorded fossils of the Paleozoic turn up in late Cambrian times at the south edge of our area in a deep-water limestone and dolomite formation called the St. Lawrence. This formation is exposed in several places, including a roadcut on Wisconsin Highway 82 about 6 miles (10 kilometers) west of Mauston in Juneau County, and on bluffs of the St. Croix River in eastern Minnesota. Among these late Cambrian fossils were brachiopods and trilobites, marine animals with such complex structures that geologists were led to suspect that more primitive life had existed in the Precambrian even before evidence of algae had been discovered in the Animikean rocks. Because Pre-cambrian rocks have been so extensively eroded and metamorphosed, we may never find all the missing links between the earliest primitive algae and their Cambrian successors. There is no doubt, however, that there was an explosion of plant and animal variety during the Paleozoic. By the end of the era, animals belonging to every phylum and class except mammals and birds would appear and leave their fossil remains. Paleontologists have discovered 1600 species of marine animals from the middle Ordovician alone.

The Cambrian brachiopod was an animal that was en-closed in a bivalve shell, but there ends any similarity in appearance to a modern clam or oyster. The Cambrian brachiopod's upper shell was smaller than the lower, and the two were hinged together at one end rather than on the side, as is a clamshell. The animal attached itself to rocks in the sea by a fleshy stalk which projected from an opening at bne end of the lower shell. The organism inside the shell consisted of a skin which lined the shell, digestive and cir-culatory systems, and two spirally coiled ridges which functioned as gills, their hairline tentacles waving the water

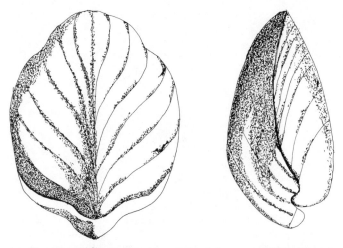

12. Two views of *Pentamerus laevis Sowerby*, a typical brachiopod of the Middle Silurian period, Michigan. *Glenda Daniel*.

to set up currents and sweep minute organisms toward the mouth.

By the end of the Cambrian period, brachiopods made up a third of the marine animal population. This life form thrived for hundreds of millions of years in the sea, and a few still survive in such cold nearshore waters as those of the Atlantic coast of Maine. Brachiopod fossils from different geological periods are so distinctive that they are helpful to geologists in determining the ages of marine sedimentary rock formations.

Trilobites, much prized today by fossil collectors, were the largest and most highly developed animals in Cambrian times. Some were nearly 2 feet (60 centimeters) long. Their bodies were divided into three long, flattened lobes. Their heads were covered by shieldlike plates and they had a pair of compound eyes, each with thousands of lenses. The thorax and abdomen had a segmented upper shell; the last few segments were joined to form a tail shield. They bore some faint resemblance to the modern crawfish and, in fact, are classed in the same phylum, Arthropoda.

Early forms of both brachiopods and trilobites are exposed at Bony Falls on the Escanaba River in the Upper Peninsula.

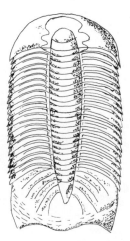

13. *Dikellocephalus oweni*, a typical trilobite of the Late Cambrian period, Wisconsin. *Glenda Daniel.*

The Ordovician:
Domes, Arches, and Basins

The Ordovician period in the North Woods was a time of shifting elevations. A number of areas were uplifted to form what geologists call *domes* and *arches*. Separating these highlands were embayments called *intracratonic basins* because, although they were below sea level and thus often inundated, they were still part of the stable interior or *craton* of the continent.

As the Ordovician began, three of these basins had already developed in the upper Midwest. One of them, the Michigan Basin, lies within our area. It occupied all of lower Michigan, parts of Ontario, and the eastern Upper Peninsula.

The western Upper Peninsula and most of Wisconsin, including all of that state contained in the modern North Woods, formed one of the highland regions known as the Wisconsin arch. The broad northern part of the Wisconsin arch is called the Wisconsin dome. A southeastward extension of it along what is now the Lake Michigan shore was named the Kankakee arch. Although the elevations on these arches were seldom more than a hundred feet (30 meters) above the surrounding basins—and often less than that—they were high enough to cause embayments to form around them. Later, during the Silurian period, reefs would form on the Kankakee arch.

Northeastern Minnesota formed another area of slightly raised elevation. Two southward extensions of the high ground, the Lincoln anticline and the Mississippi River arch, extended through western Wisconsin and southeastern Minnesota into Illinois.

Because the Michigan Basin and most of the highland areas were later covered by glacial till, there are few outcrops from post-Cambrian Paleozoic time in our region. Most of the evidence we have for regional events during the Paleozoic comes from wells, coal and salt mines, quarries, and road cuts; rocks taken from such sites are displayed in a number of regional museums. Two such institutions are the University of Michigan Exhibits Museum and the Museum of Paleontology in Ann Arbor.

The shallow seas that had lapped at the edges of the North Woods in Cambrian times became firmly established in the embayments between the domes and arches in Ordovician times. The seas persisted—although their boundaries changed repeatedly—into the Silurian period. The AuTrain formation of sandy dolomite, which can be seen at AuTrain Falls and on the upper layers of rock at Miner's Falls, offers evidence that a sea covered the Upper Peninsula at some point during the Ordovician. The oil-rich Trenton shale formation in northern Michigan, deposited as muddy sediment, also dates from that period. Trenton shale is exposed at Chandler Falls on the Escanaba River, 3 miles (5 kilometers) north of Escanaba.

The Ordovician seas covered most of Minnesota, too, and created a beach environment around the highlands in the northeastern part of the state. They receded, however, during the Silurian and most of the Devonian period, when all of Minnesota except the southeastern corner was apparently above sea level. Erosion has erased most clues to Paleozoic events in that state.

Cephalopods, ancient relatives of the octopus, first appeared during the Ordovician. So did crinoids, a favorite of fossil collectors. Crinoids still exist, although they are far less numerous than in their Paleozoic prime. Called stone lilies for their resemblance to plants, they have long slender stems and a crown of feathery tentacles used to stir water and bring microscopic organisms close enough to eat. Starfish and sea urchins are distant relatives of the crinoids; all are members of the phylum Echinodermata.

The Silurian: Seas and Coral Reefs

All of Lower Michigan was inundated during the Silurian. Dolomite was the most common rock formed. Sandstone and conglomerate formations which indicate beach environments were found well beyond Michigan borders along the Kankakee arch at the eastern edge of Wisconsin, in the Upper Peninsula, and in eastern Ontario. Coral reefs formed around the edges of various seas and embayments in mid-Paleozoic times; the remains of some of these reefs today are sources of oil and natural gas.

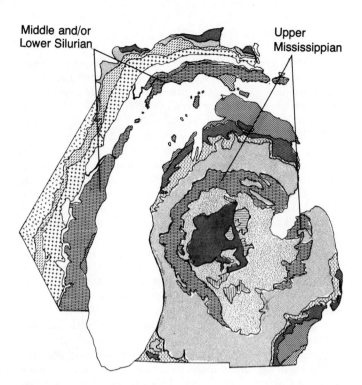

Middle and/or Lower Silurian

Upper Mississippian

	Upper Jurassic		Middle Devonian
	Upper Pennsylvanian		Upper Silurian
	Lower Pennsylvanian		Middle and/or Lower Silurian
	Upper Mississippian		Upper Ordovician
	Lower Mississippian		Middle Ordovician
	Mississippian and/or Devonian		Ordovician and Cambrian
	Upper Devonian		Upper Cambrian

14. Bedrock map of the Michigan basin (adapted from Kelley, 1977, Michigan Department of Natural Resources).

Under Inland Seas

The Niagara Escarpment

A famous regional landmark of modern times, the Niagara Escarpment, was a Silurian reef which formed in warm, clear, shallow waters at the edge of the Michigan basin. The escarpment forms a ridge which runs the length of the Door County Peninsula in Wisconsin and continues northeast to form the Garden Peninsula southwest of Manistique in the Upper Peninsula. It is exposed at the surface as two islands—Drummond and Manitoulin—on the north edge of Lake Huron, continues from there into Ontario as the Cape Hurd and Bruce peninsulas separating Georgian Bay from Lake Huron, and then south between lakes Erie and Ontario. The Niagara River plunges over the escarpment at Niagara Falls.

The Niagara, which like modern reefs was formed by lime-secreting organisms such as corals and algae, attests among other things to the abundance of marine life that had accumulated in our region by Silurian times. In places, the reef is 400 feet (120 meters) high.

The escarpment's longevity is due to the erosional resistance of the dolomite which is its main constituent. Its shape, gently sloping on the Michigan Basin side and with steep cliffs on the opposite or "shoreline" face, reflects gradual sinking of the basin. This sinking grew more pronounced with each new layer of sediment deposited as the Paleozoic proceeded.

Nesting Bowls

Layers of Paleozoic bedrock in Lower Michigan are still warped downward toward the middle of the basin, sloping at an average inclination of about 60 feet per mile (11 meters per thousand). This curious fact has made rocks from even the oldest Paleozoic periods more accessible for study by geologists than if the layers had remained in their original horizontal state. The warping has created a sort of nesting-bowl effect, with each layer closer to the surface near the edge of the basin and more deeply submerged near the center. Thus, Cambrian-age sandstones form outcrops in the eastern Upper Peninsula. On the other hand, a well dug near the center of the basin northwest of Saginaw

15. Geological cross-section of the Michigan basin, showing nesting bowl effect (adapted from Kelley, 1977, Michigan Department of Natural Resources).

touched Cambrian sandstone 13,000 feet (4000 meters) underground.

One of the main effects exerted on the regional landscape by the Niagara Escarpment and other Silurian coral reefs was to cut off outlets for water at the edge of the Michigan basin. This development created conditions of slow evaporation that led to the formation of deposits rich in rock salt (halite) and gypsum. The state of Michigan today produces 20 to 25 percent of the nation's salt supply.

The Devonian: Mud and Petoskey Stones

Effects of the Appalachian Orogeny to the east began to appear in the Midwest by Devonian times. Thousands of feet of mud that washed into our area as far west as southeastern Minnesota are present today as Antrim and Maquoketa (also called Richmond) shales.

Another shale, grayish green in color and labeled Ellsworth, swept into the Michigan basin from the northwest in Devonian and Mississippian times, indicating that highlands in Wisconsin, dating from a major uplift in late Silurian or early Devonian times, had begun to erode. The only Devonian deposits still present in Wisconsin today are from the shoreline environments at the the eastern edge of those highlands near Milwaukee. Fossil outcrops are visible at Estabrook Park in Milwaukee and at Harrington Beach State Park in Ozaukee County.

The first extensive forests of North America appeared in other parts of the continent during Devonian times and may have developed in Wisconsin and Minnesota. Much

Devonian-age rock from the North Woods has long since eroded, however, and there are no fossil records of Devonian trees in our region.

Reef-building continued in the Devonian, and fossil-rich coral reefs are exposed near Petoskey and in the Alpena and Rogers City area at the north end of Lower Michigan. Among the better observation areas are bluffs on the northeast shore of Partridge Point 4 miles (6 kilometers) south of Alpena. Fragments eroded from these reefs and polished by wave action in Lake Michigan and smaller lakes are called Petoskey stones. They are often found on the beaches of the area.

Caves formed in recent times (within the last 2000 years) in limestone deposits of the Devonian period; the roofs of most Michigan caves have collapsed to form sinkholes. There are several sinkholes in Presque Isle County in northern Lower Michigan. One is near Ferron Point on the shore of Lake Huron. Another lies farther inland to the west between Rainy Lake and Kelsey Lake in Case Township. There is even a Sinkhole Trail, east of Michigan Highway 33 south of Onaway in Black Lake State Forest. The trail is a 3-mile (5-kilometer) loop with four sinkholes on its route. The Sinkhole Trail is part of a much longer state hiking trail called the High Country Pathway.

Climbing into these sinkholes, one can see coral formations in their original growth positions; such explorations should be restricted, however, to experienced cavers with some knowledge of the special rope gear necessary to drop safely into the steep-sided caverns.

The Late Paleozoic:
Pennsylvanian and Permian

The seas receded from most of the Michigan basin during the Mississippian period; rock deposits were sandstones and siltstones that indicate a beach or nearshore environment. Geologists think that a major episode of folding and uplift in Lower Michigan at the end of the Mississippian may have been caused by reactivation of Precambrian faults and folds in the crust deep below.

The Pennsylvanian period is associated throughout eastern North America with the formation of coal. The *peat*, or partially decomposed plant material that was eventually compacted to form low-grade bituminous, or soft, coal developed in the swamps and tidal marshes that appeared in Michigan during the Pennsylvanian.

As this peat becomes more deeply buried under succeeding layers of plant material, enough heat and pressure was generated to drive off excess water and volatile gases, increase the percentage of carbon, and thus produce lignite or brown coal. Continued heat and pressure eventually made bituminous coal. Anthracite, or hard coal, forms only under conditions of extreme heat and pressure, such as that which occurred during the Appalachian Orogeny. Anthracite is, in effect, a metamorphic rock, altered from sedimentary soft coal.

Coal-forming may take place in both warm and cold climates. (The absence of annual growth rings on Pennsylvanian-age tree fossils indicates a uniform year-round climate rather than summer growth and winter dormancy.) However, other less variable circumstances are required for coal formation: Rainfall is usually high, drainage must be poor, and the accumulation of plant material must be greater than the rate of decay. Such conditions exist today in areas like Virginia's Dismal Swamp or the peat bogs that spread over vast areas of the North Woods. Many of these bogs are former glacial lakes. The peat is accumulating because the lakes have few if any natural outlets, and in the still waters, the oxygen that would support decay-producing bacteria is scarce.

One particular rock formation, the Saginaw in northeastern lower Michigan, gives us clues to a landscape scientists think may have been typical of much of Michigan during the Pennsylvanian period. The rocks indicate alternating and intertonguing stream and river channels. They include river floodplain silts and clays, shallow water marine or tidal swamp shales and limestone, along with swamp-laid coals. There are also fossil remains of animals that favored brackish and saltwater habitats.

By late Pennsylvanian times, the land had risen still further, and the swamps had given way to drier uplands. The long Paleozoic history of marine occupation and sedimentation in Michigan was drawing to a close, as it had done during Devonian times in Wisconsin and Minnesota. No rocks of the Permian period have been found anywhere above or below ground in our region. Erosion was widespread and apparently continued into the Mesozoic and Cenozoic periods which followed.

The Lost Interval

Presumably because of this erosion, there is almost no evidence in the North Woods for events of the next 280 million years. Exceptions include layers of sedimentary rock known as "red beds" scattered through six countries in central Michigan, and a fossil-rich formation of iron ore conglomerate, shale, and sandstone along the western Mesabi Range in northeastern Minnesota.

The red beds date from the Jurassic period of the Mesozoic era, between 180 and 130 million years ago. Their shape—scattered lenslike patches—has caused geologists to speculate they were laid down in depressions, possibly in ancient lakes or ponds. Their content—succeeding layers of sandstone, shale, clay, limestone, and gypsum—points to a history of rising waters followed by evaporation in an increasingly arid climate.

Molluscan and gastropod fossils in the Mesozoic formation found in northeastern Minnesota enabled scientists to date it as Cretaceous, between 130 and 63 million years old. They surmised from its content that shallow seas were then washing from the west onto the edge of northeastern Minnesota highlands in late Jurassic and early Cretaceous times. This was also the period when mid-Precambrian taconites of the Biwabic formation were weathered to form the "natural" ores of the Mesabi Range.

These two isolated formations don't tell us much. Dinosaurs roamed elsewhere in the world during this lost interval in the North Woods. Plants flowered. The first birds, reptiles, and mammals, including the genus *Homo*, appeared. The next geological evidence of events in our region, however, dates from the Pleistocene epoch of the modern or Quaternary period. This eventful epoch is the subject of our next chapter.

CHAPTER THREE

Shaping the Face
of the Land: The Ice Age

SOMETHING HAPPENED to the earth's climate about two million years ago. The change, whatever its cause, cooled the earth enough to allow part of each winter's snow to survive through the summer in high-latitude areas with ample precipitation. Only a minor change in our present annual average temperature—a drop of 9° F, or 5° C—would be enough to account for such a buildup of snow.

New-fallen snow is a network of lacy crystals as fluffy as down. It has a specific gravity as low as 0.1, compared to the 1.0 of water. In time, snow begins to settle. Air in the loosely packed snow melts the ice near the points of the crystals, and the water refreezes again near the centers, making the flakes smaller and more compact and gradually forcing out the air. The snow is changing from a sediment to a sedimentary rock.

The weight of new snow and of intermediate layers puts increasing pressure on the deepest layers, and eventually the specific gravity of these oldest snows reaches 0.8. At this point it is so compact that it is impermeable to air; it is ice, metamorphosed, like rock, by the pressure of overlying layers. Unchecked by summer thaws this buildup will continue until the ice is thick and heavy enough—a few tens of feet are sufficient—that its own weight will cause it to spread. Thus glaciers are seen to flow even in the absence of a slope.

The cool weather that began two million years ago continued until it created glaciers of continental size. In North America, at least three major—and some minor—centers produced glaciers that began to radiate out to cover much of the continent beginning about 500,000 years ago. In the eastern United States, the ice reached the southern tip of

Illinois. Worldwide, it may have covered 30 percent of the total land surface.

Geologists call this epoch of glaciation the Pleistocene. It is variously dated as beginning two million or 500,000 years ago. The dating difference is philosophical. One school dates the epoch as beginning when the cooling began. The other dates it from the spread of the glaciers.

An ice sheet of continental size is an awesome thing. Only two exist today, one in Greenland and one in Antarctica. The Antarctic sheet contains two-thirds of all the fresh water in the world. At its thickest point it is more than 2.5 miles (4 kilometers) deep. Its weight is such that the rock beneath it has subsided by as much as a third of the thickness of the ice.

The ice sheets of the Pleistocene held so much water that sea level fell to about 330 feet (100 meters) below today's levels. The glaciers created a belt of permafrost extending far to the south of the ice front. They altered precipitation patterns and blanketed millions of acres with *loess*, wind-blown glacial deposits. They also depressed the earth's crust, perhaps by as much as 800 feet (250 meters) at the center of the North American glacial spread near Hudson Bay. In our area, since the recession of the glaciers the crust has rebounded 160 feet (50 meters) in central Wisconsin and Lower Michigan and as much as 330 feet (100 meters) in northeastern Minnesota. The rebound continues today. Superior, Wisconsin, is currently rising about 0.5 inch (1.3 centimeters) a year. This rate of rebound is actually greater than the rate of uplift in any actively growing North American mountain system.

The ice advanced in great lobes that sometimes reached 2 miles (3 kilometers) in thickness and covered thousands of square miles. The movements of contemporary glaciers have been clocked at speeds as low as 100 feet (30 meters) a year and as much as 150 feet (45 meters) a day. The average glacial movement is probably nearer the lower figure than the higher.

The huge ice sheets seem powerful enough to spread where they like regardless of the shape of the land beneath them, but in fact local relief and the comparative strength of the local bedrock played important roles in channeling the ice. When glaciers reached the upper Midwest, the areas now occupied by the Great Lakes were already lowlands, probably river valleys in the watershed of an ancestor of the St. Lawrence River, and the ice was channeled into these valleys. The valley in the Lake Michigan basin was underlain by weak Paleozoic shales that the glacier scoured out enough to put the deepest point in Lake Michigan 343 feet (105 meters) below sea level.

The Superior syncline was apparently filled with sandstones and shales dating from the Cambrian or later which were weak compared to the Precambrian rocks on either side of the basin. The glaciers pulverized and transported these sedimentary layers out of the basin. These sediments were coated with iron oxides and left red deposits wherever ice from the Superior basin passed.

Glaciers move slowly, but they attack the ground around them with enormous violence and power. Ice scraping over bedrock can grind stones into a fine powder called rock flour. One contemporary alpine glacier, the Muir Glacier in southeastern Alaska, produces enough rock flour every year to create a loss of 0.8 inches (2 centimeters) of bedrock under the entire glacier. In north-central Canada, the Pleistocene ice may have removed 33 to 66 feet (10 to 20 meters) of bedrock. The average depth of deposits over the whole glaciated region of the United States is 40 feet (12 meters), and in some places the deposits are more than 500 feet (150 meters) deep.

Under very cold conditions glaciers may become frozen to their beds. More commonly, the ice in direct contact with rock melts, and the meltwater flows into cracks in the bedrock and refreezes. The cracks widen; the rocks break away from their beds and freeze into the underside of the ice. As the ice moves, the rocks scrape away at the ground like an outsize piece of sandpaper, picking up more debris as they go. Scratches, called *striae*, on bedrock exposures in the North Woods record the passage of these rasps and indicate the direction of ice movement.

The amount of material a glacier can carry is far beyond the capacity of any stream, and only glacial ice can carry particles of all sizes, from the finest clay to boulders weighing tons.

The material picked up, transported, and subsequently dropped from a glacier is called *glacial drift*. It can be deposited in two ways, as *till* or as *outwash*. Till is material dropped directly from the ice. It is a completely unsorted jumble containing particles of every size. Outwash is drift that has been carried away from the ice by meltwater. It takes a considerable volume of fast-moving water to move the big rocks, so they drop out first. Then as the water slows down, progressively smaller pieces drop out. This kind of deposition creates strata in outwash, so that instead of the jumble of till, outwash shows a series of sorted layers. The biggest pieces are at the bottom and closest to the old ice front, and the smallest pieces are on top and generally farther from the ice. The sorting helps create outwash plains with uniform soils of sand or clay.

Glaciation in the North Woods

Calling the Pleistocene the Ice Age is somewhat misleading, because there were actually four ice ages separated by lengthy periods of warm weather called *interstadials*. Some geologists believe that we are living in the interglacial period before the fifth ice advance.

The landscape of the North Woods is the creation of the last great glacial advance, which is called the Wisconsinan, or simply Wisconsin. The Wisconsin began about 70,000 years ago and ended less than 10,000 years ago. During the Wisconsin, the ice advanced into the upper Great Lakes from two major centers, one west of Hudson Bay and another in the highlands of Labrador. A third minor center in northwestern Ontario produced some of the ice that covered Minnesota.

The history of the Pleistocene in the North Woods has been pieced together from an examination of the traces the ice left behind. As the Wisconsin glaciers filled the lowlands that now contain Lakes Michigan, Huron, and Erie, Lower Michigan was virtually surrounded by ice. Ice spread through Wisconsin from the Superior and Michigan basins. In Minnesota, three major lobes contributed, one in the Superior Basin, one that followed the Red River lowland south, and a third that came south into northeastern Minnesota from Ontario.

THE PHYSICAL ENVIRONMENT

Like the Pleistocene as a whole, the Wisconsin glaciation was divided into cooler periods when the ice advanced and warmer periods when it retreated. Unfortunately, the advances and retreats don't seem to be synchronized throughout our region. Temperature changes may not have been uniform throughout the North Woods. Precipitation would also affect the ice, as would numerous other factors, including the distance from the ice source to the ice front, the flow velocity, and the volume of ice. This inconvenient lack of synchronicity has led to the elaboration of a separate terminology to describe the glacial and interglacial periods of the Wisconsin in each state.

Although a precise concordance of glacial advances seems impossible, it is generally agreed that the period from 22,000 to 12,000 years ago was a time of heavy activity. The landscape of most of the North Woods dates from this period, although both older and younger drift is present. The older drift that was deposited before 22,000 years ago is at the very edge of our region, beyond the areas covered by the more recent ice advances. In most of the North Woods, the glaciers of 22,000 to 12,000 years ago have obliterated signs of this older drift. The younger drift of the Valders ice advance, which ended 9500 to 10,000 years ago, extends from the western end of Lake Superior across northwestern Wisconsin, Upper Michigan, northeastern Wisconsin, and northern Lower Michigan. This was the last advance of the ice in the upper Great Lakes.

The Early Wisconsin

(70,000 TO 22,000 YEARS AGO)

Minnesota: Hewitt Phase of the Wadena Lobe

The Alexandria moraine, marking the greatest advance of the Hewitt phase of the Wadena lobe in Minnesota, is old drift deposited between 22,000 and 60,000 years ago (the dating is uncertain). It just touches the western end of the North Woods. The ice that deposited this moraine apparently flowed into Minnesota from the northwest up the Red

Table 6: Events of Early Wisconsin glaciation in Minnesota

Events	Ice source	Deposits
Hewitt advance of Wadena Lobe	Winnipeg Lowlands	Alexandria moraine

River valley. It carried fragments of Paleozoic rock that originated in the lowlands around Winnipeg. The ice flowed southeast and then southwest to leave the Alexandria moraine complex.

16. Glacial deposits from the Hewitt Phase of the Wadena Lobe, Wisconsin Glacier, Minnesota.

THE PHYSICAL ENVIRONMENT

Table 7: Events of Early Wisconsin glaciation in Wisconsin

Events	Ice source	Deposits
Altonian advance	Superior Basin, Michigan Basin	Old drift in west central portion of state

Wisconsin: Altonian Drift

This is found along the southern edge of the North Woods in Langlade, Taylor, Lincoln, and Barron counties, south of the well-marked moraine of the later Woodfordian

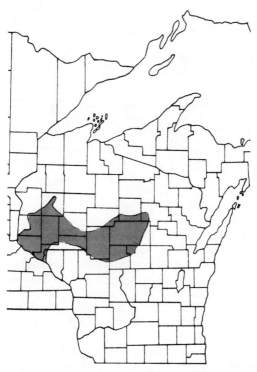

17. Glacial deposits from Altonian Drift in Wisconsin.

ice. On the older drift, the drainage system has had time to develop sufficiently to drain all the lakes left by the ice, and erosion and weathering have reduced the prominence of the glacial deposits.

Michigan

During this period, the ice margin was south of the state in Ohio and Indiana, so no traces of the ice movements of the time remain at the surface.

Moraines, Kettles, and Drumlins

The Alexandria moraine complex is an *end moraine*, the general term for the irregular ridges of till that build up at the tip of an ice lobe that is apparently standing still. The shape, location, orientation, and extent of an end moraine can tell us which direction the ice was moving, the shape of the ice front, and something about how long it stayed in one place. The till that makes the moraine can tell us where the ice came from.

A glacier with a stationary front is still moving. It appears to stand still because the annual meltback at the front is about equal to the advance. The moving ice carries drift that melts out and piles up higher and higher. Ridges on end moraines can rise hundreds of feet over surrounding lowlands if the ice stays in one place long enough. These ridges mark the former position of the ice.

Between the high knobs of the ridges are depressions called *kettles* that may be lakes, marshes, bogs, or just bowl-shape depressions, depending on their relation to the local water table. Kettle holes form when huge blocks of ice break off from the face of a melting glacier and get buried in drift. When they melt, a process that sometimes takes thousands of years, they leave the kettles. Kettle hole lakes in end moraines are quite common in the North Woods, although this is only one of the ways that glaciers create lakes.

The Alexandria complex is also a *terminal moraine*—an end moraine that marks the farthest advance of an ice lobe.

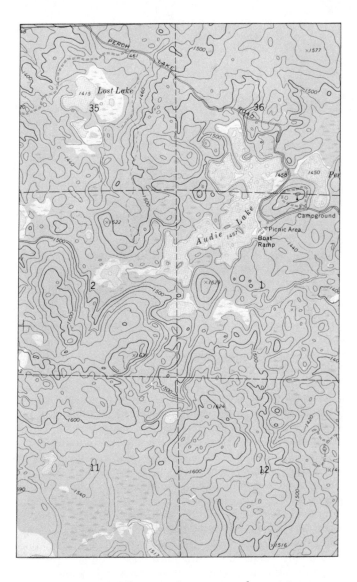

18. U.S.G.S. topographic map showing typical morainic terrain, this from the Woodfordian terminal moraine in Wisconsin. Contour lines show knobby hills; lakes fill kettleholes.

19. Glacial erratics adorn a farmer's field, part of an outwash plain at the edge of a moraine, Taylor County, Wisconsin. *Glenda Daniel*.

Beyond the morainic ridges would be outwash from the same glacier, and beyond that either unglaciated territory or drift left by another lobe.

A glacier that is melting back typically makes a rather jerky progress. It will recede for a while and then stop or even readvance briefly. The end moraines that mark the pauses in the retreat are called *recessional moraines*.

The old till of the Alexandria moraine has been largely overridden by later drift, but behind the moraine, a group of about 1200 drumlins called the Wadena drumlin field are exposed. *Drumlins* are long, narrow streamlined hills commonly formed behind the ice front when the ice molds drift that has already been deposited. The long axis indicates the direction the ice was moving. The blunt tip at one end points toward the source of the ice. The long pointed tip at the other end points to the end moraine. Some drumlins are 2 miles (3 kilometers) long and over 100 feet (30 meters) high. The Wadena drumlins form a fan-shape pattern that indicates that the Hewitt ice advanced from the northeast to the Alexandria moraine.

THE PHYSICAL ENVIRONMENT

The Later Wisconsin

(22,000 TO 12,000 YEARS AGO)

This eventful period that produced most of the North Woods landscape began in Minnesota with the advance of ice from three sources: up the Red River valley, across the Canadian Shield from Ontario, and out of the Superior basin. These advances left the Itasca and St. Croix moraines to mark their maximum spread. A slightly later advance of the Rainy lobe (from Ontario) and the Superior ice left the Vermilion, Highland, and Mille Lacs moraines.

About 16,000 years ago ice advancing from the Superior basin met Red River ice looping back to the *north* and formed a short-lived lake called Lake Grantsburg. Red River ice later advanced over much of the state of Minnesota, at one time extending south to Des Moines, Iowa. The period closed in Minnesota with an advance of Red River ice across the northern part of the state as far as the Mesabi Range, and a movement of Superior basin ice south and west.

In Wisconsin, this was the time of the Woodfordian ice, which left a prominent moraine stretching 900 miles (1450 kilometers) through the state. Interlobate moraines reveal the boundaries between the four separate ice lobes that moved into the state.

In Michigan, a time of ice retreat left a series of prominent recessional moraines across the southern part of the state. The period closed in Michigan with an ice advance from west, north, and east that left the Port Huron moraine.

Minnesota: Tripartite Advance

The early advance of the Hewitt ice was succeeded by a warmer period of glacial retreat that came to an end about 22,000 years ago. In Minnesota the warm period ended with the simultaneous advance of ice from all three centers. The Wadena lobe came south and east from the Red River valley. The Rainy lobe came straight south from Ontario to north-central and northeastern Minnesota. The Superior lobe sent a tongue of ice out of the Superior basin as far

Table 8: Events of 22,000–12,000 years ago in Minnesota

Events	Ice source	Deposits
St. Louis sublobe of Des Moines	Winnipeg Lowlands	
Thompson–Nickerson advance	Superior Basin	Nickerson Moraine
Des Moines advance	Winnipeg Lowlands	Anoka sand plain
Split Rock– Pine City Phases	Superior Basin, Winnipeg Lowlands	Glacial Lake Grantsburg
Automba Phase	Superior Basin, Ontario	Vermilion, Highland, Mille Lacs moraines
Itasca–St. Croix advance	Winnipeg Lowlands, Superior Basin, Ontario	Itasca and St. Croix moraines

south as the Twin Cities, and that lobe extended east well into Wisconsin.

The advancing Wadena lobe laid down part of the Itasca moraine, which extends west from near Walker at the south edge of Leech Lake in Cass County. Outwash from this lobe has created an extensive plain extending south from Park Rapids in Hubbard County to Menahga. Both the slope of the plain and the average particle size of the soil decrease toward the south. This outwash covered deposits left by the earlier Hewitt phase that still contained buried blocks of ice. When these melted, they formed the group of Crow Wing Lakes in southeastern Hubbard County. Outwash dotted with depressions left by the melting of buried ice blocks is called a *pitted outwash plain*. Although these are lakes formed from buried ice blocks, they differ from morainic lakes in that they are surrounded by much more level terrain.

North of the Itasca moraine the retreating ice left behind blocks that melted and formed depressions that are now the series of lakes through which the upper Mississippi flows: Cass Lake, Bemidji Lake, and Lake Winnibigoshish among them.

THE PHYSICAL ENVIRONMENT

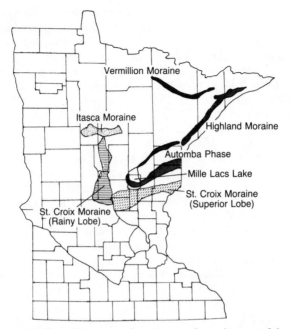

20. Deposits from Minnesota glaciation, early in the period from 22,000–12,000 years ago.

Groups of long, more-or-less parallel valleys were left by the ice of this time. Dr. N. E. Wright of the University of Minnesota has called them *tunnel valleys* and explains them as originating from local melting near the base of retreating glaciers. The escaping water cut the valleys in the drift below the ice. The Mississippi River flows north in a tunnel valley from its source at Lake Itasca on the Itasca moraine.

South of Leech Lake, the gray-to-light-brown sandy till of Paleozoic sedimentary rock that characterizes the Wadena lobe overlies till of the St. Croix moraine deposited by the Rainy lobe. This ice came south across the Precambrian rocks of northeastern Minnesota, and the brown sandy till contains fragments of basalt, gabbro, iron formation, and other igneous and metamorphic rock.

The Wadena ice and its fronting moraine dammed the Crow Wing River and thus formed a lake west of the St. Croix moraine in Wadena County. This glacial Lake Wadena may once have been 130 feet (40 meters) deep, and it deposited a blanket of sand over the old drumlins of the long-ago Hewitt phase. Temporary lakes, *proglacial lakes,* often form in front of retreating ice, sometimes from the damming of rivers and sometimes from the impoundment of meltwater between the terminal moraine and the ice front. Such lakes usually empty when the meltwater rises high enough to breach the moraine, when it begins to cut rapidly down through the unconsolidated glacial till.

The St. Croix moraine continues south as a steep, rugged ridge as far as Albany in Stearns County. It then extends southeast under a cover of younger drift. When it re-emerges near St. Paul, the composition of the drift has changed. It is now red and sandy with abundant fragments of Precambrian sandstone and shale. The ice that created this came out of the Superior basin. Still farther southeast, the moraine crosses the St. Croix south of Stillwater and continues into Wisconsin. This would seem to make it continuous with the Woodfordian terminal moraine, although dating of deposits indicates that the St. Croix moraine is older.

AUTOMBA PHASE

The ice advance that produced the Itasca and St. Croix moraines came to an end when the Superior lobe retreated to the divide in Pine County between the Lake Superior and Twin Cities lowlands. The Wadena lobe may have wasted all the way to Winnipeg. The Rainy lobe retreated about 200 miles (320 kilometers) from the St. Croix moraine before readvancing to deposit the Vermilion moraine in northeastern Minnesota. This is the northernmost area of extensive glacial deposits in northeastern Minnesota. In the lake country north of this moraine—which includes the Boundary Waters Canoe Area—the drift is thin and scattered and the lakes are basins scooped out of bedrock by the ice, their shapes largely determined by the nature of the rock.

One group of these lakes, strung out in a line along the Canada–Minnesota border, formed when ice moving south scooped out basins in soft, Precambrian slates between ridges of Keweenawan diabase (see Chapter 1). These diabase strata dip slightly south, so their upturned edges

THE PHYSICAL ENVIRONMENT

form steep north-facing slopes, while gentler south-facing slopes reveal the dip of the strata.

Other bedrock basin lakes include those which formed in Duluth gabbro where bands of slightly weaker rock offered less resistance to the passing ice.

Bedrock at the bottom of Saganaga Lake and other lakes on the Saganaga batholith is granite; their shape reveals the *joints*, lines of structural weakness, in this rock.

As the retreating glaciers grew thin, the amount of meltwater decreased, often to the point that the water could not carry the huge quantities of drift that were melting out of the ice. The excess load was deposited in long sinuous ridges that look like inverted stream valleys. These ridges, or *eskers*, are a record of streams that flowed under the ice.

During the Automba phase, ice advancing out of the Superior basin and climbing over the high ground along the north coast deposited the Highland moraine that extends as far north as Isabella. In order to flow onto this high ground, the ice would have had to be about 2500 feet (750 meters) thick, and it may have been 3000 feet (900 meters) thick at Silver Bay, about halfway up the north shore. It was probably 1000 feet (300 meters) thick at Duluth.

This Automba phase ice also moved southwest as far as Mille Lacs Lake. The terminal moraine rises steeply out of the lake along its south and west shores, creating a dam that prevents the natural drainage of the area and thus impounds the lake. Morainic dams are another way that glaciers create lakes. Lake Gogebic in northern Michigan and Lake Winnebago in Wisconsin are other examples of lakes created by morainic dams.

SPLIT ROCK—PINE CITY PHASES

The next glacial advance involved the Superior lobe again. This time it moved south to the divide in Pine County, depositing red clay up to 20 feet (6 meters) thick. At the same time, ice from the Red River valley was heading south toward Iowa. It sent a lobe northeast to near Grantsburg, Wisconsin, that breached and covered the St. Croix moraine near the Twin Cities. As this lobe later receded, its meltwater formed glacial Lake Grantsburg, which apparently lasted only about 100 years in Minnesota but may have lasted 2000 years on the Wisconsin side. The drift from this Grantsburg sublobe is gray and silty and contains numerous pieces of shale from the Red River valley. As the Grantsburg sublobe wasted and Lake Grantsburg drained away, Red River ice reached as far south as Des Moines and covered most of southern Minnesota.

ST. LOUIS SUBLOBE AND
THOMPSON–NICKERSON ADVANCE

The last major ice movements in Minnesota (about 12,000 years ago) involved Red River ice moving east across northern Minnesota to the Mesabi Range as the St. Louis sublobe, while Superior ice moved out of the basin as far as the Pine–Carlton County line where it deposited the Nickerson moraine. West of Moose Lake the moraine turns back northeast as the Thompson moraine.

The 10,000 very eventful years we have just described

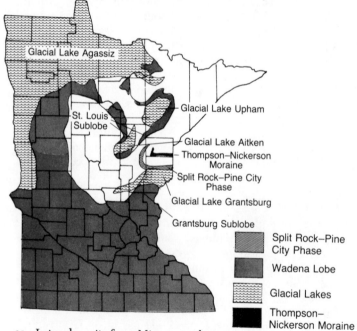

21. Later deposits from Minnesota glaciation, 22,000–12,000 years ago.

ended about 12,000 years ago with a general retreat of the ice. Carbon dating of pond sediments from northwestern Minnesota shows that by 11,740 years ago the St. Louis sublobe was completely wasted. By this time, the Rainy lobe had retreated into Ontario, but the Superior lobe remained at the Thompson moraine. The carbon date corresponds to the Two Creeks interstadial in Michigan and Wisconsin, a warm interval before the last glacial advance.

Wisconsin: Woodfordian Substage

During this same 10,000 years, the Woodfordian ice advanced over Wisconsin, leaving a terminal moraine that can be traced about 900 miles (1450 kilometers) through the state. The ice that created this very prominent glacial feature advanced for 2000 to 3000 years, reaching its maximum between 19,000 and 20,000 years ago. The ice advanced in four lobes, two coming south from Lake Superior and two heading south and west from Lake Michigan. The Lake Michigan lobe advanced as far south as northern Illinois and Indiana, while the lobes from Superior covered only the northern third of Wisconsin.

Between the lobes are interlobate moraines. These, receiving drift from both lobes, may develop massive morainic ridges. The border between the two lobes of Lake Superior ice is marked by a line of morainic hills and lakes that starts in southern Bayfield County near Cable and runs southwest into southern Washburn County.

An interlobate moraine that begins in Dickinson County, Michigan, runs southwest to Langlade County, Wisconsin. The Antigo outwash plain, a fertile farming area that partly surrounds the town of that name, is a product of runoff channeled between the two lobes.

The most impressive of these Woodfordian interlobate moraines is the Kettle moraine that formed between the Green Bay lobe and the Lake Michigan lobe, both of which came out of the Lake Michigan basin. The moraine extends northeast from near the Wisconsin–Illinois border almost to Green Bay.

The peak development of the moraine is in the North Unit of Kettle Moraine State Forest between the towns of Kewaskum and Greenbush. Some of the ridges here are

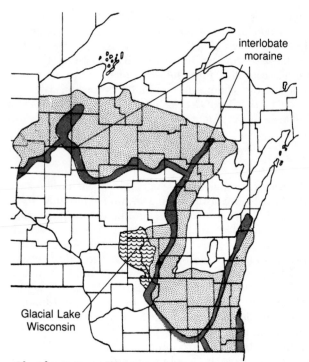

22. Glacial activity in Wisconsin, 22,000–12,000 years ago.

250 feet (75 meters) above the lowlands. All the major glacial features can be seen here—drumlins, eskers, and *kames*, the isolated hills of outwash formed by waters swirling down through holes in the ice.

Lakes are common on and north of the Woodfordian terminal moraine, mostly in drift 14,000 years old and younger, but they are especially abundant in two parts of the state. One of these zones is on the terminal and interlobate moraines and on pitted outwash in the northwestern part of the state in Polk, Burnett, Washburn, Sawyer, and Bayfield counties.

The other is in Vilas and Oneida counties, the area around Eagle River. As much as 40 percent of this district is either open water or swamp. The lakes around Eagle River

THE PHYSICAL ENVIRONMENT

Table 9: Events of 22,000–12,000 years ago in Wisconsin

Events	Ice Source	Deposits
Woodfordian substage	Superior Basin (Superior and Chippewa lobes), Michigan Basin (Green Bay and Lake Michigan lobes)	Woodfordian Moraine, three interlobate moraines; Glacial Lake Wisconsin

are a mixture of ice block pits in outwash, kettles in end moraines, and depressions in *ground moraines*. (As the Woodfordian ice retreated across this highland, it did not pause long enough to build a recessional moraine. Instead a fairly constant retreat left a continuous deposit of drift arranged in shallow hummocks and depressions. This is a ground moraine, and the lakes in this kind of deposit seldom reach 40 feet/12 meters in depth; most are in the 20–30-foot/6–10-meter range.)

Note that while this region is similar to northeastern Minnesota in its abundance of lakes, the causes that produced the lakes are quite different. The bedrock basins of Minnesota are surrounded by sharp ridges and numerous rock outcrops. The Wisconsin lakes are surrounded by hummocky rounded hills of drift. The many rocks at the surface are glacial erratics rather than bedrock outcrops. Topsoil is scanty in Minnesota as a result of glacial scouring, while some of the morainic soils of Wisconsin are deep and rich.

The meltwater from the Woodfordian glaciers created a very large lake, glacial Lake Wisconsin, in the central part of the state. At its greatest extent it covered 1800 square miles (12,000 square kilometers) and was 150 feet (45 meters) deep. Its shores formed a rough triangle between Portage on the south, Tomah on the northwest, and Wisconsin Rapids on the northeast.

Glacial Lake Wisconsin shrank after the Wisconsin River breached a moraine to the south and began to carry the meltwater to the Mississippi. However, this low flat area

23. Rocks of Cambrian sandstone eroded into castellated buttes from wave action of Glacial Lake Wisconsin, Mill Bluff State Park, Wisconsin. *Wisconsin Department of Natural Resources.*

still has enormous swamps and marshes. Cranberries are grown commercially here, but much of the land is covered with scrubby forest. The Necedah National Wildlife Refuge is located on the old lake plain; so are substantial state game reserves and a protected nesting area of sandhill cranes. The soil at the surface is sandy, supporting a southern extension of the upper Great Lakes pine forest, but under the sands are clays and silts, lake deposits that are hard for percolating water to penetrate. The soils keep the water table close to the surface.

Among the more interesting remnants of the lake scattered through this area are the castellated buttes. Some of these can be seen along Interstate 94 north of Mauston. They are Cambrian sandstones that were cut into their current rugged shapes by waves on glacial Lake Wisconsin.

The bed of the lake covered portions of what is known as the Driftless Area, a part of the state that—for unknown reasons—escaped glaciation. The north end of this area just overlaps the southern end of the North Woods. The Driftless Area is an old landscape, a low plateau deeply dissected by stream valleys, quite unlike the ice-formed land of most of our region.

THE PHYSICAL ENVIRONMENT

Michigan: Cary–Mankato (Port Huron) Advance

In Michigan, the record begins with the Cary period, about 16,000 years ago. Prior to that time the entire state was covered with ice. The Cary was a time of ice retreat in the state, a retreat broken by some readvances. Four separate lobes affected parts of the Lower Peninsula: the Michigan, Huron, Saginaw, and Erie, but the last of these covered only the extreme south.

During the Cary, the retreating Saginaw lobe left a series of long arcing moraines in the southern half of the peninsula. As it melted back into present-day Saginaw Bay, glacial Lake Saginaw formed in front of the ice. Today this is an area of very flat terrain with some clay and some sandy soils. The moraines of the retreating Michigan lobe parallel the present Lake Michigan shore.

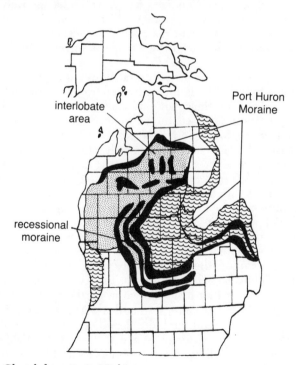

24. Glacial deposits in Michigan, 22,000–12,000 years ago.

Table 10:   Events of 22,000–12,000 years ago in Michigan

Events	Ice Source	Deposits
Port Huron advance	Michigan and Huron Basins	Port Huron Moraine
Cary stage; ice retreats leaving recessional moraines	Michigan, Huron, and Erie Basins	Glacial Lake Saginaw

Following this long retreat, the ice readvanced from three sides to the Port Huron moraine. This feature enters the state from the west near Muskegon, arcs around to the north and east, and then swings south to Saginaw. Parts of the southeastern section were laid down under the waters of glacial Lake Saginaw. Moraines that formed underwater tend to have a rather muted aspect. The effect of the waters is to even out the rough topography seen in a dry-land moraine.

A large portion of north-central Lower Michigan is an interlobate area. The last ice retreated from this part of the state during Cary time, but outwash from both the Michigan and Huron lobes continued to flood the area after the ice was gone. Morainic hills appear as islands in a sea of outwash here. The outwash is mostly sand; even many of the ridges are covered with a blanket of sand. Much of this was a pine barren at the time of settlement, and large areas are covered with a jack pine forest today. The sandy loam soils here produced some of the greatest white pine forests in the upper Great Lakes.

The Port Huron advance occurred about 13,000 years ago. It was followed by a retreat that uncovered all of Lower Michigan, the Straits of Mackinac, and part of the Upper Peninsula. This ice retreat, the Two Creeks inter-stadial, is named for a small town in northern Manitowoc County, Wisconsin. Here, during this warm period, a forest of spruce, fir, and birch developed, a forest much like the boreal forests of today. When the ice of the Valders advance came south from the Superior basin, it buried this forest. It also buried some of the wildlife in the area, in-

THE PHYSICAL ENVIRONMENT

cluding mammoth, bison, musk ox, moose, and caribou. Carbon dates from the wood indicate that this burial occurred about 11,850 years ago.

The Valders Advance

(12,000 TO 9500 YEARS AGO)

The Valders, the last major advance of the Wisconsin glaciation, originated in the Superior basin and left a distinctive iron-rich red drift wherever it passed. It apparently did little scouring of the bedrock in its path, and it moved rather rapidly, indications that the Valders ice was a rather thin fluid mass.

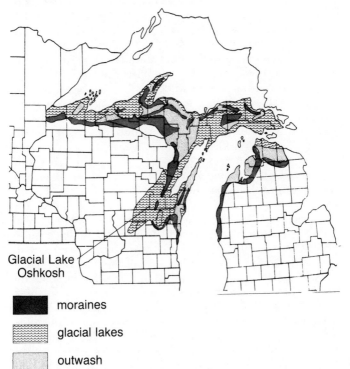

Glacial Lake Oshkosh

■ moraines

glacial lakes

outwash

25. Extent of Valders ice in Wisconsin and Michigan.

Lake Superior is almost surrounded by highlands that exerted a powerful check on ice moving out of the basin. The Valders ice left no record on the steep ridges of the north shore. To the south, the copper range in Douglas County, Wisconsin, the headland of the Bayfield Peninsula, the Penokee–Gogebic iron range, the Porcupine Mountains, the Keweenaw Peninsula, and the Huron Mountains all presented obstacles to the ice. Only at the eastern end of the basin could the ice flow across the Upper Peninsula and onto the northern edge of Lower Michigan.

Valders in Minnesota and Wisconsin

In Minnesota, the ice in Valders time did not move. It remained at the Thompson-Nickerson moraine. In western Wisconsin, the Valders moraine has traditionally been located in a line of hills and lakes, including Lake Amnicon and Lake Nebagamon in Douglas County and the lakes south of Iron River in Bayfield County. However, while these deposits did occur late in Wisconsin time, there is now some question as to whether they are synchronous with the Valders advance to the east. Along the Penokee–Gogebic iron range, the morainic hills are mixed with rugged bedrock hills, and bedrock outcrops often break through the thin drift.

The terminal moraine continues east along the southern border of Upper Michigan as the Watersmeet moraine. The northernmost lakes of the Eagle River area lie on the moraine.

In eastern Wisconsin, the Valders ice covered much less ground than the Woodfordian. The ice reached the latitude of Milwaukee in the Michigan Basin. Another narrow lobe extended south to the southern tip of modern Lake Winnebago, where it built a terminal moraine that impounded glacial Lake Oshkosh. This tongue followed a lowland underlain by Ordovician rocks that are much less erosion resistant than the Silurian Niagara escarpment to the east. Green Bay is cut in this rock. This lake endured until the ice receded from Green Bay. Lake Winnebago and several smaller lakes remain today in depressions in the old lake bottom.

THE PHYSICAL ENVIRONMENT

Events	Ice Source	Deposits
Valders Advance	Superior Basin	Valders Moraine, Glacial Lake Oshkosh
Two Creeks Interstadial	Time of ice retreat	Two Creeks Buried Forest

Valders in Michigan

In Lower Michigan the Valders moraine lies just north of the Port Huron moraine. It enters from the west just north of Muskegon, arcing north and east before entering Lake Huron about 2 miles (3 kilometers) south of Rogers City. The moraine is often weakly developed. In some areas it overlaps into the inner margins of the Port Huron moraine, but the red drift does not extend high up the slopes of the older hills. These are further indications that the Valders ice was rather thin as glaciers go.

In the western Upper Peninsula the retreat of the Valders ice is marked by a number of moraines that trend north and south, thereby revealing the effect of the highlands we mentioned above. The ice came around these uplands on its way south and it went back around them on the way north.

The resistant rocks of these uplands break through the cover of drift in several areas. There are exposures of Keewatin greenstone and Algoman granite and granite gneiss just south of the Penokee–Gogebic iron range. The Keweenaw copper range is mainly Portage Lake lava of Keweenawan age, and late Keweenawan sedimentary rock is exposed near the tip of the Keweenaw Peninsula. West of Marquette, Huronian iron ranges and Algoman granites crop out, and at Laughing Whitefish Point the Jacobsville sandstone of late Keweenawan or early Cambrian age is exposed.

In the eastern Upper Peninsula the retreating ice left

two major morainic systems—the Munising and the New-berry. These join at their eastern tips. Much of this part of the state was underwater in late glacial and early postglacial time, and part of these moraines were deposited underwater. The moraines are surrounded by sandy outwash plains and clayey lake-bottom sediments, and dunes and beach ridges mark the advance and retreat of ancient lake waters.

Hundreds of square miles of this lowland is occupied by swamps, marshes, and bogs today. The only major bedrock outcrops are the Cambrian sandstones at Pictured Rocks and the Silurian dolomite of the Niagara Escarpment along the north shore of Lake Michigan. Much of this rock was exposed by wave erosion in the postglacial Great Lakes. The history of these lakes will be told in the next chapter.

The Valders ice had retreated to the Superior basin by about 9500 years ago, leaving all the land ice free. As the ice continued to retreat it left the basin entirely, although meltwater continued to enter the basin from the north. In geological terms the Valders ended with the complete wasting of the continental glaciers and the return to present sea level, an event that occurred only about 5000 years ago.

CHAPTER FOUR

The Birth of
the Great Lakes

THE GREAT LAKES are the only glacial features that are visible from the moon. Together they spread over 95,000 square miles (245,000 square kilometers) and have a combined shoreline 8300 miles (13,400 kilometers) long. Their watershed area, some 295,000 square miles (764,000 square kilometers), is relatively small, considering the lakes' great size, yet they hold more than six billion gallons of water, one-sixth of the world's supply of fresh water.

Drainage from the modern lakes is easterly. Lake Superior drains into Lake Michigan at Sault Ste. Marie; Lake Michigan drains into Huron through the Straits of Mackinac; and Huron drains south along the St. Clair River into the Erie basin. Erie drains into Ontario, and Ontario's water flows down the St. Lawrence River to the Atlantic Ocean.

Lake Superior, largest of the group, has an area of 31,820 square miles (82,410 square kilometers) and stands at an elevation of 602 feet (183 meters). It is also the deepest, to 700 feet (215 meters) below sea level near the center of the syncline in which it formed.

Lake Huron covers 23,010 square miles (59,600 square kilometers) and averages 580 feet (177 meters) above sea level. Its floor at the deepest point is 170 feet (51 meters) below sea level.

Lake Michigan contains 22,400 square miles (58,020 square kilometers); its surface elevation is the same as that of Lake Huron—580 feet (177 meters). It is actually made of two separate basins divided by a submerged ridge of Silurian dolomite that runs east and west between the vicinities of Milwaukee, Wisconsin, and Grand Haven, Michigan. Its deepest point, 343 feet (105 meters) below sea level, is in the northern basin.

Table 12: Formation of the Great Lakes.

Date (years before present)	Glacial Event	Superior (602)
3,000	Lake Agassiz drained away	Algoma (595)
4,000		Nipissing (605)
9,500		Houghton (360) →
		Minong (470) →
		Post-Duluth →
		↓ Duluth (1,070)
11,500	Valders maximum	
11,850	Two Creeks Interstadial, Lake Agassiz formed	Keweenaw
		↓
13,000	Advance of Port Huron ice lobe	
13,300		Lake?
	Lake Border Moraine	
	Tinley–Defiance Moraine	
	Valparaiso Moraine	
14,000		

Adapted from Dorr and Eschman, *Geology of Michigan,* University of Michigan Press, 1971.

THE PHYSICAL ENVIRONMENT

Shaded areas indicate periods of glacial ice; arrows indicate direction of lake outlets $\binom{N}{\uparrow}$.

Michigan (580)	Huron (580)	Erie (573)	Ontario (246)
Algoma (595) →		Lake Erie (573) →	Lake Ontario (246) →
Nipissing (605) →			
Chippewa (230) →	Stanley (190)	→	→
Post-Algonquin Lakes →		Early Lake Erie	Early Lake Ontario
Algonquin (605) ↓			
Algonquin–Kirkfield stage (565) →			
Lake Chicago, Toleston stage (605) ↓	Early Algonquin (605) ↓	←	Iroquois →
Lake Chicago, Calumet stage (620) ↓	Lundy (620) ←		→
Chicago, Glenwood stage II (640) ↓	Grassmere (640) ←		→
	Warren (682–690) ←		
	Saginaw (695) ←	Whittlesey (738)	→
	Arkona II (695) ←		
Low-water stage before Port Huron advance (elevation and drainage unknown)			
Chicago, Glenwood stage I (640) ↓	Arkona (710, 700, 695) ←		
	Early Saginaw ←	Maumee (780, 760, 800) ←	
Early Lake Chicago ↓			

Lake Erie is 9940 square miles (25,740 square kilometers) in area with a surface elevation of 573 feet (175 meters) and a bottom elevation of 362 feet (110 meters) above sea level. Lake Ontario is 7540 square miles (19,530 square kilometers), has a surface 246 feet (75 meters) above sea level and a floor 532 feet (162 meters) below sea level.

Because the latter two "lower lakes" in the system are outside the area we are concerned with in this book, we will not describe their histories in detail.

Before the Ice Ages, the basins of today's Great Lakes were stream valleys. The glaciers advanced along the river beds, following paths of least resistance and gouging out wider and deeper depressions as the weight of the ice grew. In a few hundred-thousand years more—and barring a return of the glaciers—the basins may be stream valleys again. All lakes eventually fill with sediments and vegetation, or their outlets cut deeply enough into bedrock to drain all the water away. On a geologic time scale, they are fragile and short-lived things.

The Proglacial Lakes

The history of the Great Lakes begins about 14,000 years ago during the retreat of the Woodfordian glacier. The first basins to be uncovered were those of Lake Michigan and Lake Erie. Meltwater, impounded between ice fronts and the moraines that had marked the farthest advance of the glacier, formed the first of what are called *proglacial* lakes (lakes formed in front of a glacier). The first proglacial lake in the Michigan basin was called Lake Chicago; that in the Erie basin was called Maumee. Many more would form in the five basins over the next 11,000 years.

Although water levels and thus shorelines in these lakes probably varied with changes in weather every year, as they do in the modern Great Lakes, geologists have assigned separate proglacial lake names only to bodies of water that either stayed at the same average elevation or used the same outlets long enough to develop distinctive and still discernible beach ridges or other shoreline features.

THE PHYSICAL ENVIRONMENT

Why Lake Levels Changed

Major and long-term changes in the elevation of the lakes occurred for several reasons. The most obvious was that, as the glaciers alternately retreated and advanced, they uncovered new outlets or blocked old ones. Lake levels dropped rapidly and then stabilized as each outlet eroded down to bedrock. The glaciers' retreat also, literally, took a heavy load off the landscape. In response the earth's crust rebounded, causing lake levels to rise or the directions of drainage to shift as the elevations of their outlets rose.

Expanding Lake Chicago

Lake Chicago drained south along the Des Plaines and Illinois rivers to the Mississippi throughout its 3700-year history, but its size and extent varied widely during different periods. It occupied only the southernmost portion of the Lake Michigan basin in its earliest stages; at its maximum, it reached almost to the southern tip of Door County in Wisconsin and to the northern tip of Lower Michigan, where it merged with proglacial Lake Lundy in the Huron basin.

During the earliest, or Glenwood stage of Lake Chicago when the surface stood at 640 feet (195 meters) above sea level, a proglacial lake was also forming in the lowland area of Michigan that now surrounds Saginaw Bay. When this lake merged with meltwater in the Erie basin, Lake Maumee was replaced by a larger Lake Arkona. Drainage was west along the Grand River into Lake Chicago.

At the mouth of that river near what is today the town of Allendale, Michigan, a 100-square-mile (260-square-kilometer) delta formed. The remains of the Allendale delta, since covered with the sands and silts of later lake borders and also eroded by streams, can still be seen about 13 miles (21 kilometers) east of Lake Michigan's present shore.

Water levels in the new lakes dropped for awhile as outlets eroded; they rose again when the ice advanced to deposit the Port Huron moraine (see Figure 24).

26. Shaded areas show extent of early Lake Chicago and Lake Maumee (modified from Flint, *Glacial and Pleistocene Geology*, John Wiley & Sons, Inc., 1957).

Lakes in the Huron and Erie Basins

The Huron lobe's advance across Lake Arkona separated it into two lakes, Whittlesey (elevation 738 feet/225 meters) in the Erie basin and Lake Saginaw (elevation 695 feet/ 212 meters) in the Saginaw lowlands of the Huron basin. Shorelines for Lake Saginaw were about 50 miles (80 kilometers) inland and 115 feet (35 meters) above present Lake Huron. Lake Whittlesey discharged across the "thumb" area of Michigan into Lake Saginaw which, in turn, drained west along the Grand River to Lake Chicago.

As the glaciers receded northward from the Port Huron moraine, more outlets were uncovered and proglacial Lake Warren spread over the Huron and Erie basins that Saginaw and Whittlesey had filled. Its surface elevation

THE PHYSICAL ENVIRONMENT

ranged from 682 to 690 feet (208 to 210 meters); but crustal rebound, the earth's recovery from weight of the ice that once covered it, lifted Lake Warren beaches—long after the lake was gone—as high as 760 feet (232 meters) at Bad Axe, Michigan.

When most of the Huron basin became free of ice, the elevation of the water in that basin dropped to 640 feet (195 meters) when a single lake called Grassmere occupied the Michigan, Huron, and Erie basins. This period is also re-ferred to as Glenwood II in glacial histories of Lake Michi-gan. The area now occupied by the Straits of Mackinac was still under ice; the connection between the two basins was a narrow strait that followed a route past modern Lakes Mul-let and Burt, and the Indian River between the towns of Cheboygan and Petoskey, Michigan. The great volume of water pouring through that channel soon cut it down to bedrock; Lake Chicago stabilized at the Calumet stage, and Lake Lundy was created in the Huron basin, both at eleva-tions of 620 feet (189 meters).

Lake Superior's First Ancestor

At about this time, but possibly both before and after the readvance of ice to the Port Huron moraine, a small progla-cial lake called Keweenaw began forming at the southwest corner of the Lake Superior basin near Duluth.

As the glaciers continued to retreat, an early Lake Al-gonquin stabilized at 605 feet (184 meters) in the Huron and Erie basins and drained both south through the Chicago outlet and east along the St. Clair River—into the Erie basin and over the Niagara escarpment into a Lake Ontario ancestor, Lake Iroquois. The Illinois River in the Chicago outlet system reached bedrock, meanwhile, at the same level, and the Toleston stage of Lake Chicago was born.

A number of former islands, beaches, wave-cut cliffs, stacks, and sand dunes that date from early Lake Algonquin can still be seen along the northern tip of Lower Michigan in Emmet, Cheboygan, and Presque Isle counties. Notches in the bedrock of cliffs on Mackinac Island also date from Lake Algonquin times.

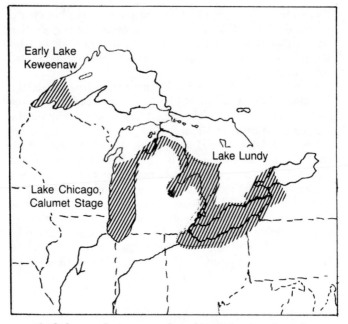

27. Shaded areas show extent of proglacial lakes Lundy, Calumet, and Keweenaw (modified from Flint, *Glacial and Pleistocene Geology*, John Wiley & Sons, Inc., 1957).

The Two Creeks Interval

About 12,000 years ago, when the ice had retreated far enough to uncover new drainageways in the St. Lawrence lowlands of Ontario, water levels in the Michigan and Huron basins dropped drastically and a low-water period called the Two Creeks interval began. Drainage shifted temporarily north and east, partly because of crustal rebound. The Kirkfield low-water stage of Lake Algonquin occupied both basins at an elevation of 565 feet (172 meters).

Advance of the Valders ice ended the warm weather and closed outlets that had kept the lake levels low. Water in the Michigan and Huron basins rose again to the 605-foot (184-meter) Lake Algonquin level, and streams that had cut into the Allendale delta west of Grand Rapids during the

Two Creeks period were filled with fine-grained lacustrine sediments.

As the Valders ice waned in its turn, several small lakes began forming again in the Lake Superior basin south of the copper range in Douglas, Bayfield, and Ashland counties, Wisconsin. A hill east of the Bois Brule River and south of the town of Brule, Wisconsin, shows marks of wave action that indicate it was an island in one of these lakes. An old beach ridge which crosses Highway 13 about 3 miles (5 kilometers) north of Mellen, Wisconsin, marks the southern boundary of another of these early lakes.

Lake Duluth

These small lakes eventually merged into glacial Lake Duluth, which formed at an elevation of 1070 feet (326 me-

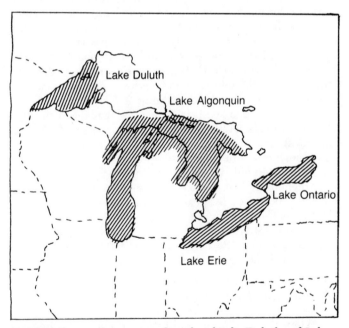

28. Shaded areas show extent of proglacial Lake Duluth and Lake Algonquin (modified from Flint, *Glacial and Pleistocene Geology*, John Wiley & Sons, Inc., 1957).

ters) between the ice front and the Valders moraine in northwestern Wisconsin. The lake drained down the Bois Brule to the St. Croix River and thus to the Mississippi in its early stages.

The ice continued to retreat, and about 10,000 years ago a new eastern outlet opened along the valley of the Whitefish River between Marquette and AuTrain bays south to Little Bay de Noc in Michigan's Upper Peninsula. Six post-Duluth glacial lakes, ranging from 1007 to 950 feet (307 to 290 meters) above sea level date from this period. Apparently, ice covered the eastern part of the Superior basin for a long time; there is no record there of Algonquin or any other lake at that elevation.

Agassiz, the Sixth Great Lake

Another "great" lake, long since disappeared, also formed during the Two Creeks period when the Wadena ice lobe in Minnesota melted back far enough to expose the Red River lowlands. Glacial Lake Agassiz at its maximum occupied 200,000 square miles (518,000 square kilometers) of northwestern Minnesota, eastern North Dakota, southeastern Manitoba, and southwestern Ontario. An eastward arm of it extended almost to Ely, Minnesota.

Agassiz drained south in its early stages down the Red River to the glacial River Warren, a predecessor of the Minnesota River. When the ice melted back far enough to expose northern outlets, drainage shifted in the shallow lake; Agassiz lasted only a few hundred more years.

Much of the bed of Lake Agassiz in northern Minnesota today is occupied by peat bogs that spread over several large counties; they are among the state's important economic resources. Lake of the Woods in Ontario and Upper and Lower Red Lakes in Minnesota also occupy part of the old Lake Agassiz basin.

Algonquin II and Minong

When the ice border had retreated enough to uncover the Trent Lowlands between Georgian Bay and Lake Ontario in Canada, levels in the Michigan and Huron basins dropped again below the Algonquin level, stabilizing at intervals long enough to establish at least six beach ridges which are still visible in a number of places. On Mackinac Island, Michigan, 12 such Algonquin-age beach ridges are still discernible.

Meanwhile, in the Superior basin, Lake Minong formed at 470 feet (143 meters) above sea level when the Valders ice finally reached the present north shore of Lake Superior.

The Smallest "Great Lakes"

By 9500 years ago, the glaciers had retreated far enough to free all of the Great Lake basins of ice. An outlet at North Bay, Ontario, near the Quebec border, was uncovered, and

29. Shaded areas show extent of proglacial lakes Houghton, Chippewa, and Stanley (modified from Flint, *Glacial and Pleistocene Geology*, John Wiley & Sons, Inc., 1957).

water levels dropped to an all-time low in the Michigan and Huron basins. Lake Chippewa in the Michigan basin had an elevation of 230 feet (70 meters), and Lake Stanley in the Huron basin stabilized at 190 feet (56 meters). Lake Houghton in the Superior basin was 360 feet (110 meters) above sea level and drained east through a gap in the Superior sill at Sault Ste. Marie.

The earth's crust in the lake basins had been rebounding gradually for hundreds of years by this time. Each proglacial lake had its own *hinge line*, a line across the lake which indicated where rebound began. Shorelines south of each hinge line are horizontal; those north of the line tilt upward at a precise angle as elevations increased in response to relief from the weight of the ice.

The Lake Algonquin hinge line in the Michigan basin, for instance, extends east in a line from just south of Kewaunee, Wisconsin., to Manistee, Michigan. The still-traceable border of that lake, extending north from the hinge line on the Michigan side, stands at 619 feet (189 meters) above sea level at Traverse City and at 813 feet (248 meters) 80 miles (130 kilometers) north on Mackinac Island. What was once a horizontal feature now slopes an average of 2.4 feet per mile (45 centimeters per kilometer).

Lake Nipissing and the Great Lakes Dunes

Rebound after the lakes were ice-free caused lake levels to rise gradually as the elevations of their outlets rose; it also reopened southern drainage outlets. A Nipissing Great Lake formed in the Michigan, Huron, and Superior basins about 4000 years ago when the North Bay outlet had been uplifted 415 feet (126 meters) to match the 605-foot (184-meter) elevation of outlets at Chicago and along the St. Clair River in Michigan.

Wave action in Nipissing time once again shaped strong shoreline features, many of which are still visible today. Dunes formed then which can be seen now on Lake Michigan's eastern shore include those at Warren Dunes State Park south of Benton Harbor, at Holland State Park, Ludington State Park, Orchard Beach State Park, Benzie State Park, and Sleeping Bear Dunes National Lakeshore.

THE PHYSICAL ENVIRONMENT

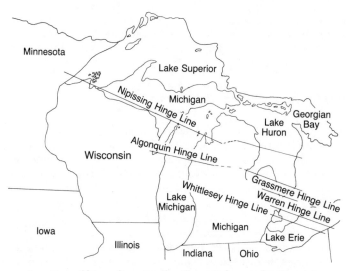

30. Location of hinge lines on the Great Lakes, reflecting rising elevations due to rebound from weight of glacial ice (Dorr & Eschman, *Geology of Michigan*).

At Sleeping Bear the dunes rise 450 feet (137 meters) above the water level of modern Lake Michigan. The dunes themselves are not actually that thick, however; they are "perched" on a platform of glacial till that was submerged in Lake Nipissing time. Crustal rebound has also uplifted the dunes since they were deposited.

The mouths of many stream valleys that had been eroded to the Chippewa and Stanley levels were drowned by the rising waters of Lake Nipissing and some were cut off from the main lake by construction of baymouth bars and spits. Two former bays that are now lakes adjacent to Lake Michigan are Crystal Lake north of Frankfort, Michigan, and Hamlin Lake north of Ludington.

Wave-cut cliffs and stacks cut in Cambrian sandstone on the south shore of Lake Superior at Pictured Rocks National Lakeshore were also shaped in Nipissing time.

In Wisconsin, abandoned beach ridges from Algonquin and Nipissing time can be seen on the shore of Lake Michigan at Point Beach State Park in Kewaunee County and at the Ridges Sanctuary north of Bailey's Harbor in Door County. The Ridges complex has 16 parallel beach ridges

Birth of the Great Lakes

that curve to reflect the shape of the original bay. The oldest is probably Algonquin; a beach and dune complex at the water's edge today has the same curving shape and direction as the others.

The Lakes Tip Southward

By 3500 years ago crustal rebound had raised elevations enough at the north end of the Great Lakes basins that the North Bay outlet was no longer operative, and drainage shifted entirely to the south. The Des Plaines River had already reached bedrock, so the St. Clair River became the dominant outlet. Rapid downcutting occurred until it, too, reached bedrock, and Lake Algoma came into being in the Superior, Michigan, and Huron basins at elevation 595 feet (181 meters). It lasted until about 3200 years ago when the St. Clair River changed course—away from its bedrock sill to an area underlain by glacial till.

Birth of the Modern Great Lakes

Downcutting in the new course of the St. Clair River proceeded rapidly until the new stream bed reached bedrock at 580 feet (177 meters) and modern Lakes Michigan and Huron were born. The new lowered lake level combined with further crustal rebound in the Superior basin caused the sill at Sault Ste. Marie to emerge again, and modern Lake Superior stabilized at its present level, 602 feet (183 meters). Lake Superior continues today to rebound from the weight of the ice, its northeastern edge rising at a rate of 12 to 20 inches (30 to 50 centimeters) a century—less than 0.2 inches (0.5 centimeters) a year—relative to its western shore. This has caused erosion to increase slightly in recent centuries on the lake's southwest shore near Duluth–Superior on the Minnesota–Wisconsin border. A new delta, a mile (1.6 kilometers) long and half a mile (0.8 kilometers) wide, has also formed in modern times on Lake Superior's north shore near the town of Silver Bay, Minnesota. The source of this delta is taconite tailings (taconite

31. Sleeping Bear Dune, Sleeping Bear Dunes National Lake-shore, near Traverse City, Michigan. *National Park Service.*

is a low-grade form of iron ore) from a Reserve Mining Company plant.

The geology of the Great Lakes in general, however, has changed very little over the past 2500 years. One reason for this is that the outlets, as noted earlier, have long since cut down to bedrock. Another reason is that the lakes' combined watershed is unusually small considering the size and extent of these bodies of water. Sediment in modern Lake Superior, for instance, piles up at the rate of 0.01 to 0.02 inches (0.3 to 0.5 millimeters) each year, not noticeably different from the sedimentation rate in the lake before settlement.

Biological changes, in contrast, have been enormous and in many cases ecologically devastating since European settlement of the region. Those changes will be discussed in Chapter 17, Life in Northern Waters.

CHAPTER FIVE

Climate

THE NORTH WOODS lie in a zone of humid continental climate with cold winters, cool summers, and precipitation scattered throughout the year. The climate is the major hazard faced by people who want to enjoy the north country outdoors. Extreme cold is frequent during the winters, midsummer frosts are not unheard of, and cold rain can fall anytime.

The Great Lakes exert a powerful moderating effect on this general pattern, locally creating a marine climate with cooler summers, warmer winters, a longer growing season, increased precipitation, and less sunshine. Since the prevailing winds in the region are westerly—often from the northwest in winter—the effects of the lakes are most pronounced on their southern and eastern shores. However, even on the northwestern shore of Lake Superior in Minnesota, temperatures average 10° F (−5.5° C) higher in January and 10° F (−5.5° C) lower in July than the figures recorded at inland stations just a few miles away.

Elevation also has an effect, even though the highest point in the region—Minnesota's Eagle Mountain (2301 feet/701 meters)—is only 1700 feet (520 meters) above the region's low points, the surfaces of Lakes Michigan and Huron. The coolest, wettest places in Wisconsin and Upper Michigan are in the northern highlands, the high country that forms the southeastern edge of the Canadian Shield. In Lower Michigan, the coldest places are inland on tablelands averaging 1700 feet (520 meters) above sea level.

Temperature

Average annual temperatures in the region range from a high of 46° F (8° C) along the Lake Michigan shore in central Lower Michigan to 39° F (4° C) in northeastern Minnesota. However, these annual averages are not very revealing, since the distinctive feature of a continental climate is the great difference between summer and winter temperatures. The highest temperature ever recorded in the region was 112° F (44.4° C) at Mio in the pine forests of northern Lower Michigan. Michigan's record low temperature occurred just a few miles away at Vanderbilt, where a reading of −51° F (−46.1° C) was recorded on February 9, 1934. This is a difference between hottest and coldest of 163° F (91° C). The record coldest reading in the region was made in northern Minnesota, where the thermometer once dropped to −59° F (−51° C). This kind of extreme is rare, but since records have been kept, the temperature has fallen to −40° F (−40° C) somewhere in Wisconsin during more than half of the winters, and −30° F (−34° C) occurs almost every year. The average temperature is below freezing four months a year in the south, five months in the north.

Extreme summer heat is less common. In northern Wisconsin, the temperature tops 90° F (32° C) only two to four days a year. Summer days are usually mild, with temperatures in the 70s or low 80s (21 to 28° C).

Precipitation

Precipitation in the region is generally greater in the east than in the west, with 32 inches (81 centimeters) an average for Lower Michigan and as little as 22 inches (56 centimeters) in northwestern Minnesota where the northern forest gives way to the prairie. In the highlands of northern Wisconsin and Upper Michigan, as much as 34 inches (86 centimeters) falls. In northeastern Minnesota, the average is just over 27 inches (69 centimeters).

About two-thirds of this precipitation falls during the five warmest months of the year—May through September—and June is the wettest month throughout the region. In northwestern Wisconsin, the average for the month is nearly 5 inches (13 centimeters), and over most of the region the five warmest months average more than 3 inches (8 centimeters) of precipitation.

Summer Storms

Summer rains often come in thundershowers, although these become less common as you move north. The storms may be accompanied by hail, high winds, and occasional tornadoes. Thunderstorms occur in very unstable conditions when air near the surface is heated enough to rise rapidly. It cools as it rises and moisture is precipitated out. The updrafts created by this process are strong enough to hold rain or hail up in the air until the drops, or the hailstones, become quite large.

Something has to replace the rising air at the surface, and in thunderstorms there is usually a circulation pattern in which updrafts are balanced by downdrafts. Some of these downdrafts are powerful enough to produce extremely destructive winds called downbursts. In one recent storm in Wisconsin, a downburst wind was clocked at 157 mph (253 km/hr). This storm, which occurred on July 4, 1977, did extensive damage along a course 166 miles (267 kilometers) long and 17 miles (27 kilometers) wide. Winds of over 40 mph (64 km/hr) blew throughout this area, and at 25 separate points, downburst winds of more than 73 mph (117 km/hr) touched the surface.

Downburst winds in some ways act like tornadoes. They do not affect wide areas as hurricanes do. Instead, they touch down at isolated points along the route of a storm and unaccountably skip over other areas. However, they differ from tornadoes in that their winds all blow in one direction. Tornadoes are vortices with winds spiralling into the intense low pressure area in the center of the funnel cloud. Trees blown down by a tornado will be twisted in every direction; tree trunks knocked over by a downburst all fall in the same direction.

The Independence Day storm in Wisconsin leveled 850,000 acres (344 hectares) of forest. A downburst storm in the Superior National Forest in Minnesota in the spring of 1976 left a swath of downed and damaged timber ¼ mile (0.4 kilometers) wide and 10 miles (16 kilometers) long.

Destructive winds of this kind can play an important role in the life of a forest. The downed timber dries out, creating a fire hazard that lasts for years. When fires do break

THE PHYSICAL ENVIRONMENT

out, they clear the ground for plant species adapted to postfire conditions. As we shall see in Part II, fire has played an important role in determining the nature of the vegetation in the forests of the region.

Spring, Fall, and Winter Storms

Precipitation amounts for the winter months are generally between 1 and 2 inches (2.5 and 5 centimeters). However, this figure can be misleading, since the great majority of this precipitation falls as snow. The water content of snow varies considerably, but on the average, 10 inches (25 centimeters) of snow would melt down to 1 inch (2.5 centimeters) of water, though in some cases it may take as many as 30 inches (75 centimeters) of snow to equal an inch of water. Snowfalls range from just under 50 inches (127 centimeters) a year in the south to nearly 300 inches (762 centimeters) a year in the Upper Peninsula of Michigan.

The movement of cyclones and anticyclones across the region from west to east produces much of the spring, fall, and winter weather. Cyclones (not to be confused with the tropical storms of the same name nor with tornadoes, which some Midwesterners call cyclones) are huge cells of low-pressure air that may be hundreds of miles across. Wind is the flow of air down a pressure gradient, so the winds in a cyclone flow toward the middle of the cell where the air pressure is lowest.

However, this flow is not straight toward the center. A force created by the earth's rotation, the Coriolis force, diverts the winds so that the air spirals toward the center of the low-pressure cell. In the northern hemisphere, this movement is counterclockwise; in the southern hemisphere, it is clockwise. The velocity of the wind varies directly with the difference in pressure, blowing stronger into an intense low and weaker into a shallow low. Air flows outward from a high pressure cell, spiraling in a clockwise direction in the northern hemisphere. As a general rule, if you stand with your back to the wind, low pressure will be to your left; high pressure to your right.

Air masses of different temperature and pressure do not mix easily, so the borders of adjoining high- and low-pressure cells form well-marked zones called fronts. At a front, warmer low-pressure air rides up over cooler high-pressure air. When this occurs, the low-pressure air is cooled, and if the cooling is sufficient the water vapor in the air will precipitate out as rain or snow.

In a typical storm sequence, cool air would be overridden from the west or southwest by warmer, moist, low-pressure air, often of Pacific origin. Snow or rain, depending on the season, would occur along this front. On the western edge of the warm low-pressure air, another front, a cold front, would form at the boundary with cold, dry, high-pressure air. The warm air riding up over the cold would produce more precipitation.

To an observer on the ground, the first sign of the approaching storm would be high thin layers of clouds of the type called cirrus moving from west to east. These might appear as much as 24 hours ahead of the storm. Behind them the cloud cover would thicken as the front approached and eventually rain or snow would begin to fall.

The actual passage of the front is likely to be marked by an increase in temperature. The temperature would drop again with the arrival of the cold front, and behind that front the skies would gradually clear.

Some cyclonic storms are extremely fierce, producing winds in excess of 50 mph (80 km/hr) and blinding snowfalls. A weather station in Cook County in northeastern Minnesota recorded 28 inches (71 centimeters) of snow in 24 hours. In Upper Michigan, the record for a single day's snowfall is 27 inches (69 centimeters), recorded at Ishpeming on October 23, 1929. The date provides an indication of how early in the season heavy snow can fall.

The coldest temperatures in North Woods winters occur when dry, clear, high-pressure air masses, usually of Arctic or polar origin, move in after a snowstorm. The white snow reflects much of the heat of the sun, and the clear air allows heat to continue escaping into space throughout the long winter nights.

Lake-Effect Snows

Winter winds blowing across the Great Lakes are warmed slightly and pick up moisture as they move. When

THE PHYSICAL ENVIRONMENT

the air hits the cooler land, the moisture may precipitate out. This lake effect is particularly pronounced in the high-lands of western Upper Michigan where air moving inland from Lake Superior is raised over 1000 feet (300 meters) in a few miles. Wind and altitude combine to make this the snowiest area in the United States east of the Rockies, with an annual average of over 170 inches (432 centimeters) in some places. On the Gogebic Range in northern Wisconsin, where similar conditions prevail, the average is 100 inches (254 centimeters).

A season record for the region was recorded at Calumet, Michigan, on the Keweenaw Peninsula, in the winter of 1949–1950 when 276.5 inches (702 centimeters) of snow fell. A single storm that raged for five days in January pro-duced 46.1 inches (117 centimeters) of this total.

This record was surpassed in the winter of 1978–1979, when 390.4 inches (992 centimeters) of snow fell on the Keweenaw. December was the snowiest month with 116.4 inches (296 centimeters). January showed a slight drop to 111.4 inches (283 centimeters). In late winter when Lake Superior is completely frozen, the westerly winds do not pick up moisture. Snowfall in February 1979 was 53 inches (135 centimeters) and in March was 52.6 inches (134 centimeters).

The heavy snows of the North Woods are very important to the plants and animals of the region. They serve as an insulating blanket, protecting the soil and its life from the effects of the bitter cold. In northeastern Minnesota and in Wisconsin along the southern shore of Lake Superior, snow covers the ground an average of 140 days a year.

The Growing Season

The presence of the snow inhibits the growth of plants in the spring. Near the Great Lakes this effect is enhanced by cool spring winds blowing off the water. These winds lower the temperature on warm spring days enough to prevent plants from growing until the danger of frost is past. They also moderate cold temperatures enough to prevent the late spring frosts that are common inland. In early fall, as the land begins to cool, the lake winds remain warm enough to delay the first killing frost as much as three to four weeks, compared to nearby inland areas. Because of the breezes off the Great Lakes, fruits can be grown on Wisconsin's Bayfield and Door peninsulas and along the west coast of lower Michigan substantially north of suitable inland locations. Washington Island at the northern tip of the Door Peninsula has an average frost-free season of 153 days, while at Medford in the center of the state at almost the same latitude, the growing season is only 126 days.

Along the shores of Lake Superior, the situation is similar: Houghton, Michigan, has a frost-free season of 148 days, and Grand Marais, Minnesota, 129 days. Inland, the length of the growing season drops sharply. It is only 85 days at Onaway, in northern Lower Michigan. St. Germain in northern Wisconsin has a 91-day growing season.

The shortest growing seasons in the North Woods occur in the highlands of western Upper Michigan. At Watersmeet, there are, on the average, only 65 days between the last frost of spring and the first freeze of fall. A few miles east at Kenton, the figure is 59 days. Here in an average year frost occurs as late as mid-June and as early as mid-August.

Even where the growing season is long, subfreezing weather can be expected in early May and mid-October. Midsummer cold snaps can drop temperatures into the 40s (5° to 10° C), and since this cool weather is often accompanied by rain, it can present a real hazard to people caught outside and unprepared.

Climatic Effects on Ecology

In Lower Michigan the southern border of the North Woods lies at about 43° north latitude, but in Wisconsin and Minnesota, it angles steadily northwestward until it crosses the Canadian border at 49°N in western Minnesota. It is the balance between precipitation on the one hand and evaporation and transpiration on the other that is largely responsible for the angle of this ecological border.

Plants are constantly pumping water from the ground up through their stems and into the leaves. Some of this is used in photosynthesis, some is used to maintain the turgidity of the plant parts, and some of it passes through pores in

THE PHYSICAL ENVIRONMENT

the leaves and into the air as vapor. This process is called transpiration, and it can add thousands of gallons of vapor to the air over an acre of forest in a single day.

Both transpiration and evaporation—the two processes are often lumped together as *evapotranspiration*—are speeded up by heat and by dry air. As precipitation declines in our region from east to west, evapotranspiration removes too much water from the warmer western areas to support a forest. Only in the cooler north of these western areas is there enough effective moisture to maintain the forest types of the North Woods. In western Wisconsin and Minnesota, oak forest, savanna, and prairie dominate at latitudes that support northern forests in Lower Michigan.

In Wisconsin, the northern forest area has a July mean temperature of 68° F (20° C), compared to 71.1° F (21.7° C) in prairie–forest transition areas in the southwestern part of the state. The higher temperature combines with lower relative humidity, more sun, and fewer days with rain to increase evaporation in July from an average of 3 to 5 inches (8 to 13 centimeters) in the north to 5 to 6 inches (13 to 15 centimeters) in the southwest.

Macroclimate and Microclimate

Annual averages of temperature and precipitation are features of the large picture, or *macroclimate*, but plants, and many animals, live their lives under extremely localized conditions that make up what is known as a *microclimate*. For example, in a mature forest where the trees form a continuous canopy, the climate at ground level is quite different from the climate of the treetops. Protected from the direct rays of the sun and the full force of the wind, the ground is likely to be wetter, cooler in the heat of the day, and warmer at night when the crowns of the trees prevent heat from radiating upward.

Local terrain features also produce microclimatic effects. The sheltered slopes and bottoms of valleys are likely to be moister and cooler than the exposed hills around them. South-facing slopes that receive the direct rays of the sun are warmer and drier than north-facing slopes. At night, cool air sinks downslope; many small lake or bog basins in the North Woods are frost pockets where the sinking cool air produces subfreezing temperatures while the uplands nearby remain above freezing.

Microclimatic conditions often have a direct effect on vegetation, and are influenced in turn by the plants. Since they are so closely linked with the vegetation, we will describe significant microclimatic factors in Chapter 8, Plant Communities in the North Woods.

CHAPTER SIX

Soils of
the North Woods

SOIL IS THE AREA where geology and biology come together. The raw materials of a soil are the bedrock and various surface deposits that overlie it, but a developed soil is a joint product of geology, climate, and the actions of living things.

Bedrock is the continuous solid rock of the continental crust. Where it is exposed, it is worked on by chemical and physical means that cause the solid rock to break up into smaller pieces.

Chemical weathering happens when rain picks up carbon dioxide (CO_2) in the air and reaches the ground as a weak carbonic acid solution. Decaying vegetation at or just below the surface provides more CO_2 and other acids as well. In the ground, the carbonic acid (H_2CO_3) splits into a positive hydrogen ion (H^{+1}) and a bicarbonate ion (HCO_3). Hydrogen ions are so small that they can slip between the atoms of a rock crystal and disrupt the structure.

One such disruption involves the displacement of the potassium from potassium feldspar, a mineral that also contains aluminum, silica, and oxygen. Water and carbonic acid react with potassium feldspar to produce a potassium ion, free silica, and a clay mineral called kaolinite. The potassium may be picked up by plants or leached out of the soil by groundwater. The silica and clay may remain or be leached out.

Chemical weathering will change any exposed rock, given enough time, and that's why geologists have to carry hammers. Only a freshly exposed sample will provide a reliable identification of a rock.

Mechanical, or physical, weathering can be caused by frost, by heat, or by plants and animals. Water seeps into cracks in rocks and then freezes and expands, breaking the rocks apart. Heat—as from a forest fire—if it is high enough and lasts long enough can cause rocks at the surface to flake off. Plants also break up rocks. Roots growing in cracks can enlarge the cracks and cause the rock to split.

The processes of weathering eventually create a blanket of broken loose rock particles overlying the bedrock. This is called the *regolith*. Soils develop in the upper layers of the regolith, the zone where plants anchor their roots and from which they derive nutrients and water.

Soils that develop in place over the bedrock that constitutes them are called *residual soils*. They are almost completely absent from the North Woods. Virtually all our soils have developed on glacial deposits and hence are called *transported* soils.

While soils in glaciated regions often contain materials that were carried hundreds of miles by the ice, studies of soil materials indicate that most of them originated in bedrock fairly close to their current location. In one study in southeastern Wisconsin, 15 percent of the pebbles in soil samples came from the Canadian Shield. The rest were Paleozoic sedimentary rocks of more local origin. The ice seems to have blurred the outline of the bedrock rather than obliterating it. This has important consequences. Soils formed on the Paleozoic sedimentary rocks of the Michigan Basin tend to be more fertile than those formed on the Canadian Shield, and soils formed over carbonate-rich limestone and dolomite are likely to be the most fertile of all.

Soil Formation in the North Woods

The development of the soils of the North Woods began with the retreat of the ice. Winds blew over the bare outwash sands, lake-bottom clays, and morainic silts, lifting huge dust clouds that eventually settled to earth as *loess* deposits. Loess is made up mainly of silt-sized particles (0.004 to 0.06 millimeters in diameter) whose unweathered, angular surfaces make soils that will accept and hold large amounts of water. Their mineralogical diversity combines with the lack of weathering to make them extremely fertile. The heaviest loess deposits in the Midwest lie south of our area. In southwestern Wisconsin, they are as much as 16 feet (5 meters) thick, but deposits of a foot (30 centimeters) or less are common in the north. The corn and wheat belts of the Midwest derive much of their productivity from these deposits.

Rain falling on the bare surfaces of fresh glacial deposits began the weathering process. Calcium carbonate from ground limestone is readily soluble in carbonic acid. It has been leached to an average depth of 6 feet (1.8 meters) in soils of the North Woods, although soils on the carbonate-rich rocks of the Michigan Basin retain more than soils on the Canadian Shield.

The process of soil creation began when the first plants invaded the new glacial deposits. In most instances, these pioneers were tundra plants that could grow over a permanently frozen—*permafrost*—layer in the subsoil. Today many soils in the North Woods are underlain at a depth of 2 to 3 feet (60 to 90 centimeters) by a dense layer of earth that is hard when dry and brittle when wet. This layer, called a *fragipan*, is impervious to plant roots. Fragipans are forming today over permafrost in the Arctic, and it may be that the North Woods fragipans date from early postglacial time when a permafrost layer still existed in our area.

The earliest postglacial forests were mainly boreal, a forest type dominated by conifers, particularly spruce and fir. Coniferous forests create a distinctive soil type that soil scientists used to call a podzol. Recently the U. S. Department of Agriculture has renamed this type a spodosol; however, podzol is still in common use.

As the trees in a boreal or pine or hemlock forest drop needles, twigs, cones, and branches, this debris creates a layer of litter on the surface. At the bottom of this layer, bacteria, fungi, and various other organisms go to work on the litter and it begins to decay, forming a thin dark layer that is rich in the finely divided, partly decayed plant remains called *humus*. Conifer needles are rich in acids but very low in the mineral bases such as calcium, potassium, and phosphorus that are essential to plant growth. The acid humus of conifer forests is called *mor* humus.

Rainwater percolating through these acidic surface layers

Soils of the North Woods   111 carries the acids down into the soil, where they dissolve soluble mineral salts and carry them farther underground. In time, this leaching process creates a pale gray layer below the humus mat that is largely devoid of the minerals plants need. The word 'podzol' is Russian for wood ashes. This soil type was named by Russian soil scientists after the pale, leached, ashy layer.

Below the leached layer is another dark soil layer where the leached minerals, particularly iron and aluminum compounds, along with organic compounds and some clays, accumulate. This zone of accumulation is the lowest layer of the soil. Below it is mineral matter unaffected by soil-creating processes. This may be bedrock, but in the North Woods it is often glacial drift. On uplands being eroded, the removal of topsoil may be balanced by a continuous extension of the soil down into this mineral material.

Under deciduous forests, things operate somewhat differently. Deciduous trees drop all their leaves at the end of each growing season, while conifers retain needles for two or three years. Deciduous leaves are also much richer in mineral bases, so the litter on the forest floor is both more abundant and more nutritious than the mat of conifer needles. Instead of a thin mat of humus, deciduous forest soils develop a dark fertile layer of topsoil that is a mixture of humus and minerals. In some old sugar maple forests, this layer may be 10 inches (25 centimeters) deep. Humus in deciduous forests is called *mull* humus.

Below this is a leached layer that is lighter than the humus but not as pale as the corresponding layer in a podzol. The zone of accumulation below this is usually rich in clays washed down from above but not as rich in iron compounds or organic matter as the same zone in a podzol.

Soil Horizons

The layers in a developed soil are called *horizons*. They are identified by letters. The O (organic) horizon includes fresh litter and the decaying vegetation just below it. The A horizon is the source of the materials that leach down into the zone of accumulation, which is called the B horizon. The underlying mineral matter is the C horizon.

Each horizon may be subdivided, so that a particular soil

may have O_1 and O_2 layers, B_1, B_2, and B_3 layers, and so on. Transitional horizons or areas where two horizons interpenetrate may be designated by two letters: A&B.

Soil scientists use lowercase letters to designate special characteristics of particular soils. Thus a lower case "h" indicates a concentration of organic matter, while "ir" means that iron is common. The typical B layer in a podzol is written Bhir, symbolic shorthand for a zone of accumulation high in organic matter and iron. B layers that are particularly rich in clay are called Bt layers.

Here is a typical sequence of horizons in a podzol:

O_1 Forest litter.

O_2 Humus, the black residue of the decay of the O_1 layer.

A_2 Pale surface layer that has been leached by percolating water.

A_3 or A B   Transitional horizon.

A&B   Zone of interpenetration.

B_1 Transitional.

Bhir   Subsoil layer enriched in organic matter and iron.

B_3 Transitional.

C   Underlying mineral horizon of the same material as the soil.

IIC   Underlying mineral horizon unlike the material that formed the A and B horizons. This is quite common in the North Woods, where glacial drift may form layers, as for example when lake-bottom clays or silts from a ground moraine underlie outwash sands.

In gray–brown podzolics (similar to podzols, but not the real thing) in deciduous or mixed woodlands, a typical sequence might be:

O_1 Forest litter.

O_2 Humus.

A_1 Dark surface soil, a mixture of organic and mineral matter. This fertile layer is often completely absent in soils under conifers.

A₂ Lighter layer leached of clay.

A₃ or A B   Transitional.

A&B   Zone of interpenetration.

B₁   Transitional.

B₂t   Layer enriched by clay washed down from above.

B₃   Transitional.

C   Underlying mineral matter.

The boundaries between these horizons may be abrupt or quite diffuse. The horizons may be level or irregular. In some soils, tongues of the higher horizons extend down into the subsoil.

The term podzol was made officially obsolete by the soil classification issued by the U.S. Department of Agriculture in 1960.* This system created a taxonomic hierarchy running from order through suborder, great group, subgroup, family, and series. Order is the most inclusive category. All the world's soils are divided into ten orders, six of which occur in the North Woods: the spodosols, alfisols, mollisols, inceptisols, entisols, and histosols.

The spodosols, the podzols of old, are soils whose B horizon shows an accumulation of iron and organic matter under a heavily leached A_2 layer. On low ground leaching may extend down to the water table. Organic matter may accumulate and be preserved in a gray, mottled, wet layer below the leached horizon.

The alfisols show an accumulation of clay in the B layer. On wet ground this layer is mottled.

Mollisols have thick, dark, fertile A_1 layers. The black earth of prairie soil belongs in this category, as do the rich brown forest soils that develop under maple forests, where the A_1 layer may be 10 inches (25 centimeters) deep.

In some soils the horizons are weakly developed, and there is little clay accumulation in the subsoil. These are called inceptisols. Entisols are another soil order with

---

*The new classification created a terminological tangle that makes soils sound like characters in *The Lord of the Rings*. Glossoboralfs and entic haplorthods have replaced the podzols of old. About 50 formative elements—prefixes, suffixes, and infixes—are used to describe the finer points.

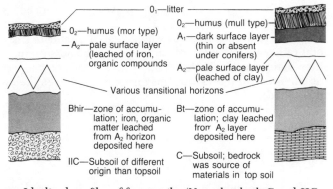

Coniferous

Deciduous

O₁—litter

O₂—humus (mor type)

—A₂—pale surface layer
(leached of iron,
organic compounds

O₂—humus (mull type)—

A₁—dark surface layer
(thin or absent
under conifers)

A₂—pale surface layer
(leached of clay)

Various transitional horizons

Bhir—zone of accumu-
lation; iron, organic
matter leached
from A₂ horizon
deposited here

IIC—Subsoil of different
origin than topsoil

Bt—zone of accumu-
lation; clay leached
from A₂ layer
deposited here

C—Subsoil; bedrock
was source of
materials in top soil

32. Idealized profiles of forest soils. (Note that both C and IIC subsoils occur in all types of forests.)

poorly developed horizons. This order includes new soils developing on sand dunes or on river floodplains where alluvial deposits are being laid down.

All of the soils we have described so far develop in surface deposits of mineral origin. They may be enriched by humus, but their richest layers are less than 25 percent organic matter. Another kind of soil, the histosols, has developed in the millions of acres of wetlands left by the glaciers. In kettle holes, in the pits on outwash plains, in shallow depressions on old lake plains, on the swampy banks of sluggish streams, rooted plants growing in shallow water or floating plants growing in mats on the surface die and fall into the water. Oxygen is scarce enough in still or slow-moving water to inhibit the activities of the bacteria of decay and prevent the oxidation of organic matter. In time, the partly decayed vegetation thickens and compresses into peat or muck. These histosols, soils of organic origin, range from extremely fibrous peats whose individual plant constituents may be identifiable to fine mucks made of tiny, amorphous particles.

Peats may contain less than 4 percent inorganic matter in places where erosion supplies only scant mineral sediments to mix with the plant remains. They have a tremendous capacity to absorb water. A ton of peat dries out to about 200 pounds (90 kilograms) of solid matter. Some North Woods peat deposits are 18 feet (5.5 meters) thick. If they began forming just after the recession of the last glacier, they have been growing an average of 2 inches (5 centimeters) a century.

Drainage in the low areas where peats accumulate is lateral rather than downward, so the leaching and accumulation that occur in better-drained soils may not happen. Subdivisions of the O layer may extend several feet below the surface.

The formation of peat will be described in more detail in Chapter 15.

Rates of Development

The time required to turn a surface deposit of raw glacial till into a fully developed podzolic soil varies greatly, depending largely on the texture of the soil particles. It happens most rapidly on sands, slowest on clays, with silts and loams falling between the two extremes. Sands are made of particles ranging from 0.063 millimeters to 2 millimeters in diameter, while clays have diameters less than 0.004 millimeters. Many clay particles are visible only under a microscope.

Coarse, sandy soils have large pore spaces between particles, so groundwater moves through them rapidly. A saturated sandy soil conducts water at a speed of about 15 feet (4.6 meters) per day, while movement through saturated clay is only about an inch (2.5 centimeters) per day. On sandy loam, the figure is about 60 inches (150 centimeters) per day, while silt loams conduct water at about half that rate. Faster water movement means that leaching of the A horizon will happen faster. Larger pieces also mean less surface area in relation to overall mass. A cubic foot of granite has a surface area of six square feet. Break that rock up into silt-size particles, mix with humus, and you have about 1000 billion pieces with a square mile of surface. A given volume of sand has about one-one hundredth the surface area of the same volume of silt, so particles in the B layer can become coated much more rapidly in sand than in finer-textured soils.

The smaller surface area also explains why sands are generally less fertile than silts, even though large amounts of minerals may be present in the grains. Chemical weathering has to take place on the surface of soil particles. Large particles with less surface per unit of volume make many minerals inaccessible to solvents and therefore to plant roots. The combination of less surface and faster movement of groundwater means that a podzolic soil can develop on loose sandy materials in 200 years or less. The same process on clays may take 1000 years.

Some North Woods Soils

Podzolic soils developed on sands are most commonly associated with pine forests in the North Woods. Vilas loamy sand is a good example. (Soil types carry geographic names derived from the locality where they were first described —in this instance, Vilas County in northern Wisconsin.) In the new terminology, Vilas loamy sand is an entic haplorthod, or a recently formed, simple podzolic soil that lies above the water table and is, therefore, usually dry.

The combined O, A, and B layers of Vilas loamy sand range from 18 to 36 inches (45 to 90 centimeters) deep. They are developed on deep deposits of glacial drift. The three layers are subdivided into seven distinct horizons: O_1, O_2, A_1, A_2, Bhir, Bir, and B_3. The A_1 layer is typically only about 1 inch (2.5 centimeters) deep and the A_2 about 3 inches (7.5 centimeters). The Bhir layer below these extends down to about 1 foot (30 centimeters) below the surface. The percentage of sand in this soil averages between 80 and 90, with the remainder of the particles mostly silt-size. Clays constitute 5 percent or less of each of the layers.

Along the south shore of Lake Superior, in Douglas County, Wisconsin, what was once the bottom of glacial Lake Duluth is now a plain with a red, iron-rich soil that supported a boreal forest until it was logged. The soil here, named Ontonagon loamy silt clay, is a gray wooded podzolic according to the old classification. In the new system, it is a typic eutroboralf, a typical, fertile, northern variety of the order Alfisol. It differs from a true podzol in that it has a well-developed A_1 layer and a Bt layer. The A_2 horizon is only 13 percent clay, but the B_2t horizon is 67 percent clay. Doubtless this concentration is partly produced by the large amounts of clay in the lake-bottom sediments on which this soil developed. It is also partly a result of frost action. Freezing has a tendency to push large particles upward and smaller ones down, creating sandy A layers and clayey B layers.

Old lake bottoms tend to be rather flat, but often the same kind of surface deposit may be spread over high and low ground. As the raw mineral matter develops into soil, leaching and erosion are likely to be more pronounced on the hilltops. The soils downslope collect minerals and organic matter from higher up. In low spots, the subsoil may be wet enough to develop a mottled appearance. Thus the same raw material can develop into a variety of soils. The sequence of soils from hilltop to wet bottomland developed on the same surface deposit is called a *soil catena*. Soils are often identified by their position in a soil catena.

Soils and the Ecosystem

The interaction between soils and vegetation is continuous. The blanket of litter that covers a forest floor helps retain

33. Newly fallen black spruce is the beginning of a tip-up mound. The hole left when roots pulled out of the ground is filled with water. *Jerry Sullivan*.

THE PHYSICAL ENVIRONMENT

34. This older fallen tree shows mound eroded into characteristic rounded shape. Plants are beginning to invade it; eventually they will completely cover it. *Jerry Sullivan.*

moisture in the soil and moderates temperature extremes. Finely divided humus can hold more moisture than coarse sand particles, although the moisture is sometimes so tightly held on the humus grains that it is unavailable to plants.

Trees constantly pump nutrients and water up from the subsoil. The nutrients are eventually deposited on the surface in leaf litter or dead trunks and branches. As these minerals are released by decay, they become available to small plants with shallow roots.

High winds can blow trees over, pulling the roots right out of the ground in the process. As the trees decay, they create microrelief: a low mound marks the position of the trunk and a shallow depression shows where the roots used to be. *Tip-up mounds* like these are common features in the North Woods. As much as 10 percent of the surface has been affected by them. Where the water table is high, the depressions may be puddles for at least part of the year, and the standing water will change the soil below it. Tipped trees also pull pieces of the subsoil up to the surface and thus alter the physical and chemical nature of the topsoil.

In some cases, plants change the soil so much that they

Soils of the North Woods

35. As fallen logs begin to decay, they serve as a nursery for a variety of plants. This downed maple nurse log harbors hemlock seedlings, along with starflower and various grasses and ferns. *Jerry Sullivan.*

can no longer grow on it and are replaced by other plants that are better adapted to the new situation. A developed soil can become something else in response to a change in vegetation. The Bhir layer that developed under a hemlock stand becomes undetectable in about 400 years if sugar maples replace the hemlocks.

Animals affect soils by compacting surface layers and by creating trails that may speed runoff and thus increase erosion. Burrowing animals carry fresh mineral matter to the surface and leaves, grass, and other organic matter into the

subsoil. Earthworms can mix the layers of a soil so completely as to change the soil type in the space of a few years.

Microscopic plants and animals are enormously abundant in the soil. They may reach a mass of 40 tons per acre
in places in the North Woods. Algae, bacteria, and fungi
form the base of a food chain in the soil. They are fed on by
protozoans and other tiny animals.

Spaces between soil particles that are not saturated with
water are filled with air. The soil atmosphere is similar to
the atmosphere above ground except that it contains less
oxygen and more CO_2 and water vapor. Carbon dioxide
may account for 10 percent of this underground atmosphere, compared to 0.03 percent above the surface. Plants
liberate oxygen, and where this element is sufficiently plentiful, organic matter is converted to CO_2. Under reducing
conditions, where oxygen is scarce, little CO_2 is liberated
and carbon is released in volatile hydrocarbons such as
methane—marsh gas.

The relationships between soils and specific plant communities and animal populations in the North Woods will
be discussed in the chapters that follow.

PART II

The Producers

Introduction to the Plant Life of the North Woods

PHOTOSYNTHESIS lets green plants combine a few minerals with water, atmospheric gases, and sunlight to produce a simple sugar. The whole substance of the green plants, the energy they need for carrying on their lives, and all the food eaten by all animals stem from this process. Green plants thus trap the energy of the sun and bring it into the ecosystem.

Chapter 7 is an introduction to plant communities, the distinctive groupings of plants that are characteristic of particular environments. The precise nature of these communities is a matter of dispute among plant ecologists. Our account gives a brief look at the issues in the controversy and then goes on to describe the processes that take place in communities, using examples drawn from the North Woods. The chapter closes with a brief introduction to common North Woods communities and explains some of the relationships that exist between them.

Chapter 8 is a primer on field identification. If you are an experienced user of field guides, you can skip this one.

Trees are a good place to start identifying a forest, so Chapter 9 begins with a simple key and follows with descriptions and line drawings for the 28 tree species most commonly found in the North Woods. Each description concludes with a list of plant communities where the tree is common. In some North Woods communities, those where a single species makes up most of the forest, identifying a single tree will be enough to direct you to the chapter where that community is described. In most cases, you will need to identify several trees before arriving at a determination of the community type. Once you have made a decision about the community, you can turn to the appropriate chapter.

Some shrubs and herbs are common in several North Woods communities. These are of little value in determining forest type, but they are responsible for a good part of the regional character of the vegetation. These ubiquitous shrubs and herbs are described in Chapter 10. The more familiar you are with the plants described in Chapter 9 and 10, the easier it will be to figure out what you are seeing in the woods, and the easier it will be to use the following chapters, which describe the various North Woods plant communities in detail, including keys and descriptions of the plants other than trees that are typical of these communities.

In Chapters 11–15 we discuss in detail the common forest communities of the North Woods: the pine forest, the mixed-hardwood forest, the boreal forest, second-growth forests, and the wetland communities. Each of these chapters features keys and descriptions of the plants other than trees which are typical of the community. We will describe something of the ways that communities work: the influence of dominants, the cycles of energy and materials, the phenology (or timing) of important events, and the favored soil and moisture conditions. We will also point out similarities and differences between communities and will cover typical successional patterns and provide some tips for recognizing succession in the communities.

Human activity has been important in this region since long before European settlers arrived, but the impact of humanity on the North Woods has increased spectacularly in the past two centuries. Our chapters on the plant communities will also include accounts of the changes—sometimes drastic—that humans have brought to the forests of the North Woods.

CHAPTER SEVEN

Plant Communities

WALK INTO A WOODLAND in Michigan's Upper Peninsula. If the first two trees you see are sugar maples, you can be reasonably confident that you will soon spot the peeling bark of a yellow birch or the thick dark crown of a hemlock.

Stand in the thin shade of a jack pine wood in northwestern Wisconsin. Begin a careful search of the ground, and down amid the litter and detritus you will probably find the fleshy leaves of a trailing arbutus or a glossy, succulent wintergreen.

Skirt the edge of a black spruce bog in Minnesota's Superior National Forest, and you are likely to find the low straggling branches of Labrador tea growing between the trees.

The fact that certain plants are commonly found growing together has been known for a long time both by scientists—and their predecessors, the philosophers—and by people who needed to know where to search for the plants they used for food or medicine. Some of these combinations are so obvious that a practiced eye can spot them from a car window while moving at the legal speed limit. A more leisurely look reveals natural systems so complex that our attempts to understand them have sparked a scientific debate that has lasted most of this century.

The central issue in this debate is the nature of the distinctive groupings we call plant communities. One school regards them as, in effect, organisms. Proponents of this school apply scientific names to communities, analogous to the scientific names applied to individual species. From this perspective, the individual species in the community have a status like the individual organs or tissues in our bodies, and the community as a whole is greater than the sum of its parts, just as a human being is more than a collection of organs, bones, and muscles. The other school believes that plant life is not organized at a more inclusive level than the individual. Tolerances of individual species are the chief determiners of the range and distribution of plants. Plants become frequent companions because they are adapted to grow in similar circumstances. These are the extreme positions in the debate, and many plant ecologists hold opinions incorporating elements of both sides.

Everyone can agree on a minimal definition of the plant community as an assemblage of species growing in a particular physical environment. For example, both black spruce and various heaths—the family of plants that Labrador tea belongs to—are adapted to the wet, poor conditions in northern bogs. Both jack pine and trailing arbutus are most often found in coarse, sandy upland soils that do not hold moisture well.

However, there does seem to be more to plant communities than the affinity of individual species for a particular kind of place. A good part of the environment that a plant lives in is created by other plants. Under sugar maples, the soil is enriched by minerals in the autumn leaf fall. Under hemlocks, it is impoverished by a mat of decay-resistant, acidic needles whose minerals are locked up beyond the reach of living plants.

In real communities where hundreds of species may grow together in a small area, the complexity of the interactions is enormous. However, certain kinds of patterns recur, and these patterns reveal attributes that are common to all communities. These include dominance, a characteristic physical structure and species composition, competition, a typical process of development, and a degree of stability. Niche is an attribute of an individual species that is expressed as its "role" in the community.

Characteristics of Communities

Dominance

While all plants exert an influence on their environment, some plants in any community are more important than others. The most important plants, those that exert the largest effect, are called dominants. The dominant plants

THE PRODUCERS

may be the most numerous or have the greatest biomass or occupy the most space. In forest communities where there are enough trees to produce a more or less continuous canopy of leaves, the dominants are always trees. In some cases, especially where the dominant trees have sparse crowns, plants of the ground layer may share dominance. For example, aspens in the North Woods let enough light through to the ground to produce a rich understory. In some woods, bracken fern may grow so abundantly under aspens that it shades out other low plants and thus has enough effect on the community to be considered a dominant.

Where trees are absent or scattered, ground-layer plants are dominants. Sphagnum moss is a dominant in open bogs in our region. The great spongy hummocks of this plant are the main constituents of northern bogs. Sphagnum helps create the highly acid conditions in these bogs by absorbing mineral bases in the water and thus limiting other plant life to those species which can survive in acid soils.

Only a few plants in any given community are capable of becoming dominants. Usually they are the plants with wide tolerances that enable them to thrive in a range of physical conditions. Subordinate species tend to be more specialized, filling in by occupying parts of the environment that the dominants cannot use and, to a considerable extent, depending on the dominants to create the particular conditions favorable for their growth. Most woodland wildflowers, for example, grow only in the shelter of the trees.

Most of the forest communities of the North Woods are dominated by a very small number of tree species, and in some cases, a single species may form an almost pure stand. In moist, springy soil situations, northern white cedar may dominate to the virtual exclusion of other species. Black spruce forms pure stands on peatlands following fires.

Composition of a Community

The physical structure of plant communities is usually described in terms of layers. In a forest, the top layer is the canopy, the crowns of the large trees that most directly encounter the climate. Rain hits the canopy first; the wind strikes it most directly. Most important, the canopy gets more direct sunlight than the lower layers. Consequently it is the center of food production in the forest. Here the trees, through the process of photosynthesis, convert sunlight into food energy.

Below the canopy, sheltered from wind, rain, and sunlight, is the *tall shrub layer*. This layer includes trees such as the mountain maple that seldom attain sufficient size to reach the canopy. It also includes such typically shrubby species as the hazels and the honeysuckles, along with young trees that will eventually be part of the canopy.

Next comes the *low shrub layer*, which consists of woody plants with straggling or spreading growth habits. Blueberries are typical of the growth form of these plants. Finally, the *herb layer* includes the wildflowers and ferns, the plants without woody tissue. It may also include mosses and lichens.

The plants in a community can also be classified according to how they survive the winter. Some do it as seeds, although only a few of these annuals are common in the North Woods. Many perennials have developed underground food storage organs—bulbs, corms, rhizomes, and others—that stay dormant all winter and send up new shoots in the spring. Most of the herbs of the North Woods, including the ferns, are part of this group.

Many low shrubs produce buds at or just above ground level, low enough to be protected by the snow from the extremes of winter. Plants that survive the winter underground or under the snow are common in cold climates like the North Woods; warmer, moist places produce more vines—and more species of trees and tall shrubs. Many of our shrubs—wintergreen is a good example—creep over the ground with their woody stems below the surface. Their short, upright leafy branches make them look like herbs.

Differences in the relative abundance of plants in the various layers are often very large. Aspen stands with their high light levels are likely to have a rich tall shrub layer. In many stands of black spruce, tall shrubs are completely absent. These differences in relative abundance are important in part because every layer in the forest supports animal populations that depend on the vegetation of that layer for food or shelter. Tall shrubs are winter browse for deer and moose. Obviously aspen forests are more likely homes for these animals than black spruce woods.

No two stands of any plant community type have exactly the same species composition. Physical factors such as soil texture, moisture, and climate determine what *can* grow on a given piece of ground. What *does* grow there and in what quantities is determined by the specific history of the stand.

In spite of such variables, however, we do find enough similarities in stands to justify grouping them as examples of various community types. If we study a number of stands that seem similar because they are dominated by the same kinds of trees, we are likely to find that only a few species of plants are present—and usually quite common—in all or nearly all the stands. A considerably larger number of species will be present in, say, half of the stands. A great many species will appear in only a few stands and be common in none.

Specialized plants found in a single community type and rarely seen elsewhere are called *indicators*.

Niche and Competition

Niche is an attribute that belongs to an individual species, but it can only be expressed in a community—just as an individual can be a lawyer but can only practice law in a society with a system of courts. Niche is used in two different senses in ecology. It can refer to a plant or animal's position in time and space or to its function in a community. In an aspen community, aspen has a position in the canopy, and it plays the roles of pioneer and community dominant.

The effect of the specialization of plants that fill various niches is to reduce the inhibiting influence of competition. Other specializations, including variations in the timing of essential activities such as leaf opening, flowering, and seed development, allow hundreds of species to grow together in natural communities by spreading out the demands they make on the environment.

Competition is very important in limiting the distribution of plants. It occurs between individuals of the same species (*intraspecific*) or between different species (*interspecific*). In a mixed-hardwood forest in the North Woods, the death of an old sugar maple will let a patch of sunlight through to the forest floor. Literally hundreds of maple seedlings will crowd that open spot, competing for the light, for moisture, and for nutrients. In time, all but one of these will be eliminated, and that one—genetically favored or with the luck to be in a position to get more light, water, or nutrients—will replace the old tree in the forest canopy. Interspecific competition is equally important. Quaking aspen can successfully pioneer in a broad range of circumstances in the North Woods, but in very dry, sandy soils jack pine seems to enjoy a competitive advantage that enables it to displace aspen as a pioneer.

Competition is likely to have its greatest effect on plants that are under stress from some other cause. For example, a plant near the edge of its range and facing an unfavorable climate may be at a competitive disadvantage to other plants and unable to grow on a site it would easily occupy nearer the heart of its range. Conversely, the suppression of competition allows domesticated plants to grow in back-yards and farmers' fields far outside the plant's normal range.

Succession

The development of plant communities and relative stability are both aspects of the process of succession. Succession is a natural change in the plant life of an area that involves the gradual, continuous replacement of one group of species by another. The impetus for this change comes from the plants themselves as pioneering species create conditions that prevent them from reproducing. In time the pioneers are replaced by plants that can reproduce in the altered circumstances. The theoretical end point of this process is reached when plants that can reproduce in the environmental conditions they create take over a community. The endpoint, self-maintaining and permanent, is called the *climax*. All the communities that follow each other in the succession from pioneer to climax on a particular type of site are known collectively as a *sere*, and each step along the way is a *seral stage*.

Events that derail this process are termed *disturbances*. Fire is a common disturbance in forests. An insect or disease attack that kills large numbers of dominant plants is another. Storm damage can disturb succession and, of course, human activities—logging, for example—can be quite disturbing.

The early stages of succession are commonly characterized by communities containing a small number of species, and the direction of change is toward more diversity. A piece of forest ground that has been cleared by fire is a very uniform environment. The whole place gets direct sunlight and the full force of wind and rain. Only plants that are adapted to this kind of situation can grow.

A maturing forest has a greater variety of niches available. Trees that need full sunlight can grow there along with herbs that need the shaded, protected environment of the forest floor and mosses that can grow only on tree trunks.

TYPICAL SUCCESSION PATTERNS

Among the common successional sequences that occur in the North Woods are two that begin on dry land and one that starts in the still waters of the thousands of lakes in the region.

Lakes are invaded by a floating mat of vegetation that begins the process called *hydrarch* (wet-site) succession. The mat typically consists of herbs such as sedges combined with low shrubs and sphagnum moss. As it grows and thickens, the dead and only partly decomposed remains of the plants begin to fill the lake basin, forming thick deposits of peat.

The first trees to colonize the floating mat are usually tamaracks or black spruces. As the remains of dead plants continue to build up, soil conditions may become moderate enough to support northern white cedar or balsam fir. Ultimately, a mesic forest of mixed hardwoods may occupy the site. However, this idealized succession pattern may be modified, halted, or even reversed by local conditions. See Chapter 15 for a description of some of these conditions and the succession patterns they produce.

On extensive outwash plains and old lake beds where the soil is mostly sand, the process of *xerarch* (dry-site) succession begins when jack pine colonizes an area. Jack pine has a number of characteristics that are typical of pioneering trees. It can scatter large amounts of seed, it is extremely intolerant of shade, and it grows and matures rapidly in full sunlight.

The jack pine, a tree of dry places, is particularly dependent on fire for reproduction. The cones of about half the population in the Lake States are sealed by a resin and they remain on the tree for many years. The heat of a fire melts the resin and scatters the seeds. Jack pine can hold as many as two million seeds per acre in reserve this way. The seeds sprout on the fire-cleared soil, and they may mature enough to produce cones after just five years of growth.

The jack pine's intolerance of shade shows up in its sparse crown. Lower branches shaded by those above die quickly. The result is a lot of light reaching the ground, not enough to raise another generation of jack pines, but enough to grow red and white pine, red oak, red maple, and paper birch. Given enough time without disturbance, these second generation trees may be succeeded by mixed-hardwood or boreal forest.

One of the most common successional patterns in the North Woods begins with the establishment of a pioneer community dominated by quaking aspen with paper birch, big-toothed aspen, and various other species as less common associates. Quaking aspen is a typical pioneer species. Its seeds are very light and come equipped with cottony filaments that help disperse them in the wind. Like the jack pine, the aspen grows rapidly in full sunlight and reproduces early. It is also extremely intolerant of shade.

Aspens have another advantage that helps them become established in disturbed areas. They can produce root suckers, shoots that arise from the root systems of established trees and grow into new individuals. Aspen roots usually survive logging or fire and very quickly send up suckers. Stored food in the roots and a greater access to water give the suckers a competitive advantage over young trees growing from seed and help them establish dominance in the pioneer community.

In the absence of further disturbance, aspens are likely to give way after one generation to whatever community is best adapted to the soil type. On sandy soils, they may be replaced by white pine. Elsewhere they may be replaced by mixed-hardwood or boreal forests.

Those who argue that plant communities are, in effect, organisms, the highest and most complex expression of plant life, point to the regularity of succession, the similarities of physical structure and species composition in different stands, and the intensive interaction between species as indications of the essential unity of plant communities.

Interaction and Diversity

While we have described succession in terms of the major trees, the process actually involves hundreds of species. As the dominant trees change, shrubs and herbs adapted to conditions in a jack pine forest, for example, will be replaced by those adapted to grow under maple or hemlock. The process is not perfectly timed. Some plants of the jack pine forest endure longer than others; some plants of the maple forest appear earlier than others.

While all the successional patterns we have described seem to be heading toward a uniform climax—in most of our region a mixed-hardwood forest—it is highly questionable whether they will ever actually arrive there. It may take a thousand years to go through the change from jack pine dominance to the dominance of mature sugar maple, and a single fire, disease outbreak, or insect attack at any time in that millenium can send the whole forest back to bare ground. It may take tens of thousands of years for peat to fill in a lake, and when it is filled in, the soil may be so lacking in nutrients that demanding trees like sugar maple won't be able to grow in it. It may take millions of years for erosion to reduce the topographical irregularities and eliminate the differences between swampy lowlands, cool north slopes, and high, sandy hills.

At any given moment, the patterns of vegetation in the North Woods are a mosaic of stands at every stage of succession, and in a number of cases the direction of change seems to be quite different from the courses we outlined above. It is also difficult to decide just what constitutes a disturbance. Jack pines and aspens, for example, have evolved to take advantage of fires, and for these species and many of their associates, periodic fire is less a disturbance than a part of the normal order.

The various plant communities are also not sharply separated from each other on the ground. Instead they intergrade in a continuum that responds to changes in local climate, slope, soil moisture, and soil texture. Animal activity also helps shape the plant cover.

Emphasizing diversity and the lack of permanence is especially fitting in a region such as ours that has only been deglaciated for a few thousand years. The oldest villages on the site of Jericho in the Middle East are older than the forests of the Great Lakes. Since the glaciers receded, there have been at least two significant climate changes. A cool moist period when the forests were dominated by spruce and fir followed the glaciers. A dry interval came next. Pines became much more important and the prairies advanced eastward. Most recently, the climate has again become moister and warm enough to allow many hardwoods to extend their ranges north.

Classifying Communities

In spite of continuous variation and blurred community boundaries, it is possible to recognize certain plant combinations that occur again and again. In his book *The Vegetation of Wisconsin,* John Curtis arranged the forests north of the tension zone—which separates the North Woods from southern forest types—along a soil moisture gradient. He divided the gradient into five segments. We have used a version of his gradient to classify community types. Curtis's segments, and the dominant trees in each, are:

Dry Forest	Dry–Mesic Forest	Mesic Forest	Wet–Mesic Forest	Wet Forest
Jack pine	White pine	Sugar maple	White cedar	Tamarack
Hill's oak	Red oak	Hemlock	Balsam fir	Black spruce
Red pine	Red maple	Yellow birch	Black ash	

We have discussed Curtis's dry and dry–mesic forests in our chapter on the pine forests (Chapter 11); his mesic forest in the chapter on mixed hardwoods (Chapter 12); and his wet–mesic and wet in the swamp forest and bog forest sections, respectively, of our chapter on wetland communities (Chapter 15).

Not on Curtis's gradient but discussed in Chapter 13 is the boreal forest, which is dominated by spruce and fir and reaches the southern end of its continuous range in northeastern Minnesota (though there are good examples of the type in Wisconsin and upper Michigan, especially around the south shore of Lake Superior).

Most of the North Woods has recently endured the massive shock of European settlement. Widespread clear-cutting followed by repeated, very destructive fires have converted millions of acres into second-growth aspen stands. These are described in Chapter 14, Second-Growth Forests.

Our chapter on the wetland communities (Chapter 15) also covers three widespread nonforest communities: open bogs, marshes, and alder thickets.

CHAPTER EIGHT

A Guide to Plant Identification

LEARNING TO IDENTIFY plants in the field can be a difficult and discouraging business for amateurs. It is possible to learn by doing, however, without a thorough grounding in botany and without the expert guidance of experienced teachers. This section will guide the novice through the difficult first stages. Once you master the basic botanical information here you should be able to head for the woods with some confidence that you will be able to name what you see. Those who can handle field guides to flowers, trees, and shrubs with ease can skip this section.

A plant taxonomist working with a herbarium specimen is able to look at a great many clues to help him identify an unknown plant. He may dissect the flower to discover how many ovules are inside the ovaries and where they are placed on the ovary wall. He can examine the roots as well as the above-ground parts of the plant. He may even use a microscope to examine the chromosomes in the plant cells.

Working in the field, the range of clues we have available is much smaller. Most important, we do not want to damage the plants we look at, so we must work only with the visible parts. When looking at typical wildflowers, small plants with no woody tissue, we do not want to remove or otherwise damage leaves, stems, flowers, or fruit. When it is absolutely necessary, we can remove a twig from a tree or shrub without doing harm to the plant, but cutting should be limited. Find one good specimen twig and cut it carefully, preferably where the twig joins a larger branch. There is no need to lop off branches or to take a dozen samples of the same plant.

Plant Characteristics

We should begin with a few definitions. Most of the land plants big enough to be visible to the naked eye belong to the large group called *vascular* plants. Vascular plants are equipped with tubes that carry water, minerals, and food from one portion of the plant to another. Only the mosses, liverworts, and lichens among the common land plants do not have vascular tissue.

The more primitive vascular plants—the ferns, club mosses, and horsetails, for example—reproduce by spores, tiny one-celled or few-celled structures. The higher plants reproduce by seeds, more complex structures consisting of an embryo, a quantity of stored food, and a protective seed coat. Seeds generally have a higher rate of reproductive success than spores.

The seed producers are divided into two classes, the gymnosperms and the angiosperms. The term *gymnosperm* means 'naked seed.' It describes a group of plants including the pines, spruces, and firs which produce their seeds on the inner surfaces of cone scales. *Angiosperm* means essentially 'enclosed seed' (*angio-*, 'vessel'). It describes the group of plants that produce seeds within the protective covering of an ovary. Although the cones of gymnosperms are actually female flowers, the term *flowering plants* is commonly applied only to the angiosperms, the huge group of plants that dominate most of the earth's surface. Gymnosperms are often called conifers, cone-bearing plants. In our area, all but one of the conifers are evergreen. The one exception is the tamarack which, like such common angiosperms as the maples, aspens, and birches is deciduous, losing its leaves each autumn. Angiosperm trees are often called *broad-leaved* to distinguish them from the needle-leaved conifers. The angiosperms are the trees known as hardwoods.

We have divided the plant characteristics which are useful for field identification into six broad categories: behavior, growth form, leaves, stems, flowers, and seeds and fruit.

Behavior

This is simply where the plant grows and when it carries on the activities essential to its life cycle. Is it colonizing the bare sand of a beachfront dune or growing in six inches of water at the edge of a lake? Is it growing in a clearing exposed to full sun or in the dense shade of a hemlock forest? Does it flower in May or August?

Behavior is in part governed by ecological tolerance, which varies widely from species to species, so behavior is a more useful clue to identification for some plants than for others. Marsh marigolds, with a narrow tolerance, are virtually always found in wet situations; Canada mayflowers may be common in any forested habitat.

Blooming dates vary too. Spring flowers that appear in April at the southern end of our region may not bloom until June in the north. However, they are unlikely to be in flower in late August. We have listed a range of blooming dates (e.g., Apr-Jun) for the flowering plants described in this book.

Growth Form

All species have a typical growth form which will help in identification. These typical forms can be extensively modified by local circumstances, however, so they should be used only as one of several clues to identification. For example, white pine is typically symmetrical, sending out whorls of horizontal branches from a straight central trunk. However, in areas where strong winds with a persistent direction are common, the windward side of the trunk may be bare, and branches will grow only on the sheltered side.

Some typical growth forms are:

TREES An erect central trunk of woody tissue with branches arranged in various ways. Conifers usually have a single vertical trunk that sends out horizontal branches along its entire length. Hardwoods usually have shorter trunks that branch and branch again to produce a *crown*. Hardwoods growing in the crowded conditions of a forest have longer central trunks than open-grown trees.

Within the broad categories, notice such individual traits

as the gracefully bowed branches of the white pine, the tall narrow cone shape of the spruces and the balsam fir, and the slender sparse crown of the aspens.

ERECT SHRUBS   Shrubs are woody plants that typically have a number of more or less equal stems growing from the ground. Beaked hazel is probably the most common such plant in the North Woods. The term may also be applied to plants such as the juneberries which sometimes grow as single-trunk trees but are not big enough to reach the forest canopy.

CREEPING, ARCHING, TRAILING, AND STRAGGLING SHRUBS   One of the distinguishing characteristics of the forests in our area is a large number of shrubs whose growth form is creeping, or prostrate. Their woody stems—in some plants they grow underground—send up shoots that carry the leaves, flowers, and fruits. Wintergreen and trailing arbutus are common examples. These two plants look so much like herbs that we have put them in that category in our keys.

Other shrubs have woody stems that grow up from the ground and then curve horizontally or arch back to earth. Many of the brambles—raspberries and blackberries—and honeysuckles are in this category. We have termed straggling those shrubs that are low and extensively branched with nearly horizontal stems.

CLIMBING VINES   Woody plants that climb on other plants. These are not very common in our area, though poison ivy sometimes grows in this form.

HERBS   Plants without woody tissue. We classify both flowering plants and ferns in this category.

Some herbaceous plants are *annuals,* growing from seed in spring, producing flowers and seeds, then dying at the end of the warm season. Some are *biennials,* producing leaves the first year and flowers and seeds the next before dying.

In our woods, most of the herbs are *perennials.* Roots and underground stems that live for many years send up shoots each spring. These shoots produce flowers and fruits and then die in the fall. Although ferns are not flowering plants, they are among the perennial herbs, producing annual shoots from long-lived rootstocks.

While they are all small, the growth forms of the herbaceous plants are in other ways extremely varied. They may be upright or reclining. They may have leaves only at their bases or the leaves may be at the top of the plant shading the flowers.

Leaves

A leaf can be divided into three parts: the petiole, the blade, and the stipules. The *petiole* is the stalk that joins the leaf to the plant's stem; the *blade* is the broad part; *stip-*

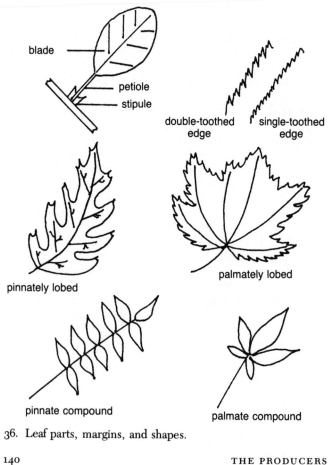

blade

petiole

stipule

double-toothed edge

single-toothed edge

pinnately lobed

palmately lobed

pinnate compound

palmate compound

36. Leaf parts, margins, and shapes.

ules are a pair of appendages at the base of the petiole. Any of these structures may be absent or so heavily modified as to be virtually unrecognizable. The maples, for example, have no stipules. Other plants lose theirs shortly after the leaves open. Stipules may also be large and leaflike or modified into thorns and tendrils.

Leaves lacking petioles are called *sessile*. Sessile leaves are attached directly to the plant stem. Some plants, with sessile leaves such as the grasses, have leaves whose bases clasp the stem. Others are *perfoliate*, with stems that appear to grow up right through the leaf.

Petioles carry water and minerals to the blade, where photosynthesis takes place, and carry the products of photosynthesis to the rest of the plant. They also adjust the position of the leaves in relation to the sun so that the blade will receive the optimum amount of light.

LEAF TYPES   Leaves are of two types, simple and compound. A *simple* leaf has a single blade. A *compound* leaf is divided into a number of *leaflets* which look superficially like separate leaves. Leaflets can be distinguished,

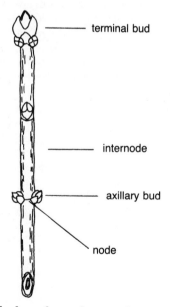

37. Twig with buds, nodes, and internodes.

A Guide to Plant Identification   141 however, by the absence of prominent clusters of veins, *vascular bundles*, connecting them to the midrib. A leaf cut from a stem will leave one to several distinct bundle scars showing as small circles within the overall scar.

Compound leaves are of two types, pinnate and palmate. *Pinnate* ('featherlike') leaves have a central axis called a *rachis* or *midrib* with leaflets arranged at right angles along the length. *Palmate* compound leaves have leaflets radiating out from a central point like the spokes of a wheel or the fingers of a hand.

Leaves are produced at points along stems called *nodes*. The spaces between nodes are called *internodes*. Buds also arise at nodes, growing in the angle between the petiole and the stem. This angle is called the *axil*, and these buds are known as *axillary buds*. Leaflets do not have axillary buds at their bases.

Some leaves are twice or thrice compound. In these the midrib produces pinnately compound leaflets which look like compound leaves themselves. Bracken fern leaves are twice compound.

LEAF ARRANGEMENTS   The arrangement of leaves on the stem is an extremely important characteristic. Some plants, such as bedstraw, have three or more leaves growing from a single node. This arrangement is called *whorled*. Some plants have two leaves growing from a single node on opposite sides of the stem. This arrangement is described as *opposite*. The dogwoods, maples, and viburnums are among the opposite-leaved plants. Plants with only a single

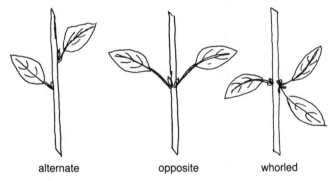

alternate   opposite   whorled

38. Leaf arrangements.

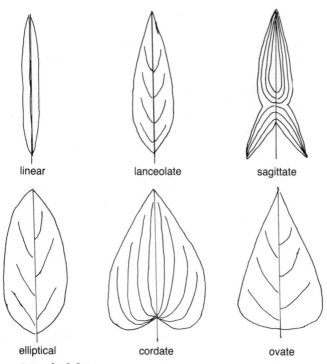

linear   lanceolate   sagittate

elliptical   cordate   ovate

39. Some leaf shapes.

leaf at each node are called *alternate leaved.* The aspens
and birches are among these.

It is a good idea to look at several twigs and at the leaf
scars on several older branches before deciding whether a
tree or shrub is alternate or opposite leaved. On very short
twigs, the nodes may be so close together that alternate
leaves look like opposite or whorled leaves.

LEAF SHAPES Botanists have developed a long list of
terms to describe leaf shapes. For example, *sagittate* leaves
are shaped like an arrow head; lanceolate, like the head of a
spear; ovate, egg-shape. Leaves that are judged to be intermediate are described with combined terms such as
ovate–lanceolate.

Since most of these terms have common English equivalents, we have avoided the technical vocabulary wherever
possible. We have not made this substitution for technical

terms—like lanceolate—that seem as clear as any reasonable alternative.

Botanists also have many specialized terms for describing the tips and bases of leaves. We have substituted common English terms in our descriptions.

LEAF MARGINS Margins may be *entire*, i.e., without teeth or lobes, or they may be finely or coarsely toothed or deeply incised in lobes. The lobes may be pinnate, like the oaks, or palmate, like the maples.

VENATION Flowering plants of the large group called *monocotyledons*, which includes the grasses and the lilies, generally have *parallel veins*. The main veins arise at the base and extend the length of the leaf. Other tiny veins, usually invisible to the naked eye, connect these main veins. The *dicotyledonous* plants usually have *net venation*, with the major veins producing branching veins which branch again. The members of the genus Cornus, the dogwoods, have *arcuate venation*, with veins sweeping outward from the midrib in an arc that follows the outline of the leaf.

SURFACE TEXTURE Taxonomists use more than thirty terms to describe the character of leaf surfaces. Most of the terms have to do with the nature, extent, and location of leaf hairs. For example, *ciliate* means that the leaf margin is fringed with hairs; *tomentose* means that the surface is densely woolly and matted; *pubescent* means covered with short, soft hairs, etc. A real understanding of the differences that these terms describe would require a chance to look at—and touch—a wide variety of samples. We have

 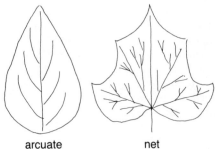

parallel   arcuate   net

40. Leaf venation.

THE PRODUCERS

not used these terms, preferring to stick with more accessible phrases such as "woolly," or "covered with fine soft hairs."

LEAF SIZE   In our plant descriptions, we give a range of figures for size, and you can expect to find a great deal of variation between these extremes. Leaves that are in shade much of the time tend to be larger than leaves usually exposed to full sun, and young trees usually produce bigger leaves than older trees of the same species.

Stems

Stems are typically slender structures that support the plant and its various parts and transport water and other materials. Stems have nodes that give rise to branches, leaves, flowers, and buds. Needless to say, stems vary greatly. The main stem of the wild sarsaparilla scarcely breaks the surface, while the central trunk of the white pine is a stem that may grow over 200 feet (60 meters) tall.

On woody plants, stems produced by the current year's growth are called twigs. Twigs are generally tipped with a terminal bud and marked off from the previous year's growth by a ring of scars left by that year's terminal bud. The previous year's growth is known as a *branchlet.* It is possible to determine the age of young branches by counting the rings of bud scars.

Plants produce a variety of specialized stems. Strawberries grow *runners* (also called *stolons,*) horizontal stems that creep along the surface and send down roots at the nodes. A new plant forms at this point, and later the runner dies.

Rhizomes are underground stems that produce shoots from their nodes. Many rhizomes grow steadily longer, gradually colonizing a larger and larger area. Many of the perennial herbs of the North Woods send up annual shoots from long-lived rhizomes.

The surface features of stems are important identification clues. Herbaceous stems and very young woody twigs may be hairy. The stems of some plants are thorny or prickly. *Cork,* which forms the visible bark of woody stems, is impervious to water and air. *Lenticels* are openings in the cork where loosely arranged cells and many intercellular openings allow the exchange of gases. Lenticels often appear as raised dots of a color that contrasts with the rest of the bark.

Stems are often distinctively colored, and on trees and shrubs the twigs and branchlets may be a different color than the older stems.

A typical twig is tipped with a terminal bud which will begin to grow the following spring. Axillary buds grow in the leaf axils, and in some plants these produce the flowers. When leaves fall they leave scars on the twig which are of a characteristic shape for each species. The number and arrangement of vascular bundle scars is also characteristic.

The *pith*, which is the core of a woody stem, consists of storage cells. It may appear as a solid substance of various colors, or it may form a series of chambers with thin partitions between them.

The *epidermis* and *cortex* which form the surface of plant stems are permanent tissues which cannot increase in size. As a tree trunk grows these tissues split, and cork forms as a protective layer to cover the damage. These cork formations, the bark of the tree, are distinctive in each species in color, shape, and thickness.

Flowers and Fruit

Flowers are among the most conspicuous and distinctive features of the higher plants. Flowers are reproductive structures which produce pollen and ovules. Fertilized by pollen, the ovules develop into seeds. In the angiosperms, the seeds are surrounded by a fruit which may be a large conspicuous structure, such as an apple, or just a thin covering over the seed.

A complete flower consists of four parts: sepals, petals, stamens, and pistils. The *sepals* are usually green and leaflike, although in some plants—such as the wood anemone—they may be brightly colored. They enclose the rest of the flower in the bud stage and may not persist for the life of the bloom. Sepals may be separate, identical parts like those shown in Figure 41, or they may be fused into a single structure called the *calyx*. On some flowers they are modified in various ways so that the individual sepals appear dissimilar.

The *petals* lie within the surrounding sepals. They are

146   THE PRODUCERS

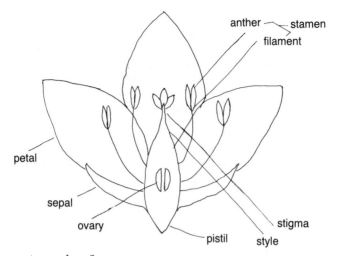

41. A complete flower.

usually the most showy and brightly colored parts of the flower. They may be identical, as in lilies such as the Clintonia, or they may be unlike, as in the orchids. They may be separate or they may be united into a tubular structure called the *corolla*, as in the honeysuckles. On some flowers the petals and sepals are united into a single floral envelope called the *perianth*.

Stamens, which produce pollen, and *pistils*, where ovules fertilized by the pollen develop into seeds, are generally inside the petals.

Flowers lacking one or more of the four components are termed incomplete. Flowers lacking either the male (stamen) or female (pistil) parts are termed imperfect. Flowers lacking both of these reproductive parts are called sterile.

Many plants produce two kinds of imperfect flowers: the staminate blooms produce pollen, the pistillate, ovules. In some species both of these flower types are produced on the same plants. The alders are an example of this condition, which is called *monoecious*. In other species individual plants produce either male or female flowers but not both. The aspens are examples of this type, which is called *dioecious*.

Many flowers grow in clusters called *inflorescences*. These have several typical shapes:

A *cyme* (pronounced *syme*) is an inflorescence developing from a terminal bud and forming a flat-topped or convex cluster in which the central flowers bloom first.

A *head* is a dense cluster of sessile or nearly sessile flowers. Asters are a good example of this sort of inflorescence. What appears to be a single flower surrounded by a rim of petals is actually a cluster of tiny flowers.

A *spike* is an elongated flower cluster with a central axis producing sessile or nearly sessile flowers along its length. If the flowers have stems of more or less equal length, the cluster is called a *raceme*.

If the central stem produces branches which branch again before producing flowers, the cluster is called a *panicle*.

A *corymb* has a main vertical stalk with branches of unequal length produced along it. The side branches may be simple or they may branch again.

An *umbel* has several branches arising from a common point at the summit of the main flower stem. Umbels may be simple or compound.

Catkins, or *aments*, are elongated clusters—they may be spikes or racemes—of unisexual flowers without petals. Birches and alders are among the plants of our area that produce catkins. The staminate and pistillate flowers can be distinguished by their shapes.

Technically a fruit is a matured ovary that may or may not contain a seed or seeds. This simple statement hides a bewildering complexity of fruit shapes, sizes, and types. The elaborate botanical terminology that describes these types is generally not needed by amateurs interested in field identification, and it can be confusing since it frequently uses common terms in ways that differ from ordinary usage. For example, the technical term *berry* describes the fruit of the juneberry and also the fruit of the tomato, but it does not describe the strawberry or the raspberry.

Some fruits—such as those of the asters—are extremely inconspicuous, consisting mainly of a thin covering over the seed.

We have described fruits only when they are conspicuous and likely to be helpful in identification.

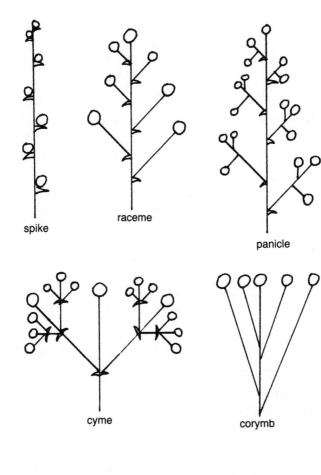

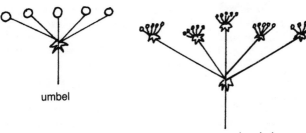

42. Types of flower clusters.

A Guide to Plant Identification

Equipment for Botanizing

The only equipment a botanizer needs is a hand lens and a field guide. A lens with 10-power magnification is best, although you can get by with a 4-power lens. A small 4-power lens attached to a protective leather or synthetic envelope can be found for under $2; a 10-power model of the same type can be purchased for under $10, so the expense is not very great.

This book will introduce you to the common plants of the North Woods, but if you find yourself getting interested in the game of field identification, you will want a more comprehensive guide. You will need at least three books to cover all the vascular plants of the region, one for trees and shrubs, one for wildflowers, and one for ferns and club mosses.

A good field guide should have clear illustrations, concise descriptions, and a system of organization to help you find the plants you come across in the field. It should also be convenient to carry (not too big or heavy), well bound, and reasonably priced.

Most guides use line drawings or paintings rather than photographs because drawings allow the artist to emphasize the distinctive features of the plant. Some guides use key systems like the one we use in this book. Others create categories based on flower color, and others simply list the species in taxonomic order (a standardized listing by class, order, family, genus, and species).

We have deliberately made our descriptions longer than the minimum needed for field identification in order to call attention to the whole structure of the plant. Some field guides include only enough to separate a species from others of quite similar appearance. Guides should also include information on a plant's range, either presenting it in words (e.g., "from Quebec to Minnesota and south to Missouri") or in range maps. Maps are preferable because they are quicker to use and can show range boundaries more accurately.

In general, guides to the northeastern United States will give you thorough coverage of the North Woods. An annotated listing of guides to this area will be found in Appendix B, Further Reading.

CHAPTER NINE

Common Trees of the North Woods

THIS CHAPTER PROVIDES a key, detailed descriptions, and line drawings to illustrate 28 tree species typical of the North Woods region. The line drawings emphasize, in most cases, only those details which are essential to identification. Photographs or drawings of bark, flowers, and fruit, therefore, will accompany some descriptions but not others. Each description concludes with a list of the plant community or communities where that tree is most often found. Presumably, once you have identified one, or at most two or three, trees in a particular area, you will also have identified the community and will be able to turn to the appropriate chapter for its history, general characteristics, and information on plants other than trees that are typical of that community.

Key to the Common Trees

A key is designed to help identify plants by presenting a series of choices. If you make the correct choice at each step, you will arrive at the proper species.

The following key to North Woods trees offers two choices numbered 1. Pick one and then move on to the choices numbered 2. In some cases, identification comes quickly, e.g., you will know you are looking at a northern white cedar if you determine (1) that its leaves are needle- or scale-like—the defining characteristic of all conifers— and (2) that those leaves are flattened, scale-like, and assume a certain pattern on the stem. For other trees you will need to eliminate five or six choices before making the identification. Species are indicated in boldface type in the key to let you know when you have made a positive identification.

In some cases, the final choice in the key will refer you to a group of closely related species in the descriptions (e.g., *Maples*). This is indicated by italics in the key. Comparison of the detailed descriptions will lead you to identification of the species. For convenience, the descriptions are organized parallel to the key.

1. Leaves needle- or scale-like (conifers)

    2. Leaves flattened or scale-like, lying in 4 overlapping ranks on stem—**Northern white cedar**

    2. Leaves needle-like

        3. Needles growing in clusters

            4. Needles in clusters of 2 to 5 (pines)

                5 Needles in clusters of 5—**White pine**

                5. Needles in clusters of 2

                    6. Needles less than 2 in. (5 cm) long—**Jack pine**

                    6. Needles more than 4 in. (10 cm) long—**Red pine**

            4. Needles in clusters of more than 5 growing at tips of short spur branches—**Tamarack**

        3. Needles growing singly

            4. Needles attached directly to twig, leaving flat, round scar when picked—**Balsam fir**

            4. Needle has short petiole attached to rounded woody base that stays on twig when needle is picked—**Eastern hemlock**

            4. Needle attached to short projecting stem that remains on twig after needles have fallen—**Spruces**

1. Leaves broad (hardwoods)

    2. Leaves opposite

        3. Leaves compound—*Ashes*

3. Leaves simple, palmately lobed—*Maples*

2. Leaves alternate, simple

   3. Leaves pinnately lobed—*Oaks*

   3. Unlobed leaves with toothed edges

      4. Leaf bases asymmetrical (examine several before making a decision)

         5. Leaves broadly heart-shape with hairs on vein axils beneath—**Basswood**

         5. Leaves ovate to oblong—**American elm**

      4. Leaf bases symmetrical

         5. Buds gummy, smelling of balsam—**Balsam poplar**

         5. Buds downy, brown—**Big-toothed aspen**

         5. Buds otherwise

The rest of the common trees in this large group of species with alternate, simple, toothed leaves can be identified by their distinctive bark.

      6. Bark smooth, gray, even on oldest trunks—**American beech**

      6. Bark smooth, greenish white, becoming dark and furrowed on oldest trunks—**Quaking aspen**

      6. Bark bright white, peeling in horizontal strips—**Paper birch**

      6. Bark yellow-gray, lustrous, peeling in horizontal strips—**Yellow birch**

      6. Bark smooth, reddish brown, dotted with pale lenticels

         7. Leaves lanceolate, marginal teeth irregular, rounded; white flowers and bright red berries growing in umbels—**Pin cherry**

         7. Leaves lanceolate, marginal teeth blunt-tipped; white flowers and purplish red to black fruit in racemes—**Black cherry**

Plant Descriptions

Conifers

Trees with needles flattened or scale-like.

Northern White Cedar, *Thuja occidentalis.* A tree growing to 65 ft (20 m) tall with a straight central trunk and a
compact, conical crown. *Leaves:* Flattened, scale-like, 0.1 -
0.2 in. (2-4 mm) long, arranged in four ranks on the
branches. *Cones:* Oblong, up to ½ in. (12 mm) long, standing upright on branches. *Bark:* Fibrous, shredding, ridged,
light brown. *Plant communities:* Swamp forest or on rocky
upland sites, especially on limestone outcrops.

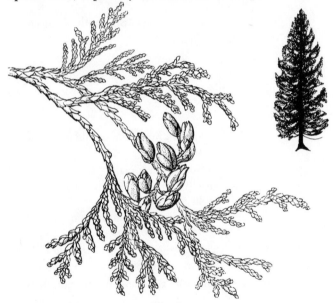

43. White cedar, *Thuja occidentalis.*

White Pine, *Pinus strobus.* Potentially the largest tree in
the region. Specimens up to 225 ft (70 m) tall have been
found. Branches extend horizontally from the tall straight
central trunk with a graceful bow toward their tips that

THE PRODUCERS

44. White cedar bark. *Jerry Sullivan*.

combines with the long, supple needles to give the tree a very distinctive appearance. *Leaves:* Needles in bundles of 5, up to 5 in. (13 cm) long. They are pale green with a silvery sheen that is quite apparent in bright sun. *Cones:* 4 - 8 in. (10-20 cm) long, slender, curved. *Bark:* Dark gray to

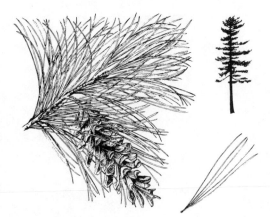

45. White pine, *Pinus strobus*.

black, heavily furrowed. *Plant communities:* A dominant in pine forest. Occurs as scattered tree in all forest types; stunted specimens often found in open bogs.

Jack Pine, *P. banksiana.* A straight-trunked tree with short horizontal drooping branches. *Leaves:* Stout needles in bundles of 2 are 0.8-1.5 in. (2-3.5 cm) long. *Cones:*

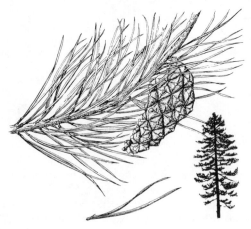

46. Jack pine, *Pinus banksiana*.

THE PRODUCERS

Somewhat curved, 1-2 in. (3-5 cm) long; often in pairs. *Bark:* Dark reddish brown to gray; scaly. *Plant communities:* pine forest.

Red Pine, *P. resinosa.* A straight-trunked tree up to 130 ft (40 m) tall with horizontal branches forming a broad oval, rather open crown. This tree is also called Norway pine. *Leaves:* Needles in bundles of 2 are slender, flexible, 4-6 in. (10-15 cm) long. *Cones:* Egg-shape to oval up to 2.5 in. (6.5 cm) long. *Bark:* Reddish brown, broken up into scaly plates; twigs are yellow to orange–brown. *Plant community:* Pine forest.

47. Red pine, *Pinus resinosa.*

Trees with needles in clusters of more than 5.

Tamarack, *Larix laricina.* Straight central trunk to 65 ft (20 m) tall and a slender open crown of horizontal branches. *Leaves:* Needles up to 1.3 in. (3.3 cm) long, slender; growing in clusters at the tips of short spurs or singly on twigs of present year's growth. They are deciduous, turning golden yellow in the fall before dropping off. *Cones:* Egg-shape, up

48. Tamarack, *Larix laricina*.

to 0.8 in. (2 cm) long. *Bark:* Dark gray bark flakes off in small scales. *Plant communities:* Bog forest, open bogs.

Trees with needles growing singly.

Balsam Fir, *Abies balsamea.* Up to 82 ft (25 m) tall with a straight central trunk and whorls of branches in shape of a tall, slender cone. *Leaves:* Needles up to 1 in. (25 mm)

49. Balsam fir, *Abies balsamea*.

THE PRODUCERS

long, blunt or minutely notched at the tip with narrow white stripes beneath; attached directly to twigs, leaving a round scar when picked; spirally attached but typically lying on one plane by twisting at the base. *Cones:* Cylindric, up to 4 in. (10 cm) long; borne erect on top of branches. *Bark:* Smooth and gray, becoming scaly on old trees. *Plant communities:* Boreal forest; swamp forest; second-growth stands and as an understory tree in mixed–hardwood forest.

50. Eastern hemlock, *Tsuga canadensis.*

Eastern Hemlock, *Tsuga canadensis.* Tree up to 100 ft (30 m) tall with a straight central trunk and a dense loose crown that has a lacy look. *Leaves:* Needles flat, short, up to 0.6 in. (15 mm) long, with 2 white bands beneath. A short petiole attaches to a rounded woody base that remains on the twig when the leaf is removed. *Cones:* Ovoid, up to 0.8 in. (20 mm) long, hanging from short stems. *Bark:* On mature trees bark is purple–brown, scaly and deeply furrowed. *Plant communities:* Mixed–hardwood forest or in drier parts of swamp forest; sometimes in pine forest. Absent in Minnesota.

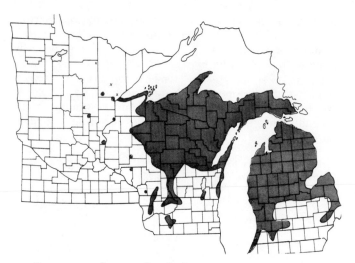

51. Range map of eastern hemlock.

White Spruce, *Picea glauca,* and **Black Spruce,** *P. mariana.* Both of these spruce species are trees up to 82 ft (25 m) tall with straight central trunks and whorls of branches forming a narrow cone. Spruce leaves are joined to the twig by a short projecting stem that stays on after the leaves have dropped off. The principal differences between the two species are: *Leaves:* Black spruce needles are usu-

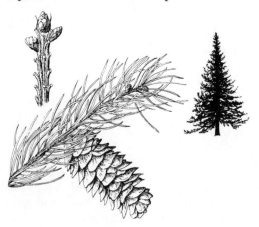

52. White spruce, *Picea glauca.*

160   THE PRODUCERS

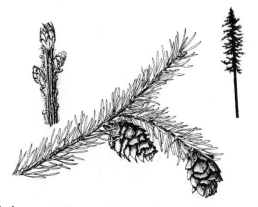

53. Black spruce, *Picea mariana*.

ally shorter than white spruce, but there is considerable overlap. White spruce are 0.4-0.7 in. (10-18 mm) and black spruce, 0.2-0.7 in. (6-18 mm). Black spruce needles are sometimes covered with a white powder. *Cones:* The best distinguishing marks. White spruce, elliptical, 1.4-2 in. (3.5-5 cm) long with thin, flexible scale edges; Black spruce, egg-shape 0.6-1.4 in. (1.5-3.5 cm) long with firm scales with toothed or ragged edges. *Twigs and Buds:* Hairy on black spruce, smooth on white. These hairs are very short, thin, and sparse and often difficult to see even with a hand lens. *Plant communities:* White spruce: boreal forest. Black spruce: bog forest, boreal forest; in northeastern Minnesota grows on upland sites with jack pine.

Hardwoods

Trees and erect shrubs with broad, opposite, compound leaves.

ASHES

Ashes are the only trees with broad, opposite, pinnately compound leaves you are likely to encounter in our region. All the ashes are tall trees with deep crowns and ascending branches. While they are quite distinctive as a group, telling one species from another can be difficult. Important differences are italicized in the descriptions below.

54. Black ash, *Fraxinus nigra*.

Black Ash, *Fraxinus nigra*. *Leaves:* 7-11 leaflets are lanceolate/oblong with a *long tapering* point. They are hairless, *sessile*, and often toothed. *Flowers and fruit: Flowers emerge before the leaves.* They grow in clusters from the axils of last year's leaves. The fruit is a one-winged samara, *rounded or notched at the tip. The wing extends to the base, or nearly so. Twigs:* Round, smooth. *Plant community:* Swamp forest.

Green Ash, *F. pensylvanica* (sometimes called red ash). *Leaves:* 5-9 leaflets are lanceolate to oblong or elliptic. Their bases are wedge-shaped or sharp-pointed and often asymmetrical. The petiolules—the stalks that join the leaflet to the midrib—*are short, or the leaflet nearly sessile. Petioles, the undersides of the leaflets and the midrib may be covered by downy, pale brown hairs. Flowers and fruit: Flowers emerge after the leaves have begun to open. The samara has a wing extending only to the middle of its body. Twigs:* May be hairy. *Plant community:* Mixed–hardwood forest.

White Ash, *F. americana*. *Leaves:* The 5-9 leaflets are oblong to egg-shape tapering to an abrupt point. They have *rounded bases,* are *pale or white below,* and may be finely toothed above the middle. They are *attached to the midrib by slender petiolules* 0.1-0.6 *in.* (0.3-1.5 *cm) long. Petioles and midrib are hairless. Flowers: Emerge before leaves. Fruit: a samara with a rounded tip and a wing that does not extend quite to the base. Twigs:* Round, smooth. *Plant*

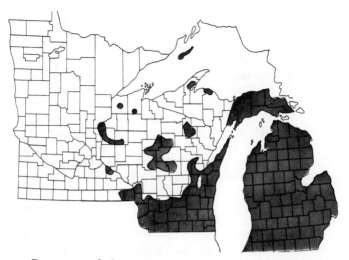

55. Range map of white ash.

community: Mixed–hardwood. The map shows the range of the white ash. In the western Upper Peninsula and most of Wisconsin and Minnesota, you are far more likely to encounter green ash in mesic situations.

Trees with opposite, simple, palmately lobed leaves.

MAPLES

Sugar Maple, *Acer saccharum.* A tree up to 130 ft (40 m) tall. In the open it has a short trunk and a deep, rounded

56. Sugar maple, *Acer saccharum.*

crown. *Leaves:* 3-5 lobes, each lobe with a few large pointed teeth. Edges are otherwise toothless. The sides of the center lobe roughly parallel. *Flowers and fruit:* Yellow, unisexual flowers in umbels on long stalks growing from terminal or uppermost axillary buds. They appear with the leaves. Two-winged samaras ripen in fall. *Bark and twigs:* New branchlets brown, becoming smooth and gray and then furrowed and scaly. *Plant community:* Mixed–hardwood.

Red Maple, *Acer rubrum.* A tree up to 85 ft (25 m) tall with ascending branches forming a deep oval crown. *Leaves:* 3-5 pointed lobes, leaf edges coarsely toothed. The sinus (deep indentation) between the center and lateral lobes is pointed. Leaves may turn either red or yellow in fall. *Flowers and fruit:* Usually scarlet—sometimes yellow—flowers appear well before the leaves. Samaras ripen in late spring. *Bark:* Smooth, light gray, except on old trunks where it darkens and splits in scaly plates. *Plant communities:* Swamp forest, pine forest, boreal forest, second-growth forest.

57. Red maple, *Acer rubrum.*

THE PRODUCERS

58. Red maple bark. *Jerry Sullivan.*

Striped Maple, *Acer pensylvanicum.* A small tree, generally not tall enough to reach the canopy of a mature forest. *Leaves:* Three-lobed with rounded or heart-shape base. Finely toothed—or doubly toothed—with 7-12 teeth per cm. Hairless on both sides when mature. *Flowers and fruit:* Bright yellow flowers in drooping racemes appear when the leaves are nearly grown. Staminate and pistillate flowers are separate. Samaras with widely spread wings are green and yellow. *Twigs and bark:* Twigs and buds hairless. Green smooth bark is marked with vertical white stripes. *Plant communities:* Boreal forest, mixed–hardwood.

Mountain Maple, *Acer spicatum.* A small tree. May grow to 30 ft (10 m) but most are under 20 ft (6 m). *Leaves:* 3-5 lobes. The coarse teeth, 2-3 per cm are tipped with minute sharp glands. They are hairless or slightly hairy beneath. *Flowers and fruit:* Greenish flowers appear after the leaves in slender, ascending, hairy racemes. Samaras usually red, sometimes yellow. *Bark and twigs:* Twigs and buds hairy. Bark dark reddish-brown or greenish, with or without stripes. *Plant communities:* Boreal forest.

Trees with alternate, simple, pinnately lobed leaves.

OAKS

Northern Red Oak, *Quercus borealis* or *Q. rubra* var. *borealis.* This species—or variety, depending on which authority you consult—is the most common and widespread oak in the North Woods. It is a tree that can grow to 70 ft (20 m) in height, but on very dry sites it may be stunted and almost shrubby. *Leaves:* 6-10 sharp pointed lateral lobes. Sinuses between lobes extend halfway to the midrib. Young leaves just emerging in the spring are pink and quite hairy. Hairs are shed until mature leaves show only tufts of hair in the axils of veins on the undersides. Leaves turn red in fall. *Flowers and fruit:* Acorn is 1 in. (2.5 cm) or less in length. Cap is turban-shape or hemispherical and encloses about ⅓ of the nut. *Bark:* Dark brown or gray to black and deeply furrowed. Upper trunk and branches smoother and paler gray. *Plant communities:* Pine forest.

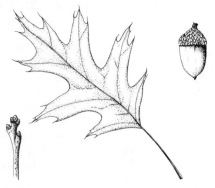

59. Red oak, *Quercus rubra.*

THE PRODUCERS

Hill's Oak, *Q. ellipsoidalis.* A small- to medium-size tree, sometimes stunted on poor soils. *Leaves:* 2-3 pairs of toothed, pointed lateral lobes. Sinuses between lobes are rounded to elliptic and extend nearly to midrib. Leaves are smooth except for small tufts of branched hairs on vein axils on the undersides. *Flowers and fruit:* Acorn is slim and tapering and about 0.6-0.8 in. (1.5-2 cm) long. The cup is gray, deep, scaly, turban-shape and covered with downy hairs. It covers from ⅓ to ½ of the nut. *Bark and twigs:* Smooth to shallowly furrowed, gray. *Plant communities:* Pine forest.

Several other species of oak, including **bur oak** (*Q. macrocarpa*) and **white oak** (*Q. alba*), grow in the North Woods. They are most likely be encountered near the southern edge of the region.

Trees with alternate, simple, toothed leaves.

Basswood, *Tilia americana.* A tree that grows up to 130 ft (40 m). In the open it has a deep oval crown. *Leaves:* Sharply toothed with an asymmetrical, heart-shape base. The tips taper abruptly to a narrow point. They are typically large, 5-6 in. (12.5-15 cm) long and 3-4 in. (7.5-10 cm) wide. Hairs grow on the vein axils beneath. *Flowers and fruit:* White or cream flowers grow in axillary cymes on long stalks attached to a structure called a bract that looks like a long slender leaf. Flowers are fragrant, bloom Jun–Jul. Fruits nutlike. *Bark:* Dark gray or nearly black, ridged and furrowed on old trunks. *Plant community:* Mixed–hardwood.

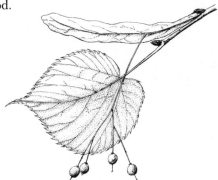

60. Basswood, *Tilia Americana.*

61. American elm, *Ulmus Americana.*

American Elm, *Ulmus americana.* A tall tree—to 130 ft
(40 m)—that in the open produces a straight trunk which
divides into ascending limbs that grow up and out and then
droop at the tips, producing a shape like the top of an am-
phora. *Leaves:* Egg-shape or oblong with an asymmetrical
base and a pointed tip; short petioles. Smooth or sandpapery above; edges usually double-toothed. *Flowers and*
fruit: Clusters of tiny flowers with stalks that become long
and pendulous appear before the leaves. Fruit is a long-
stemmed samara with hairy edges. *Buds:* Smooth or
downy, over 0.25 in. (6 mm) long. Scales light brown with
dark edges. *Bark:* Twigs hairless or barely hairy. Bark on
mature trees dark gray in flat-topped ridges. *Plant commu-*
nity: Mixed–hardwood. Frequently on stream banks.

Balsam Poplar, *Populus balsamifera.* Tree up to 97 ft (30
m) high with a straight central trunk and a narrow, oval
crown. *Leaves:* Petioles round or nearly so, blades lanceolate to egg-shape, base rounded to nearly heart-shape.
Finely toothed, pale and lustrous beneath, they are borne

62. Balsam poplar, *Populus balsamea*.

on short branches. *Flowers and fruit:* Catkins emerge before leaves. Seed capsules are egg-shape, 2-valved, 0.3-0.4
in. (5-8 mm) long, grow crowded on short stalks in a compact, spike-like raceme. *Twigs and bark:* Smooth gray–
green bark becomes furrowed on old trunks. *Plant communities:* Swamp forest, boreal forest.

Big-Toothed Aspen, *Populus grandidentata*. A tree up to
65 ft (20 m) tall with a straight central trunk and a narrow,
oval crown. *Leaves:* Petioles flattened, blades broadly egg-
shape and 3-5 in. (8-12 cm) long with 5-10 large, projecting,
round-pointed teeth. Leaves covered with woolly white
hairs beneath when young. *Flowers and fruit:* Catkins
emerge before leaves. *Bark and twigs:* Light greenish gray
turning dark brown. Often has a faint salmon cast. Twigs
may be hairy. *Plant communities:* Second-growth and pine
forests.

American Beech, *Fagus grandifolia*. A tree up to 97 ft
(30 m) tall with a short trunk and a broad rounded crown.
Bark remains smooth and gray even on the oldest trunks.

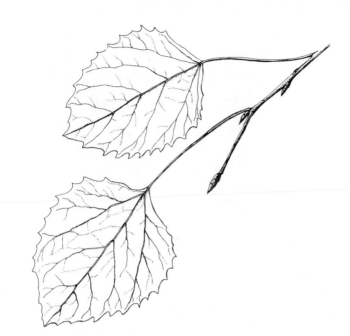

63. Big-toothed aspen, *Populus grandidentata*.

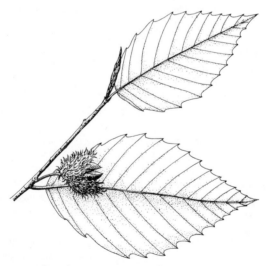

64. American beech, *Fagus grandifolia*.

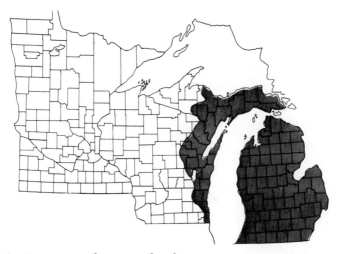

65. Range map of American beech.

Leaves: Egg-shape, coarsely toothed with a vein running from the midrib to each tooth. Silky when young, but the silkiness remains only on the midrib below when the leaves are mature. Leaves turn a rich bronze orange in fall. *Flowers and fruit:* Flowers grow in leaf axils and emerge with the leaves. Staminate flowers in small heads on drooping stalks; the pistillate usually in pairs on a short stalk. Fruit is a small, triangular nut. *Buds:* Many scales; slender, long, growing at a broad angle from the twig. *Plant community:* Mixed–hardwood in lower Michigan, eastern Upper Peninsula, and eastern Wisconsin. Absent west of there.

Quaking Aspen, *Populus tremuloides.* A tree up to 65 ft (20 m) tall with a straight central trunk and a narrow rather sparse oval crown. Commonly called popple. *Leaves:* Petioles flattened and weak, causing the leaves to flutter in the slightest breeze. Blades egg-shape to nearly circular, abruptly pointed, 1-4 in. (2.5-10 cm) long. Edges with 20-40 regular teeth. *Flowers and fruit:* Drooping catkins emerge in spring, mature before the leaves are fully out. Seed capsules are slender, conic, 0.1-0.2 in. (2.5-5 mm) long on stalks 0.04-0.1 in. (1-2 mm) long. *Bark and twigs:* Light greyish green to almost white. Bark becomes dark and furrowed with age. *Buds:* Terminal buds brown, shin-

66. Quaking aspen, *Populus tremuloides*.

ing, smooth. *Plant communities:* Pioneer species. Most common tree in second-growth forest. Often present in other types as well.

Paper Birch, *Betula papyrifera*. A tree up to 97 ft (30 m) tall with a straight central trunk and narrow crown. Trunks growing from stump sprouts often clumped. *Leaves:* Egg-shape, 2-4 in. (5-10 cm) long, tapering to a point, sharply

67. Paper birch, *Betula papyrifera*.

68. Paper birch bark. *Jerry Sullivan.*

toothed. They are sparsely downy beneath, especially on the veins. *Flowers and fruit:* Staminate catkins formed in fall become tassel-like in spring. Seeds carried in slender cones called strobiles, 1-2 in. (2.5-5 cm) long. *Bark and twigs:* Clear white, peeling bark is marked by dark horizontal blotches. Bark on youngest branches is a warm brown. On old trunks it becomes black and fissured. *Plant communities:* Second-growth, pine, and boreal forests.

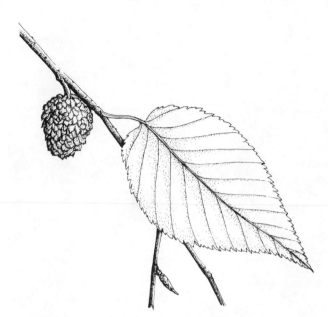

69. Yellow birch, *Betula lutea*.

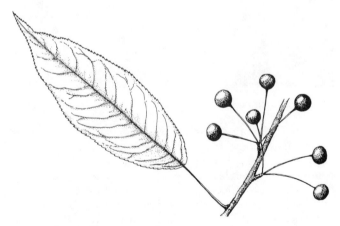

70. Pin cherry, *Prunus pensylvanica*.

THE PRODUCERS

Yellow Birch, *Betula lutea.* A tree up to 97 ft (30 m) tall with a straight central trunk and slender crown. *Leaves:* Lanceolate to egg-shape, pointed, with sharp, coarse teeth. They are longer and narrower than paper birch leaves. 2.5-4 in. (6-10 cm) long. Soft hairs on veins below. *Flowers and fruit:* Pendulous staminate catkins. Strobiles erect and egg-shape to cylindric, about 1 in. (2-3 cm) long. Fruit a more or less round samara. *Bark and twigs:* Yellowish gray bark with satiny luster peeling in thin strips. On older trees it may pull away in thick sheets. Twigs are hairy. *Plant community:* Mixed–hardwood.

Pin Cherry, *Prunus pensylvanica.* A tall shrub or tree up to 33 ft (10 m) tall. *Leaves:* Lanceolate to oblong–lanceolate, 2.5-5 in. (6-12 cm) long, less than half as wide, tapering to a long, slender point. Teeth are fine, irregular, and rounded. Petioles are usually glandular near the blade. *Flowers and fruit:* Umbel-like clusters of 2-5 white flowers on stalks 0.4-0.6 in. (1-1.5 cm) long. The 5 petals have fine hairs on the back near the base. Jun. Fruit, red berries with a hard stone, Jul–Sep. *Bark and twigs:* Smooth, reddish brown, with horizontal lenticels. Forms broad plates on old trunks. *Plant community:* Second-growth forest.

Black Cherry, *Prunus serotina.* A medium-sized tree up to 80 ft (25 m) tall. *Leaves:* Thin, long, fine, and blunt-toothed, 2-6 in. (5-15 cm), midrib hairy beneath. *Flowers and fruit:* Flowers with five white petals in racemes 4-6 in. (10-15 cm) long; calyx sharp-lobed. May–Jun. Fruit dark red, black when ripe, with hard stone. Aug–Sep. *Bark and twigs:* Smooth, reddish brown with pale lenticels on young trees. Becomes scaly on older trunks. *Plant communities:* Second-growth forest.

CHAPTER TEN

Ubiquitous Plants of the North Woods

THE PLANTS described in this chapter are typical North Woods species but are not indicative of any particular plant community. Rather, they occur in a wide variety of habitats throughout the region.

The key which begins the chapter uses roman numerals to separate four major categories: shrubs, herbs, ferns, and club mosses. Within each of these categories, the key works the same way as that in Chapter 9. Pick first from among the descriptions numbered 1, then from among the choices numbered 2, and so on, until the ever-narrowing and more precise descriptions lead you to an identification.

The descriptions which follow the key are, in most cases, descriptions of individual plant species. The exceptions are grasses and sedges, brambles, currants and gooseberries, ferns, and club mosses.

Grasses and sedges are very complex families of plants consisting of hundreds of species. Reliable identification of individual species of grasses and sedges takes more training and skill than we can impart in this brief treatment, so we have limited ourselves to outlining the major characteristics of the families. When field studies require a more precise identification, a specialist in these plants is called on to help.

Brambles (genus *Rubus*) and currants and gooseberries (genus *Ribes*) are also represented by many species in the North Woods, and among the brambles there are hybrids that can confuse even the experts. Our general descriptions will enable you to separate these genera from other low shrubs. Some particularly common, typical, and readily identifiable species within the genera are described in later chapters on individual plant communities.

We have followed a similar treatment for ferns and club mosses, the most readily noticeable nonflowering plants in the North Woods.

Key to the Ubiquitous Plants

I. Shrubs

   1.   Tall shrubs with alternate, simple, toothed leaves

      2.   Teeth coarse, bark tan to gray, sandpapery to the touch—*Hazel*

      2.   Teeth coarse, bark tan to gray, sandpapery to the touch—*Hazel*

   1.   Low shrubs

      2.   Alternate leaved with prickles—*Rubus* spp.

      2.   Alternate palmately lobed leaves—*Ribes* spp.

II. Herbs

   1.   Erect plants with opposite simple leaves

      2.   Flowers with 4 petal-like bracts—**Bunchberry**

      2.   Flowers with 5 lobes—**Twinflower**

   1.   Erect or arching plants with alternate simple leaves

      2.   Leaves entire, sheathing stem

         3.   Stems round, leaf sheaths open—*Grasses*

         3.   Stems triangular, sheaths closed, leaves in 3 ranks—*Sedges*

      2.   Leaves toothed

         3.   Flowers purple to lilac with 9-20 rays—**Large-leaved aster**

         3.   Glossy leathery leaves, sparingly toothed or entire—**Wintergreen**

      2.   Leaves entire, not sheathing stem

         3.   White flowers with 4 petals in dense racemes—**Canada Mayflower**

3. Flowers in leaf axils, rose–purple to pink with 6 petal-like divisions—**Rose twisted stalk**

1. Plants with whorled leaves

2. Stems prostrate or draped over other plants— *Bedstraw*

2. Stems erect

3. Leaves compound, divided into 3-5 leaflets; plant less than 1 ft (30 cm) tall—**Wood anemone**

3. Lanceolate leaves in a whorl of 5-10; flowers white, star-shape—**Starflower**

1. Erect plants with basal leaves

2. Leaves twice compound—**Wild sarsaparilla**

2. Leaves simple, entire; flowers yellow, nodding; perianth has 6 petal-like lobes—**Clintonia**

III. Ferns (see descriptions)
IV. Club mosses (see descriptions)

Plant Descriptions

Tall Shrubs

Beaked Hazel, *Corylus cornuta.* A shrub up to 9 ft (3 m) tall that grows as a clump of slender upright stems. Often forms dense thickets. *Leaves:* Oblong to egg-shape with a short point and coarse double teeth. Base is round. Leaves are somewhat downy beneath, especially on veins. Petioles smooth. *Flowers and fruit:* Sessile male catkins emerge in autumn, mature and bloom in early spring. Female flowers produce nuts usually in pairs with the husks elongated into flared tubes or beaks. *Bark:* Gray or brown, feels sandpapery. Young twigs hairy, becoming smooth. *Plant communities:* In all but very wet situations. May be the most common shrub in the North Woods.

American Hazel, *C. americana.* Much less common than the beaked hazel, but this species may be found in our area.

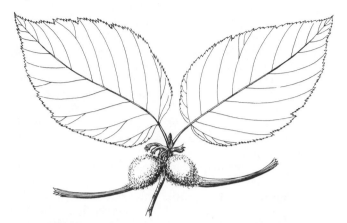

71. Beaked hazel, *Corylus cornuta*.

72. Beaked hazel bark. *Jerry Sullivan*.

Ubiquitous Plants of the North Woods

It differs from *C. cornuta* in having fuzzy petioles, hairy twigs, and staminate catkins attached to the stem by a short stalk. The paired nuts are enclosed in thin, flattened husks with ragged edges. *Plant community:* Pine forest.

Juneberry or **Serviceberry,** *Amelanchier* spp. This genus of tall shrubs and small trees includes a number of similiar species, many of which hybridize to produce confusing specimens. We will describe only the characteristics of the genus as a whole. *Leaves:* Shapes vary, but oval leaves with pointed tips are common. *Flowers and fruit:* Pink or creamy white flowers appear before the leaves are fully out. They have 5 petals and are borne on racemes. Fruits are dark red to purple and hit their peak in July. They do not have large, hard pits like cherries. On many species the fruit is sweet and quite tasty. *Bark:* Relatively smooth; light brown with dark narrow vertical lines on the trunk. *Buds:* Slender, pink to reddish with dark-tipped somewhat twisted scales. *Plant Communities:* Widespread, probably most common with pines.

Low Shrubs

Brambles, *Rubus* spp. The plants of the genus *Rubus,* collectively called brambles, are a taxonomist's nightmare. Botanists have divided the North American members of the genus into anywhere from 11 to over 200 species. Some have inserted subgenus as a level of classification between genus and species.

The problem is that Rubus is a highly variable set of plants. Local populations may be distinctive enough to be considered separate species, only to lose their unique characteristics when given the chance to hybridize with other populations. The variations are so complex that it is possible for a taxonomist to build a successful career around the study of this one genus. We have used Gleason's treatment of the genus in the *New Britton and Brown Illustrated Flora of the Northeastern States and Adjacent Canada* as the source of our descriptions.

Various members of the genus are common as a part of the understory of different forest types in our area. They are also important invaders of cut-over and burned ground.

73. Juneberry leaves and fruit, *Amelanchier* sp. *Jerry Sullivan*.

sometimes helping to form a cover of brush thick enough to hinder the growth of young trees.

Brambles send up shoots from perennial roots. In two of the species described in subsequent chapters, *R. allegheniensis* and *R. strigosus*, the canes are biennial. The first-year canes are called primocanes; they are strictly vegetative. The second-year floricanes produce flowers and fruit. Leaves on primocanes may be quite different in shape and size from those on floricanes. Individual species are described in the chapters on the plant communities where they are most common.

Currants and **Gooseberries**, *Ribes* spp. This genus of spreading and straggling shrubs has several species in our area. The following are characteristics of the genus. *Leaves:* Palmately lobed, alternate, or in clusters on short lateral branches. *Flowers and fruit:* Tiny flowers growing in racemes in the axils of leaves. The 5-lobed calyx is sometimes curved back toward the base of the flower. In some species, the base of the flower is quite bristly. The fruit is a berry in various colors; sometimes bristly and always crowned with the shriveled remains of the calyx. *Branches:*

May be smooth or bristly or bearing a few thorns. *Plant communities:* Species in various forest communities. Members of this genus are important as alternate hosts of the fungus that causes white pine blister rust.

Herbs

Erect plants with opposite simple leaves.

Bunchberry, *Cornus canadensis.* This herb belongs to the same genus as the dogwoods and shares with them the distinctive leaf venation. It is a perennial growing from a creeping rhizome that forms clumps of upright stems 2-12 in. (5-30 cm) tall. *Leaves:* Egg-shape and pointed, opposite but so close together that they appear whorled. 2-3 pairs of curving veins. *Flowers and fruit:* At the tip of the stem the cluster of very tiny flowers is surrounded by 4 white petal-like bracts that give the whole cluster the appearance of a single flower. May–Jun. Fruits are bright red berries borne in a cluster. *Plant communities:* Least common in mixed-hardwood forest.

74. Bunchberry, *Cornus canadensis.*

THE PRODUCERS

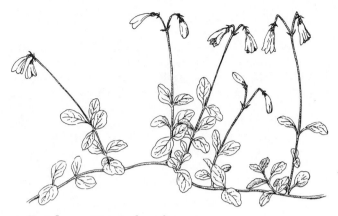

75. Twinflower, *Linnaea borealis*.

Twinflower, *Linnaea borealis*. A slightly woody, some-what hairy creeping stem sends up flower stalks at intervals along its length. *Leaves:* Opposite on the prostrate stem or the upright flower stalks, they are less than 1 in. (2.5 cm) long, nearly round, with tiny teeth and short petioles. *Flowers:* A pair of tiny, pink, nodding bells with five lobes at the top of the flower stalk. Funnel-shape and fragrant. Jul–Aug. *Plant communities:* Least common in mixed-hardwood forest.

Herbs with alternate, simple, entire leaves.

Grasses *and* **Sedges.** Herbs, annual or perennial. These worldwide families have many species. Gleason lists 107 genera of grasses in the northeastern United States and 17 genera of sedges. One of the latter, the genus *Carex,* is represented by 220 species.

Numbers are only part of the story. Identifying individual species requires a 10-power hand lens or a dissecting microscope and a good deal of expertise. Many field studies of plant communities content themselves with identifying plants as members of the grass family (Graminae) or sedge family (Cyperaceae).

Both families are plants with slender stems and narrow elongated leaves. Flowers are clustered and generally lack a perianth. They consist of stamens and pistils enclosed in bracts.

The leaves of both families have basal sheaths that clasp the stems. In the grasses, these sheaths are open at the top. In sedges, they are completely closed. In grasses, there is an appendage called the *ligule* at the juncture of the sheath and blade. Leaves on sedges are generally in three ranks. The stems—called *culms*—of grasses are usually round. Sedge culms are usually, but not always, triangular.

Plant communities: Sedges are most common in moist situations: bog and swamp forests, alder thickets, open bogs, etc. Grasses of various species are common in many situations.

Herbs with alternate simple, toothed leaves

Large-Leaved Aster, *Aster macrophyllus.* A perennial herb growing from a creeping rhizome or a short, branched caudex, the thickened, woody base of the plant. The basal leaves of this plant come up early in spring and persist until frost. In many wooded areas, they carpet the ground. The plant will come into flower in favorable conditions, but flowering specimens are much scarcer than plants consisting only of basal leaves. *Leaves:* Basal leaves are heart-shape, 1.6-8 in. (4-20 cm) long, 1.2-6 in. (3-15 cm) wide. The toothed, thick, firm leaves may be smooth or hairy and rough. *Flowers and fruit:* The flowering stem is 1-5 ft (30-150 cm) tall with alternate leaves that become smaller and

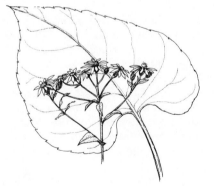

76. Large-leaved aster, *Aster macrophyllus.*

THE PRODUCERS

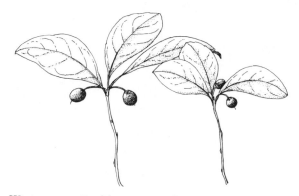

77. Wintergreen, *Gaultheria procumbens*.

sessile higher up the stem. The flowers in a corymb form a cluster of 9-20 lilac to purple rays. The disk becomes reddish. Flower stalks are sticky and covered with tiny glands. Aug–Sep. *Plant communities:* Common in all but the wettest forest situations.

Wintergreen, *Gaultheria procumbens*. Technically a shrub, but looking like a clump of herbs. A creeping stem on or below the surface produces erect or ascending flowering branches, 2-6 in. (5-15 cm) tall. *Leaves:* Initially tender, becoming hard, glossy, and leathery. Elliptic or narrowly egg-shape with the narrow end at the base 0.8-2 in. (1.5-5 cm) long. A few small widely separated teeth. Broken or crushed leaves have a strong taste and smell of wintergreen. *Flowers and fruit:* Flowers 0.2 in. (6 mm) long, nodding, bell-shape, white with 5 small teeth at the tip. They grow from the axils of leaves. Jun–Aug. Fruit, bright red and berry-like, remains on the plant through the winter. *Plant communities:* Pine forest, swamp forest, boreal forest.

Canada Mayflower, *Maianthemum canadense*. A tiny perennial growing from a creeping rhizome that creates clumps of plants. Stems 2-6 in. (5-15 cm) tall with 2 or 3 leaves and the flowers in a raceme. *Leaves:* Sessile, heart-shape at the base, 1-4 in. (2-10 cm) long. *Flowers and fruit:* Raceme a cluster of tiny 0.1-0.2 in. (4-6 mm) white flowers with 2 petals and 2 sepals, colored alike. May–Jun. Fruit, a cluster of speckled white berries that turn pale red. *Plant communities:* Probably the most common and widespread herb in the North Woods.

78. Canada mayflower, *Maianthemum canadense*.

Rose Twisted Stalk, *Streptopus roseus*. A perennial growing from a rhizome with a single somewhat arching stem 12-30 in. (30-80 cm) long that may branch. Stem may have hairs, particularly at the nodes. Flowers hang from leaf axils. *Leaves:* Sessile, lanceolate, with a rounded base, and tapering to a point. Principal leaves 2-3.5 in. (5-9 cm) long, green beneath, with fine hairs on the edge. *Flowers and fruit:* Rose purple to pink flowers in leaf axils on stalks 0.4-1.2 in. (1-3 cm) long and twisted in the middle. May–Jul. Berry is red. *Plant communities:* Widespread. May be found in all but the wettest forest situations.

79. Rose twisted stalk, *Streptopus roseus*.

THE PRODUCERS

Herbs with whorled leaves.

Fragrant Bedstraw, *Galium triflorum.* One of several quite similar species of the genus in the area. The stem— usually smooth to the touch—is weak and drooping. *Leaves:* In whorls of 6, narrow, elliptic to lanceolate, 0.8- 2.4 in. (2-6 cm) long. Leaves have rough margins and bris- tles at the tip. *Flowers:* In clusters at the tips of branches or in leaf axils. The tiny greenish white flowers have 4 petals. Jun–Aug. *Plant communities:* Many forested situations. Others of the genus in alder thickets.

Wood Anemone, *Anemone quinquefolia.* One of the first signs of spring on the forest floor, blooming before leaves emerge on trees. This small perennial is less than 1 ft (30 cm) tall with a single erect stalk with a flower at the tip and a whorl of 2 or 3 compound leaves. *Leaves:* Divided into 3-5 egg-shape leaflets; some cleft, all toothed, especially above the middle. Basal leaf—if present—has a long petiole. *Flowers and fruit:* The single white to pale purple flower is 0.5-1 in. (1-2.5 cm) across and has 5-6 petal-like sepals. Apr–Jun. *Plant communities:* Common in all forest types except the wettest.

Starflower, *Trientalis borealis.* A perennial from a creeping rhizome. Grows with a single stem 1-10 in. (2.5- 25 cm) tall topped by a whorl of 5-10 leaves. 1 or 2 flowers on slender stalks extend up from the whorl. *Leaves:* Whorled, lanceolate. *Flowers:* White, star-shape with 5-9 pointed petals. 0.5 in. (1.2 cm) across. May–Jun. *Plant communities:* All forests.

80. Wood anemone, *Anemone quinquefolia.*

81. Starflower, *Trientalis borealis*.

Wild Sarsaparilla, *Aralia nudicaulis*. A perennial growing from a rhizome. The stem scarcely reaches the surface. The visible portions of the plant are the leaf petiole—8-16 in. (20-40 cm) tall—the leaf itself, and the flower cluster. *Leaves:* The long petiole, which looks like a stem, divides at one point into 3 divisions; each of those further divided into 3-5 leaflets. Leaflets are egg-shape to oval with a pointed tip and serrated edges. Lateral leaflets have asymmetrical bases. Leaflets are a rich brown when first opening in spring. *Flowers and fruit:* On a separate stalk growing below the leaf. Tiny, greenish white flowers with 5 petals in umbels. May–Jun. Fruit a cluster of purple–black berries. *Plant communities:* Nearly all wooded situations.

82. Wild sarsaparilla, *Aralia nudicaulis*.

THE PRODUCERS

83. Bluebead lily, *Clintonia borealis*.

Clintonia or **Bluebead Lily,** *Clintonia borealis.* Perennial from a creeping rhizome that often produces dense clumps of flowering plants. The basal leaves arch outward from a center that produces the flower stalk. *Leaves:* 2-5 in a rosette. They are dark glossy green, oblong or elliptic, 4-12 in. (10-30 cm) long with abrupt points. Veins are parallel; edges are covered with fine hairs. *Flowers and fruit:* On a stalk 6-16 in. (15-40 cm) tall. 3-8 greenish yellow, nodding flowers in an umbel. The perianth is in 6 petal-like divisions that curve outward. May–Jun. Fruit a cluster of blue berries. *Plant communities:* Most common in boreal and pine forests.

Ferns

The ferns are among the Pteridophyta, the group of vascular plants that produce neither flowers nor seeds. The club mosses are among the other orders in this division of the plant kingdom. The pteridophytes reproduce by spores rather than seeds. The tiny spores are produced asexually—which means they are genetically identical to the plant that produces them—and in huge numbers.

When mature, the microscopic spores are released and carried by the wind. Any that chance to land in a favorable spot put down a tiny, rootlike hair that anchors them to the soil. The spore then grows into a membranous green, heart-shape structure called the *prothallus*. The prothallus is typically less than ¼ inch (6 mm) long, but it provides for sexual reproduction. The sex organs develop in the underside, male at one end, female at the other. It takes perhaps two weeks for a spore to grow into a mature prothallus and three and one–half months for a fertilized egg to grow into a mature fern.

Ferns produce their spores on their leaves. In some species, the fertile spore-producing leaves are virtually identical to the sterile leaves. In others, the fertile leaves are extensively modified. The sensitive fern, described in Chapter 15, is an example of the latter condition.

A fertile fern leaf will be dotted with *sori* (sing., *sorus*), or fruit dots, containing spore cases. In some species, the sori are covered by a thin membrane called the *indusium* (pl., *indusia*). The shape, size, arrangement, and color of the sori are important characteristics for field identification in many species.

A typical fern can be divided into three parts: a rhizome or root stock, a stem (also called a stipe), and a leaf or frond. Fern leaves are often very distinctive and prominent, the part of the plant that most people recognize. They have a central rachis and are often divided into leaflets. These leaflets are divided into subleaflets in twice-cut, or bipinnate leaves. The subleaflets are divided into lobes in thrice-cut, or lacy-cut, leaves. Fern leaves show in spring as tightly rolled fiddleheads that unroll as the leaf opens. Some species produce evergreen leaves.

Shield or **Wood Ferns,** *Dryopteris* spp. The species in this genus are difficult to identify. Taxonomists disagree on which plants belong in the genus, so the same plant may carry two or more completely different scientific names, depending on which authority you consult. The tendency of these plants to produce hybrids complicates the problem. In order to keep things simple, we have confined ourselves to describing only the characteristics of the genus. *Leaves:* Usually grow in circular clusters from a central coarse scaly rootstock that may be upright or creeping. Fronds usually lacy-cut (florists use members of this genus for floral arrangements) and often evergreen. *Stipe:* Shorter than fronds and quite scaly. *Spores:* Fruit dots round and attached to underside of leaf at or near the tips of veins. May be naked or covered by a round or kidney-shape indusium. *Plant communities:* All forested situations.

Club Mosses

Club mosses are a family of primitive plants that once produced mighty trees. They were among the dominant plants of the ancient forests that formed the earth's coal deposits. Today they survive as creeping plants of the forest floor.

The stems send up short, erect evergreen flowering branches that produce the strobiles, which in turn produce the spores that provide for reproduction. The stems creep on or just under the surface, often branching extensively and producing large clumps of upright branches.

The leaves of club mosses are tiny and narrow, a trait that accounts for the common name of ground pine. However, they are much more closely related to the ferns than to the pines. Individual species abundant in various plant communities are described in the appropriate chapters.

CHAPTER ELEVEN

The Pine Forest

KEY TREES: Jack pine, white pine, red pine, red oak, Hill's oak, red maple, paper birch, quaking aspen, big-toothed aspen.

SOME GREAT LAKES pine forests are stands of scruffy jack pines with their short branches and sparse crowns; and others consist of tall stately red pines growing over open ground where only a few scattered herbs and shrubs break through the carpet of dead needles; but the symbol of the North Woods for many people is a forest of huge white pines towering over young hardwoods or the narrow spires of spruce and balsam fir. This beautiful pine is the biggest tree in the area, and it can grow in almost every habitat in the North Woods, from sand dunes to open bogs. The white pine was the tree that drew lumbermen to the North Woods. The wood is ideal for construction, the long straight trunks yield a lot of saw timber, and their light weight made it possible to float them down the rivers to the sawmills.

Both red and white pine reach a peak of abundance in the upper Great Lakes region. They range from Maine to Minnesota in a narrow band that roughly defines the north and south borders of the North Woods. There are scattered populations, especially of white pine, south of our area, but these are generally remnants confined to small pockets of specialized habitat such as lake dunes. To the east the ranges of these two continue to the Atlantic in Maine, and they both occur in the Appalachians, the white pine showing up as far south as Georgia.

Jack pine, the third Great Lakes pine, is essentially a tree of the boreal forest. Most of its range lies in Canada, extending north to the end of trees. There are scattered, islanded populations in New England, but only in the Great Lakes does the continuous range of the species extend this far south. The southern edge of its range in Michigan, Wisconsin, and Minnesota is almost exactly the southern edge of the North Woods.

All three of the pines can be pioneering trees, but jack pine is the most specialized for this role. Jack pine forests dominate on the sandiest, driest, and least fertile soils capable of supporting a forest at all. It is also seen, though less often, in another extreme environment, open bogs, where it sometimes combines with another pioneering species, black spruce. In northeastern Minnesota, closer to the hearts of their range and with fewer competitive species to contend with, these two pioneers jointly colonize upland sites of moderate moisture.

Both red and white pine can grow with jack pine or seed in under it. White pine is the most shade–tolerant of the three. All of the pines sometimes grow in almost pure stands. The natural production of such stands—which was often, if not always, dependent on fire—has been augmented by widespread row plantings, particularly of red and jack pine, that began in the 1930s.

The hardwoods growing with the pines, besides the oaks, include red maple, paper birch, and the aspens. On the deepest, loamiest, most fertile sandy soils, the pine forest merges with the mixed–hardwood forest, and white pine is found growing with yellow birch and sugar maple. Around Lake Superior, white pine and red pine are important in the boreal forest. Virgin stands of boreal forest in the Boundary Waters Canoe Area often have supercanopies of huge pines growing high over the lower crowns of balsam fir, birch, and the spruces.

Pine Forest Communities

John Curtis, in *Vegetation of Wisconsin*, put the pine forests in the dry and dry–mesic segments of his continuum. The dryness, of course, comes from the sandy soils where pines grow best. We have described how the coarse texture of these soils reduces their ability to hold water between rains. The rather open canopy of a pine wood increases the aridity by letting sunshine through to the ground where it promotes evaporation.

The Jack Pine Forest

Jack pine is so well adapted to dry conditions that it pioneers on soils of the Boone sands series, perhaps the least fertile soil in the region. (It is nothing but sand under an A horizon a few inches thick, and even the A horizon is 93 percent sand.) Pioneering jack pines grow rapidly in full sunlight, reach maturity early, and cannot grow in the shade of other trees. Fires must have always been common in jack pine woods, so common that the tree has evolved a reproductive strategy that depends on fire for success. The cones of perhaps half the jack pines in the Lake States don't drop off the tree as cones of the other pines do. Instead they remain on the tree and sealed closed by resins for as long as twenty-five years—although seed viability begins to decline after about four years. Sometimes growing branches will completely engulf the closed cones. It takes a temperature of 116° F (46.5° C)—the heat of a ground fire is more than sufficient—to soften the resin enough to allow the scales to open. The seeds are quite resistant to heat, remaining viable until temperatures are high enough to ignite the cone. Experimentally, they have withstood temperatures of 900° F (482° C) for as long as 30 seconds.

So a jack pine forest begins on a bed of ash, with part of the mat of organic matter on the surface having been consumed by fire. The jack pine seedlings can send their rootlets down through the thinned humus and tap the moisture and nutrients in the mineral soil below. Most germination takes place in the first or second years following a fire, and in another five years the sprouts are producing seed. Thus jack pine is capable of maintaining itself on a site if the fires come less than once in seven years.

PINE BARRENS

In some places in the North Woods, fires have come more frequently than once every seven years. On the sand hills of Lower Michigan's interlobate area, in the bed of glacial Lake Wisconsin, on the interlobate moraine that marks the division between the Superior and Chippewa ice in northwestern Wisconsin, pine barrens were once common. These were savanna communities, grass and shrub lands with scattered trees, mostly stunted jack pine and Hill's

84. Jack pine forest, Northern Highlands State Forest, Wisconsin. *Glenda Daniel*.

oak. The Wisconsin barrens extended the ranges of prairie plants such as flowering spurge (*Euphorbia corollata*) and redroot (*Ceanothus ovatus*) into the North Woods.

There were few trees in the barrens. Surveyors' records for one tract in Adams County, Wisconsin, showed two to eight trees to the acre in 1851. In the extensive barrens of Bayfield and Douglas counties, Wisconsin, early reports tell of areas of several square miles almost devoid of trees.

The barrens were prime blueberry habitat, and there is some evidence that Indians set fires periodically to keep the barrens free of trees and full of blueberries.

The Pine Forest

Fire protection, which became effective over most of the North Woods in the 1930s, is rapidly converting the barrens from savanna to closed-canopy forest. The Adams County tract that was supporting 2 to 8 trees per acre in 1851 was growing 160 to 250 per acre in 1950. Most of the trees were 20 to 30 years old, indicating that they had grown since fire protection began to be provided. The species mix had not changed however. The new forest was primarily jack pine and Hill's oak with some bur oak.

The change from savanna to forest may eliminate some of the prairie plants and some prairie wildlife, too. Both the sharp-tailed grouse and the prairie chicken were common in the barrens, but loss of habitat is making them increasingly scarce. Mowing and deliberate burning are now being used as habitat management schemes to foster these species.

The extreme dryness of the pine barrens shows in a comparison of the water-retaining capacity of barrens soils with those supporting richer vegetation. Soils of the barrens can hold moisture equivalent to an average of 36 percent of dry weight. In closed canopy jack pine forests, the average is 120 percent. Under white pine it is 130 percent. The average under a mixed-hardwood forest is 250 percent. The differences reflect the buildup of organic matter, which holds moisture in the soil.

ASSOCIATES OF JACK PINE

Jack pine is the most important tree in dry forests. Its common associates are the other pines, especially red pine, oaks, quaking aspen, big-toothed aspen, paper birch, and red maple. A jack pine forest is a well-lighted place. The scanty crowns of the trees let the sun through to the forest floor, creating good conditions for herbs and shrubs. However, the infertility of the soils, or perhaps their aridity, produces some stands with almost nothing but grass for a ground cover.

Jack pine can also colonize bedrock outcrops covered with as little as 6 inches (15 centimeters) of soil. The thin soil creates conditions as dry as a sand dune. In northeastern Minnesota, jack pine on bedrock grows with lesser amounts of black spruce, paper birch, red maple, and quaking aspen.

The jack pine–black spruce combinations in Minnesota usually grow on south or southwest slopes and are usually poor in understory plants, except for mosses. In some cases, Schreber's feather moss seems to blanket the ground. Feather mosses have leafy shoots that are pinnately lobed. They are so abundant at times that they completely cover boulders. Black spruce, sometimes with jack pine and sometimes not, grows on both upland mineral soils and on peats with an understory that is primarily moss. This is a widespread community in Minnesota, where the trees are harvested from these stands for pulpwood.

The richest soils supporting jack pine forests are also in northeastern Minnesota. On cool, moist, north and northeast slopes with rather rich soils—sands with substantial amounts of silt and clay which are as much as 40 inches (100 centimeters) deep over bedrock—jack pine grows with balsam fir, black spruce, quaking aspen, paper birch, and white spruce.

The Red Pine Forest

Red pine forests, except where they have been deliberately planted, are much less common than jack pine. Red pines shed their seeds as they produce them, so they have no reservoir of seeds ready to capitalize on catastrophe. The seeds germinate most successfully two or three years after a fire when leaching has reduced the ash layer somewhat but plants that could shade out the seedlings have not yet begun to grow. Good seed crops are produced only once every five to seven years, and if a good crop doesn't coincide with good germination conditions, red pine will be scarce or absent. The seeds do not travel far, so some old trees would have to survive a fire to supply seed for a new stand. One study of burned stands in the Boundary Waters Canoe Area found only 1 out of 56 with a good crop of young red pine.

Red pine stands are often found along lakeshores, a situation that provides some fire protection. Virgin stands in the Boundary Waters wilderness are generally open, with scanty understories. Mosses and lichens account for a majority of the ground cover.

85. One hundred-sixty-year-old white pine stand, Michigan.
U.S. Forest Service.

The White Pine Forest

White pine forests are much scarcer than they used to
be. They were the loggers' first target, and outside of the
Boundary Waters wilderness only a few remnant stands
remain. One of these is Hartwick Pines State Park, a 49-
acre (20-hectare) tract in northern Lower Michigan, the
only such forest in the Lower Peninsula. The trees are immense, the tallest 155 feet (47 meters) from root to crown
and almost 4 feet (1 meter) in diameter. Between the huge
trunks the forest is quite open. The ground is covered with
a thick mat of pine needles and cones.

In the Boundary Waters Canoe Area wilderness, white
pine stands are usually on northeast- to south-facing slopes
and on ridgetops. The pines here grow with other species
that are typical of the boreal forest, including balsam fir, paper birch, quaking aspen, white spruce, and jack pine. None
of these grows as tall as the white pine, so these stands show
a well-developed supercanopy of white pine, with lesser
amounts of red pine, towering over the main canopy
formed by the smaller species.

THE PRODUCERS

Plants of the Pine Forests

The understory in all these varieties of pine forest is remarkably similar. Frequent fires would tend to restrict ground-layer plants to species that could survive the flames.

Bush honeysuckle and the hazels are common tall shrubs. Green alder and mountain maple are much more common at the northern end of the region than in the south.

Pine woods may not produce as many blueberries as the barrens, but around midsummer they are a very good place to start looking for late low blueberries. Sweet fern is a low shrub of very sandy soils. It is rather intolerant of shade, so you can expect to see it most often in very young woods. In older forests it forms dense patches in clearings and along roadsides. The pungently aromatic odor of the leaves is the most powerful smell in the pine woods, especially on hot sunny days.

Prostrate shrubs are common in the pine woods, especially trailing arbutus and wintergreen. Some of the wildflowers occur in other forest types; a few are unique to the pine woods. Wood anemone is likely to be the first flower of spring, appearing before the hardwoods leaf out. Other species blooming before midsummer include some that are ubiquitous in the North Woods (Canada mayflower, wild sarsaparilla), some that are shared with the mixed-hardwood forest, many that are shared with boreal forest (goldthread, twinflower, wild strawberry), and a few (such as barren strawberry) that are common only in the pine woods.

A number of common North Woods plants show an unusual distribution. They are abundant in dry soils under pines and in wet soils under balsam fir or white cedar, common in boreal forests, but rather scarce in mixed-hardwood forests. Examples include bunchberry, dwarf raspberry, and, among the trees, red maple. Curtis thought that this distribution suggested light as a limiting factor. These plants are unsuccessful in the dim light under sugar maples or hemlocks.

Phenology, the timing of major events, is somewhat different in the pine forest than in the mixed-hardwood forest.

Almost half of the common plants in the pine forest bloom after midsummer. In the hardwoods, 70 percent of the flowers appear before that time. Among the late bloomers is narrow-leaved cow-wheat, which flowers early in July under jack pines. This is one of the few common annuals in the North Woods and a good indicator of dry conditions. It is far more common under jack pine than white pine. Pipsissewa, another July flower, is a prostrate shrub with the appearance of an herb, an evergreen heath that sends up short flowering branches.

Late in the year, the large-leaved aster and the pearly everlasting bloom. Bracken ferns unroll early in summer, and in many jack pine stands are thick enough to form a sort of subcanopy over the lower plants of the ground layer. They die at first frost, turning brown but remaining upright.

There are some regional variations in the associates to be found in jack pine forests. In Lower Michigan, you may find more species of oaks, and pin cherry and chokecherry may be more common than elsewhere. *Kalmia polifolia*, a low shrub in the heath family commonly called sheep laurel, grows with jack pine in central Lower Michigan but not farther west.

Succession in the Pine Forest

We have already described jack pine as a pioneer tree intolerant of shade. It aggressively colonizes denuded areas, but without fire it will survive for only one generation before being replaced by more tolerant species capable of growing in the shade of the pines. A typical generation of jack pines takes just over a century to mature and die. In one stand in Minnesota that originated after a fire in 1810, 95 jack pines per acre remained in 1923. By 1952, only 9 of the trees were surviving.

The pioneering jack pines serve as a nurse crop, providing a slightly protected environment for species that will replace them. Depending on local circumstances, these species may be hardwoods such as red maple, red oak, and paper birch and conifers such as red pine, white pine, black and white spruce, and balsam fir.

THE PRODUCERS

The way to predict the pines' replacements is to look at the younger, smaller trees, the saplings, and the seedlings that will take over the stand when the pines die.

You may find some jack pines in these lower trees, but these are likely to be *transgressives*. They are the same age as the canopy, but their faster growing neighbors put them in the shade and prevented them from reaching full height. They will stay small and will die sooner, or at least live no longer, than the canopy trees.

A few miles from the virgin white pine stand at Hartwick Pines in Michigan, a jack pine stand more than a century old is beginning to pass. Many of the old pines have fallen, and in the open sunny forest young white pines and oaks are growing up to replace them in the canopy.

On bedrock outcrops in the Boundary Waters Canoe Area, jack pines are likely to be replaced by a mixture of paper birch, red maple, black spruce, and balsam fir. In the same area, the jack pine colonies on rich soil will give way to a boreal forest of balsam fir, spruces, paper birch, and quaking aspen. The understories in these stands already show strong boreal affinities, including tall shrubs like mountain ash and mountain maple and low shrubs like dewberry.

A similar direction is indicated for the jack pine–black spruce combinations, although reproduction is not as vigorous in these stands.

In white pine forests, the direction of change in most of the North Woods is toward a mixed-hardwood forest. This trend can be seen clearly at Hartwick Pines, where a census of part of the virgin stand produced the figures shown in Table 13.

Red maple may have been a part of this forest for some time—this species does not often produce trees that grow old or large enough to reach the tall pine canopy—but hemlock and the hardwoods are invaders. As they grow, they steadily change the soil and light conditions below them, creating an environment that will favor understory plants of the mixed-hardwood forest. These two pure pine stands will eventually be replaced by a mixed-hardwood forest with a substantial pine component.

A study of forest stands on Star Island in Cass Lake, Minnesota, at the western end of the North Woods, shows a

Table 13: Composition of Virgin Forest at Hartwick Pines

	Stand 1	*Stand 2*
Canopy		
Number of trees	54	102
Species (percent of total number)		
White pine	61.1%	73.5%
Red pine	38.9%	26.5%
Subcanopy		
Number of trees	44	60
Species (percent of total number)		
White pine	40.9%	28.3%
Red pine	9.1%	1.8%
Hemlock	18.2%	33.3%
Sugar maple	11.3%	3.3%
Red maple	13.6%	15.0%
Beech	6.8%	18.2%

From *Deciduous Forests of Eastern North America,* E. Lucy Braun.

similar sequence from jack pine to red pine to white pine to mixed hardwood. Here, with beech and hemlock absent, basswood joins sugar maple as a major component of the hardwood forest.

Where boreal forest is dominant, the successional trend is toward balsam fir, the spruces, and paper birch. Those huge old pines towering over the smaller trees in the Boundary Waters Canoe Area wilderness will eventually die and the boreal trees will remain.

But the reign of white pine is long. A mesic forest with a nearly continuous canopy is usually found under white pine within 200 years, but the pines may live 600 or 800 years. A fire, windstorm, or an attack of disease at any time during those centuries can open the ground and start the whole process over with white pine seedlings growing under a nurse crop of jack pine or aspen.

Pine forests are dynamic places, constantly evolving into something else. In most of the North Woods, the direction of evolution is from jack pine and red pine through white pine (with red maple and red oak) into mixed-hardwood forest. Where boreal forests dominate, the pines are still pioneers and the evolution is from pine to balsam fir,

THE PRODUCERS

spruce, and paper birch. This continuing evolution would seem to doom the pine forest to extinction but it doesn't, and the major reason is fire.

Fire and Succession

A study of virgin stands in the Boundary Waters Canoe Area showed that every one of them had been burned at least once within a period of just over 450 years, a time that is within the potential life-span of a single white pine.

Most of us think of forest fires as devastating conflagrations, holocausts that destroy everything in their path. Fires can be like that, but they can also be considerably less damaging. Ground fires can burn dead wood, partly destroy shrubs and reduce the thickness of the humus layer while leaving the big trees—or at least some of the big trees—with only minor damage. Mature red pines are especially resistant to ground fire. The practice of deliberately setting

86. Fire in a pine woods, Superior National Forest, Minnesota. *U.S. Forest Service.*

fires on logged-over jack pine stands in order to provide an ideal seedbed for a new generation of pine is becoming more common.

In the past, fire maintained the pine woods, but fire is now controlled. On the millions of acres of commercial forest land in the North Woods, deliberate management will maintain the pines as long as they are a valuable timber source. But what of the pine forests that will not be logged? Hartwick Pines will in time be Hartwick maples, and in time the pine woods of the Boundary Waters wilderness may be spruce–fir stands. This possibility has led to the suggestion that wildfires should be allowed to burn within the Boundary Waters area unless they present a danger to neighboring areas. Wildfire would maintain the mosaic of stands in various stages of succession that characterized the primeval forest. In these circumstances, the pine woods could maintain themselves.

However, there are problems with this approach. Clifford Ahlgren of the Wilderness Research Foundation has been studying burned plots in the Superior National Forest and in Ontario's Quetico Provincial Park for a number of years, and his results call into question the ability of fire to maintain the pines, particularly red pine.

We mentioned earlier his study of 56 burned areas that found good red pine reproduction on only 1 site. White pine does better than this, but white pine blister rust, a disease introduced to North America 60 years ago, kills many of the young trees. Only jack pine reproduces vigorously on burned sites in today's forest.

Ahlgren has concluded that maintaining red pine by fire requires a forest of tens of thousands of square miles. Letting wildfires burn in northeastern Minnesota, he believes, is more likely to perpetuate boreal forests or to reestablish jack pine–black spruce communities than to maintain red or white pine.

A Human History of the Pine Woods

The loggers began moving into the North Woods in the 1830s. Most of them were Maine men, descendants of lumbermen who had been cutting white pine in New England since colonial times when the British navy laid claim to the big, straight trees to provide masts for its sailing ships.

In 1835, men from Maine built the sawmill town of Augusta near Kalamazoo, Michigan. In 1839, the first log drive came down the Muskegon River from the pineries in the central part of Lower Michigan. Logging operations began in northeastern Wisconsin in 1845 and in Minnesota somewhat later.

The loggers found white pine in abundance. Huge trees of this species were scattered all over the North Woods, many of them dating from widespread fires in the 15th century. The men who went into the wilderness to find these trees were called timber cruisers. They often traveled alone by canoe or on foot through woods that were almost devoid of humanity. The Indians had been moved onto reservations, and only a few trappers lived in the forest.

Some of these cruisers were independents who worked for themselves. When they found a good stand of pine, they located it on their maps and headed back to town to buy it. Others free-lanced, finding the good trees and then selling their knowledge to the highest bidder. Most of the cruisers worked for timber companies.

The big timber companies who came west from Maine eventually got most of the land, often buying prime pine stands at $1 to $2 per acre. Much of the early production from Michigan went east through the Erie Canal to Albany, New York, which became the biggest timber market in the world. Later, river towns like St. Louis became important as the North Woods pines provided the lumber that built the Midwest. From 1850 to about 1900, the peak period of production, the loggers had a ready market for every stick of pine they could cut.

In the area around Saginaw and Bay City in eastern Michigan, 100 large sawmills were in operation at the turn of the century. By 1900, Michigan had produced 162 billion board feet of pine. By 1899, Wisconsin's woods were producing 3.4 billion board feet every year. (A board foot is 12 inches long, 12 inches wide, and 1 inch thick.)

Yields from some of the stands were enormous. Curtis reports that "one forty[-acre plot] in Bayfield County [Wisconsin] which was cut in 1921 was reported to have yielded an average of 70,000 board feet per acre," and some single acres yielded as much as 100,000 board feet. The biggest standing tree in Hartwick Pines contains 6,000 board feet! However, the average yield was about 12,000 board feet an acre, and 25,000 was considered a good cut.

Winter was the work season in the woods. The newly hired crew went in during the fall, and their first job was to build the camp they would live in through the cold weather. With that out of the way, they started cutting.

Each crew was a group of specialists. Choppers felled the trees, others trimmed the branches and sawed the fallen trunks into standard lengths. Teamsters, usually driving oxen, snaked the logs to railhead or river.

The rivers carried the logs out of the woods in spring. Cutting near small streams, the loggers built temporary dams that turned the creeks into a series of ponds. With winter's production in the ponds, the dams were broken, and the logs started downriver.

The North Woods lumberjack was a romantic figure. Like the cowboys and the bluewater sailors he inspired legends, and like them he had a hard and very dangerous job. The choppers cut down the huge pines with two-man saws that were expressively dubbed 'misery whips.' Accidents were frequent in the woods and even more frequent in the spring drives down the rivers to the mills.

The earliest cutting was done near the rivers for ease of transportation. After the more accessible stands were cut, loggers built narrow-gauge railroads from the nearest water into promising stands. They cut the pure pine stands first, then they selectively logged the pines out of the mixed-hardwood forests. Only when all the pine was gone did they turn to the hardwoods.

By the 1930s the harvest was about over. The 0.3 billion board feet that Wisconsin produced in 1932 was the lowest cut since 1850. In the entire cycle, Curtis estimates, Wisconsin produced—at 1959 prices—$10 billion worth of timber.

The cutting of the North Woods is generally seen now as an example of unbridled rapacity, and to a considerable extent it was that. But the lumbermen of the time did not see themselves in quite the way we look at them today. They were performing a public service, not only supplying the growing nation's need for timber, but clearing the ground for settlement as well. "The plow follows the axe" was the ideology of the time, and it took the bitter experience of many busted farmers to reveal that the North Woods pine lands were not much good for agriculture.

Since they were not concerned about growing a new forest to replace the one they were cutting, the lumbermen made little effort to control fires. Indeed, fire was seen as partly beneficial. It further simplified the task of the settler by removing slash—the waste left behind by the loggers. Many fires were set deliberately to clear ground. Some of these fires raged out of control, burning vast areas and in some cases producing real catastrophes. The Peshtigo fire of 1871, for example, burned through parts of eight counties in northeastern Wisconsin, destroying whole towns and killing at least 800 people.

Wildfires had maintained the forests, but the fires that followed the loggers struck again and again with only a few years between them. The cumulative effect was devastating. In 1905, Burton Livingston described parts of Roscommon and Crawford counties in Lower Michigan, once prime pine country:

In lumbering all the pine was removed, and the subsequent fires have killed the young growth of this tree as well as the scattering hardwoods. Over vast stretches originally covered with white pine there are now no trees at all. They are regions of dwarfed Quercus alba [white oak], Quercus rubra [red oak], Acer rubrum [red maple] and a number of shrubs. The oaks and maples are rarely more than twice as high as a man, are burned down every few years, and exist here only because of the fact that they sprout from the roots, which are not always killed by the fire.

In northern Wisconsin, the situation was similar. Curtis describes it:

The desolation of much of the pine area in the 1920s and early 1930s is difficult to describe to anyone who did not see it. In many places the entire landscape as far as the eye could see supported not a simgle tree more than a few inches in diameter. Only the gaunt stumps of the former pines, frequently with their root systems fully exposed as a result of the consumption of the topsoil by fire, remained to indicate that the area was once a forest rather than a perpetual barren.

The Pine Forest

The rehabilitation of this wasteland began in the 1930s. The first effective fire control system cut losses, and new forests began to grow. Pines—particularly red and jack pine—were planted widely.

The Future of the Pine Forests

Much of our account of the pine forests of the Boundary Waters Canoe Area was drawn from a study of virgin plant communities done by Lewis F. Ohmann and Robert R. Ream. A few years ago, Ohmann and G. F. Grigal extended the study by adding 68 disturbed stands to the original sample of 106 virgin stands. They also introduced some new methods. Instead of basing their community classifications solely on the distribution of trees, they also considered important understory plants, both shrubs and herbs. They then categorized communities according to the distribution of all of these important plants.

The new categories agreed with the old with one major exception: in the new classification, the white pine community disappeared. In the disturbed stands, understory plants typical of the pine woods were growing under canopies of aspen and birch. Ohmann and Grigal concluded that the aspen–birch woods in the disturbed stands that had been added to the study were white pine stands with the pine removed by logging and subsequent fires.

This removal of the pines is a common situation throughout the North Woods. The hardwoods could survive the fires by producing stump sprouts or root suckers. Pines, unable to reproduce in this way and without time between fires to mature and produce seed, became less and less common with each fire. White and red pine, which mature more slowly, were affected more than jack pine. Today, stands of paper birch, red oak, and red maple occupy thousands of acres of old white and red pine lands. Growing under these hardwoods are plants like pipsissewa and trailing arbutus, indicators that a pine forest once grew here. Often in such woods one can find huge old stumps looking like the ruins of a vanished civilization. These are all that remain of the pines.

White pine can still reproduce vigorously where seed

87. White pine forests dominated the North Woods before logging companies clearcut entire counties near the turn of the century. White pine stumps like these can still be seen in second growth forests throughout the region. *Jerry Sullivan*.

sources are available, and at least some of these second-growth hardwood stands have a substantial number of young pines that could eventually overtop the smaller and shorter–lived oaks and birches.

White Pine Blister Rust

However, white pine has another problem. White pine blister rust is a fungus disease that was accidentally imported into North America around 1900. It has since spread throughout the range of this tree. The fungus has a complex life cycle. It has five different spore forms. Two of these occur on white pine and cause the disease. The other three live on shrubs of the genus *Ribes* (currants and gooseberries). The disease cannot spread directly from pine to pine. It must in every case go through the intermediate shrub host.

Blister rust produces a yellow discoloration of bark and clusters of orange–yellow or yellow–brown cankers (the blisters) whose appearance varies with season and the stage of infection. When the blisters break, a flow of resin from them can leave long white streaks on the trunk. A blister rust infection of the main trunk inevitably kills the tree, but infection on branches will destroy only the affected limb.

Blister rust is a serious problem, but it is not a threat to the continued survival of the species, as Dutch elm disease is to the American elm. The fungus needs cool wet weather to reproduce, so at the southern end of the North Woods the climate provides a good deal of protection. Topography also provides protection. Trees on ridgetops have a better chance than those in low spots where cool, moist air collects.

Foresters can take measures to protect their trees by eradicating currants and by pruning the lower limbs of their pines. Nearly all infections occur on branches, or on the trunk within 6 feet (1.8 meters) of the ground, so pruning provides a substantial measure of protection. Pruning also helps open the stands to breezes that keep the humidity down and thus cut down on fungus reproduction.

For the long term, efforts are now underway to breed a resistant strain of white pine. These are showing some success, although seeds are not available yet from such trees.

The direct threat to white pine from blister rust is considerable, but perhaps the indirect effects are even greater. Fear of blister rust damage has kept foresters from managing land to promote white pine growth. Good pine lands are much more often planted in red pine, even though white pine is in many ways a more desirable tree from a timber grower's standpoint. As better methods of disease control become available, white pine may again approach its former abundance in the North Woods.

Key to Some Common Plants
of the Pine Forests

I.   Tall shrub; alternate, toothed leaves—**Green alder**

II. Low shrubs

   1.   Opposite simple leaves—**Bush honeysuckle**

                                                  THE PRODUCERS

1. Alternate-leaved

    2. Compound leaves

        3. Toothed compound leaves—**Eastern blackberry; Red raspberry**

        3. Leaves with three leaflets; may be toothed or not—**Poison ivy**

    2. Simple leaves

        3. Palmately lobed—**Prickly gooseberry**

        3. Pinnately lobed—**Sweet fern**

        3. Entire—**Late low blueberry**

III. Herbs

    1. Opposite simple leaves

        2. Pink bell-shaped flowers—**Spreading dogbane**

        2. White flowers with yellow top—**Narrow-leaved cow-wheat**

    1. Alternate simple leaves

        2. Low, creeping, leaves thick and succulent—**Trailing arbutus**

        2. Arching stem with terminal cluster of white flowers—**False solomon's seal**

        2. Erect; nodding yellow flowers—**Sessile-leaved bellwort**

        2. Leaves pale green, covered with white woolly hairs—**Pearly everlasting**

    1. Whorled leaves—**Pipsissewa**

    1. Basal leaves

        2. In three leaflets

            3. Yellow flowers—**Barren strawberry**

            3. White flowers—**Wild strawberry**

        2. Simple; in pairs—**Lady's slipper**

IV. Ferns—**Bracken fern**

V. Club mosses (see descriptions)

Plant Descriptions

Tall Shrubs

Green Alder, *Alnus crispa.* A shrub up to 9 ft (3 m) tall with ascending trunks usually growing in clumps. *Leaves:* Broadly elliptic to egg-shape with a blunt rounded or slightly heart-shape base; finely and sharply double-toothed. In maturity, 1-3 in. (2.5-8 cm) long. *Flowers and fruit:* Staminate catkins in racemes on slender stalks. They are concealed in buds in winter and develop with the leaves in spring. The pistillate catkins are short and ovoid to ellipsoid. *Buds:* 3-4 scales. They are pointed, reddish or greenish and slightly stalked. *Bark and twigs:* Smooth, not speckled. Young branches smooth or only sparsely downy. *Plant communities:* Pine forest, second-growth forest. More common in north.

Low Shrubs

Bush Honeysuckle, *Diervilla lonicera.* A low, upright shrub to 4 ft (120 cm) tall. *Leaves:* Toothed, egg-shape, pointed, 2-5 in. (5-12.5 cm) long. Sometimes fringed with fine hairs. *Flowers and fruit:* Stalks arising from the tips of

88. Bush honeysuckle, *Diervilla lonicera.*

branches or from leaf axils hold clusters of flowers—typically three to a cluster. The yellow funnel-shape flowers have 5 lobes. They change color with time, becoming deep yellow and then scarlet, crimson, or maroon. May–Aug. *Plant communities:* Pine forest, boreal forest.

Eastern Blackberry, *Rubus allegheniensis.* Canes of both years are erect or nearly so and at least 18 in. (50 cm) tall. *Primocanes:* Compound leaves with 5 palmate leaflets. The leaflets are toothed and roughly heart-shape with long tapering points. Stems are prickly. *Floricanes:* Leaves smaller. Some are simple, some compound with 3 lanceolate toothed leaflets. *Flowers and fruit:* Short lateral branches hold a few leaves and a terminal raceme of white flowers with 5 petals. The flowers are about 1 in. (2.5 cm) across. Jun. The fruits are black when ripe. Jul–Aug. *Plant communities:* Pine forest, especially south. Less common in the Upper Peninsula and Minnesota.

Red Raspberry, *Rubus strigosus.* Canes of both years up to 6 ft (2 m) long, erect to nearly prostrate with upright tips. *Primocanes:* Compound leaves with 3-5 leaflets. Leaflets egg-shape or slimmer, tapering gradually to a sharp point. The edges are coarsely toothed, especially above the middle. Undersides covered with downy hairs. *Floricanes:* Leaves variable. *Flowers and fruit:* White—or greenish white—flowers in an umbel. The 5 petals are shorter than the green sepals that surround them. Jun. Fruit is red. Jul–Aug. *Plant communities:* Most common in pine forest and boreal forest, but often found elsewhere, including along roadsides.

Prickly Gooseberry, *Ribes cynosbati.* One of the members of the genus Ribes in our area. It is a shrub that may grow to 5 ft (1.5 m) tall. *Leaves:* 3-5 palmate lobes, leaf edges toothed. Round–ovate and rounded to somewhat heart-shape at the base. They are nearly always covered with short, soft, downy hairs. *Flowers and fruit:* 1-3 tubular green flowers with bristly bases in racemes with long stalks. May–Jun. Red–purple berry is also bristly. *Branches:* Either scattered prickles or none. *Plant communities:* Pine forest, less common in Minnesota than in the rest of our region.

Poison Ivy, *Rhus radicans.* This plant may grow as a low upright or trailing shrub or as a climbing vine. When it does

89. Prickly gooseberry, *Ribes cynosbati*.

climb, the branches produce aerial clinging roots. Old stems of climbing vines are densely covered with dark fibers. *Leaves:* 3 leaflets tapering to a gradual point or with a sharp well-defined angle at the tip. Terminal leaflet longer-stalked than side leaflets. Leaves may be shiny or dull, toothed or not, and leathery or thin. *Fruits and flowers:* Tiny green flowers—0.12 in. (3 mm) across—have 5 petals and grow in racemes from leaf axils. May–Jul. Fruits are dun-colored to white berries. Aug–Sep. *Buds:* Hairy, without scales and pinched at the base. *Plant communities:* Widespread. Most common in pine forest.

Sweet Fern, *Comptonia peregrina* or *Myrica asplenifolia.* A much–branched plant up to 40 in. (1 m) high. The whole plant is richly aromatic. *Leaves:* Linear to narrowly oblong, pinnately lobed, 2-5 in. (6-12 cm) long and softly hairy on one or both surfaces. Covered with dots of resin. Dark green above, pale below. *Flowers and fruit:* Flowers emerge before leaves. Staminate flowers in cylindric catkins; pistillate in round, bur-like aments. Fruits solitary or few in cluster, round, warty, covered with wax. *Plant community:* Pine forest.

THE PRODUCERS

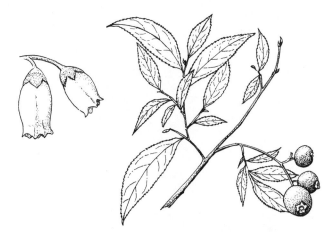

90. Late low blueberry, *Vaccinium angustifolium*.

Late Low Blueberry, *Vaccinium angustifolium*. A low, much-branched shrub that spreads by stolons. In favorable situations, it forms large colonies. Young stems are green. *Leaves:* 0.2-0.7 in. (0.7-2 cm) long, bright green and lanceolate. Teeth on leaf edges are tipped with small spines. *Flowers and fruit:* Tiny, bell-shape flowers grow singly or in clusters. They are white or pink-tinged. May–Jun. Dark blue to black sweet berries are sometimes covered with a white powder. *Plant communities:* Pine forest, boreal forest, swamp forest.

Herbs

Spreading Dogbane, *Apocynum androsaemifolium*. A low branching plant with arching branches. The reddish stems have a fibrous bark, but they are not woody. *Leaves:* Broadly lanceolate to egg-shape with a short, abrupt tip. May be hairy or woolly beneath. 1-3 in. (3-8 cm) long. *Flowers:* Pink with dark rose stripes inside the flower. Bell-shape with 5 petal-like lobes at the tips. 0.1-0.2 in. (3-6 mm) long, borne in small clusters at the tips of branches or in the axils of leaves. Jun–Jul. Seedpods in pairs, long and slender, looking rather like a small string bean. *Plant communities:* Pine forest, boreal forest, also in fields and roadsides.

91. Narrow-leaved cow-wheat, *Melampyrum lineare. Glenda Daniel.*

Narrow-Leaved Cow-Wheat, *Melampyrum lineare.* An annual herb with a simple or branched stem 4-16 in. (10-40 cm) tall. *Leaves:* Slender, pointed. Upper leaves smaller and with a few teeth at the base, 1-3 in. (2-6 cm) long. *Flowers:* In the axils of the upper leaves, white with a yellow tip. They are slender, tubular with an arched upper lip and a lower lip divided into 3 lobes. Jul–Aug. *Plant communities:* Pine forest.

Trailing Arbutus, *Epigaea repens.* Another low, creeping plant that is technically a shrub. Both stems and flowering branches are prostrate. *Leaves:* Oval to slightly circular, 1-3 in. (2.5-7.5 cm) long. Sometimes hairy, sometimes smooth, thick and succulent. On long petioles. *Flowers and fruit:* Flowers expand very early, often blooming while snow is still on the ground. Pink or white and fragrant with a tubular corolla that expands into 5 petal-like lobes. Inside of the corolla is hairy. Flowers grow in axillary or terminal clusters. Fruit looks like a strawberry with the seeds exposed on its surface. *Plant communities:* Pine forest.

False Solomon's Seal, *Smilacina racemosa.* A single ascending and arching stem up to 40 in. (1 m) long bearing 5–12 or more leaves. Stem is downy and often has slight zig-zag. Flowers in a panicle at tip of stem. *Leaves:* Spreading horizontally on each side of the stem. Elliptic, 2.5-6 in. (5-15 cm) long, rounded at the base and tapering to a long point at the tip. Fine, downy hairs beneath. *Flowers and fruit:* Panicle sessile or on stalk is pyramidal, 3-7 in. (7-17 cm) long with numerous white flowers 0.1-0.2 in. (3-5 mm) wide. Jun–Jul. *Plant communities:* Most common in pine forests but present in mixed-hardwood and boreal stands.

Starry False Solomon's Seal, *Smilacina stellata.* A perennial from a rhizome. It produces stolons that give rise to new plants. The single stem, downy or smooth, is either erect or arching. *Leaves:* Sessile or slightly clasping, spreading or ascending, lanceolate to oblong, tapering at the tip. 2.7-6 in. (6-15 cm) long, slightly downy beneath. *Flowers and fruit:* Raceme sessile or nearly so with few to several scattered white flowers with 6 petal-like lobes each. May–Jun. Fruit a cluster of berries either black or green with black stripes. *Plant communities:* Pine forest.

Sessile-Leaved Bellwort, *Uvularia sessilifolia.* A single erect stem 4-12 in. (10-30 cm) tall that forks above the middle. The lower section is covered with tight sheaths and sometimes with leaves. Above the fork, one stem is sterile—leaves only—and one is fertile, producing flowers. *Leaves:* Narrow, lanceolate with a rounded base and a pointed tip. Sessile, pale beneath. *Flowers and fruit:* Perianth made up of 6 long, slender, pointed yellow parts. Flowers nodding, i.e., hanging "upside down" with the open end of the perianth pointing downward. May–Jun. *Plant communities:* Pine forests, but rare or absent from northern Lower Michigan and the central and eastern Upper Peninsula.

Pearly Everlasting, *Anaphalis margaritacea.* A perennial with an erect single or branched stem 12-36 in. (30-90 cm) tall. Very leafy. *Leaves:* Pale, gray–green, narrow, sessile, pointed, almost like grass leaves. Covered with white, woolly hairs, especially below. *Flowers and fruit:* White, globular with yellow centers. Borne in a flat-topped cluster. Aug–Sep. *Plant communities:* Pine forest, boreal forest.

Pipsissewa, *Chimaphila umbellata.* Perennial creeping

92. Pipsissewa, *Chimaphila umbellata*.

rhizomes send up evergreen shoots 4-12 in. (10-30 cm) tall.
Leaves: In whorls around stem. Lanceolate, pointed, finely
toothed, thick, shiny, and evergreen. *Flowers and fruit:*
Pink or white with violet anthers, 5 petals. Nodding. They
grow in an umbel of 2-8 flowers at the tip of the stem.
Jun–Aug. *Plant community:* Pine forest.

Barren Strawberry, *Waldsteinia fragarioides*. A low perennial growing from a rhizome. As the common name
suggests, the plant strongly resembles a strawberry. The
leaves and flowers are on separate stems. However, both
flowers and fruit are quite unlike strawberries. *Leaves:* 3
leaflets are wedge-shape and toothed with shallow, irregular lobes. The lateral leaflets are asymmetrical. *Flowers:*
Yellow with 5 petals. Growing in a cyme at the top of stalk
that often has small bracts. May. Fruit is dry and inedible.
Plant community: Pine forest.

Wild Strawberry, *Fragaria virginiana*. A perennial
growing from a rhizome. It also produces stolons from
which new plants grow. Typically just a few inches high
with the leaf on one stem and the flowers and fruit on a
separate, shorter stalk that is usually hidden beneath the
leaves. *Leaves:* 3 leaflets with rounded tips and triangular,
pointed bases. Lateral leaflets have rather rounded outer
edges toward the bases. Upper half of leaflets coarsely

THE PRODUCERS

93. Wild strawberry, *Fragaria virginiana*. *Jerry Sullivan*.

toothed. Leaves often leathery. *Flowers and fruit:* Flowers white with 5 round petals, 2 to several growing in an umbel. May–Jun. Fruit smaller and sweeter than domestic strawberries. Jun–Jul. Fruit is at its best in clearings where plants get full sunlight. Shade-grown plants may produce little or no fruit. *Plant communities:* Pine forest, boreal forest and in open places.

Lady's Slipper or **Moccasin Flower**, *Cypripedium acaule*. A perennial growing from fibrous roots. The two nearly opposite basal leaves have a single flower stalk 8-16 in. (20-40 cm) tall growing up between them. *Leaves:* Narrowly elliptic up to 8 in. (20 cm) long, slightly downy, pale beneath. *Flowers:* Stalk is downy. A single, lanceolate green bract arches forward over the flower. 4 sepals and lateral petals also lanceolate, yellow–green to greenish brown. The lip, the slipper part of the flower, is red or pink, rarely white, drooping, heavily veined, 1.2-2.4 in. (3-6 cm) long and cleft along the upper side with the inturned margins in contact. May–Jun. *Plant communities:* Pine forest, swamp forest, open bogs.

Ferns

Bracken Fern, *Pteridium aquilinum.* A perennial growing from a creeping rootstock that may be buried 10 in. (25 cm) deep, a trait that protects the plant from drought and frost. A single upright stalk 2-3 ft (70-90 cm) tall produces a single leaf which is divided into 3 leaflets, which are further divided into subleaflets. Dense stands of bracken produced vegetatively from the creeping rootstocks may shade out shorter plants. *Stipe:* Smooth, rigid, initially green but turning dark brown. *Leaves:* Leaflets have narrow, blunt tips. The tips and midveins are slightly hairy, quite vulnerable to frost. In early fall, still-erect stems are topped by withered brown leaves. *Spores:* Fruitdots in line near the edges of leaflets. Silvery, becoming dark brown. Partly covered by reflexed edges. *Plant communities:* Widespread, particularly common in pine forests and second-growth communities.

94. Bracken fern, *Pteridium aquilinum.*

THE PRODUCERS

Club Mosses

Ground Cedar, *Lycopodium complanatum.* The horizontal stem is on or just below the surface. Upright stems are heavily branched, the branches often arched or hanging and flattened. *Leaves:* In 4 ranks, grown together and lying flat against the stem for most of their length. Upper rank grows flat against the stem; lateral ranks have short free points. Lower rank, flat against the stem and much reduced. *Spore production:* 1-4 slender strobiles looking like candelabra at the tip of a long stem with a few scaly leaves. Strobiles 2.5 in. (6.4 cm) long; stem 3 in. (7.5 cm) long. *Plant communities:* Pine forests, boreal forests.

Ground Pine, *Lycopodium obscurum.* Horizontal stems are underground. Scattered upright stems often growing in rows look like tiny trees with arching branches growing from an upright central stem. *Leaves:* Crowded on the stems in 4-8 ranks, they are 0.2 in. (6 mm) long and lanceolate with sharp-pointed tips and a narrowing at the base. *Spore production:* The stemless strobiles grow directly from the tips of upper branches. They are upright and slender up to 2.6 in. (6.5 cm) long. There may be as many as a dozen on a single branch. *Plant communities:* Widespread, most common in pine forests and boreal forests.

95. Ground pine, *Lycopodium obscurum.*

CHAPTER TWELVE

The Mixed–Hardwood Forest

KEY TREES: Sugar maple, American beech, eastern hemlock, yellow birch, basswood.

THERE IS A FOREST west of Watersmeet in Michigan's Upper Peninsula where sugar maples tower a hundred feet above the forest floor. White pines are scattered among the maples on high ground, while on slopes and in ravines there are hemlocks and ancient yellow birches, the bark of the latter so old it peels in great sheets. The forest has never been logged; a group of steel executives bought it before any lumber company could get to it, and they kept it as a summer retreat. Many of the trees there got started after a fire in the 17th century. This 21,000-acre virgin tract, called the Sylvania, is now part of Ottawa National Forest. It is located on the Valders moraine and contains 33 lakes big enough to have names. It is also a classic example of a mature northern hardwood forest.

In early spring, before the thick canopy has filled with leaves, the floor of this forest is covered with wildflowers. The wood anemones bloom first, their white flowers pushing above the thick layer of leaves left from the previous autumn. They are followed in close succession by Clintonia lilies, Canada Mayflower, rose twisted stalk, and large-flowered trillium. By midsummer, when the forest is in deep shade, they are gone. Maple seedlings are everywhere but tiny, and there are no tall shrubs. The damp, still air near the ground is excellent for ferns. One can walk with ease in this forest, as if in a park.

The size of trees in the Sylvania is unusual, but the forest type, a mixture of hardwoods with a scattering of conifers, is the region's most common. It is the forest that Midwestern city dwellers visualize when they come out to see spring

96. Mixed hardwood forest, Wisconsin. *Jerry Sullivan.*

flowers or when they pile into cars in October and head for the country to see fall color.

Because its trees are prolific, long-lived, and able to reproduce in their own shade, the mixed hardwood forest is considered to be a climax type for the region. In the absence of major disturbance, this forest should maintain itself indefinitely; succession will not cause it to evolve into another forest type. Because it occupies the middle of the moisture gradient, the mixed-hardwood forest of the North Woods is also referred to as *mesic*.

Characteristics of a Mesic Forest

Shade Tolerance

Among the characteristics shared by mesic forest trees, the most obvious is *shade tolerance*. This can be seen both in the growth form and the typical stand structure of trees such as sugar maple and beech. The crowns of sugar maple are broad and deep; their shaded lower leaves, unlike those of such sun-loving trees as quaking aspen, can still carry on photosynthesis. Shade-tolerant trees also tend to grow closer together, producing dense stands. These factors combine to make summer light levels in a northern hardwood forest extremely low. One study showed it averaged 1 to 5 percent as much as the light which shines on a meadow.

Few tall shrubs can grow in such an environment, so the floor of this forest is usually open and parklike. Most wildflowers in northern hardwood forests bloom early in spring before tree leaves are out. Studies in Wisconsin have shown that 70 percent of them flower before midsummer. Their leaves can often be seen, grown large, later in summer; the leaves build up a food reserve which will fuel the next spring's sudden burst of growth and flowering.

The tiny maple seedlings we described as being so abundant on the forest floor of the Sylvania tract are also typical of mesic forests throughout the region. Many of them will die, but some may survive in the understory for years, then undergo a sudden spurt of growth when the death of a canopy tree above exposes them to direct sun. This ability to withstand *suppression* and then grow rapidly when light becomes available is typical of all mesic forest trees. Hemlocks a century old and only 2 inches (5 centimeters) in diameter have been found in Great Lakes forests.

ABOUT SUNFLECKS

If the floor of a mesic forest were uniformly and consistently dark, not even the most shade-tolerant species could survive for long. The shade is interrupted by *sunflecks*, however, which sweep over the ground and dapple the leaves as the day progresses. Sunfleck illumination is perhaps half as bright as sunlight in the open, but it provides enough light to maintain photosynthesis at a level which will balance respiration. Plants absorb carbon dioxide and give off oxygen during photosynthesis, and they give off carbon dioxide during respiration. In order to grow and produce flowers and fruit, this exchange must rise above a *compensation point* at which gains from photosynthesis and losses from respiration are balanced.

Rich Soil

The soils of northern hardwood forests tend to be well-drained, dark-colored loam, rich in humus. Under the old terminology, they are gray–brown podzolic types with well-developed A_1 and A_2 layers. The Department of Agriculture now calls them alfisols. Spencer silt loam, as an example, is a soil type that occurs under hardwoods on moraines. Its A and B layers, almost 2.5 feet (0.75 meters) thick, developed from the fine, wind-blown glacial particles called loess. The composition of these top layers is about 70 percent silt; the rest of the material is mainly clay with a little sand mixed in.

MAPLES AND MORAINES
Hardwoods are often found on moraines in the North Woods. Because the hillsides trap wind-blown material, the topsoil on moraines tends to be deeper than it is in surrounding flatter countryside. The pockets of low ground within the moraine collect leaves which decay to create the deep humus on which hardwoods thrive. The hilly moraine country is also better drained than the lowlands where swamp forests grow, although it holds *more* moisture than the flat sandy plains where pines are usually found. Moraines, in other words, offer soil conditions that are classically mesic.

MULL AND MOR HUMUS
Although humus, as we indicated above, tends to be thick in most northern hardwood forests of the region, it may differ widely in pH levels, depending on the species of tree which created it. The humus that forms from maple litter tends to be alkaline; it is said to be *mull*-type humus. Because its organic matter decomposes rapidly to mix with minerals in the topsoil, it supports the richest variety of spring wildflowers. Beech leaf litter is slightly more acid, and the highly acidic *mor* humus, common under conifers, decays so slowly that thick fibrous mats of plant material may lie on the surface of a hemlock forest floor for several years. Few ground-layer plants of any sort can survive these conditions.

ACROSS THE MOISTURE GRADIENT
Differences in soil moisture also bring changes in the composition of a forest. Mesic forests in the North Woods

The Mixed–Hardwood Forest   225

merge with pine forests where soils are near the drier end of the moisture gradient; white pines, red oaks, and red maples blend with the sugar maples in such areas. In damp hollows or other poorly drained spots, trees characteristic of a swamp forest—white cedars, black ashes, and balsam firs—become more frequent.

Another set of changes takes place in the understory. Light levels increase in both wet and dry woods from their low point in the mesic forest. Shrubs become more common. In the wet forests, several species of currants may grow along with red osier dogwood and speckled alder. Beaked hazel, prickly gooseberry, and wild red raspberry become more common under the pines and oaks. Bunchberry on the ground and red maple in the canopy become more common in both wet and dry forests than they are in the mesic forest.

Trees of the Mixed-Hardwood Forest

Regional Variation

Many of the typical species in the North Woods mesic forest—sugar maple, beech and basswood, for instance—are widespread throughout the eastern United States. Others, such as yellow birch, reach their greatest development within the northern Great Lakes area. The region's hardwood forest is unique, then, less in the kinds of trees that grow here than in the ways they combine in communities. It is also distinctive for the scattered but consistent presence of certain conifers—mainly hemlock and white pine.

Though all of the trees listed at the head of the chapter are typical of mesic forests, variations, sometimes only in proportion, occur from east to west, north to south, and across the moisture gradient.

Sugar maple is ubiquitous throughout the three-state area, although it is scarcer and more likely to be confined to sheltered sites in northern Minnesota than elsewhere. Sugar maple combines with beech and hemlock in Lower

Michigan, but in Wisconsin, beech is more typical in counties that border Lake Michigan. In the Upper Peninsula, beech only occurs east of the Canadian Shield. Hemlock disappears almost entirely west of Sawyer and Bayfield counties in northwestern Wisconsin. Basswood is abundant in Minnesota and grows scarcer in eastern Wisconsin and Michigan. Yellow birch is most plentiful in northern Wisconsin and the Upper Peninsula. In Minnesota, it occurs only along Lake Superior's north shore and inland on sheltered sites. White spruce and balsam fir occur in greater numbers among the hardwoods as one travels north.

The reasons for these variations may be complicated and are not clearly understood. Climate can be suggested as one logical limiting factor, especially in the case of sugar maple and yellow birch, which come near the northern edge of their ranges in the North Woods, and for spruce and fir, which are at the southern edge of their range in parts of our region. Temperature tolerances, length of days in spring and fall, and number of frost-free days are among climatic factors that could be relevant. The effect of competition is also likely to increase as plants near the limits of their climatic tolerance. It has been suggested that beech and hemlock extend no farther west than their range limit in the North Woods simply because they have not had time to colonize areas farther west since recession of the last glacier.

Sugar Maple

Sugar maple is the strongest dominant in mixed hardwood forests through the region. It produces abundant seed, it is very shade tolerant and very long lived. Mature sugar maples range from 60 to 130 feet (18 to 40 meters) tall and 3 to 4 feet (90 to 120 centimeters) in diameter. Ages of 200 years are common, and some giants live to 400.

The species enriches the soil with minerals such as calcium, potassium, and magnesium. These are drawn up from the subsoil by the roots and deposited on the surface when the leaves are shed in fall; in other North Woods trees such as beech and the oaks, nutrients withdraw from the still-green leaves into the trunk for storage.

Hemlock

Hemlock does best on the moister soils within the mesic forest. At Pictured Rocks National Lakeshore in the eastern Upper Peninsula, several rivers have cut through the glacial till and into the Miners Castle and Chapel Rock sandstones on their way to Lake Superior. The hemlocks are concentrated in the steep, narrow valleys. Beech and maple dominate the rolling uplands. This is a common pattern of distribution for these trees.

Hemlock seeds are shed from the cones in autumn, and germination occurs in spring on moist acidic ground. The seedlings most likely to survive to sapling stage are those that germinate on mossy stumps of pine and hemlock or on the sides of the hummocks of dirt called tip-up mounds which form at the base of trees uprooted by wind. Because of its shallow root systems and because of the acid, highly leached soil that results from the tree's acid leaf litter, hemlock is especially prone to windthrow. So tip-up mounds, which are common throughout the North Woods, are especially noticeable in old hemlock stands.

Deer are fond of hemlock seedlings and saplings. These animals are a serious threat to survival of the trees in some areas because hemlock, unlike sugar maple, does not reproduce from vegetative sprouts. If hemlocks are cut back too far, they die.

The infertile acid soil that develops under hemlock, combined with the deep shade cast by these trees, prevents the growth of plants on this forest floor.

Beech

American beech is a codominant with sugar maple in hardwood forests of Lower Michigan, the eastern Upper Peninsula, and eastern Wisconsin. Various studies have been conducted to learn why beech doesn't grow farther west, but no definite conclusions have been reached. The growing season where beech occurs in our region averages 25 days longer than the areas where it is absent. Long frost marks appear on beech trunks in winter near the north end of their range. Temperatures of $-40°$ to $-50°$ F ($-40°$

to −45° C) can kill them. As noted above, it has also been suggested that beech may simply not have had time since the recession of glacial ice to migrate farther west.

Beech reproduces better from sprouts than from seeds, a fact that helps the species survive fire. However, catastrophic fires that level huge areas seem to be less common in mixed-hardwood forests than they are on the drier soils of the pine forests. *Gap phase replacement* is a common form of forest renewal here. This involves the creation of small openings in the canopy by wind, lightning, or disease. Young trees grow in the gaps and replace the older trees.

Basswood and Yellow Birch

Basswood and yellow birch are both adapted to gap phase replacement, so they often have a scattered patchy distribution in the forest. Yellow birch seeds germinate particularly well on the bark of downed logs or on stumps. Roots from the saplings eventually reach the ground on either side of the logs and form a strong prop root system. When the logs decay, the exposed roots become the sole

97. Yellow birch prop root system. *U.S. Forest Service.*

98. Basswood suckers form a ring around the parent tree. *U.S.
Forest Service.*

support of the trunk. Walking through the North Woods,
one may come upon rows of stilt-legged yellow birches that
grew, one behind the other, on a mossy log long since gone.

Basswood stands may have an unusual growth form—a
perfect circle. Mature trees produce what are called root
crown sprouts around the central trunk. When the old tree
dies, the young sprouts are left growing in a circle. Each of
these offspring will be capable of creating a circle of its own
when it gets big enough. This habit of vigorous vegetative

THE PRODUCERS

reproduction helps basswood maintain its numbers even in competition with sugar maple. With an established root system as a source of water and nutrients, the sprouts have an advantage over young trees growing from seed.

Typical Shrubs

Tall shrubs are less common in mesic forests than in wetter and drier woodlands; low light intensity is the main reason. Among typical species are beaked hazel and maple-leaved viburnum, ironwood, alternate-leaved dogwood, and red-berried elder.

Canadian yew was once more common than it is today. Heavy deer browsing has all but eliminated it in many areas, although it thrives on a number of islands in the Great Lakes. We have seen it on one of the Apostle Islands off the Bayfield Peninsula in Lake Superior and on south Manitou Island off the east shore of Lake Michigan near Traverse City, Michigan. In these deerless refuges, yew creates luxuriant thickets that make cross-country hiking very difficult.

History of the Hardwoods

The mixed-hardwood forests are now the region's most common forest type, as they were at the time of settlement. However, their dominance may have begun within the last 500 to 1000 years. Some of the oldest stands found in the 19th century could have been the first of their type on the site they occupied.

Cutting of hardwoods was limited until about World War I. By then improved transportation and a high demand for quality hardwood made it attractive to clear-cut these forests. The fires that followed favored a regeneration of hardwoods over pine and hemlock, which cannot sprout from stumps. Surveyors' records show that many of today's hardwood stands were once mixed forests with substantial numbers of white pine.

Where fires were especially severe or frequent, the hardwoods could not survive. Here the typical second-growth forest dominated by aspens took over. In many cases, hardwoods have seeded in under the scanty canopy of the aspens. As the old trees die, the stand will gradually convert to a mixed-hardwood forest. Since effective fire protection arrived in the 1930s, this kind of conversion has been going on all over the region.

Future of the Hardwood Forest

Whether or not the mixed hardwood forest is the enduring climax for the region, there is no doubt that succession in many pine forests and swamp forests and second-growth forests is moving in this direction.

Many woodlands are now deliberately managed for northern hardwoods. However, the clean forestry usually practiced today leaves few dead logs and tip-up mounds to be colonized by yellow birch and hemlock seedlings. Combined with preferential browsing by deer, this could reduce these species and favor sugar maple.

Forest Stearns described a forest he explored in 1946 near Drummond, Wisconsin; it had already been approaching a climax state when surveyors took notes on it 90 years before.

By the time Stearns arrived, the canopy trees—mainly hemlock, yellow birch, and sugar maple—ranged from 50 or 60 feet (15 to 18 meters) to 120 feet (36 meters) tall. The trunks were straight and, except for hemlock, clear of branches to a height of 50 feet. The forest floor was open and parklike, with wildflowers early in the season and few shrubs anywhere. Stearns wrote:

Fallen trees varying in size from small saplings to logs well over 30 inches [76 centimeters] in diameter were found in all stages of decay, while an occasional stub or broken trunk stands upright, riddled with woodpecker holes . . . There was relatively little air movement, an atmosphere of remarkable quiet and heightened humidity.*

*Forest Stearns, "The Composition of the Sugar Maple–hemlock–yellow birch Association in Northern Wisconsin," *Ecology* 32 (1951): 245–265.

When we visited in 1978, the parklike atmosphere was largely gone. Most of the hemlocks, the yellow birches, and the largest maples had fallen, presumably victims of old age. The only pure hemlock stand, belying all the statistics, occupied a hilltop. A small cedar swamp was growing in a low area. The rest of the stand consisted almost entirely of young healthy sugar maples.

Key to Common Plants of the Mixed-Hardwood Forest

I.   Tall shrubs

   1.   Alternate leaves

      2.   Leaves simple

         3.   Toothed—**Ironwood** or **Hop hornbeam**

         3.   Entire—**Alternate–leaved dogwood**

      2.   Leaves compound—**Red-berried elder**

II.   Low shrubs

   1.   Needle-like leaves—**American yew**

III.   Herbs

   1.   Opposite leaves, prostrate—**Partridgeberry**

   1.   Alternate leaves

      2.   Leaves compound—**White baneberry**

      2.   Leaves simple

         3.   Leaves toothed, flowers yellow—**Downy yellow violet**

         3.   Leaves entire

            4.   Yellow–green flowers in leaf axils—**Solomon's seal**

            4.   Leaves pierced by stem, flowers yellow—**Large-flowered bellwort**

4. White flowers with 3 petals—**Large-flowered trillium**

IV. Club mosses—**Shining club moss; Stiff club moss**

V. Ferns—**Virginia grape fern**

Plant Descriptions

Tall Shrubs

Alternate-Leaved Dogwood, *Cornus alternifolia.* A small tree growing, rarely, to 25 ft (8 m) tall. The branches may be grouped in irregular, horizontal platforms. *Leaves:* Elliptic to egg-shape and tapering to a sharp point. They are pale green and hairy beneath with 4–5 pairs of lateral veins that follow the same curve as the edge of the leaf. The leaves appear whorled near the ends of flowering branches. *Flowers and fruit:* A flat-topped cyme, 1–2.5 in. (3–6 cm) across. The flowers are white with 4 petals. Jun–Jul. Fruit a cluster of blue–black berries. Sep. *Bark:* Newer branches greenish. *Plant communities:* Mixed-hardwood forest.

Ironwood or **Hop Hornbeam,** *Ostrya virginiana.* A slender tree that may grow to 65 ft. (20 m) but is more common as a plant of the understory. *Leaves:* Petioles hairy when young, blades oblong or ovate and tapering to a point. They are sharply and often doubly toothed and downy beneath. *Flowers and fruit:* Staminate catkins may be present in winter. Slender pistillate catkins give rise to a cluster of pouches or bladders, each holding a small nut. Flowers emerge with the leaves. *Buds:* End buds are false. *Twigs and bark:* Twigs are initially hairy. On older trunks, the bark is light brown or gray, scaly, and broken into shreds. *Plant communities:* Mixed-hardwood forest.

Red-Berried Elder, *Sambucus pubens. Leaves:* Toothed, elliptic, pointed; the 5–7 leaflets are usually downy below. Midribs purple or purple striped above. *Flowers:* A conical cluster, creamy white, yellow, sometimes pink.

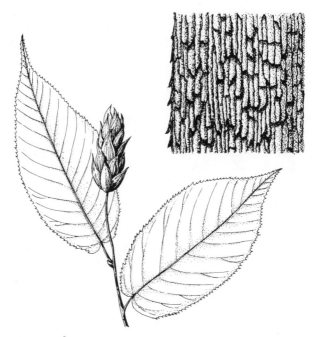

99. Ironwood, *Ostrya virginiana*.

Each flower has 5 petal-like lobes. May–Jun. Fruit is a cluster of red berries. Aug–Sep. *Bark:* Pale gray and smooth except for round, raised dots. *Plant communities:* Mixed-hardwood forest.

Low Shrubs

American Yew, *Taxus canadensis.* A low, straggling shrub with stems erect or arching upward. *Leaves:* Needles tapering to a sharp point. At the base, the petiole is attached to a stalk that lies on the twig for a short distance below the needle. *Flowers and fruit:* Staminate flowers grow singly in the axils of leaves. Pistillate flowers in pairs developed into red fleshy berries. *Bark and twigs:* Twigs are smooth except for leaf stalks. *Plant community:* Mixed-hardwood forest.

100. American yew, *Taxus canadensis*. *Larry Evans*.

Herbs

Partridgeberry, *Mitchella repens*. An herb or creeping shrub with a prostrate stem that roots at the nodes and forms mats on the ground. *Leaves:* Evergreen, petioled, round to egg-shape, shining, 0.4–0.8 in (1–2 cm) long. May be veined with white. *Flowers:* In pairs, white, slender, with a tubular corolla divided into 4 (occasionally 3, 5, or 6) spreading lobes. May–Jun. Fruit a red berry. *Plant communities:* Mixed-hardwood and pine forests; scarce in Minnesota.

Herbs with alternate compound leaves.

White Baneberry, *Actaea alba*. Erect stems up to 3 ft (1 m) tall with spreading leaves. *Leaves:* Pinnately twice compound with ovate leaflets that are sharply toothed and sometimes lobed. *Flowers and fruit:* Tiny white flowers with 4–10 petals are borne on a short thick raceme that is

236   THE PRODUCERS

101. White baneberry, *Actaea alba*.

longer than it is wide. May–Jul. Fruit is a cluster of lustrous white berries, each with a purple spot at the tip. They are borne on short thick stalks. Berries mildly poisonous. *Plant communities:* Mixed-hardwood and pine forests. The very similar red baneberry found in the boreal forest is described in Chapter 13.

Herbs with simple leaves.

Downy Yellow Violet, *Viola pubescens.* A perennial from a rhizome, it typically has 1 or 2 stout, upright, hairy stems with leaves near the top. Occasionally it will have a single basal leaf. *Leaves:* Circular to broadly egg-shape, short pointed with a heart–shape base. Hairy beneath, 1.6–4 in. (4–10 cm) long. Stipules are tiny, broadly egg-shape, toothed. *Flowers:* Yellow with brown–purple veins near the base. The 5 petals are irregular with the lowest elongated into a spur. Lateral petals hairy. Flower stalks are hairy and the sepals are fringed with hairs. May–Jun. *Plant communities:* Mixed-hardwood and pine forests.

The Mixed–Hardwood Forest 237

Hairy Solomon's Seal, *Polygonatum pubescens.* A single arching stem grows from a rhizome. Flowers grow in leaf axils. *Leaves:* Narrowly elliptic to broadly oval, 1.5–4.7 in. (4–12 cm) long on a short petiole or sometimes sessile. Smooth above, often with fine hairs on veins below. You will need a hand lens to see them. *Flowers and fruit:* Flowers yellow–green, hanging in clusters of 1–4 from leaf axils. Apr–Jul. Fruit a dark blue or black berry. *Plant communities:* Most common in mixed-hardwood but also in pine forest.

Large-Flowered Bellwort, *Uvularia grandiflora.* A perennial from a rhizome growing with a single erect stem 8–20 in. (20–50 cm) tall that forks above the middle into a sterile stem—leaves only—and a fertile stem with flowers. *Leaves:* Pierced by the stem, broadly oval to oblong, up to 4.7 in. (12 cm) long with tiny hairs below. *Flowers and fruit:* Yellow, nodding flowers with 6 long, pointed segments of the perianth. 1–4 per plant. Apr–Jun. *Plant communities:* Mixed–hardwood forest.

Large-Flowered Trillium, *Trillium grandiflorum.* A perennial that produces a single erect stem 8–16 in. (20–40 cm) tall with a whorl of 3 leaves and a single large terminal flower. *Leaves:* Egg-shape to nearly round, commonly like a parallelogram with sides all the same length and a pointed tip. 3–5 in. (8–12 cm) long. *Flowers:* On an erect or ascending stalk, 2–3 in. (5–8 cm) long. 3 lanceolate green sepals 1.2–2 in. (3–5 cm) long and spreading. 3 petals usually white, ascending from the base and then spreading, egg-shape, pointed, 1.6–2.4 in. (4–6 cm) long. May–Jun. *Plant communities:* Most common in mixed–hardwood. Also in pine forest.

Club Mosses

Stiff Club Moss, *Lycopodium annotinum.* The horizontal stems, on ground or just covered by humus, are up to 6 ft (1.8 m) long. Vertical stems up to 12 in. (30 cm) may fork once, twice, or not at all. *Leaves:* Whorled, with 4 to the whorl. Almost needle-like, they are tipped with a tiny sharp spine. They are stiff and prickly to the touch. *Spore production:* In sessile strobiles at the tips of vertical stems.

102. Large-flowered bellwort, *Uvularia grandiflora*. *National Park Service.*

Strobiles are cylindrical, straw-colored and up to 1.5 in. (4 cm) long. *Plant communities:* Mixed-hardwood, boreal forest.

Shining Club Moss, *Lycopodium lucidulum.* Horizontal stems lie on the ground. Fertile stems up to 10 in. (25 cm) tall curve upward and may fork up to 3 times. *Leaves:* Arranged in 6 ranks around the stem. They spread outward or curve downward, giving the stem a slightly shaggy appear-

The Mixed–Hardwood Forest

ance. They are tiny—0.2–0.5 in. (7–12 mm)—and shaped like a candle flame, flaring out from a narrow base and then tapering to a point. Toothed near the tips. *Spore production:* In tiny sporangia 0.06–0.07 in. (1.5–1.8 mm) wide in the axils of leaves. *Plant communities:* Mixed-hardwood, boreal forest.

Ferns

Virginia Grape Fern, *Botrychium virginianum.* The buried rootstock produces a single lacy-cut sterile leaf arching to nearly horizontal on a vertical stem. A separate stalk arising from the juncture of leaf and stipe holds the fertile leaf. *Stipe:* Up to 13 in. (34 cm) long, erect and smooth. *Leaves:* Up to 8 in. (20 cm) long and 12 in. (30 cm) wide; triangular. Small stems extending laterally from the midrib bear pinnate leaflets that are toothed and somewhat blunt tipped. *Spores:* Stalk for fertile blade up to 8 in. (20 cm) long with a twice or thrice cut blade up to 6 in. (15 cm) long. Spore cases are bright yellow. Fertile branch appears in early summer, withers before sterile leaf. *Plant community:* Mixed–hardwood forest.

CHAPTER THIRTEEN

The Boreal Forest

KEY TREES: Balsam fir, white spruce, paper birch.

COMMON ASSOCIATES: Quaking aspen, balsam poplar, jack pine, black spruce, white pine, white cedar, red maple, mountain maple, mountain ash.

THIS FOREST is noisy with rushing meltwater in spring. Loons rest on its still lakes in summer, and it has its share of bright color in autumn, too. Yet it is in winter that the boreal forest, which occupies the northern fringe of our area, comes into its own. The pyramidal shapes of scattered spruce and the bunched groves of balsam fir provide greenery when maple woods have long since shed their leaves. Several of the deciduous trees that do thrive here—the paper birch and the various aspens—have white or near-white bark that also seems adapted esthetically to a winter landscape.

The boreal forest is actually *circumboreal,* that is, it extends all the way around the world in the higher latitudes. Many of the trees and wildflowers, mosses, and lichens that grow in the spruce–fir forests of our region are also found in Finland, the Ukraine, and northern China. A comparison of boreal stands in Wisconsin and in Germany found 60 species in common; more than half of the genera were the same.

On this continent boreal forest occurs mainly in Canada, where it extends north to the timberline. Tongues of it extend into the United States along spines of the Appalachians in the east, the Rockies and Coast Ranges in the west. The broadest expanse of boreal forest within the lower 48 states, however, lies around the Upper Great Lakes at the edge of our own North Woods. It was the first forest type to appear in the region after the glacier receded,

103. The boreal forest in winter, Superior National Forest, Minnesota. *U.S. Forest Service.*

and it once spread much farther south than its present range.

Today the boreal is the climax forest in much of northern Minnesota from Lake Itasca State Park on the west, where prairie plants begin to invade the woods, to the Boundary Waters Canoe Area wilderness north of Lake Superior. In Upper Michigan, stands are found on the Keweenaw Peninsula and in Houghton, Baraga, and Marquette counties; a few stands also occur on moist, protected sites at the northern tip of Lower Michigan. Spruce–fir in Wisconsin is confined mainly to a narrow strip of land along Lake Superior in Douglas, Bayfield, and Ashland counties. The lake has a powerful effect on the summer climate here, keeping it much cooler than inland areas; still, most of the boreal stands are in narrow river valleys that are more sheltered from the warm sun than hilltops and upper slopes. A tiny remnant of boreal forest grows on a site at Bailey's Harbor on the Door County Peninsula that is strongly affected by Lake Michigan. Midday temperatures here on warm summer days may be 20° F (11° C) cooler than they are on Green Bay less than 10 miles (16 kilometers) away.

The boreal forests of Wisconsin—and many of those in Michigan and Minnesota—show ecotonal characteristics. They contain plants typical of nearby mixed-hardwood forests that are not found in the more northern boreal forest. Some show signs of a successional change toward dominance by sugar maple and other northern hardwoods. Some spruce–fir stands on the Keweenaw Peninsula apparently grew in after logging on land that had been occupied by mixed hardwoods, and the understory suggests that they may return to the pre-logging forest in time.

The boreal forest of the Lake States is not so much a different forest as it is a more limited forest than those occupying other parts of our region. The trees are found in other forest communities, and many of the shrubs and herbs of the understory are among the ubiquitous plants of the North Woods discussed in Chapter 10. But there are generally fewer species, particularly of trees. And with fewer species competing, they may occupy different ecological niches than they do in other forest types. To the south, for example, trees that are dominants in the boreal forest are often confined by competition to the poorest sites (e.g., bogs for black spruce, sand for jack pine); in northeastern Minnesota both of these trees can be found on relatively rich upland soils as well as in their usual situations. To the south, hemlock seedlings claim fallen logs or the pits next to tip-up mounds; beyond the hemlock's range, spruce and fir take over these spots.

Soil throughout most of the boreal forest is gray wooded podzolic, although in some areas true podzols form. Soils vary from clay to sandy loam.

The boreal forest is a climax type that depends on continuing disturbance to maintain itself. Fire, insect attack, and windthrow are all common occurrences that serve to ensure the continuation of the type. We will describe this process of maintenance-through-disturbance in our discussion of succession in the boreal forest below.

Trees of the Boreal Forest

Balsam fir is the most abundant tree in the boreal forest. The southern end of its range closely defines the southern edge of the North Woods. It can grow in the drier parts of cedar swamps, as an understory tree in the shade of tall maple or white pine, or as a successor to quaking aspen in second-growth stands. To the north it becomes steadily more common.

Spruce–fir forest is a common synonym for the boreal forest, but in the Lake States fir–spruce might be a better name, since spruce is generally much less common than balsam fir. Both balsam fir and white spruce occur in a broad range of soil moisture conditions, but there is a general tendency for balsam fir to reach its peak of abundance in somewhat wet conditions while white spruce is most common in drier soils.

Other common trees of the boreal forest include black spruce, paper birch, the three Great Lakes pines, and three members of the genus *Populus:* quaking aspen, balsam poplar, and big-toothed aspen. The relative abundance of these species is in part determined by factors such as soil moisture, but the extent of the disturbance that led to the establishment of the boreal forest stand and the length of time since that disturbance occurred may be even more important in determining what species are present. We will discuss this in more detail below.

Adaptations

Trees of this forest show adaptations not only to cold and snow but to dessication. The needle-like leaves of all conifers expose very little surface to the elements. The needles of spruce, fir, and jack pine, whose ranges extend the farthest north, also have unusually thick outer layers—in the case of jack pine this layer constitutes half the bulk of the entire needle. The stomata, the pores through which a leaf breathes, are also well protected in these species, sunk deep into the needle's lower surface.

Most of the deciduous trees found in a boreal forest are quite supple. The branches of birch and aspen can bend almost double without breaking under the weight of snow. This suppleness has an advantage too for animals that roam the woods in winter; it puts a meal of tender buds within their reach. The waterproof bark of the paper birch which makes such good canoes also helps protect the tree from cold, dry winds.

THE PRODUCERS

Plants of the Understory

Mountain maple and mountain ash are the most distinctive understory plants in most boreal forest stands near Lake Superior. Mountain ash is a shrub over most of its range, but along the lakeshore often grows tall enough to reach the forest canopy. Its bright orange–red berries cling to the trees through half the winter and are eaten by many birds and mammals.

Among plants of the boreal forest floor, red baneberry is probably the most distinctive. Other indicator species include nodding trillium, one-sided pyrola, and northern white violet. Many other wildflowers typical of the boreal forest are found throughout the North Woods; they merely occur here in greater profusion than in any other habitat. The twinflower is one such example. Others include fragrant bedstraw, Canada Mayflower, Clintonia lily, bunchberry, starflower, and large-leaved aster.

Herbs which are common in the boreal forest but which occur in greater numbers in other forest types include goldthread, wood anemone, wild strawberry, wild sarsaparilla, lady fern, oak fern, bracken fern, tree club moss, and hairy club moss.

Low-lying species of perennial shrubs and herbs that survive the harsh winters under a blanket of snow make up much of the ground cover in a boreal forest. The snow protects them, as it does the small woodland animals, not only from cold, but from the drying effects of cold air. At the northern edge of the boreal forest, near the tundra, temperatures are so low and winds so fierce that even trees can't survive at heights greater than the snow's depth. (Low light levels in boreal forests, especially in balsam fir groves, also play a part in keeping out tall shrubs.)

Mosses and lichens also become increasingly important parts of the landscape in the boreal forest. In many black spruce stands, feather mosses dominate the ground cover. Reindeer moss, a kind of lichen (*Dicranum* spp.), grows almost a foot (30 centimeters) thick near the Canadian border in Minnesota. This pale gray–green ground cover is a combination, as are all lichens, of a fungus and an algae. The fungus provides minerals; the algae carries on photosynthesis, producing food for itself and for its symbiotic partner. When woodland caribou lived in the North Woods, mosses and lichens were an important part of their food supply.

Lichens are capable of colonizing bare rock that is essentially devoid of soil, and they may play a role in breaking down the rock and enabling other plants to follow their pioneering lead. Particles of windblown dust, leaves, and other debris lodge in the tangled lichen tufts and provide the raw materials for soil development.

Succession in the Boreal Forest

The deep narrow cone-shape spruce and balsam fir throw a shade on the ground so dense that young trees cannot effectively start until the old generation of trees is cleared away. The boreal forest depends on disturbance, and the most common kind of disturbance is fire. The ground in a boreal forest is covered with a steadily thickening mat of high-acid decay-resistant mor humus that consists mainly of fallen spruce and fir needles. In dry weather this makes a great

104. Spruce and fir colonizing an old field, Douglas County, Wisconsin. *Glenda Daniel.*

THE PRODUCERS

fuel, as do the lichens. Unlike the other forest trees of our region, spruce and fir are not self-pruning, and fires are fueled as well by low branches that stay on the tree even after it has reached a considerable height. The narrow crowns of the spruce and fir, however, are too far apart to allow crown fires to leap from treetop to treetop. Water helps limit the extent of fires, too. There are so many lakes, ponds, and swamps in the boreal forest regions that a fire is likely to encounter an aquatic obstacle before it has gone too far.

Fire is important to the boreal forest. Without it this woodland type degenerates rather than developing. Decay rates are slow in this cold climate, and podzolization steadily decreases the fertility of topsoils. The raw acid mat of mor humus on the surface grows thick, making it more and more difficult for the rootlets of sprouting plants to reach mineral soil. There may be no seedlings to replace trees blown down or pulled over by the weight of snow on their branches, and shrubs and mosses will spread at the expense of trees. This sequence of events is prevented by fire, which clears the ground and releases minerals held in the mor humus.

Sometimes the burning of a spruce–fir stand results in the immediate growth of another spruce–fir stand, but in most instances this severe disturbance favors the growth of aspen and paper birch, of black spruce–jack pine forests, or of the other pines. In the absence of further disturbance, these pioneers will endure for one generation, serving as a nurse crop for a new growth of spruce–fir. Of course in the case of red and white pine, a generation may be several centuries. In northeastern Minnesota stands of pine were apparently maintained in the past by fires that burned the balsam fir and spruce growing in under the pine and left the ground clear for a new growth of pine. We described in Chapter 11 the forests of the Boundary Waters Canoe Area that consist of an overstory of very large pines towering above the smaller spruces and firs. Without another fire to clear the ground, these stands will evolve into pure spruce–fir as the old pines die.

Many of these pine stands show a three-layered structure. The pines that seeded in right after the last fire form the top layer. Somewhat younger white spruces make up the second layer, and balsam firs form the lowest layer. Balsam firs are quite vulnerable to fire, and they do not colonize burned areas quickly. Their heavy seeds spread slowly, but they are well adapted to germination in soils that have not been burned in some time. In fact, balsam firs, unlike jack pines, which must reach mineral soil in order to grow, can reach considerable size with their root system entirely within the humus layer.

These shallow roots of balsam firs make them quite vulnerable to another common boreal forest disturbance: windthrow. However, clearings created by windthrow can be recolonized directly by balsam fir with no intervening generation of aspen or pine.

The deep snows of the north, especially the wetter varieties, take their toll on the forest. The cumulative weight of lacy flakes can topple 100-foot (30-meter) spruces; the shallow-rooted balsam firs are even more vulnerable. Where fallen trees have left an opening in the forest, snow piles up against the trees at the leeward edge of the clearing, and the weight of this snow will uproot trees, one at a time, each fall exposing a new, previously protected tree to the elements. This slowly advancing destruction of the forest can continue indefinitely.

Insect attacks constitute another common disturbance in the boreal forest, with spruce budworm doubtless the most devastating. This imported pest became epidemic in the boreal forests of our region in the mid-1950s. In spite of its name, this foliage-eating caterpillar mainly attacks balsam fir. Several successive years of defoliation will kill an infected tree. Frequently, whole stands are destroyed. The death of the old trees opens up the canopy and promotes a heavy growth of tall shrubs—particularly beaked hazel and bush honeysuckle—and a crop of aspen and birch; below these, a new growth of balsam fir will begin.

The inherent instability of the boreal forest has an obvious affinity to the even more unstable Arctic ecosystems to the north. The spruce budworm can devastate an entire forest because a single species—the balsam fir—makes up such a large part of it. The crash of the balsam fir affects many other plant species, and animal species as well, leading, for example, to temporary explosions in the populations of insect-eating birds such as the wood warblers.

Key to Common Plants of the Boreal Forest

I. Tall shrubs

    1. Opposite leaves

        2. Leaves entire, nearly round with abrupt pointed tip—**Round-leaved dogwood**

        2. Leaves lobed—**Highbush cranberry**

    1. Alternate compound leaves—**Mountain ash**

II. Low shrubs

    1. Opposite leaves—**American fly honeysuckle**

    1. Alternate leaves

        2. Large, palmately lobed—**Thimbleberry**

        2. Leaves entire, undersides downy—**Thin-leaved bilberry**

III. Herbs

    1. Compound leaves—**Red baneberry**

    1. Whorled leaves—**Nodding trillium**

    1. Basal leaves

        2. Toothed—**One-sided pyrola**

        2. Entire—**Northern white violet**

IV. Club moss—**Running ground pine**

Plant Descriptions

Tall Shrubs

Round-Leaved Dogwood, *Cornus rugosa.* A shrub or small tree growing to 10 ft (3 m) tall. *Leaves:* Broadly egg-

105. Round-leaved dogwood, *Cornus rugosa. Jerry Sullivan.*

shape to nearly circular with abruptly pointed tips. 1–5 in. (3–13 cm) across. 6 to 9 pairs of lateral, arcuate veins branch off from the midrib. Veins curve around following the outline of the leaf. Leaves are sometimes hairy beneath. *Flowers and fruit:* Tiny white flowers with 4 petals clustered in a flat-topped cyme. Fruit is a cluster of light blue berries. Flowers, May–Jul. Fruit, Aug.-Oct. *Bark:* On younger branches greenish, usually blotched with purple. *Plant communities:* Boreal forest.

Highbush Cranberry, *Viburnum opulus* (B&B) or *V. trilobum* (Fern).* There are several species of this widespread genus in the North Woods. They are all shrubs or small trees with opposite simple leaves and flowers in flat-topped clusters. *Leaves:* Nearly circular but with 3 deep lobes. They are coarsely toothed except near the deepest parts of the indentations between lobes. The lobes taper to

---

*'B & B' refers to *The New Britton & Brown Illustrated Flora* [of the Northern United States and Canada], by Henry A. Gleason (New York Botanical Garden, 1952); 'Fern,' refers to *Gray's Manual of Botany* (8th ed.), by M. L. Fernald (American Book Company, New York, 1950). These two standard references occasionally disagree on nomenclature, and where this is the case we have given both names.

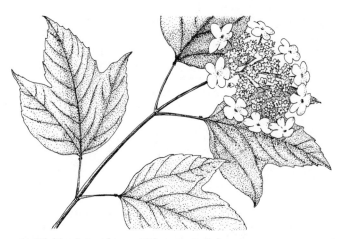

106. Highbush cranberry, *Viburnum trilobum*.

points. Somewhat downy below, especially on veins. Note the warty glands near the base. *Flowers and fruit:* In a flat-topped cyme. The white outer flowers are large and sterile. Small inner flowers with 5-lobed corollas bear the fruit. Jun–Jul. Fruit, a cluster of red berries about the size of a cranberry appearing in Sep–Oct. *Bark:* Gray, smooth on younger stems. *Plant communities:* Boreal forest.

Mountain Ash, *Sorbus americana* or *Pyrus americana*. A tree of the understory that may grow to 33 ft (10 m) in height. *Leaves:* Pinnately compound with 11–17 toothed leaflets. The leaflets are lanceolate to narrowly oblong, 2–3.5 in. (5–9 cm) long, tapering to a long point. They are paler below. *Flowers and fruit:* The cyme is rounded to nearly flat across the top, up to 8 in. (20 cm) across, and covered with white flowers with 5 petals. Jun–Jul. Fruits are bright red berries in dense clusters. Aug–Sep. *Bark and twigs:* Light gray–brown, smooth to scaly. *Plant communities:* Boreal forest, swamp forest.

Low Shrubs

American Fly Honeysuckle, *Lonicera canadensis*. A low, straggling, loosely branched shrub up to 6 ft (2 m) tall. *Leaves:* Egg-shape to oblong with rounded or slightly heart-shape bases. Toothless edges fringed with fine hairs. 1–4 in. (3–12 cm) long, smooth or sparsely downy below. *Flowers and fruit:* Tubular greenish yellow flowers typically in pairs at the end of a long stalk growing from the leaf axils. They have 5 petal-like lobes and are 0.5–0.8 in. (1.2–2 cm) long. Fruit is a red berry. Flowers, May–Jun. Fruit, Jul–Aug. *Plant communities:* Boreal forest, mixed-hardwood forest.

Thimbleberry, *Rubus parviflorus.* An unarmed bramble with stems 3–6 ft (1–2 m) long with shredding bark. Younger parts of the stem have glands on stalk-like bases. *Leaves:* Up to 8 in. (20 cm) broad, they have 3–5 palmate lobes. The sinuses between lobes cut to about 1/3 of the width of the leaf. The lobes are toothed and pointed. Petioles have tiny glands. *Flowers and fruit:* White flowers in a small, long-stalked cyme. Sepals have long tail-like tips. The 5 petals are elliptic to egg-shape and up to 0.8 in. (2 cm) long. Jun–Jul. Fruit, sweet, red, up to 0.8 in. (2 cm) in diameter with downy drupelets. Aug–Sep. *Plant communities:* Boreal forest.

Thin-Leaved Bilberry, *Vaccinium myrtilloides.* A shrub 8–24 in. (20–60 cm) tall. *Leaves:* Oblong to elliptical, edges

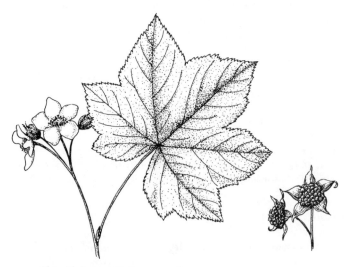

107. Thimbleberry, *Rubus parviflorus.*

THE PRODUCERS

without teeth. The undersides and sometimes the upper surfaces downy. 0.6–1.2 in. (1.5–3 cm) long. *Flowers and fruit:* Bell-shape greenish flowers are 0.2–0.3 in. (4–6 mm) long and borne in racemes at the tips of branches. May–Jun. They expand when the leaves are half grown. Sour fruits are blue with a heavy bloom (white powder) over their surface. Jul–Aug. *Twigs and branches:* New branchlets are velvety or hairy. *Plant communities:* Boreal forest, swamp forest.

Herbs

Red Baneberry, *Actaea rubra.* Erect stems up to 3 ft (1 m) tall with spreading leaves. *Leaves:* Pinnately twice compound with ovate leaflets that are sharply toothed and sometimes lobed. *Flowers and fruit:* Tiny white flowers in a rounded raceme. May–Jul. Berries are red and held in a cluster by slender stalks. *Plant communities:* Boreal forest.

Nodding Trillium, *Trillium cernuum.* *Leaves:* Broad, almost diamond shaped, 2.4–4 in. (6–10 cm) long. A very small petiole. Leaves may appear sessile. *Flowers:* Flower's stalk bent downward so flower nods below the leaves. Petals white or pink, up to 1 in. (2.5 cm) long with the tips curved back toward the flower stalk. 3 lanceolate sepals

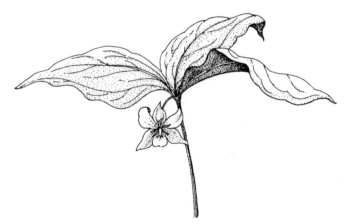

108. Nodding trillium, *Trillium cernuum.*

about as long as the petals. May–Jun. *Plant communities:* Boreal forest, swamp forest.

One-Sided Pyrola, *Pyrola secunda.* A perennial from a creeping rhizome, one of several similar species of this genus in the region. *Leaves:* Evergreen, elliptic or egg-shape to nearly round, 0.6–1.6 in. (1.5–4 cm) long. Slightly toothed or entire. *Flowers and fruit:* White or pale green flowers in a raceme on a stalk 3–8 in. (8–20 cm) long. The flowers are clustered along one side of the stalk. They have 5 petals and a long style that protrudes from the flowers like a tiny elephant's trunk. Jun–Jul. *Plant communities:* Boreal forest, pine forest.

Northern White Violet, *Viola pallens.* A perennial growing from a rhizome. Stolons form clumps of plants. *Leaves:* Heart-shape or broadly egg-shape with rounded tips; smooth, light green with dull or glossy sheen. *Flowers:* White on erect stalk. 3 lower petals with brown–purple veins near the base. Two lateral petals usually have tufts of hairs. May–Jun. *Plant communities:* Boreal forest, swamp forest.

Running Pine, *Lycopodium clavatum.* Long, forking horizontal stem lies on the ground or arches slightly. Erect stems branching up to 16 in.. (40 cm) high, including the strobiles. *Leaves:* In 10 ranks, slender and tapering to a hairlike tip. Spreading or ascending. *Spore production:* Strobile cylindric, straw-colored and up to 4 in. (11 cm) long. They grow atop slender flower stalks up to 6 in. (15 cm) long that are covered with yellow, scaly leaves. Strobiles may grow singly or in candelabralike clusters of up to 6. *Plant communities:* Boreal forest, pine forest.

THE PRODUCERS

CHAPTER FOURTEEN

The Second-Growth Forest

KEY TREES: Quaking aspen, paper birch.

ENTERING THIS FOREST on a clear summer day, one's first impression is of sunlight dappling everything—reflecting off the pale bark and quivering silvery leaves of the aspens, settling on the tall hazel shrubs that everywhere block the way, warming the raspberries and intensifying their scent. The aspen, which is the main component of second-growth forests in the North Woods, requires full sun for growth. Created by disturbance, the forest endures only a generation—with some exceptions—before giving way to one of the region's more enduring forest types.

Known more commonly in the North woods as popple, aspen is one of the most widely distributed native trees in North America. Its range extends from Maine to Alaska and south in the western mountains as far as Mexico. It is a quintessential pioneer, a specialist in catastrophe that evolution has equipped to exploit the openings produced by fire, disease, logging, and windthrow. When the loggers and the fires that followed them denuded millions of acres in the North Woods, the aspens moved in. Today aspen woods cover about 13 million acres (5.3 million hectares) in our region. Most of these woods date from the 1930s or later.

Quaking Aspen: A Life History

Quaking aspen's pioneering begins when the fruit capsules open in late May and early June. The seeds that fall from the capsules are extremely light—averaging about three

255

109. Second growth forest, Douglas County, Wisconsin. *Glenda Daniel.*

million to the pound—and they are surrounded by tufts of long silky hairs that make them very buoyant. Even a light breeze can carry them a long distance, enabling them to colonize areas far from the parent tree.

The seeds remain viable for a very short time. They must sprout the summer they fall. They need moisture, but they are very tolerant about just how much. They can even grow completely submerged. Postfire conditions are ideal for them because fires remove duff and humus from the surface, putting mineral soils within reach of the rootlet growing down from the seed. Fires also enrich the soil by releasing minerals held in decaying vegetation. Aspens seem to have a particular need for large amounts of potassium.

By the end of their first year, aspen seedlings may be up to 2 feet (60 centimeters) tall and have roots extending 5 to 10 inches (12.5–25 centimeters) deep and up to 16 inches (40 centimeters) laterally. They are very intolerant of shade, but in full sunlight they can grow 3 feet (90 centimeters) a year for as long as 10 years.

Aspens are rather small short-lived trees that may be only 30 feet (9 meters) tall at maturity. They get larger—and live longer—at the northwest end of our region. In the Boundary Waters Canoe Area Wilderness of northeastern

THE PRODUCERS

Minnesota they may reach heights over 80 feet (25 meters), and some individuals may live as long as 200 years. In general, however, 100 years is a very long life, and 50 years is more typical.

While aspens do reproduce from seed in the way we have described, they far more commonly reproduce vegetatively from root suckers. Suckers are sprouts that grow from lateral roots usually within 3 inches (8 centimeters) of the surface. Aspen stands produce these sprouts continuously, but in the shade of living trees, they are usually weak, short lived, and inconspicuous. Hormones produced in the growing tips of living trees inhibit the production of suckers, but when the tree is removed, the growth regulators go with it. With the shade gone, more heat and light reach the ground, and these further stimulate the roots to produce suckers. In dense stands of quaking aspen, over 20,000 suckers per acre have been counted one year after logging.

With a mature root system to provide water and stored food, the suckers have a considerable advantage over newly sprouted seedlings. On good sites suckers can reach a height of 4 feet (1.2 meter) at the end of their first full growing season.

110. Aspen suckers pioneer after a logging clearcut. *Jerry Sullivan.*

The Second-Growth Forest   257

Aspen's intolerance of shade means that only the fastest growing sprouts survive. Those that fall behind are shaded out and killed. An initial stem count of 12,000 an acre may be down to 900 after 10 years and 300 after 20 years. The demise of slower-growing stems produces a forest of remarkably even height.

About Clones

The sprouts growing from a single root system are of course genetically identical, so the group they form is called a clone. As the sprouts become trees, their root systems produce more sprouts, and as aspen generations succeed each other on a site, the clones can grow larger and larger. Most clones in the Lake States cover less than 0.2 acres (0.08 hectares), but some of the older ones occupy as much as 4 acres (1.6 hectares). In the Rockies, where competition from other species is not as great, clones covering 200 acres (80 hectares) have been found.

Root connections between individual stems in the clone may endure for a century, but even after they have been broken, the identical genetic makeup of the trees in the clone sets them apart from their neighbors. All the members of the clone produce the same kind of flowers, either staminate (male) or pistillate (female). In the Lake States, staminate trees are about three times as common as pistillate. Members of the same clone can be distinguished from unrelated trees by their leaf shape and color and particularly by the timing of the major events in their annual cycle. Flowering, the emergence of leaves, the autumn color change, and leaf fall occur simultaneously throughout the clone.

Associates and Understory Plants

Quaking aspen grows in a wide range of situations in the North Woods, from sandy, excessively drained soils to peats. Its common associates generally have narrower tolerances. Big-toothed aspen, another member of the genus

Populus, is most common in dry sandy soils, although it may occasionally be found in wet situations at the southern end of our region. Balsam poplar does best on low ground. It reaches a peak in size and abundance on the clay and silt loam soils that were once the bottom of glacial Lake Agassiz in northern Minnesota, and it is much less common in southern and eastern areas. It is the largest of the three North Woods poplars, frequently reaching a height of 85 feet (26 meters). The record height for the species is 118 feet (36 meters). Balsam poplars often live 100 years; many 200-year-old individuals have been found at the northern end of the species' range.

Both of these associates of quaking aspen produce root suckers, although they are not as prolific as their more abundant relative. Big-toothed aspens often sprout directly from stumps, and their root suckers generally grow closer to the parent tree. A big-toothed aspen sucker is usually less than 30 feet (9 meters) from its parent, while quaking aspens sometimes send up suckers 100 feet (30 meters) from the main stem.

The other trees found with quaking aspen include all the common species of the North Woods. Their presence and relative abundance depend on local soil conditions. Black ash, tamarack, white cedar, and other species adapted to wet conditions are likely to be found on peat. On sands and sandy loams, paper birch, the pines, red oak, and other species common to dry situations can be expected. Red maple is likely in both wet and dry circumstances. On clays the usual associates are balsam fir, white spruce, sugar maple, and cherries.

Aspen woods, with their sparse canopies, usually develop a rich understory, but there is nothing particularly distinctive about it, hence the end of this chapter lacks the usual key and plant descriptions. Some of the common species—beaked hazel, wild sarsaparilla, Canada Mayflower—are nearly ubiquitous. Others reveal something of the character of the site. Where aspens have invaded moist soils, speckled alder, red osier dogwood, and sensitive fern are common in the understory. On drier soils, typical pine-woods species like bracken, wintergreen, and sweet fern occur.

The Second-Growth Forest   259

Succession in the
Second-Growth Forest

The life cycle of most aspen woods begins with the disturbance that clears away the old forest. In the past, this disturbance was most commonly fire, although windthrow and
insect attack were also important. Today the disturbance is
usually logging. Fires destroy humus and expose mineral
soils. Seeds of various species that were buried in the
humus may survive the fire and sprout. Other seeds, such
as the aspens, arrive on the wind. Seed-eating animals—
white-footed mice, pine siskins—become more common.
The exposed soil dries out, but just below the surface, the
ground is actually wetter than it is under a forest cover, and
this moisture allows seeds to germinate.

A number of annuals are so specialized for postfire conditions that they are usually called fireweeds. In the North
Woods, the most common fireweed is the bright pink
flower whose scientific name is *Epilobium angustifolium*. In
the first year after a fire, the fireweeds may grow so thickly
that they shade out aspen seedlings and suckers. Later,
they become sparser and shorter, allowing the aspens to
become established.

Other common plants on recent burns are perennials of
the forest floor whose roots were buried deep enough to
allow them to survive the blaze. Various grasses, big-leaved
aster, sweet fern, wild sarsaparilla, bunchberry, and wintergreen are among the most common, along with shrubs
such as beaked hazel, bush honeysuckle, and red osier
dogwood. Bracken fern, whose rootstocks are often buried
10 inches (25 centimeters) deep, is particularly adapted to
surviving fire. Bracken can also get dense enough to shade
out aspen suckers. Forest floor plants that require shady
conditions usually decline after a fire opens things up.

Wind-borne colonizers such as aspen are usually distributed fairly evenly over a burn. Colonizers such as raspberries and blueberries whose seeds are carried in by animals
are usually found in scattered clumps. However, sometimes brambles—raspberries and blackberries—can grow
thickly enough to prevent aspen from surviving.

Early Growth Stages

Once the young aspens are established, they quickly begin replenishing the soil with an abundant leaf litter that is rich in nitrogen, phosphorus, potash, and calcium. With substantial amounts of sunlight penetrating the thin canopy, production in the ground layer is quite rich. Only about 1 percent of the biomass in an aspen wood is herbs, ferns, and low shrubs of the ground layer, but these plants are very important to the mineral cycle. About half of the leaf fall in the woods comes from these plants, and about 40 percent of the total litter. The remains of these ground-layer plants are quite rich in minerals, and they decompose rapidly, making their nutrients available to new generations.

In the darker mixed-hardwood forest ground-layer plants account for only about 10 percent of the total litter. The trend in woodlands is toward decreasing ground production and greater canopy production as succession proceeds. (When ground-layer plants are grown in full sun in greenhouses, biomass production goes way up. It is three times as much in the greenhouse as in the aspen woods; ten times more in full sun in the greenhouses than in the mixed-hardwood forest.)

Most of the biomass of the ground-layer plants is underground, and the imbalance is particularly pronounced on dry sites. In drought conditions, the larger roots can better support a small plant above the surface.

Almost all the vegetation growth in the ground layer takes place in the first half of the growing season, and within 50 days of the last frost the growing season is essentially over. Total production can vary by as much as half from year to year, depending on how often the sun shines, how much rain falls, and when the last frost of spring occurs. Stress in one area cuts a plant's ability to take advantage of abundance elsewhere. The sun shines more often during droughts, but without water plants can't use the sunlight.

A typical aspen stand may have 70 to 80 species of plants in the ground layer, but most of them will be uncommon, and only a few will be abundant. Something that harms one of the abundant species can reduce total production dramatically. For example, bracken ferns are very vulnerable to frost damage; so a late frost that ruins the bracken will have a very large effect on total production.

Decline of the Aspen Woods

Like most pioneers, the aspen creates conditions that prevent its own survival. Dependent on full sun for growth, it cannot produce a second generation in its own shade. In northern Wisconsin aspen stands mature in 40 to 60 years and begin to deteriorate soon after. Tent caterpillars may defoliate the trees. A disease called hypoxylon canker (after the genus of the fungus that causes it), which makes the bark look rough and scaly, weakens the trees and makes them vulnerable to windthrow. As some trees fall and the canopy begins to open up, the remaining trees become more vulnerable to wind damage. Aspens have no means of controlling moisture loss through the leaves, so as they become more exposed to wind they become more vulnerable to moisture stress. Within five years after maturity much of the stand may be gone. In Lower Michigan this process may occur within 30 years of the establishment of the stand.

What comes after the aspen depends primarily on three interacting factors: the quality of the site (soil type and moisture), the availability of seed, and competition between succeeding species. Succession proceeds very slowly on dry sites, and even 60 years may not be enough for other trees to become established under the aspen. Here, the aspen forest is replaced by scattered aspens surrounded by brambles and other shrubs.

The Forests that Follow

White pine is tolerant enough to grow under aspen, but a scarcity of seeds prevents it from doing so in many areas. Even where seed is available, young white pine may have difficulty due to competition from shrubs such as hazel or from bracken. On coarse, dry soil where pine seeds are unavailable, aspen is likely to be followed by red maple and red oak. On low, boggy sites, black ash, white cedar, American elm, balsam fir, and white spruce are common replacements. Where boreal forest is the climax vegetation, balsam fir and white spruce succeed.

Competition is most severe on rich well-drained soils where northern hardwoods are the likely replacements for aspens. Sugar maple is the most common successor in such situations, and it creates such a dense shade that it can reduce the success of yellow birch, basswood, white ash, and other hardwoods.

You can make a reasonable prediction about the future of an aspen stand by looking at the seedlings and saplings growing under the aspen canopy. These more tolerant trees are all likely to live longer than the aspen, and in time they will dominate the forest. This successional sequence can be reversed, of course, by another disturbance. Fires are much less common than they used to be, but aspen today is often maintained by cutting because of its value as pulpwood. Over half the total pulpwood cut in the North Woods is quaking aspen, and the rapid growth of the species makes it very attractive to managers of commercial woodlands. Of course, cutting the mature trees stimulates the growth of suckers and starts a new generation of aspen growing.

When a generation of aspen has been replaced by more tolerant trees, the roots continue to send up suckers, sometimes for as long as a century. In the shade, these suckers die quickly, but if some disturbance opens up the canopy, they can grow into the opening very quickly. Quaking aspen can maintain itself as a scattered forest tree in this way almost indefinitely.

Some foresters think that the long history of fire extending back thousands of years has produced a terminal dominance for quaking aspen on some sites. Here the root systems and suckers have become so dense that they prevent any other trees from becoming established. When the old quaking aspens on these sites die off, they are quickly replaced by a new generation without the need for any intervening disturbance.

CHAPTER FIFTEEN

Wetland Communities

Introduction

MILLIONS OF ACRES in the North Woods are wetlands of various kinds. In these low-lying areas, the groundwater table is at or near the surface throughout the year. In some, standing or slowly moving water is visible all year. In others, the water table may rise over the surface only in spring when snowmelt and heavy rains combine to create very wet conditions.

The height of the water table and the amount of water movement exert a considerable effect on the vegetation. The origin of the soil materials is also an important factor.

We will describe six distinctive types of wetlands in this chapter. They are lakes and marshes, alder thickets, open bogs, bog forests, swamp forests, and other peatland types.

Marshes are areas where the water table is usually above the surface. They may have substantial amounts of open water surrounded by vegetation that is rooted in the bottom. Marshes are likely to develop in slowly moving waters that carry mineral nutrients for plants. The movement also helps keep the water aerated, i.e., rich in dissolved oxygen.

Alder thickets are shrub communities that are most common along watercourses where in an average year the water table is above the surface only in spring. With the poorly developed drainage patterns of the North Woods, a slow-moving stream may meander in several ill-defined channels through a valley a half mile wide. Alder may cover the whole valley in such situations. A persistent alder thicket may also take over a black spruce forest after clear-cutting.

Bogs are most likely to occur in basins where drainage is poor or nonexistent. Bog vegetation forms a floating mat that gradually spreads over the surface of a lake or pond. In time, this vegetation may fill the basin completely as the floating mat becomes thick enough to reach to the bottom.

Forested wetlands can be divided into two types which we have named *bog forests* and *swamp forests*. Bog forests are dominated by black spruce and tamarack, and their understories have much in common with the vegetation of open bogs. Swamp forests are dominated by white cedar and black ash with balsam fir in the drier places, and their understories are much richer than those of bog forests. These swamp forests merge on drier sites with more mesic forests, either mixed hardwood or boreal.

The general pattern of succession in North Woods bogs is from open bog through bog forest to swamp forest. However, some interesting exceptions to this pattern have been found—particularly on the peatlands that now occupy the bed of glacial Lake Agassiz. These are described in the final section of this chapter on other peatland types.

LAKES AND MARSHES

A MARSH ON A WARM, sunny summer day is a lush place vibrant with life. Redwings gleam atop the cattails. Dragonflies hunt above the floating leaves of the lilies. Mallards and pied-billed grebes swim in the still waters. Some North Woods marshes occupy the beds of old glacial lakes. Others are found on the shores of present-day lakes or along the banks of slow-moving streams. (Often, in the lake districts of the North Woods, the distinction between a lake and a stream is rather hard to maintain. Some streams flow slowly through chains of lakes joined by narrow channels.)

Typical marsh plants grow on the edges of deep lakes and streams as well as in shallower bodies of water. They can be divided into two large groups: *emergent* plants that grow well above the surface of the water, and *floating* or *submerged* plants which either just break the surface or grow entirely under it. Both types are rooted in the bottom, which keeps them out of deeper waters and sets them apart from the floating algae of deeper lake waters and from the tiny duckweeds—the smallest of all flowering plants—that form a bright green scum on the surface of lakes and ponds.

Various rushes, reeds, and sedges grow along the shore in the shallowest waters. Slightly deeper water supports cattail, wild rice, bulrush, arrowhead, and pickerel weed. Beyond these, where the water is too deep for emergent plants, bullhead lily, pondweed, and naiad grow. Where the bottom drops off steeply from the shore, these floating species may be found growing right up to the edge of the water.

All the emergent plants reproduce by sending out rhizomes that produce new shoots. The clones form dense colonies that help keep the plants in place when winds and waves threaten them. These colonies also collect sediments that reduce the depth of the water even further.

Marsh plants grow in well-oxygenated waters where the bacteria of decay break down dead matter quickly. This releases minerals and makes them available to plants once again. The rapid cycling of materials through this system makes it very productive. Marshes produce large amounts of vegetation every year, providing food for a large number of animals. The high productivity of this ecosystem is a considerable contrast to the slow growth in bogs.

Key to Common Plants
of Lakes and Marshes

1. Plants emerging above the surface of water or on land at the shoreline

    2. Leaves alternate

        3. Leaves reduced to bladeless sheaths on stem—**Great bulrush**

        3. Leaves long, slender, sheathing stem

            4. Flowers large, violet or violet with yellow and white—**Blue flag**

            4. Tiny brown flowers in dense spikes—**Cattail**

        3. Leaves not sheathing stem

4. Flowers irregular, blue, in spike; upper and lower lips divided into 3 lobes—**Pickerel weed**

2. Leaves basal, lobed, like arrowheads with 2 long pointed lobes at base extending back toward the petioles; flowers white—**Arrowhead**

1. Rooted plants growing entirely submerged or with portions of the plant just breaking water surface

2. Leaves opposite, needle-like—**Naiad**

2. Leaves alternate

3. Flowers in spherical staminate and pistillate heads scattered along a branching stalk—**Bur reed**

3. Flowers in dense cylindrical spikes—**Pondweed**

Plant Descriptions

Great Bulrush, *Scirpus acutus.* This perennial sedge has an erect, round stem up to 10 ft (3 m) tall with the flowering and fruiting heads at the top. It looks leafless, but closer scrutiny reveals the sheaths. *Flowers and fruit:* Clusters of nearly sessile heads and heads on flattened stalks, 0.4–3.1 in. (1–8 cm) long. *Plant communities:* Emergent from lakes, ponds, and streams.

Larger Blue Flag, *Iris versicolor.* A perennial herb growing from a creeping rhizome. Blue flag has a single stem up to 32 in. (80 cm) tall, long narrow leaves that sheath the stem, and a single, large flower. *Leaves:* Up to 1.2 in. (3 cm) wide and 40 in. (1 m) long. Stiff, gray–green, ascending and arching. *Flowers:* Consist of 6 segments. The sepals are spread wide and up to 3 in. (8 cm) across. They have 3 concentric semicircles of color: a greenish yellow spot at the base, then white with purple veins, then purple around the margins. The margins may vary from dark purple to lavender and, rarely, to white. The 3 petals are erect and shorter than the sepals. May–Jul. *Plant communities:* Wet places generally, especially when open to the sun. Lakeshores, marshes, river borders, open bogs, ditches.

111. Blue flag, *Iris versicolor*. *Jerry Sullivan*.

Common Cattail, *Typha latifolia*. A perennial from a creeping rhizome that can form almost pure colonies of considerable extent. Its long, slender leaves sheath a stem 3–10 ft (1–3 m) tall. *Leaves:* Bluish or grayish green, up to 1 in. (2.5 cm) wide, taller than the stem. *Flowers and fruit:* The brownish flowers are on dense cylindrical spikes at the tip of the stem. The lower half of the spike has pistillate flowers, the upper half, staminate. In this species, the two halves generally touch; in others they do not. *Plant communities:* Marshes, lakeshores, open bogs, roadside ditches.

Pickerel Weed, *Pontederia cordata*. A perennial growing from a rhizome. Emerging from shallow water with a rosette of basal leaves, one stem leaf and flowers in the cluster at the tip of the stem. *Leaves:* Heart-shape, up to 7.1 in. (18 cm) long with long petioles. *Flowers:* Blue, in a spike. Individual flowers have upper and lower lips, each divided into 3 lobes. Stem below cluster closely sheathed by a

THE PRODUCERS

spathe, a specialized leaf, 1.2–2.4 in. (3–6 cm) long. Jul.–Aug. *Plant communities:* Emergent in lakes, ponds, rivers.

Arrowhead or **Duck Potato,** *Sagittaria latifolia.* A perennial herb growing from a rhizome. Grows in water with basal leaves emerging above surface and flowers on separate stalk. *Leaves:* Arrowhead shape with 2 long, pointed lobes extending downward from the juncture of the petiole and blade. 2–16 in. (5–40 cm) long. Lobes from one-half to longer than body of leaf. *Flowers:* In whorls, usually of 3, on stalk up to 4 ft (1.2 m) tall. 3 white petals, broadly egg-shape, 0.4–0.8 in. (1–2 cm) long. *Plant communities:* Lakes, ponds, marshes, streams.

Plants growing submerged or just breaking the surface of water.

Naiad, *Najas flexiles.* An annual herb. *Leaves:* Slender and needle-like, the edges with tiny thorns. The base of the leaf is dilated. Leaves often crowded and bushy, especially toward the tip of the stem. *Flowers:* Hidden in dilated leaf bases. *Plant communities:* Lakes and ponds.

Bur Reed, *Sparganium spp.* This genus includes both floating plants and erect plants growing in shallow water. *Leaves:* Flat, narrow, elongated, with parallel veins, sheathing at the base. *Flowers:* From leaf axils, a branching stalk with separate staminate and pistillate heads scattered along its length. Heads are spherical, the pistillate 0.8–1 in. (2–2.5 cm) in diameter. The dense heads are crowded with tiny flowers, the whole head looking enough like a cockle bur to give the genus its common name. *Plant communities:* Emergent or floating vegetation in lakes and ponds.

Pondweed, *Potamogeton gramineus.* There are either 30 or 37 species of the genus *Potamogeton* in the northeastern U.S., depending on which authority you consult. They all grow in water, producing submerged leaves. Where the stem reaches the surface, floating leaves, often of a different shape from the submerged, are produced. *P. gramineus* is a common species in the North Woods. *Leaves:* Submerged leaves sessile, slender, varying to a narrow egg-shape, 1.2–3.1 in. (3–8 cm) long with pointed tips. Floating leaves elliptic, 0.8–2 in. (2–5 cm) long, slender petiole often longer than the blade. Stipules about 0.8 in. (2 cm) long.

Flowers: In dense cylindrical spikes, 0.6–1.2 in. (1.5–3 cm) long. Growing on stalks thicker than the stems. *Plant communities:* Lakes and ponds.

ALDER THICKETS

THE YOUNG DRAINAGE SYSTEM of the North Woods includes broad, flat valleys where shallow water moves slowly across the entire valley floor. In such places, alder thickets may cover hundreds of acres. Most alder thickets, though, are narrow strips that occupy the low ground along streams and lakes or the courses of intermittent streams in woodlands.

Alder thickets are rather forbidding places. The dominant plant is the speckled alder—sometimes called the tag alder—a shrub that grows in clumps of ascending stems, commonly reaching a height of 10 to 15 feet (3 to 4.5 meters). The dense clumps are difficult to walk among, and the difficulty is increased by the soil under alders—likely to be a rich, deep muck that can swallow your leg to the knee.

112. The dense tangle of a typical streamside alder thicket. *Jerry Sullivan.*

THE PRODUCERS

Speckled alder is the most important shrub, but there are others present in varying numbers. Many of the herbs are tall, late-blooming plants that also grow in roadside ditches. Reclining plants like bedstraw are another feature that makes a stroll through an alder thicket an arduous undertaking.

Alders require moving water that is rich in both nutrients and oxygen, and they can endure indefinitely on a site that provides these. The alder that takes over a bog forest after a fire may be replaced by a new generation of trees.

Alders add to the fertility of the soils they are rooted in. Bacteria in their roots turn atmospheric nitrogen into a mineral form that is accessible to plants, adding as much as 5 grams of nitrogen to a square meter of topsoil every year.

Key to Common Plants of Alder Thickets

I.   Tall shrubs with alternate, toothed leaves

    1.   Teeth coarse; smooth brown bark dotted with white lenticels—**Speckled alder**

    1.   Teeth fine; twigs yellowish brown, white flowers in cluster like bunch of grapes—**Meadowsweet**

    1.   Leaf edges variable (toothed to entire); buds covered by a single scale—**Pussy willow**

II.   Herbs

    1.   Opposite leaves, erect plant; flowers asymmetrical with distinctive upper and lower lips in spike at tip of stem—**Turtlehead**

    1.   Alternate leaves

        2.   Sheathing stem; cluster of flowers at tip—**Bulrush**

        2.   Simple, toothed; tiny yellow flowers in terminal cluster—**Goldenrod**

        2.   Simple, entire, arrowhead-shape; stems prickly—**Tear thumb**

    1.   Leaves whorled—**Joe Pye weed**

Plant Descriptions

Shrubs

Speckled Alder, *Alnus rugosa.* A shrub up to 16 ft (5 m) tall, with ascending trunks usually growing in clumps. *Leaves:* Elliptic to egg-shape, broadest below the middle. Base rounded, tip blunt or pointed. Usually double-toothed. *Flowers and fruit:* Staminate catkins form in fall, come into bloom in early spring. Fruit is a cone-like strobile 0.4–0.6 in. (1–1.5 cm) long, either sessile or on a short, thick stalk. It remains on the plant after the leaves have fallen. *Bark and twigs:* Smooth, brown bark abundantly dotted with warty white lenticels. *Buds:* Stalked. *Plant communities:* Alder thickets, wet forests, boreal forest.

Meadowsweet, *Spirea alba.* An erect shrub up to 6 ft. (2 m) tall. *Leaves:* Lanceolate to oblong, 1.2–2.4 in. (3–6 cm) long, finely toothed. *Flowers and fruit:* Flower cluster shaped like a bunch of grapes. It is hairy. Flowers are white with 5 nearly circular petals and 0.2–0.3 in. (6–8 mm) across. Jun–Aug. *Stems:* Twigs yellowish brown. *Plant communities:* Alder thickets, other wet situations.

113. Speckled alder, *Alnus rugosa.*

THE PRODUCERS

114. Pussy willow, *Salix discolor*.

Pussy Willow, *Salix discolor*. This is just one of several willows—both trees and shrubs—that grow in our area. All willows have alternate, simple leaves—some toothed and some not—and buds covered by a single scale. Pussy willow may grow as a shrub or a small tree. *Leaves:* Elliptic or lanceolate with a pointed tip and rounded base. Edges are somewhat variable from toothed to nearly entire. Leaves are up to 4 in. (10 cm) long, dark green above and whitened beneath. They may be downy when first opening. *Flowers and fruit:* Flowers emerge before the leaves. The catkins are stout, sessile, cylindric and 1–4 in. (2–10 cm) long. The staminate catkins are the familiar parts of pussy willow. *Bark and twigs:* Reddish to dark brown. The youngest downy, but becoming smooth. *Plant communities:* Swamp forests, alder thickets, sometimes pine forests.

Herbs

Turtlehead, *Chelone glabra*. A tall perennial herb with an upright stem with the flowers growing at the top. *Leaves:* Narrow to nearly egg-shape, tapering to a point, toothed, sessile or on a short petiole. Up to 6 in. (15 cm) long. *Flowers:* White, growing in spikes. Upper lip arches over lower lip, giving turtlehead appearance. Upper lip is 2-lobed; lower is 3-lobed with the middle lobe hairy. Jul–Aug. *Plant communities:* Alder thickets, low meadows, lakeshores.

Bulrush, *Scirpus atrovirens.* A perennial that forms clumps. Stems up to 60 in. (1.5 m) tall with an umbrella-like panicle of flowers at the tip. *Leaves:* Up to 0.75 in. (18 mm) wide, mostly on lower half of the stem. *Flowers and fruit:* Inflorescence crowded with globular clusters of flowers. Green scales covering the flowers are elliptic or egg-shape with their tips prolonged into a point. Jun–Aug. *Plant communities:* Alder thickets, other wet situations.

Small-Flowered Goldenrod, *Solidago canadensis.* A perennial herb from a creeping rhizome. It has an erect stem with the flowers in a terminal panicle. The stems are smooth near the base and downy above. *Leaves:* Long, slender, sessile, tapering to a long point. Toothed or nearly entire, and thin. They are thickly crowded on the stem and have prominent veins paralleling the midrib on each side of the leaf. *Flowers:* In a panicle whose individual racemes curve outward until the tips turn back to the ground. The tiny yellow flowers grow only on the upper surface of the racemes. Aug–Sep. *Plant communities:* Alder thickets, fields.

Tearthumb, *Polygonum sagittatum.* Polygonum is a widespread common genus with about 30 species in our area. This species is erect when young but usually reclining on other plants. The stems are 4-sided, slender, densely covered with prickles that point downward. Nodes are swollen and covered with a sheath. *Leaves:* Lanceolate to elliptic, 0.8–4 in. (2–10 cm) long. Species name means 'arrow-shaped'. Leaves are narrow, pointed at the tip with 2 long rounded lobes extending back on either side of the point of attachment of the petiole to the blade. *Flowers and fruit:* Terminal and axillary racemes are short with long stalks. Tiny flowers are pink. Jul–Sep. *Plant communities:* Alder thickets and other wet situations.

Joe Pye Weed, *Eupatorium maculatum.* A perennial with an upright stem up to 8 ft (2 m) tall. Flowers grow in a terminal cluster. Stems are speckled or solid purple. *Leaves:* In whorls of 3–7. Lanceolate with short petioles,

sharply toothed, 2.4–5.3 in. (6–21 cm) long. *Flowers:*
Purple in a densely flowered, flat-topped corymb. Jul–Sep.
Plant communities: Alder thickets and ditches.

OPEN BOGS

VISIT A TYPICAL bog in a small lake basin. You will see a
level expanse of dull, dark gray–green. Look closer, and
the level surface breaks up into a rough pattern of hummocks and hollows with a cover of low straggling shrubs. A
narrow moat of open water may separate this surface from
the surrounding uplands. A small lake or pond may be visible somewhere around the middle of the bog. The whole
expanse may be treeless, or patches of forest may occupy
part of it. Sometimes trees—often stunted specimens less
than 10 feet (3 meters) tall—may be scattered over the bog.

A bog is a vivid example of how living things can change
a landscape. The transformation of a sand- or clay-bottom
lake into the sort of scene we have described is the work of a
group of specialized plants which are mostly confined to
bogs and adapted to the harsh conditions that exist there.

Bogs are most likely to develop in small shallow lakes
and ponds, or sometimes along very sluggish streams. Cold
northern lakes with little drainage are generally poor in
both nutrients and oxygen. Bog development tends to make
them even colder and poorer.

The first sign of the bog to come is the establishment of a
floating mat of plants creeping out from the lakeshore. A
number of plants may lead this invasion, but in the North
Woods the most common invaders are sedges, and the most
common sedge is *Carex lasiocarpa*. As far as we know it has
no common name, although the species name means 'hairy-
fruited.' *C. lasiocarpa* reproduces by sending out rhizomes.
New plants grow from the rhizomes, and all the interlock-
ing individuals form the mat.

The mat grows slowly. An inch a year is a typical rate,
and one good windstorm can deposit decades of accumulation on the shore. Windstorms can also detach the mat from
the shore, creating floating islands. The lack of heavy wave

action in small shallow lakes is another reason why these basins are good places for bog growth.

As the mat expands out over deeper water, it shades out the rooted plants such as pondweed that grow in the shallow waters next to the shore. Most of the sedge mat is under water. Only the vertical stems break the surface. As new growth is added above, the mat sinks and eventually extends all the way from the surface to lake bottom. The mat is now *grounded.*

Compressed beneath the weight of the growing layers above, the dead plant remains become peat, a partially decomposed mixture of dead plants that contains cellulose, waxes, resins, fats, proteins, and sugars, along with various other organic compounds. Its precise nature depends on what it is made of and what has happened to it since its plant constituents died. Where there is enough oxygen for decomposition to proceed, the dead plants can be broken down into muck, a black or dark brown granular substance. When cold water and a lack of oxygen seriously inhibit decay, the plant remains in peat may be well enough preserved to allow individual species to be identified. The pioneering sedge mat typically produces a stringy, matted, fibrous peat.

When the mat has been grounded, it can no longer rise and fall with changing water levels. If the water level falls and the top of the mat is above water for part of the growing season, *Carex lasiocarpa* dies out. Its usual replacement is a low shrub–moss community dominated by heaths and sphagnum moss. The low straggling or prostrate heath shrubs are sometimes seen at the very edge of the expanding floating mat. While they usually follow the sedges they are also sometimes the pioneers in bog development, and they may colonize logs lying in the water at the shoreline.

Large cranberry is among the first of the heaths to appear on the mat, followed by bog rosemary, small cranberry, pale laurel, and leatherleaf, the most common of these heaths. (Leatherleaf occurs in virtually every bog and is found in no other habitat.) Labrador tea, creeping snowberry, and late low blueberry are sometimes found on the mat, although they are more common in bog forests under the sparse canopies of black spruce or tamarack. Scattered patches of cotton grass are also common.

All of the heaths, except the blueberries, are evergreen, and they all show adaptations typical of plants growing in very dry conditions. Their leaves are slender, cutting down the ratio of surface to volume; they are thick and succulent and their surfaces are waxy and often hairy as well. It has been suggested that these traits are adaptations to a physiologically dry environment created by the ability of sphagnum—which appears in a bog at about the same time as heaths—to hold water so that it is unavailable to plant roots. However, their evergreenness may be the crucial adaptation. Bogs are very cold, nutrient-poor environments. Their location in basins makes them subject to midsummer frosts, and growing seasons tend to be quite short. Under these circumstances, it is an advantage for the heaths not to have to grow a whole new set of leaves every spring. The hairs and the tough skin may be further adaptations to help the evergreen leaves survive the desiccating winds of winter.

Sphagnum moss grows continuously, adding new leaves on top, dying away below. The long reclining stems with their thin, almost translucent leaves may be yellow, red, or green. Several different species grow in North Woods bogs, some specializing in forming hummocks, others occupying hollows.

Once sphagnum begins to grow, the process of bog formation is accelerated. The leaves and stems of this moss contain large, porous, hollow cells that take up and hold large amounts of water. A sphagnum bog is like a huge sponge; depending on the species, sphagnum can hold 10 to 20 times its weight in water. The moss can even raise the water table by growing upward and pulling the water along with it.

The cell walls of sphagnum absorb mineral bases while setting free hydrogen ions. This makes the surrounding waters extremely acid. The absorbed minerals are unavailable to other plants, and the extreme acidity hinders the absorption of such bases as are available. Many northern lakes are quite poor in minerals even without sphagnum, but the ability of this plant to lock up beyond the reach of plants such minerals as are present makes these waters even poorer. The moss cuts off oxygen, too, and bog waters are often totally lacking in this element just 8 inches (20 centimeters) below the surface.

Sphagnum forms a thick, insulating layer over the bog water. Bogs freeze late in winter, but they thaw quite late in spring and they stay very cold all summer. There is no permafrost in the North Woods, but isolated lenses of frozen peat have been dug up in northern Minnesota as late as the last half of August.

Finally, sphagnum is quite resistant to decay. In many bogs the entire rooting zone of the higher plants consists of infertile, raw sphagnum.

Bog waters are usually brown. They are in effect a weak tea colored by the plant remains soaking in them. Since so many rivers derive their waters in part from swamps and bogs, many North Woods streams are almost coffee colored. The softness of these waters creates globs of foam where streams flow over falls or rapids.

Carnivorous plants have evolved in the stingy environment of bogs, gaining from their insect food the elements, particularly nitrogen, that their roots cannot provide. On the moss–heath mat, the most common and conspicuous meat eater is the pitcher plant. Pitcher plants are passive trappers. Their leaves do not move to close around an insect. Instead, color and the scent of a sugary solution that fills the bottom of the cup-shape leaf attracts the unwitting bug. A fringe of downward pointing hairs inside the leaf prevents the prey from leaving, and eventually it falls into the fluid at the bottom of the leaf where digestive enzymes speed its decomposition. Once freed from the body of the insect, the various elements are absorbed by specialized cells in the leaf. The most important element is nitrogen; experiments with radioactively tagged nitrogen show that as much as 40 percent of this element in the roots of carnivorous plants is derived from captured insects.

The other carnivorous plants of the bog mat— bladderwort and sundew—are active trappers. They may be found on the moss–heath mat or in wetter, sedge–dominated conditions. Sundews have a basal rosette of tiny leaves covered with short sticky glands. The glands hold the prey while the leaves close around it. The bladders of bladderworts are elastic pouches growing under water. When the trap is set, the bladders are flat, and the entrance to the pouch is closed by a flap of cells. If something touches the

278 THE PRODUCERS

sensitive hairs around the entrance, the walls spring apart and water rushes in through the entrance, carrying the prey with it. Since the bladders are submerged, the plants often catch mosquito larvae and various tiny, aquatic invertebrates.

Succession in Open Bogs

The first trees to invade the bog may appear on either the floating or grounded parts of the mat. Tamarack and black spruce are the usual species. Both of these pioneers are intolerant of shade, although tamarack is the less tolerant of the two. They both have shallow, wide-spreading root systems. Tamarack, the only deciduous conifer in the North Woods, also has the ability—rare in conifers—to send up new shoots from the root systems of established trees.

Black spruce can reproduce vegetatively by layering. As the sphagnum layer deepens—by as much as 0.5 inch (1.3 centimeters) a year—it buries the lower branches of the spruce. These can then take root at their tips and produce new trees. Black spruce in bogs often grows in clumps, with a taller central tree surrounded by smaller stems produced by layering. Black spruce can also produce new sets of roots from the main trunk as the old roots are smothered by the growing moss.

Tall shrubs also invade the moss–heath mat, with bog birch, winterberry, and chokeberry among the common species. Speckled alder also appears, especially near the old lakeshore where runoff from the upland makes the peat soil of the bog slightly richer than it is nearer the center of the basin.

The process we have just described, the filling of a basin by a floating and eventually grounded mat of vegetation, may end with the establishment of a bog forest (the subject of the next section) of black spruce and tamarack, or it may continue into a swamp forest or even a mixed-hardwood forest. However, basin-filling is not the only bog process going on in the North Woods.

String Bogs

On peatlands where there is some water movement, *string bogs* can develop along a water track. String bogs were first discovered in Scandinavia and in the Canadian Arctic and were not known to exist as far south as the Lake States until quite recently. A string bog features a pattern of alternating ridges and hollows oriented at right angles to the direction of water movement. The ridges are chiefly sphagnum covered with shrubs such as bog birch, the heaths, red osier dogwood, and winterberry. Larger ridges may have black spruce or tamarack. Herbs include pitcher plant, larger blue flag, and sundew. The hollows—called *flarks*—are mainly sedges and reeds along with bladderwort. The hollows are usually wet, even in late summer, and only extremely dry conditions will eliminate standing water. Flarks also offer little support to passing humans. If you step on one, you can expect to sink to your shoulders.

String bogs are very well developed on the vast peatlands that now occupy the bed of glacial Lake Agassiz in northern Minnesota. They have also been discovered in the eastern Upper Peninsula and in Wisconsin as far south as Ozaukee County (just north of Milwaukee) where a string bog occupies part of a basin on the terminal moraine of the Valders glaciation. This one is far enough south to have poison sumac on its ridges.

The causes of string bogs are unknown, although frost action and the movement of peat downslope seem to be involved. Core samples of the peat under the string bogs indicate that they are very stable communities with no direction of succession indicated beyond their present conditions.

Key to Common Plants of Open Bogs

I. Tall Shrubs

    1. Tall shrub with alternate, simple toothed leaves—
       Bog birch

    1. Low straggling shrubs

2. Opposite leaves—**Pale laurel**

2. Alternate leaves

   3. Undersides of leaves covered with yellowish to rusty brown scales—**Leatherleaf**

   3. Undersides of long (1–1.5 in./2.5–3.8 cm) leaves covered when young with fine, dense white hairs, leaf edges rolled—**Bog rosemary**

   3. Tiny (0.375–0.625 in./9–16 mm) leaves pale or whitened below—**Cranberry**

II. Herbs

   1. Alternate leaves, stems topped by white bristles like cotton bolls—**Cottongrass**

   1. Basal leaves

      2. Leaves in shape of pitcher topped by a broad hood that partly covers mouth; prominent purple veins—**Pitcher plant**

      2. Leaves tiny, bristly, dotted with drops of clear sticky fluid—**Sundew**

      2. Leaves heart-shape; flowers white with tall central spike—**Water arum**

Plant Descriptions

Tall Shrubs

Bog Birch, *Betula pumila* var. *pumila* and *B. pumila* var. *glandulifera* (Fernald); *B. pumila* and *B. glandulifera* var. *glandulifera* (B&B). The two authorities disagree here. We follow Fernald because his treatment is simpler. Bog birch is an erect, branching shrub up to 9 ft (3 m) tall. Prostrate or matted forms exist but are found north of our region or in mountainous areas. *Leaves:* Thin, soft, translucent and pliable, pale green to whitish below with large teeth. They are egg-shape to circular or kidney-shape and 0.4–1.6 in. (1–4 cm) long. In var. *pumila,* the lower surfaces are without glands and are usually downy. In var. *glandulifera,* lower surfaces are glandular, warty, and usually hairless. *Flowers and fruit:* Staminate flowers are catkins; pistillate strobiles are erect and sessile. *Bark:* Smooth, brown, dotted with white, warty glands. Branchlets and shoots downy. A variety with hairless twigs grows in northern Indiana and southern Michigan. *Plant communities:* Open bogs, bog forest.

Low straggling shrubs lacking erect stems of any length

Pale Laurel, *Kalmia polifolia.* A sparingly branched, straggling shrub usually less than 3 ft (1 m) tall. *Leaves:* Nearly sessile, leathery, slender or lanceolate, 0.4–1.2 in. (1–3 cm) long, tips blunt. Edges usually curled under, the lower side whitened with fine downy hairs. *Flowers and fruit:* The rose purple to pink flowers have 5 lobes, grow in terminal corymbs on stalks 0.4–1.2 in. (1–3 cm) long. May–Jul. *Plant communities:* Open bogs, bog forest.

Leatherleaf, *Chamaedaphne calyculata.* A low, much-branched shrub up to 4.5 ft (1.5 m) tall. *Leaves:* Petioles 0.1 in. (1–3 mm) long. Blades oblong or elliptic, rarely egg-shape with the broad end toward the tip, 0.6–2 in. (1.5–5 cm) long, leathery; lower surface covered with rusty brown scales. *Flowers and fruit:* White, nodding, bell-like flowers with the corolla divided into 5 lobes. Corolla is narrowed at the throat. Apr–Jun. *Plant communities:* Open bogs, bog forest.

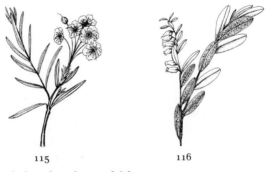

115   116

115. Pale laurel, *Kalmia polifolia.*

116. Leatherleaf, *Chamaedaphne calyculata.*

117. Bog rosemary, *Andromeda glaucophylla*.

Bog Rosemary, *Andromeda glaucophylla*. A low shrub with a creeping base and ascending stems. *Leaves:* Evergreen, linear to narrowly elliptic, 0.8–2 in. (2–5 cm) long, leathery, the edges curled under. Whitened beneath when young by dense, fine white hairs. *Flowers and fruit:* White or pink flowers are bell-shape with 5 lobes either spreading or curved back toward the base, 0.2–.3 inch (5–6 mm) long. In small umbels. May–Jun. *Plant communities:* Open bogs, bog forest.

Small Cranberry, *Vaccinium oxycoccus*. Creeping shrub with ascending, slender branches. *Leaves:* Egg-shape to elliptic with pointed tips and rolled edges. 0.1–0.3 in. (3–8 mm) long, pale and whitened beneath. *Flowers and fruit:* Pink flowers with 4 recurved lobes and protruding stamens. They grow in clusters of 1–4 on long stalks from the axils of upper leaves. Jun–Aug. Pale speckled berries become red when ripe. Sep–Oct. *Plant communities:* Open bogs, bog forest.

Large Cranberry, *Vaccinium macrocarpon*. A creeping shrub with a long, intricately forking stem and ascending branches. The commercial cranberry is this species.

118. Large cranberry, *Vaccinium macrocarpon*.

Leaves: Evergreen, nearly sessile, leathery, elliptic to oblong, rounded or blunt at the tip, flat or slightly down-
curved at edges, 0.2–0.7 in. (6–17 mm) long. Pale or
slightly whitened beneath. *Flowers and fruit:* Pale pink
flowers with 4 petal-like lobes curving back toward the base
grow on long stalks in the lower leaf axils. Stamens protrude
from the center of the flower. Stalks have 2 green bracts
above the middle. Jun–Jul. Berries, Aug–Sep. *Plant communities:* Open bogs.

Herbs

Cottongrasses, *Eriophorum* spp. These sedges are
topped by white bristles that could be taken for cotton bolls
at a distance. *Plant communities:* Open bogs, bog forest,
ditches. The three common species are:

Eriophorum spissum. Forms clumps of erect stems 8–27
in. (20–70 cm) tall with 1–2 dilated leafless sheaths. *Leaves:*
Blades are very thin and threadlike, growing from clumps
at base of stem. *Flowers and fruit:* Bristles at the tip of the
stem are the perianths of the flowers. Jun–Aug.

119. Cottongrass, *Eriophorum spissum. Jerry Sullivan.*

THE PRODUCERS

E. angustifolium. Stems solitary or in clumps, sturdy, up to 30 in. (80 cm) tall. *Leaves:* Principal blades up to 0.2 in (5 mm) wide. They are folded together, especially above the middle. Edges of leaves rough to the touch. *Flowers and fruit:* 2–10 spikelets on ascending spreading or drooping stalks. Jun–Jul.

E. virginicum. Stems solitary or a few together. Up to 40 in. (1 m) tall. *Leaves:* Blades flat, elongated, 0.1–0.2 in (2–4 mm) wide, firm. The uppermost leaves have tight sheaths. *Flowers and fruit:* Dense cluster of tawny or copper-colored bristles. Narrow bracts ascend from the base of the cluster and grow up well beyond the bristles. Aug–Sep.

Pitcher Plant, *Sarracenia purpurea.* A perennial, insectivorous plant. *Leaves:* Pitcher-shape and topped by a broad hood that partly covers the pitcher. Hollow inside partly filled with clear liquid. Leaves covered with prominent purple veins. *Flowers and fruit:* Dark red with 5 petals, nodding, 2–2.8 in. (5–7 cm) across, growing on a stalk 11.8–19.7 in. (30–50 cm) tall. Jun–Jul. *Plant communities:* Open bogs, bog forest.

Round-leaved Sundew, *Drosera rotundifolia.* One of two species of this insectivorous herb found in our region. *Leaves:* Tiny, petioles 0.6–2 in. (1.5–5 cm) long, blades 0.2–0.4 in. (4–10 mm) long. Nearly round. Both petioles and leaves are hairy, bristly and glandular. Glands exude a

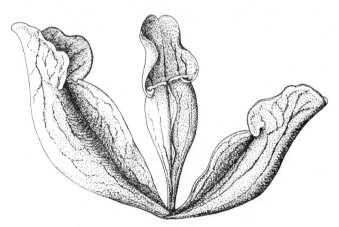

120. Pitcher plant, *Sarrecenia purpurea.*

clear, sticky fluid. *Flowers:* 3–15 in a one-sided raceme on a smooth stalk 2.8–13.8 in. (7–35 cm) tall. The stalk nods at the top. Flowers have five petals and are white or rarely pink to red. Jun–Aug. *Plant communities:* Open bogs.

Wild Calla or **Water Arum,** *Calla palustris.* A perennial from a creeping rhizome, the plant usually grows in water. *Leaves:* Long-petioled, heart-shape 2–4 in. (5–10 cm) long. *Flowers and fruit:* Stalk is 4–12 in. (10–30 cm) tall. It bears a broad, white, leaflike spathe tipped by an elongated point. The golden yellow spike-like spadix is cylindrical and 0.6–1 in. (1.5–2.5 cm) tall. Berries are red. *Plant communities:* Open bogs, openings in bog forest.

THE BOG FOREST

Key Trees: Black spruce, tamarack.

The bog forest comes creeping into the open bog. Its trees are scattered and small at first, but in time they may form a solid stand. The spruces are tall and slender and on windy days they bend in the breeze in shallow arcs. The ground is hummocky and green with moss.

This is a pioneering forest that grows on the grounded mat of open bogs. The change from bog to forest is slow and gradual. The invading trees are unlikely to advance faster than the floating mat of the open bog. The soils of this forest are similar in nutrient content to open bogs. Many of the understory plants of this community are common on moss–heath mats, too. Others are more at home in the richer swamp forests. Plants such as gold thread, bunchberry, and starflower under black spruce or tamarack generally indicate a somewhat richer soil than pitcher plant, cotton grass, or leatherleaf.

Both major trees of this forest are pioneers, with tamarack showing less shade tolerance than black spruce. They both show special adaptations for growing on a deepening sphagnum mat. These include the ability to produce new sets of roots from the trunk as old sets get buried too deeply, and the ability to produce new trees by lay-

THE PRODUCERS

ering. When the tips of low branches touch the mat, they sprout roots and eventually establish themselves as independent.

Both trees have very shallow root systems which make them vulnerable to windthrow, although the roots of tamarack may spread wider than the height of the tree. The deciduous needles of tamarack begin to emerge while the ground is still frozen and take four to six weeks to develop completely. In autumn, they turn a rich gold before dropping off. This tree grows very rapidly on good sites. It is very sensitive to fire damage. It is also heavily damaged by infestations of the larch sawfly, an imported pest that defoliates the trees.

Like other trees whose ranges are mainly in boreal regions, tamarack and black spruce grow larger and live longer in Minnesota and northwestern Wisconsin, closer to the heart of their ranges. They are smallest and shortest lived at the southeastern extremes. Black spruce may grow 60 to 80 feet (20 to 25 meters) tall on good sites, but on very poor ground, trees 80 to 100 years old may be only 6 feet (2 meters) high. Such stunted trees are common on muskegs, very infertile places where the soil is mostly raw sphagnum. The small trees here are widely scattered amidst a ground layer of moss–heath plants. Muskegs may indicate an early stage of bog forest.

On better sites, black spruce produces a denser shade than tamarack, and since its needles stay on the tree year-round, little early spring sunshine reaches the floor to stimulate understory growth. Black spruce cones are usually concentrated at the very tip of the tree, and their seeds are shed gradually throughout the year. These characteristics make fire a real benefit to the species. With the cones beyond the reach of ground fires and a constant reservoir of seeds, black spruce is able to colonize a burn quickly and abundantly. Frequent fires will gradually eliminate tamarack from a bog forest. Even-aged stands of black spruce are likely to have originated from fires.

Fire, often a stimulant to the process of succession from bog to bog forest, can only occur in bogs after the vegetation is grounded. Since the mat can no longer rise and fall with changing water levels, the peat soil may be left high and dry during droughts or when an outlet stream has cut

121. A Minnesota black spruce stand with typical mossy floor and lack of shrubs and herbs in understory. *U.S. Forest Service.*

its channel deep enough to lower the water in the basin. Peat is quite flammable, and severe fires may burn down to the waterline.

By destroying the dead plant remains, fire frees the minerals held in them and enriches the soil. Even without fire, oxidation of the peat will proceed with exposure to the air. If water levels stay low long enough, the topsoil may be converted from raw sphagnum to muck. This enrichment of the soil may go far enough for alders to invade, and their nitrogen-fixing ability can carry the process to the point where white cedar will appear and produce a swamp forest.

Sometimes water levels rise high enough above the peat to kill the trees. This can happen in very wet years, or as a result of beaver dams blocking outlet streams. Many bogs have a ring of dead trees at their edges. In others, the grounded mat is treeless moss–heath, and the only trees visible are on the floating mat near the center of the bog.

Where the peat soil is rich enough to provide good growing conditions for black spruce, and the trees are large and dense enough to shade the ground well, the ground cover may be mostly mosses of various kinds. Both shrubs and herbs are scattered, sparse, or absent in these communities, and the mosses may cover every bit of ground between the trees. This kind of black spruce–moss community also occurs on mineral soils on upland sites in northeastern Minnesota. Even boulders may be completely carpeted with moss in these communities.

These black spruce–moss communities are generally on acid peats with a pH below 4.0. When conditions are more alkaline—pH above 4.5—a richer community that includes speckled alder and red osier dogwood is common.

Both heaths and orchids are common families in open bogs and in bog and swamp forests. The two families have some similarities. Both produce very tiny seeds that are little more than embryos. Both depend on fungi which infect either the roots or the entire plant to supply the food needed for germination. The fungi supply carbohydrates which in most higher plants are stored in the seed. This is a reversal of the usual situation in which mycorrhizal fungi aid in absorption of minerals from the soil and receive carbohydrates from the plant. Both heaths and orchids produce beautiful, elaborate flowers and depend on insects for pollination.

The pines are generally a minor component of bog forests. White pine occurs as scattered, usually stunted, individuals. Jack pines, while absent from most bogs, are sometimes numerous enough to be the most common dominant. These bog jack pines are a southern extension of a community that is fairly common in the boreal forests of Ontario, where jack pine often grows on poorly drained flats.

White cedar sometimes invades the black spruce or tamarack forest, establishing itself on fallen logs or other microhabitats that are drier and richer than most of the bog soil. As a tolerant tree, it can grow in the shade of spruce or tamarack. Vegetative reproduction by layering allows it to spread until it forms dense, shady clumps too dark to allow the intolerant pioneers to grow. This kind of succession occurs throughout the North Woods, although it is probably more common in Lower Michigan or on soils derived from limestone than elsewhere.

White cedar is a more demanding tree than black spruce or tamarack. Tests in white cedar swamps in Wisconsin showed soils had eight times the calcium, almost five times the magnesium, and more than twice the potassium and phosphorus of soils in black spruce–tamarack stands. They also had higher pH readings, better aeration, and much less water-retaining capacity. A cedar swamp is a generally richer environment than a bog forest, and we will describe it in the next section.

Key to Common Plants of the Bog Forest

I.   Shrubs

   1.   Tall shrubs with alternate leaves

      2.   Compound leaves, leaflets without teeth—**Poison sumac**

      2.   Simple leaves, toothed; fruits are red berries scattered along twigs in leaf axils—**Northern holly**

   1.   Low shrubs with alternate leaves, simple, densely hairy below—**Labrador tea**

II. Herbs

   1.   Alternate simple leaves, entire

      2.   Plant creeping or prostrate—**Creeping snowberry**

      2.   Plant erect

         3.   3–8 regular flowers in raceme—**Three–leaved false Solomon's seal**

         3.   Irregular flowers in spike—**Tall northern bog orchid**

   1.   Basal leaves, simple, entire, flowers in a raceme, lower petal elongated—**Blunt-leaved orchid**

Plant Descriptions

Poison Sumac, *Rhus vernix.* A shrub or small tree up to 16 ft (5 m) tall. All parts of this plant contain a poisonous substance that causes intense skin irritation. Do not touch! *Leaves:* 7–13 oblong or elliptic pointed leaflets with tooth-less edges. *Flowers and fruit:* Tiny greenish yellow flowers with 5 petals growing in panicles from the axils of leaves. May–Jul. Fruit a cluster of ivory–white berries. Aug. Fruit may remain on plant through winter. *Bark:* Smooth, thin; gray–brown with lenticels. *Plant communities:* Bog forest, swamp forest. This is a southern species that is thankfully absent from most of our area. However, it is common at the edges of relict bogs in southeastern Minnesota. In southern Wisconsin we have seen it as far north as Ozaukee County, and it has been reported from north of there. In Lower Michigan it has been collected as far north as Grand Traverse County.

Northern Holly or **Winterberry**, *Ilex verticillata.* Usu-ally shrubby, may sometimes grow as a small tree up to 16 ft (5 m) tall. *Leaves:* varying from lanceolate to nearly circular. Dull above, may be downy below. *Flowers and fruit:* Staminate flowers in dense clusters. Pistillate usually solit-ary in leaf axils are white with 6–8 petals. The lobes of the calyx are fringed with hairs. May–Jun. Berries are red, scattered along twigs. Sep. *Bark and twigs:* Smooth, brown, dotted with lenticels. *Plant communities:* Bog forest, swamp forest.

Labrador Tea, *Ledum groenlandicum.* A low, diffuse, freely branching shrub up to 3 ft (1 m) tall. *Leaves:* Ever-green and sessile or nearly so. Lanceolate to narrowly ellip-tic, 0.8–2 in. (2–5 cm) long. Leaf edges rolled under. Smooth above, densely hairy—with brown or white hairs—beneath. Thick and succulent, stiff and leathery. *Flowers and fruit:* White flowers with 5 petals in a dense terminal raceme. May–Jul. *Plant communities:* Open bogs, bog forest.

122. Labrador tea, *Ledum groenlandicum.*

123. Sphagnum moss and bunchberry with Labrador tea in background—typical bog forest ground cover, Wisconsin. *Glenda Daniel.*

Creeping Snowberry, *Gaultheria hispidula.* A creeping, trailing, matted, leafy stem that is bristly when young. *Leaves:* Evergreen, short-petioled, broadly elliptic to nearly round, 0.2–0.4 in. (5–10 mm) long, smooth above, sparsely bristly below. *Flowers and fruit:* White, tiny bell-shape flowers have a corolla with 4 rounded lobes. They are solitary in leaf axils on curving stalks. May–Jun. Fruit is a white berry 0.2–0.4 in. (5–10 mm) in diameter. *Plant communities:* Open bogs, bog forest, swamp forest.

Three-Leaved False Solomon's Seal, *Smilacina trifolia.* An erect plant 4–10 in. (10–40 cm) tall that grows from a creeping rhizome. *Leaves:* Sessile, 2–4 leaves on stem. Oval to oblong or lanceolate, 2.4–4.7 in. (6–12 cm) long, tapering to a sharp point, ascending. *Flowers and fruit:* 3–8 white, 6-lobed flowers on a long-stalked raceme. May–Jul. Fruit is a dark red berry. *Plant communities:* Open bog, bog forest.

Tall Northern Bog Orchid, *Habenaria hyperborea.* A perennial from tuberous, thickened roots. A single leafy stem up to 16 in. (40 cm) tall topped by a many-flowered spike. *Leaves:* Lowest leaf bladeless. Main foliage leaves lanceolate up to 4 in. (10 cm) long. Upper leaves smaller and passing gradually into the bracts of the flower cluster. *Flowers:* Erect or ascending, greenish white or green. Lip is egg-shape or lanceolate, up to 0.3 in. (7 mm) long, gradually and uniformly widening toward the base. Petals are lanceolate and directed forward and incurved under the upper sepal. The spur is as long as the lip. Jun–Aug. *Plant communities:* Open bogs, bog forest, various other wet situations such as beach pools, ditches.

Blunt-Leaved Orchid, *Habenaria obtusata.* A perennial growing from a rhizome, the plant has a single leaf and a flower stalk up to 16 in. (40 cm) tall. *Leaves:* Egg-shape with a broad part near the tip tapering gradually to a slender, almost petiole-like base. Up to 5 in. (12 cm) long. *Flowers:* Raceme has a few greenish white flowers on short stalks. The lip is bent downward, 0.2–0.4 in. (5–9 mm) long, lanceolate. Upper sepal rounded, arching as a hood over the flower. 2 oblong lateral sepals curving backward. 2 upper petals ascending, narrow. Jun–Aug. *Plant communities:* Wet situations of various kinds.

THE SWAMP FOREST

KEY TREES: White cedar, balsam fir, black ash, hemlock, yellow birch, red maple, paper birch.

Cedar swamps are dark and tangled places where the branches on fallen trunks become young trees themselves. The ground is spongy and mossy, and on spring days, the goldthreads are almost as abundant as the mosquitoes.

Swamp forests dominated by white cedar grow on the richest peatlands as well as on moist mineral soils. The water table is usually below the surface except in spring, although pools of water may remain in low spots through the year. Some likely locations are at the edge of a peat-

124. Mossy ground cover in a Minnesota cedar swamp. *Glenda Daniel.*

filled basin where runoff from mineral soils delivers nutrients to the peat, in small bog basins where cedar may succeed tamarack or black spruce, or along sluggish streams.

Trees of the Swamp Forest

White cedar grows in dense clumps that produce enough shade to prevent the growth of most other plants. The other trees and the shrubs of this forest are often scattered between the clumps of cedar. The shallowly rooted cedars are subject to windthrow. Downed logs make cedar swamps into impossible tangles that can only be walked through slowly and circuitously. The branches on the upper side of fallen trunks keep growing, and new roots grow down from the trunk below. With the decomposition/burial of the old log, the old tree becomes several young trees. The whole process can be repeated. Young cedar trees may represent the growth of a seedling that sprouted hundreds of years ago.

The shade-tolerant balsam fir is a common associate of white cedar, usually on the drier sites in the forest. Black ash is usually the first hardwood to invade. Its seedlings and saplings are shade–tolerant. Deer browse it heavily, but once it gets beyond their reach it grows rapidly. A forest with a large black ash population is much different from the cedar swamp which preceded it. Instead of gloom, the spring sunshine covers the ground. Black ashes leaf out quite late, so spring bloomers like marsh marigold thrive under them. Tall shrubs are also abundant.

Red maple generally favors drier places than the black ash, and yellow birch and hemlock show a transitional situation where conditions are almost like those in the mixed-hardwood forest.

White cedar also grows on uplands, especially where soils are rich in calcium. There is evidence that these upland trees are a different ecotype than the swamp cedars. An ecotype is a variety that is precisely adapted to a narrower range of conditions than the species as a whole. If the separation between upland and lowland cedars is complete enough and continues long enough, the two could develop into separate species.

Upland cedar stands show some similarity to the swamps. Balsam fir is a common tree in both. Paper birch is present in swamp forests but much more common on the upland. But there are many differences. The understory lacks alder on the upland stands, for instance. American yew is fairly common in upland cedars in northeastern Minnesota. Farther south it is a shrub of the mixed-hardwood forest.

The ground layer in swamp forests shows a considerable similarity to the boreal forest. Plants such as goldthread, twinflower, fragrant bedstraw, and bush honeysuckle are common in both communities. There are more ferns of more different species than in any other North Woods community.

Cedar swamps are favorite winter yarding places for deer. Whitetails show a strong taste preference for cedar leaves over other kinds of winter browse. They often yard up in large numbers late in the season, especially when snows are deep. In these numbers, deer can affect the state of the vegetation. Their preference for young cedars cuts down on reproduction of cedar and favors balsam fir, which deer find unpalatable, and their hooves trample the ground enough to eliminate some herbs.

Key to Common Plants of the Swamp Forest

I. Shrubs

    1. Tall shrubs with opposite simple leaves; leaf edges entire—**Red osier dogwood**

    1. Tall shrubs with alternate simple leaves, toothed; fruit, red berries scattered along twigs in leaf axils—**Northern holly** (for description see Bog Forest)

    1. Low straggling or ascending shrubs

        2. Opposite simple leaves without teeth—**Swamp fly honeysuckle**

        2. Alternate leaves divided into three leaflets—**Dwarf Raspberry**

II. Herbs

    1. Alternate simple leaves, toothed; flowers yellow with 5–9 bright yellow petal-like sepals—**Marsh marigold**

    1. Basal leaves

        2. Simple, toothed

            3. Leaves hairy; flowers greenish—**Naked mitre-wort**

            3. Flowers with five purple petals—**Marsh blue violet**

        2. Compound leaves; flowers on separate stalk—**Goldthread**

III. Ferns—**Sensitive fern**

THE PRODUCERS

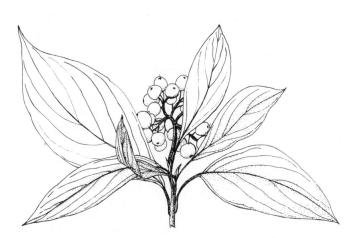

125. Red osier dogwood, *Cornus stolonifera*.

Plant Descriptions

Shrubs

Red Osier Dogwood, *Cornus stolonifera*. This shrub spreads by stolons, forming dense thickets of upright stems up to 10 ft (3 m) tall, but usually much shorter. *Leaves:* Lanceolate to egg-shape 2–4 in. (5–10 cm) long, tapering to a point. Whitened beneath. 5–7 pairs of veins branching from the midrib and curving parallel to the edge of the leaf. *Flowers and fruit:* A flat-topped cyme, dense with tiny white flowers with 4 petals. Flower stalks may be hairy or smooth. Fruit a cluster of white or lead-colored berries. Flowers, Jun–Jul. Fruit, Aug–Sep. *Bark and twigs:* Young branches deep red, becoming pale green. *Plant communities:* Bog forest, swamp forest, alder thickets.

Swamp Fly Honeysuckle, *Lonicera oblongifolia*. A shrub up to 6 ft (2 m) tall with ascending branches. *Leaves:* Oblong, 1.2–2.8 in. (3–7 cm) long, downy beneath, and, when young, above. Petioles short. *Flowers and fruit:* In pairs from leaf axils. Flowers yellow with a tubular corolla, downy, broad upper lip with 4 lobes, and a lower lobe pointing downward. Jun–Jul. The berries are orange to red. *Plant communities:* Swamp forest, mixed-hardwood forest.

Dwarf Raspberry, *Rubus pubescens.* Horizontal stems at or near the surface give rise to short, vertical stems 8–20 in. (20–50 cm) tall. The vertical stems are not woody and they are not armed with prickles, although they may occasionally have a few bristles. *Leaves:* Divided into 3 leaflets 2–3 in. (4–8 cm) long, roughly egg-shape with the narrow end at the base. Leaflets taper to sharp points. Edges tend to be smooth at the base and coarsely toothed above. Petioles are rather long and at their bases are pairs of narrow, blunt-pointed stipules. *Flowers and fruit:* Flower stalks arising from the tips of branches—or occasionally from the axils of leaves—hold 1–3 flowers. Flowers are white with 5 petals and only 0.4 in. (1 cm) across. May–Jul. Red fruits are tiny and edible, but not very tasty. Jul–Aug. *Plant communities:* Swamp forest, boreal forest.

Herbs

Marsh Marigold, *Caltha palustris.* A low perennial that forms clumps. Stems may be erect or spreading. They are

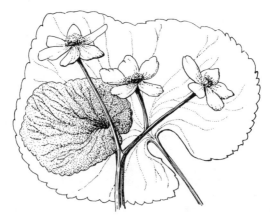

126. Marsh marigold, *Caltha palustris.*

THE PRODUCERS

thick and hollow. *Leaves:* Round or kidney-shape. Lower leaves are on long petioles. Petioles become shorter toward the top. *Flowers:* Bright yellow with 5–9 petal-like sepals. *Flowers* 1–1.5 in. (2.5–3.8 cm) across. The sepals are elliptic to egg-shape with the broad end toward the tip. May–Jul. *Plant communities:* Swamp forest, alder thickets, along streams, in roadside ditches.

Naked Mitrewort, *Mitella nuda.* A perennial herb from a rhizome, the plant spreads by creeping stolons. *Leaves:* Basal or alternate on rhizomes or stolons, heart-shape to nearly circular or kidney-shape, coarsely or doubly toothed. Leaf on the flower stalk—if present—egg-shape, sessile, few-toothed. *Flowers:* Greenish petals divided into a fringe. Sepals 5-lobed. Flowers 0.3–0.4 in. (7–11 mm) wide, in racemes. Flower stalk hairy, glandular. May–Jun. *Plant communities:* Swamp forest, boreal forest, mixed-hardwood forest.

Marsh Blue Violet, *Viola cucullata.* A perennial from a rhizome, the plant is low with the flowers on stalks taller than the leaves. Forms clumps. *Leaves:* Ovate or kidney-shape, pointed and toothed. *Flowers:* Violet. Darker toward center. On long stalks, sepals narrow, lanceolate. 2 lateral petals covered with hairs tipped with knobs. May–Jun. *Plant communities:* Swamp forest, mixed-hardwood forest.

Goldthread, *Coptis groenlandica* or *C. trifolia.* A low perennial growing from slender, yellow rhizomes that give the plant its common name. *Leaves:* Evergreen, lustrous. 3 leaflets are egg-shape, sharply toothed and sometimes shallowly lobed. Petioles are long and slender. *Flowers:* White with 5 petal-like sepals growing on a stalk 3–5 in. (7–13 cm) tall. May–Jul. *Plant communities:* Swamp forest, boreal forest.

Ferns

Sensitive Fern, *Onoclea sensibilis.* Scattered sterile fronds rise from a creeping rootstock, arching upward and backward. Highly modified fertile leaves on separate upright stalks look like clusters of small brown beads. Fertile leaves persist through the winter. Sterile leaves die at first frost. *Stipe:* Longer than frond; straw yellow; smooth except for a few scales at the base. *Leaves:* Sterile leaves up to 14 in. (35 cm) long and 16 in. (40 cm) wide are divided into 8–12 pairs of leaflets. Leaflets are oblong to lanceolate with pointed tips. Edges may be entire or slightly lobed. The longest leaflets are at or near the base and the leaf tapers to a point. The midrib is flanked by a broad wing near the tip, the wing becoming narrower toward the base. On the underside, veins and midrib bear scattered hairs. *Spores:* Fertile fronds are actually leaves whose leaflets are rolled into tight balls. *Plant communities:* Swamp forest, alder thickets.

SOME OTHER PEATLAND TYPES

THE SUCCESSION PATTERN we have described in the last three sections (from open bog to bog forest to swamp forest) is happening in basins all over the North Woods. But it doesn't always happen this way. The biggest exception to the pattern is the peatland that covers much of the bed of glacial Lake Agassiz. Here complex changes in the vegetation sometimes create a direct reversal of this pattern.

When the lake drained away 7000 to 8000 years ago it left a plain dotted with shallow depressions. The plain was mostly clay, although sandy spots existed. The slope of the plain, gradual but definite, was toward the north.

Prairie probably advanced over the western part of this plain during a warm dry period following the glaciers, but the modern vegetation seems to have been present by 4000 years ago. The depressions were filling in with sedges, and the slightly drier ground around them was forested with tamarack—and other species—whose growth rings show that they were growing on fertile sites. Then the bog plants began to spread from the basins onto the uplands.

This process, the spread of bog plants onto drier ground, is called *paludification*. It is going on now. It has been seen in black spruce stands on podzolic soils with the mottled subsoil layer that indicates poor drainage. Sphagnum moss is scattered under the spruces, but when cutting opens a part of the woods to the sun, sphagnum begins to spread. In one stand, the water table was 2.5 feet (76 centimeters) below the surface, but the sphagnum stayed moist and spongy because of its tremendous water-holding capacity. Puddles can stand on the surface of the moss when lower spots nearby are dry. Within ten years of logging, the moss may be 2 to 4 inches (5 to 10 centimeters) thick on the ground and on the slash left by the loggers.

As sphagnum deepened in the Agassiz basin, the water table rose with it. Streams flowing north cut into the thickening peat and clay below it. Today, the old lake bed is a huge peatland broken mainly by a few old beach ridges, remnants of the glacial lake. It contains a great majority of Minnesota's seven million acres of peat.

The prairies still begin just west of the old lake. To the south, northern hardwoods like sugar maple and basswood reach the northwest end of their range. The few mineral soils on islands within the peatland support forests of boreal species: the spruces, balsam fir, the pines, white cedar, quaking aspen, balsam poplar, paper birch, and black ash.

The peat communities are quite varied. There are definite slopes to the peat here, so water moves slowly through them, carrying nutrients from the mineral soils. The water may be on the surface or underground. The peat up to ¼ mile (0.4 kilometers) downslope from an island of mineral soil is likely to support a rich swamp forest with substantial speckled alder in the understory. The soil is always wet, and sometimes water movement can be seen in pools. This same kind of forest borders the broad tracks of slowly moving water.

Farther downslope, bog forests take over and cedar becomes scarce and stunted. Downslope from the spruce forest, sphagnum moss may have grown up into a low dome above the general level of the water table. The flow of groundwater is outward from this high spot, so the dome must rely almost entirely on rainwater as a source of nutrients. Consequently, it is very poor. It supports the moss–heath plants of the open bogs along with stunted black spruce scattered as if on a savanna.

What makes the succession pattern in the Lake Agassiz peatlands interesting is that succession seems to be proceeding from the rich forest to the muskeg. The peatland is expanding upslope. The thickening peat dams the ground-water flowing from the mineral soil, raising the water table enough to allow the peat-forming swamp plants to climb the hill. The richest forest here is on the youngest soil. Downslope on progressively older peats, bog forest and then muskeg replace the forest of the leading edge. The stratigraphy of the peat layers shows that some muskegs were once rich forests. Once established, the muskeg is a very stable community. It seems a very unmesic climax for the local vegetation.

The biggest of the peatlands is north of Red Lake. Water movement is very slow here, too. The water tracks are broad, low, wet areas of watery sedge peat and of string bogs with their alternating ridges and hollows. Scattered along the water tracks are teardrop-shape "islands" of bog forest. These islands are peat, too, and the higher growth of sphagnum toward the center is often covered with muskeg. This pattern of string bogs or patterned fens of sedge and scattered forest islands is apparently very stable. Core samples of the peat show that the sedges have been there since peat began to form. This could be another climax for the region.

One thing that might produce a new pattern of vegetation is the drainage of the bog, but this is a long way from being accomplished. The scattered streams may flow through canyons 30 feet (9 meters) deep, but the immense water-holding capacity of the peat keeps most of the water out of the streams, and keeps the peats wet even though they are well above stream level. As long as the peat stays wet, the cold water in it will keep soil temperatures low, and make summer frosts commonplace, effectively restricting the growth of most plants other than those of the bog community.

Myron Heinselman, who studied the Lake Agassiz peatlands, concluded that the communities he found were "only the net result of the interplay of a multitude of physical and biological events in the history of the landscape." The multitude of events could lead in many directions: "The vegetation of any particular locality reflects its total environment, past and present." In other words, there is no such thing as a regional climax.

THE PRODUCERS

PART III

The Consumers

Introduction to the Animal Life of the North Woods

PLANTS TURN SUNLIGHT into food energy. Animals depend on this energy to keep them alive. Herbivores are plant-eating animals whose sustenance comes directly from photosynthesis. Carnivores are meat eaters who feed on the plant eaters. Many North Woods birds and mammals are omnivores which eat both plant and animal food.

Most of the animal life in any ecosystem consists of invertebrates: insects, arachnids, protozoa, earthworms, flatworms, centipedes, nematodes, and many others. All of these are small; many are microscopic. But their cumulative effect on the ecosystem is greater than that of any large vertebrate. Some insects and other pests can kill trees, most often by defoliating them. These tiny creatures also do much of the work of decomposition, breaking down dead plant and animal material and freeing the essential minerals and atmospheric gases contained in it. Without them, the cycling of materials through the ecosystem could not continue. These small creatures are also vital parts of food chains.

Many of these small animals are quite specialized. They may live and feed on one particular part of a particular plant species. The larger vertebrates are generally more mobile and more opportunistic in their diet and habitat requirements. Nonetheless, there are differences in diet and habitat between closely related species that enable them to occupy slightly different niches within an ecosystem.

Our account of the major birds and mammals emphasizes the role each species plays in the function of the ecosystem. What they eat, where, when, and how they eat, and what eats them are the major elements in the role. All animals can be placed in food chains that begin with plants and end with a top carnivore that preys on other animals but is generally too large and fierce to be preyed on itself. The caterpillar that eats the maple leaf is eaten by the red-eyed vireo which is in turn swallowed by the sharp-shinned hawk. The deer eats the red-osier dogwood buds and is eaten by the wolf. All food chains are short, since less energy, out of the total fixed by plants, is available at each step. The deer use some of the calories in the dogwood to move around or maintain their body heat, and everything used up that way is not there for the wolf. A hypothetical animal that lived entirely on wolves or sharp-shinned hawks probably could not find enough food to survive.

With less energy available to them, carnivores have much smaller populations than herbivores. Mice are always more common than weasels; snowshoe hares are always more abundant than lynx. Anyone who spends much time in the woods will probably see all the major herbivores, but seeing all the carnivores takes effort. There are fewer of them to see, they are more wary, and many are out mainly at night.

The patterns of eating and being eaten are better called food webs than food chains. Weasels eat mice and great horned owls eat weasels. But the owl eats mice itself, and it may eat a crow that has been feasting on the carcass of a dead wolf. If we could trace all the connections between all species, the web would be almost impossibly complex.

Our accounts of animals include information on habits and on signs of presence that we hope will help you find these animals or at least know when they are around. Where a single family or order of birds or mammals has many species in the North Woods, we have given a general description of the family while mentioning prominent species. Lists of common species by habitat types follow

THE CONSUMERS

these descriptions. We have not included physical descriptions of the animals, since these are readily available in the guides listed in the Bibliography.

We have divided animals into those that live in the forest (Chapter 16) and those that live in and around lakes and streams (Chapter 17). 'Forest' is used here to mean all forested land and ground that has just been cut and is beginning to grow again. The habitats covered in Chapter 17 are all those that are too wet to grow trees or tall shrubs. There is some overlap here, since some of the animals included in Chapter 17 may live in wooded swamps, too.

The animal life of the North Woods shows a clear transition from south to north. Many of our common species are found as far south as the Gulf of Mexico. Some of our species—white-tailed deer, mink—also live well to the north of this region. Others—raccoon, bobcat—are near the northern end of their range here.

Some species—gray jay, lynx—are boreal forest animals who are at the southern end of their range here. Others—mainly birds such as the black-throated green warbler and the veery—have ranges centered on this transition zone. Animals are generally most abundant at the center of their range and scarcest at its edges. Gray jays are rare in northwestern Wisconsin even though this area is within their range.

Vegetation is the most important factor controlling the distribution of land animals within the limits of their range. Herbivores favor areas that will supply the food and shelter they need. The control on carnivores is indirect; they must seek out the places favored by their preferred prey. In a transitional area like the North Woods, the likeliest place to find northern species such as the gray jay is in habitats with northern affinities. In the case of this bird, black spruce swamps are favored nesting sites. Southern animals such as the wood thrush are most likely to be encountered in deciduous woods, habitats most like those in the heart of this bird's range. Of course, animals are mobile, so they may be found in quite unusual spots. Also, large carnivores such as timber wolves have hunting ranges that sometimes exceed 100 square miles (250 square kilometers). They will travel through many kinds of habitat in the course of patrolling such a large range.

Introduction 305

Animal Pests

Catching a glimpse of a wild animal in the woods is usually an exciting experience, but there are a few creatures that most of us could happily do without. We include in this category mosquitoes, various biting flies, and wood ticks. All of them can make you miserable, and their combined assault can nearly drive you crazy.

Mosquitoes begin to emerge in May, but they don't build up to really maddening numbers until June. Populations begin to decline in late July, and by the middle of August they are no longer a problem. They are most common in swamps or on quiet ponds, but any woodland is likely to have more than you would care to meet. A good breeze will keep them down, but breezes don't penetrate thick woods very well. They don't like direct sunlight, so during the day you can escape most of them by moving into the open. They are most active mornings and evenings.

If you move into the sun to escape the mosquitoes, you will run into black flies, deer flies and various biters. These can actually draw blood. Like the mosquitoes they are most abundant in June and July, but they are often around in some numbers in August. They retire in late afternoon, so they won't bother you in the evening.

The no-see-um is a tiny biting fly, as its name suggests. It can pass right through many coarse mosquito nets. It *will* bother you in the evening.

Wood ticks are arachnids, eight-legged relatives of spiders and mites. Adults hang on plants until something, or someone, passes by. Then they grab on and look for a likely spot to insert the proboscis for a blood meal. Once fully inserted, their mouth parts are difficult to remove. Just pulling them off may leave part of the tick under your skin, and there is some risk of infection. Ticks stay attached to one place until they have taken in enough blood to expand their bodies to several times normal size. Then they drop off.

Ticks can carry serious diseases, including Rocky Mountain spotted fever, but they are seldom a serious problem for humans. They seem quite fussy about where they bite, and usually you can feel them crawling on you and pull them off before they start digging into your skin. If you are with another person, mutual grooming at the end of the day will usually dispose of ticks. These pests emerge in June and are usually gone by the end of July.

You can avoid all these pests by confining your trips to the woods to early spring or late summer and fall. Unfortunately, if you do that, you will miss the blooming of most of the wildflowers and the nesting and singing of most of the birds. For trips to the woods in bug season, we recommend long pants, a long-sleeved shirt, a hat, and a good insect repellent. If you find that measure of protection insufficient, you can buy a headnet in most sporting goods stores. These are designed to fit over a hat. Elastic bands at the bottom fit under your arms and hold the thing on. They do cut down on vision somewhat, but they will definitely keep the bugs away.

CHAPTER SIXTEEN

Animals of the Forests

FOREST ANIMALS can be categorized by what they eat and by where they eat it. Among the herbivores, for example, some are primarily seed eaters, others are mainly browsers who eat leaves, bark, buds, and twigs. Some herbivores feed in the trees, others feed on the ground, and some opportunists are able to exploit both areas for food.

Among the carnivores, the smaller animals are mainly insect eaters, larger animals take larger prey. In the North Woods, the timber wolf is at the absolute top of this hierarchy, since it is capable of killing the largest herbivores: white-tailed deer and moose. Carnivores can also be categorized by where they eat, on the ground or in the trees.

Our discussion of forest animals begins with seed eaters and goes on to browsers, carnivores, and closes with the omnivores, the opportunistic feeders who eat both plants and animals and who are often important scavengers. Along the way, we give a brief account of the teeming life in forest soils. Finally, we list important species in forests of various ages and compositions.

The most numerous herbivores in any forest are the insects. We have not attempted to deal with complexities of form and behavior in this huge class of animals, since we feel that we could not adequately cover it in a work of this scope.

Herbivores

The Seed Eaters

Seeds are very nutritious. These plant embryos offer protein and vitamins. They hold large reservoirs of carbohydrates and fats. Many animals eat some seeds, but in the North Woods two groups specialize in it: rodents, among the mammals, and finches, among the birds. Both these groups of seed eaters include ground-feeding and tree-feeding species. The amount of seeds in their diets varies—most eat other things as well—but seeds are likely to be the largest single category of food.

SMALL RODENTS

The small forest rodents—mice and voles, chipmunks and squirrels—are mainly seed eaters, but they vary their diets with buds and young leaves, fruit, and insects. Squirrels take birds' eggs and young from nests in trees in the early summer. Chipmunks sometimes raid those of ground-nesters.

They are all makers of caches to store food through the winter. The mice and chipmunks build elaborate burrows with storerooms next to the living quarters. Squirrels seem more haphazard; gray squirrels bury individual acorns, each in a separate hole. Red squirrels cache cones in cracks in rocks or hollows in trees.

Gray squirrels, *Sciurus griseus,* are a deciduous forest species that has moved north after logging. **Red squirrels,** *Tamiasciurus hudsonicus,* seem to prefer conifer woods, and conifer seeds are a favorite food. They store whole cones—along with mushrooms, another favorite—in caches. In winter, they take their stored cones to a favored eating spot which soon becomes littered with cone scales. Neither of these squirrels hibernates, but both are less active in winter. There may be one to four pairs per acre in good habitat.

Two species of chipmunk live in the North Woods. The **least chipmunk,** *Eutamias minimus,* is a northern and western animal not found in Lower Michigan. Elsewhere both the least and the **eastern chipmunk,** *Tamias striatus,* are common. They live in burrows and search the forest floor for fruit, seeds, and thin-shelled nuts. They store the seeds for winter and eat berries in summer.

Chipmunks and squirrels and mice are eaten by a mob of predators: coyote, fox, bobcat, weasel, mink, fisher, and pine marten among the mammals; goshawk, Cooper's, red-tailed, and broad-winged hawks, great horned, long-eared, and barred owls among the birds. If they try to cross water—or fall in—they may be eaten by muskies.

FINCHES (FAMILY FRINGILLIDAE)

The finches are a very large family, with over 400 species world wide. Nearly 30 of these seedeaters breed in, migrate through, or spend their winters in the North Woods. The best identifying mark for the family is the beak. It is typically short and conical, adapted to do the powerful pinching that cracks the hulls of seeds. The amount of force some of these small birds can exert is astounding. European hawfinches regularly dine on olive pits, and our own grosbeaks crush the seeds of wild cherries.

Eating habits vary in the family. Some finches are almost exclusively seedeaters. The American goldfinch even delays breeding until July and August when more seeds are available to feed their young. Song sparrows, on the other hand, eat large amounts of animal food in spring and summer and switch to seeds when the cold begins to set in.

The family can be broken down into several smaller groups.

GROSBEAKS   As the name indicates, these finches have very large powerful beaks. We have three species in the North Woods. The **rose-breasted grosbeak**, *Pheucticus ludovicianus*, is a bird of the deciduous forest that reaches the limit of its range in northern Minnesota. The **evening grosbeak**, *Hesperiphona vespertina*, breeds in a narrow band that extends through the North Woods. In winter these birds spread both north and south from their breeding range. The **pine grosbeak**, *Pinicola enucleator*, breeds mainly to the north of our area and appears here only as a winter bird. The two latter species are among the northern finches whose populations fluctuate rapidly and drastically. They may be dripping from the trees one year and completely absent the next. The changes are probably produced by actual changes in number and by a nomadic habit that is a response to fluctuations in the food supply.

These birds live mainly on tree seeds, and trees do not produce large seed crops every year. Add to that the small number of tree species in the northern forest, and it is easy to see how food supplies could be enormous one year and nearly nonexistent the next. The evening grosbeak is one of the northern species that periodically irrupts into the south. These irruptions apparently occur after several years of good seed crops have built populations to high levels. A bad year leaves the birds with nothing to eat and they start to wander south in search of food. Some get as far as the Carolinas. Irruptions of this kind are especially common in Arctic species.

SMALL FINCHES   The **purple finch**, *Carpodacus purpureus*, which nests throughout the North Woods, looks like a smaller version of the beautiful wine-colored pine grosbeak.

The **indigo bunting**, *Passerina cyanea*, is another small finch of deciduous woods. This southern species has been moving north into areas where coniferous woods have been replaced by deciduous second growth. It reaches the limit of its range in northern Minnesota.

The **pine siskin**, *Carduelis pinus*, is a small northern finch with a nomadic population. Outside the breeding season siskins are usually seen in flocks.

THE CROSSBILLS   The tips of the beaks of these birds actually do cross. The unusual shape makes the birds extremely adept at opening the cones of conifers to get at the seeds inside. These are the most nomadic of the northern finches. They travel much of the time, in flocks, looking for good seed crops. They commonly begin breeding in late winter, but if they find an abundant food source they may start nesting in the coldest time of year. The **red crossbill**, *Loxia curvirostra*, is more common than the **white-winged**, *Loxia leucoptera*.

THE GROUND FEEDERS: TOWHEE AND SPARROWS The **towhee**, *Pipilo erythrophthalmus*, shares some coloring with the robin, and it feeds rather like it too, scratching in the leaf litter of the forest floor.

The sparrows are a large group of primarily ground-feeding finches. Their common name derives from their similarity to the familiar English or house sparrow, although that bird is actually part of a separate family, the Old World weaver finches. Sparrows are small brown birds variously patterned with camouflage streaks and spots. They nest on the ground or in shrubs or small trees. There are 32 species in North America, and most of them prefer open country: prairies or beach dunes. Common species in the North Woods are:

Savanna Sparrow, *Passerculus sandwichensis.* In open areas, pastures and old fields.

Northern Junco, *Junco hyemalis*—Departs from the group's usual color pattern. It is solid slate gray above, white below. In brushy areas in coniferous forests.

Chipping Sparrow, *Spizella passerina.* Most common in dry, open pine woods. They have become rather domesticated, and often feed on lawns.

White-Throated Sparrow, *Zonotrichia albicollis.* In brushy areas in many habitats, from bogs to second-growth forests to pine woods. The song of this species is one that even the most tin-eared can learn to recognize. It is a high, clear whistle, almost a pure tone without overtones. It can be rendered as *old-Sam-Pea-body-Pea-body-Pea-body.* Canadians transcribe it *oh, my, Canada, Canada, Canada.*

Lincoln's Sparrow, *Melospiza lincolnii.* Nests in open bogs.

Swamp Sparrow, *Melospiza georgiana.* The name tells it; more common in wet areas where tree cover is not complete.

Song Sparrow, *Melospiza melodia.* Nests in shrubby areas in a wide range of forest types, old fields, young second growth, forest edges.

The Browsers

Browsers mainly eat the parts of woody plants: leaves, flowers, fruit, seeds, buds, twigs, bark, and whole seedlings. In summer, when herbs and grasses are available, these also form part of the browsers' diet. Food is abundant for browsers in summer, but in winter they must subsist on buds, twigs, bark, and conifer needles; winter food supplies are a major factor in the control of browser populations.

The major browsers in the North Woods divide the resources vertically. Snowshoe hares feed at or just above ground level. White-tailed deer feed a little higher, moose higher yet. Porcupines feed in the treetops. Beavers, whose habits are elucidated in Chapter 17, get at the treetops by felling the trees. Ruffed grouse feed both on the ground and in trees and reach buds and flowers the others cannot go after. Food preference also plays a part in how the resources are shared. Deer will eat balsam fir only when they are starving; moose will browse it nearly to extinction.

Browsers are usually concentrated in younger forests where light levels are high enough to maintain a rich crop of shrubs and small trees. Ruffed grouse, porcupines, and beavers are especially attached to aspens.

GALLINACEOUS BIRDS: GROUSE

Gallinaceous means 'chicken-like', and all the birds in the order Galliformes are similar to domestic fowl. They are ground feeders, primarily, who get about by walking and running. Flight is chiefly a means of escape from predators, although grouse will fly up into trees to feed and to roost.

Gallinaceous birds have short broad wings that give them an explosive start—the sudden movement and the whirr of wings can be quite startling—but they don't fly far. A grouse flushed in a dense wood is likely to be back on the ground within 50 yards. If it is flushed three or four times in quick succession, it may become so exhausted that it can be caught by hand.

We have three gallinaceous birds in the North Woods, all of them grouse. The **sharp-tailed grouse,** *Pediocetes phasianellus,* is a bird of brushy openings and the savanna. It used to thrive on the pine barrens; in the woods it depends on fires or winds to provide openings. It is scarce now. The sharp-tail is the only gallinaceous bird on Isle Royale, apparently having become established there after past fires. It remains on exposed ridges, but is uncommon.

The **spruce grouse,** *Canachites canadensis,* is another boreal bird that is most likely to be encountered in northeastern Minnesota. South of Lake Superior, it is rare and spottily distributed. Bog forests are the likeliest habitats. The males use patches of open bog muskeg for mating displays.

Spruce grouse often feed in trees. They live on the needles and buds of conifers through the winter and are able to fly up beyond the reach of competitive browsers. In summer, they switch to young leaves and to fruits and seeds. The young prefer insects.

The **ruffed grouse**, *Bonasa umbellus*, is common throughout the North Woods. Since it is an important game bird, its habits have been thoroughly studied.

Ruffed grouse is one of the species that has benefitted from the arrival of settlers. It thrives in country that is a mixture of open fields and woodlots. It favors young forests, particularly aspen forests.

In the early spring mating season, male ruffed grouse seek a drumming site, a fallen log or other slightly elevated perch surrounded by shrubs sparse enough to give the bird at least 20 yards vision in any direction. Surrounding trees, ideally aspen, should be tall enough to screen out aerial predators. The birds become attached to their drumming site and may use the same one for years.

Once on site, the male stands with his tail braced and his claws sunk in the wood of his drumming log and begins a peculiar flapping of wings that looks as if he were trying to beat his chest. The movement starts slowly and speeds up, and each stroke produces a low drumming noise. The effect in the woods is as if someone were unsuccessfully trying to start a lawnmower. Drumming usually starts just before dawn and continues somewhat past sunrise. A second period starts about an hour before twilight, and some males drum well into the night. Drumming is most common in early spring and it tails off rapidly in May. Some birds do some drumming throughout the summer, so you may occasionally hear this North Woods sound in August or in early fall when the changing length of day seems to stimulate more drumming.

Drumming attracts the females, and once mating has taken place the male takes no further part in producing the young. The females nest on the ground, usually near clearings and preferably in or near a clone of male (staminate) aspens. The buds and emerging flowers of these trees are important food for the female while she incubates the eggs.

The chicks—an average clutch of eggs is 11—can run from birth and they can fly within 10 to 12 days. The mother provides protection for the chicks, and she leads them to good food sources, but the chicks feed themselves.

For the first 14 days, their diet will be about 75 percent insects, with ants the most common. Within two months, insect food is down to 5 percent of the diet.

The adults continue eating buds and flowers—particularly of quaking aspen—well into May. They will add leaves of strawberry and wintergreen to their diet then, and through the summer they will live mainly on wild fruit. This preference will continue into the fall when berries of the viburnums, dogwoods, roses, and other shrubs ripen.

In mid-September families break up. The species doesn't migrate, but the young do wander in the fall looking for unoccupied land that will support them through the winter. The distance of the spread is usually a quarter-mile or even less, but wanderings of over 7 miles (11 kilometers) have been recorded. This is a dangerous period for the inexperienced young who have to travel through strange terrain alone.

An ideal habitat can support a breeding male on every 8 to 10 acres (3 to 4 hectares), but a more typical average would be four to six birds on 100 acres (40 hectares). In early fall, with the young of the year added, population may reach one bird to 3 or 4 acres (1 to 1.5 hectares).

How many of these birds survive the winter depends on the food supply, which varies from year to year depending on weather and other factors. Ruffed grouse roost in conifers where the foliage provides some protection from the winter. They also burrow directly into the snow, sometimes remaining for days under this insulating blanket. The temperature under the snow at 32° F (0° C) may be 60° or 70° F (40° C) warmer than the outside air on some January nights. Buried grouse are vulnerable to predators if one finds a burrow.

Ruffed grouse are among the animals whose population fluctuates on a regular cycle. They may be abundant one year, very scarce the next, and then build gradually up to abundance. The causes of these fluctuations are unclear.

Ruffed grouse move into a young aspen forest when the trees are under 30 feet (9 meters) tall. On a well-stocked stand, the trees may total 6,000 to an acre. The birds will use this forest for 10 to 15 years. By then the trees will have grown larger, and shading will have cut stem density down to below 2,000 per acre. After that, the grouse may still feed in the stand, but their breeding activity is likely to happen elsewhere.

MAMMALS

Snowshoe Hare, *Lepus americanus.* The snowshoe is sometimes called the varying hare, since its fur varies from summer brown to winter white. The white fur is good camouflage against the snow. The snowshoe's huge hind feet help it move fast on deep powder snow.

Snowshoe hares often eat the same plants as deer or moose. They eat bark, especially in winter, and they often girdle small trees or shrubs like hazel above the snowline. Young forests and conifer swamps are favored habitats.

Snowshoes are a major food of lynx and other small predators such as bobcat, coyote, and red fox. The hares are on a 10-year population cycle of mysterious origin, and the populations of their predators follow the cycle, too. In recent decades, snowshoe hares have been most abundant in

127. Snowshoe hare, *Lepus americanus,* a browser at ground level. *Wisconsin Department of Natural Resources.*

THE CONSUMERS

the early years of the decade. Predator populations, especially of the lynx, lag slightly behind. Lynx build to maximum numbers just after overbrowsing or some social cause has produced a crash in the snowshoe population. Then lynx numbers drop, only to increase when the hare population starts to build again. Such large fluctuations in numbers seem more common in the north where there are fewer species of plants and animals. Lynx have fewer choices in prey; snowshoes have fewer choices in plants to eat.

Cottontail, *Sylvilagus floridanus.* Logging and the spread of farming into the North Woods have helped the cottontail rabbit extend its range northward. It is absent only in northern Minnesota, but it is usually confined to settled areas where the woods are broken with fields.

White-Tailed Deer, *Odocoileus virginianus.* Before logging and settlement, the big populations of white-tailed deer were south of our area. They lived in the edges where prairie and forest met, and they were scattered through the woods where fire or wind provided the young forests they needed. Logging opened the North Woods to the whitetail, although initially, the scrub and the fires and indiscriminate hunting—including large-scale market hunting—came near to wiping them out. When the scrub land began to grow into young forest and hunting was regulated, the deer began to come back. The new aspen stands with their luxuriant shrubs were ideal habitat made even better by scattered farms that provided forest edges and sometimes corn and alfalfa as well.

Predators such as timber wolf were absent over most of the North Woods by the 1920s, and the deer came back to the point that population irruptions in Wisconsin and Michigan ended in mass starvation. A white-tail buck prefers about one square mile of territory, but some forests in the North Woods were carrying 20 to 50 deer on that much land.

Deer have definite food preferences. We mentioned earlier that in mixed-hardwood forests of the North Woods deer have almost eliminated American yew. On overbrowsed ranges deer may do the same to hemlock, white cedar, and yellow birch. Small shrubby looking hemlocks may be the plants browsed down to the snowline the previous winter. Deer eat sugar maple too, but this tree seems better able to survive the onslaught. Eventually it grows beyond the reach of the deer and in time creates a dark hardwood forest with a sparse understory that offers little food and no winter shelter to the deer. Deer like white cedar, too, and they can eliminate reproduction by browsing seedlings. Their eating can help turn a cedar swamp into a balsam fir stand. Since deer turn to eating balsam fir only when starvation is the alternative, balsam fir stands offer winter shelter but little food.

Overbrowsing produces an environmental deterioration from the deer's point of view. The ability of the environment to produce food and shelter keeps declining because of the competitive edge given unpalatable species. When the deterioration is fast enough, mass die-offs ensue.

Deer populations are still quite high in the North Woods. They are higher in lightly or moderately populated areas than they are in unbroken wilderness. Predation is still scarce and local. Hunters kill thousands and cars thousands more. But hunters are usually allowed to take only bucks, and deer are polygamous. A buck will mate with as many does as he can find, so killing a controlled number of bucks will not lower the reproductive capacity of the population. When deer seem to be overloading the environment, some kind of additional hunting for does may be allowed.

The record white-tail buck weighed 400 pounds (180 kilograms), but animals that size must be very rare. A more typical buck would weigh about 150 to 165 pounds (68 to 75 kilograms) and be just over 3 feet (90 centimeters) tall at the shoulders. Does are slightly smaller. Deer in the woods always seem larger than they actually are.

Deer follow paths through the woods, and sometimes these are so heavily used that they look as conspicuous as human footpaths. You can usually find tracks and droppings along these. Through most of the year the droppings are brown pellets about the size of a marble. The trails are laid along a safe route from bedding ground to food. They are good places to look for deer, but the animals will abandon trails suddenly for safety or when a food source runs out.

Deer are very elusive on their home ground. They can leap over or slither under almost any obstacle or freeze to

318

stone when that seems expedient. In the primeval forest, wolves were their principal predator. The deer are not large enough to fight off wolves, so all their strategies involve escape and evasion.

In the warmer months, deer often feed during the night. After daylight, they bed down on high ground. They don't reuse old beds, but they do go back to favorite bedding areas. When they pick out a spot, they turn around and lie facing down the hill on their own back trail. They may get up and feed occasionally during the day. In late afternoon, they go for water. In the evening they begin to feed again.

Males begin to grow antlers in late spring. Young bucks born the previous season may grow only tiny button antlers. Those a year older grow spikes, curving horns with a single division at the tip. The older animals grow the big racks. The size of the rack varies with the quality and quantity of the food supply. Bucks in their prime produce small antlers in bad food years.

The antlers grow as living tissue surrounded by skin. When they harden and mature, the skin dies and the deer peel off the velvet by rubbing it on trees. Buck rubs can be seen on small saplings. The antlers are used in stylized combats during the rutting season, when bucks roam in search of receptive does. When a wandering buck meets another male, the two of them clash antlers and begin to push against each other. The contest is usually decided non-lethally when one buck becomes convinced that he can't win. He is allowed to wander off. Sometimes the chance lethal cut with a sharp antler will kill one of the combatants. Rarely, the two sets of antlers will become inextricably locked and both bucks will starve together.

The spotted fawns (usually one, but up to three per doe) are born in spring. Apparently, they have almost no scent for the first month of their lives. Left alone while their mothers are feeding, the fawns lie very still, and predation is very light (although the fawns are vulnerable to coyotes and other smaller hunters that would be hard pressed to take an adult white tail).

Deer need cover in winter. They stay on south slopes when the weather gets cold. When the real cold and deep snow come, they may yard up in swamp forests which they return to year after year. Cedar swamps are ideal for this,

Animals of the Forests   319

since they offer both food and shelter. Initially the congregating deer may improve the food supply. By trampling down the deep snow, they can move more easily, making food more accessible. In very hard winters, deer in yards may exhaust all their food. They remain in the yard rather than floundering through the snow looking for food in strange territory, and often they starve. Some cedar swamps have trees with no leaves below the level the deer can reach. The usual species of tall shrubs are bitten off above the snow and stay short.

Moose, *Alces alces.* The moose is the largest animal in the North Woods. Bulls may weigh 1200 pounds (550 kilograms) and cows often near 900 pounds (400 kilograms)—as big as horses. They are browsers who enjoyed a period of prosperity following logging and fires, but habitat loss has driven them steadily northward. The last known native moose in Wisconsin was shot in 1916. Today they live only in northeastern Minnesota and on Isle Royale. Occasionally a young male will wander into northwestern Wisconsin south of Duluth or come across the narrow part of Lake Superior to the Bayfield Peninsula, but none has survived very long.

A moose needs a big territory, and it does not seem to tolerate much human presence. It cannot find a home in a farm woodlot, as a whitetail can. It needs large amounts of wilderness or near wilderness.

Moose are sometimes competitive with deer. American yew and red osier dogwood are preferred foods for both animals. Sometimes they are complementary. Moose spend many summer days in the water eating pondweed and bur reed and water lilies. Deer seldom look for their food in lakes and streams. Moose prefer balsam fir as a winter browse, while deer prefer it only to starvation.

Brushy fields beginning to grow a crop of jack pine, white spruce, or balsam fir are prime moose habitat. Like deer, they become scarce in old forests dark enough to shade out most of the shrubs. They also like young aspen–birch woods. They browse on both of these trees.

Winter is the time of scarcity in the North Woods. Then the moose eat buds and twigs of willows, beaked hazel, red osier dogwood, and aspen. On Isle Royale, where moose became too numerous before the arrival of wolves, they ate

THE CONSUMERS

so much balsam fir that they practically eliminated young trees of the species from the island.

Like white-tailed deer, bull moose begin to grow their antlers in spring. They use them during the fall and early winter rutting season in ritual combats with other bulls. Calves are born in spring and stay with their mothers through their first year. Moose are otherwise solitary. Bulls in rut and cows with calves can be aggressive.

Expanding deer populations may be contributing to the decline in moose. Large deer populations increase infections in moose of a nematode called *Pneumostrongylus tenuis*. Infection is common—and not lethal—among deer, but it causes a fatal neurological disease in moose.

Moose are powerful swimmers. It is likely that the population on Isle Royale arrived by swimming in Lake Superior. The nearest land is 15 miles (24 kilometers) away.

Porcupine, *Erethizon dorsatum.* The porcupine is a very slow-moving animal. It cannot run—or even walk fast. Its one defensive maneuver is to erect its quills, tuck its head down between its front paws and present its spiny rear to its

128. Porcupine, *Erethizon dorsatum*, browsing on a red maple tree. *Wisconsin Department of Natural Resources.*

enemy. The quills are sharp and barbed. They come out at a touch, and once they are lodged in the foe, its muscles retract away from them and the barbs work deeper. Porcupines have been known to kill owls and dogs, and probably other hunters as well. Fishers know how to get past the porcupine's defense, and these larger relatives of the weasel take many porkies.

Porcupines spend little time on the ground. They feed and nest in trees, in summer eating leaves and fruit, and in winter, buds and inner bark. They often girdle trees, stripping the bark off all the way around the tree and killing it. Porcupines benefited from the conversion to aspen of so much North Woods land, but they eat coniferous needles and buds as well.

During the late fall–early winter breeding season, porkies produce some unearthly screaming in the night.

A Fruit Eater

Cedar waxwing, *Bombycilla cedrorum.* Waxwings eat some insects, but most of their food is wild fruit or flowers. They feed from the ground to the treetops on strawberries, Juneberries, mountain ash, and many other wild fruits. They are wanderers, apparently moving about following the crops. They live in flocks except during the very brief breeding season. Few winter in the North Woods.

Carnivores

The Insect Eaters

Most of the herbivores in the forest are insects, so it follows that most of the carnivores are insect eaters. One order of mammals, called the Insectivora, includes shrews and moles, and these animals do eat many insects. The omnivorous bears and skunks also include insects in their diet, as do rodents and smaller carnivores.

The most numerous insect eaters are birds. The dozens of species divide the resources of the environment in several ways. Some feed on the ground, some on the main trunks of trees, and some in the leafy canopy. Tiny insect eaters such as kinglets take very small prey. Orioles and tanagers can take much larger caterpillars and moths. Different hunting methods also provide different quarry.

The insectivorous birds favor different kinds of habitat. Some prefer open ground, others mature forests. These preferences also distribute the birds through the environment.

We will first describe insect-eating birds that feed in or from trees or tall shrubs, and then go on to ground feeders. Some common birds that feed at the tips of branches and on leaves are:

Ruby-Crowned Kinglet, *Regulus calendula,* and **Golden-Crowned Kinglet,** *R. satrapa.* The kinglets are very small; next to hummingbirds they are the smallest birds in North America. They live in mature conifer woods and are much more likely breeders at the north end of our area than at the south. They are very active as they feed on the smaller branchlets, twigs, and leaves. They eat mainly insects, especially eggs and larvae. Their size confines them to very small prey.

WOOD WARBLERS (FAMILY PARULIDAE) The wood warblers are a New World family of insect-eating birds represented in the North Woods by more than 30 species that breed in or migrate through the region. One genus of these birds—which includes the ovenbirds and waterthrushes—feeds on the forest floor. All the others feed in trees or shrubs.

Wood warblers are tiny birds, typically 5 inches (13 centimeters) or less from tip of beak to tip of tail. An average-size specimen weighs little more than a quarter of an ounce (7 grams), yet these birds migrate thousands of miles. Breeding as far north as the tundra, they may spend their winters in South America. Only a few of the species that breed in the North Woods winter as far north as the southern edge of the United States. Most of them fly south to Central America, northern South America, or the West Indies.

The wood warblers all have the slender bills typical of insect-eating birds. With a few exceptions, they are very active and fast moving, hopping about in the foliage of trees and shrubs, seldom sitting still long enough for us to get a good look at them. Many of them, particularly the males with their bright colors and the striking patterns of spring breeding plumage, are worth a look.

Some species of wood warblers hunt the treetops. Others feed in the low shrubs. Some favor very young stands just recovering from fire or logging, others prefer stands of pole-size trees, and still others are seldom found outside old growth stands. Many wood warblers prefer deciduous trees, while others specialize in conifers. Most hunt on the tips of twigs amid the foliage, but a few concentrate on the large limbs and the main trunk.

A good example of specialization and resource partitioning occurs in tall spruces and firs. **Cape May Warblers,** *Dendroica tigrina,* nest and hunt in the tops of the trees. **Blackburnian Warblers,** *D. fusca,* live just below, and **black-throated green warblers,** *D. virens,* nest down to about 15 feet (5 meters) above ground. In the very lowest level of trees and shrubs the **magnolia warbler,** *D. magnolia,* nests and hunts. Sometimes this division is carried even further, as the **ovenbird,** *Seiurus aurocapillus,* may live on the forest floor below these other species.

Many warblers breed mainly in the boreal forest to the north of our region. In northeastern Minnesota, northern Wisconsin, and upper Michigan, they are at the extreme southern edge of their range. Our lists of birds by habitat at the end of this chapter indicate that these species are more common to the North.

The wood warblers begin to arrive in the North Woods in early May when the opening leaves bring out the first crop of caterpillars and other insect larvae. The males arrive first, establishing territories for breeding. The new generation is raised quickly. Typically it takes only 10 to 12 days of incubation to hatch an egg and another 10 days to two weeks for the young to develop enough to leave the nest.

Warblers arrive in spring in waves, flying in on southerly winds. The fall migration is much more leisurely. The young of the year start south first, often beginning the move in early August. The adults come later, mostly in September. By the beginning of October, nearly all the warblers have left the North Woods.

The ovenbird, the most common warbler in our region,

is also the most anomalous—it feeds and nests on the ground and looks like a tiny thrush. Ovenbirds are common in many woods. Their call is quite distinctive, a sharp two syllables repeated several times with mounting volume and intensity. The syllables are usually rendered *tea-cher*, *tea-cher*, but the accenting makes it closer to *ter-chee, ter-chee*. Ovenbirds sing into August and often in the middle of the day.

The **black-and-white warbler,** *Mniotilta varia,* is another somewhat unusual warbler that feeds on the trunks and larger limbs rather than amid the foliage.

The most famous specialist among the North Woods warblers is the **Kirtland's,** *D. kirtlandii.* This species nests on the ground under jack pines from 5 to 15 feet (1.5 to 4.5 meters) tall, trees with enough low branches to shield the nest. Kirtland's warblers do not nest under larger jack pine nor under any under tree.

In the past, fire apparently supplied them with suitable nesting grounds. Today, deliberate management is being used to preserve the species. Kirtland's warbler, with a total population of about 1,000 birds, is one of the rarest vertebrates in North America. It lives in one tiny portion of northern Lower Michigan around the town of Mio. Controlled fires and other sorts of intervention are used to provide nesting sites. In 1980 one of these fires got out of control and destroyed a substantial amount of timber.

Black-Capped Chickadee, *Parus atricapillus,* and **Boreal Chickadee,** *P. hudsonicus.* Chickadees are conspicuous birds. In winter, their calls may be the only noise in the woods. The black-capped is common throughout in all kinds of woods. The boreal, or brown-capped, breeds in Minnesota. Most sightings in Wisconsin and Upper Michigan are winter birds.

Chickadees feed from the lower reaches of the canopy to the tall shrubs. They eat some seeds and fruit, but most of their food is insects. In winter they eat eggs picked from the bark, plant lice on buds, and scale insects on spruce needles. They hang upside-down from the tips of branches and even turn somersaults to get at every bit of food.

A chickadee has to find enough food on a short winter day to maintain a 104° F (40° C) body temperature and a very active life. They weigh less than a half ounce (14

129. Black-capped chickadee, *Parus atricapillus*, in flight. *National Park Service*.

grams). Small flocks sometimes crowd into a woodpecker hole and sleep in a pile to conserve heat.

Chickadees are very tame. They will eat out of your hand if you are patient about letting them approach.

Red-Eyed Vireo, *Vireo olivaceus*. Vireos are slightly larger than warblers with slightly thicker and stronger beaks. The red-eyed vireo is the most abundant bird in eastern deciduous woodland. In the North Woods it comes in as the forest matures and remains abundant in mature deciduous and mixed forests.

This vireo requires some tall shrubs, since it usually nests 5 to 10 feet (1.5 to 3 meters) from the ground. It feeds in the canopy, searching the leaves, twigs, and smaller branches. It eats mostly insects, particularly caterpillars. Vireos with young hunt constantly. Nestlings may eat over 100 separate items in a day.

Vireos are small and pale green and they move slowly through the canopy, making them very hard to see. They are, however, very easy to hear. It is worth learning the red-eyed vireo's song. It is quite simple, and male vireos repeat it hundreds of times daily.

Four other vireos breed in some part of the North

Woods: the **solitary,** V. *solitarius;* **yellow-throated,** V. *flav-ifrons* (south); **Philadelphia,** V. *philadelphicus* (north); and **warbling,** V. *gilvus*.

Northern Oriole, *Icterus galbula,* and **Scarlet Tanager,** *Piranga olivacea*. These two belong to separate families. We put them together because they are the largest of the insect-eating birds to hunt in the treetops. They take large prey. Tanagers eat adult cecropia and luna moths. The moths lie quietly and protectively colored on tree bark. The birds find them by hunting slowly, giving careful attention to every leaf and bit of bark.

The male oriole and the male tanager in their spring plumage are very brightly colored birds, but they are seldom seen because they are hidden in the leaves overhead. The females are more obscurely colored and seen even less. The northern oriole and scarlet tanager both favor mature deciduous woods, and the tanager seems to show a particular preference for oak.

The next group of birds are those that feed mainly on trunks and larger branches. The insect eaters who winter in the North Woods—with the exception of the chickadee—belong to this group. Their winter diet consists of eggs, pupae, and wintering adults found in or on bark.

Brown Creeper, *Certhia familiaris*. The name tells the story. Creepers are small brown birds that hunt for insects by creeping over tree trunks. They start at the bottom and climb in a zig-zag course up the trunk. When they are well up, they fly to the base of the next tree and start again. They do not winter in the North Woods.

White-Breasted Nuthatch, *Sitta carolinensis,* and **Red-Breasted Nuthatch,** *S. canadensis*. The white-breasted favors deciduous trees and is more common to the south. The red-breasted likes conifers and is more common in the north. The red-breasted is one of the northern birds that mysteriously irrupts to fill every tree one year and disappears the next.

Both birds are here year around. As their name suggests, they eat tree seeds, using their sharp beaks to break the nuts into edible pieces. They also eat insects, including eggs and larvae in winter. They often hunt by marching down a tree trunk head foremost, a posture that may give them a view of food in the bark that an upright woodpecker or creeper would miss. They often flock with chickadees in winter.

WOODPECKERS (FAMILY PICIDAE)   These birds of the trees feed on the trunks and large limbs. They have long straight sturdy bills that they use as chisels to dig into the bark to go after insect eggs and pupae cases as well as adults. One species, the yellow-bellied sapsucker, dines on tree sap. Sapsuckers drill a row of holes into trees and then lick the sap that flows out. Woodpecker tongues are long, sticky, and raspy, and the birds can extend them well beyond the tip of the beak. After the chiseling beaks have revealed a cavity filled with insect eggs, the long tongue can reach in to get the food.

Woodpeckers are very important to a variety of hole-nesting birds. With their powerful beaks, they excavate a nesting cavity in a living tree or a dead snag. Many hole-nesting species cannot do this, and are entirely dependent on woodpeckers to provide them with places to live. Hole-nesting species generally have young that develop more slowly than the young of birds that build their nests on tree limbs or on the ground. They are also likely to have a higher rate of reproductive success, since their young are more thoroughly protected from both the weather and from predators.

Eight species of woodpeckers live in the North Woods. Three of these are migratory. The **common flicker,** *Colaptes auratus,* the **yellow-bellied sapsucker,** *Sphyrapicus varius,* and the **red-headed woodpecker,** *Melanerpes erythrocephalus,* spend their winters to the south of our region, although their winter range is near enough that occasional individuals may be seen throughout the year.

Three species are resident through the year and throughout the region. The **pileated,** *Dryocopus pileatus,* a bird the size of a crow, is the largest of our woodpeckers. This is one of the species that nearly vanished in the destruction of the forests. Now that many of the trees are back, the pileated woodpeckers are returning, too. Species like the pileated, which require old-growth forest, provide an excellent argument for maintaining wilderness areas. The **downy** and **hairy woodpeckers,** *Picoides pubescens* and *P. villosus,* have essentially identical plumage, but the hairy is a larger bird with a much heavier beak. The downy is the most common woodpecker in the North Woods. In winter, the downy flocks with chickadees and nuthatches.

The **northern three-toed** and **black-backed three-toed woodpeckers**, *P. tridactylus* and *P. arcticus*, are boreal birds with a scattered distribution. They are more common in northern Minnesota than elsewhere in our region, and more common there in winter, when some birds move south of their breeding range, than at other times of the year.

TYRANT FLYCATCHERS (FAMILY TYRANNIDAE) This is a New World family whose principal prey is flying insects. Their hunting method involves sitting on a convenient perch and waiting for something to fly near. They make a short, quick flight and snatch their prey from the air. Several species nest in the North Woods. All are highly migratory. Only the phoebe winters as far north as the southern United States. Some other common species are:

Kingbird, *Tyrannus tyrannus*. Look for it in tall shrubs at the edge of forests, along roads, fields, etc. Also in shrubs such as alder or where scattered small trees are invading old fields or cut-over ground.

Least Flycatcher, *Empidonax minimus*. Sings from perches in the understory of woods mature enough to have a closed canopy. Not much larger than a warbler.

Great Crested Flycatcher, *Myiarchus crinitus*. Nests in woodland canopies, especially deciduous. More common in south. The largest of the North Woods flycatchers.

Wood Pewee, *Contopus virens*. Nests in canopy, particularly in deciduous woods.

Yellow-Bellied Flycatcher, *Empidonax flaviventris*. Nests in bog forests, more common in north.

Olive-Sided Flycatcher, *Nutallornis borealis*. Found at edges between open bogs and forest.

Other aerial feeders include swallows and swifts. Since swallows are rarely far from water, they are described in the following chapter. **Chimney swifts**, *Chaetura pelagica*, hunt flying prey above the forest canopy. These are the most aerial of birds. They even mate in the air. Their legs and feet are so weak that they can cling to a vertical surface but cannot walk at all. Around civilization, they do nest in chimneys. In the woods, they choose standing dead trees whose tops have fallen off so the birds can enter from above.

The following birds are ground-feeding insect eaters, a large group in the North Woods.

BROWN THRUSHES There are five similar thrushes, one of the genus *Hylocichla* and four of the genus *Catharus* in eastern North America; all but one of them nests somewhere in our area. Like their cousin the robin, these thrushes have slender bills of medium length. They tend to carry themselves as if they were thrusting their breasts out. The birds of this group are among our best singers.

The thrushes are birds of the forest floor, and their coloring helps them blend with their environment. They all have solid-color backs of various shades of brown, olive and gray. Their breasts are white or pale gray and all are spotted to some extent.

The ranges of the different species overlap, and between them they extend from the Gulf of Mexico to the arctic treeline.

The thrush that occurs farthest south is the **wood thrush,** *H. mustelina,* the largest thrush in our area. The center of its range is the eastern deciduous forest, but it breeds in our transition forest as well. Wood thrushes are more common at the southern end of our area than in the north.

The **hermit thrush,** *Catharus guttatus,* is the most common thrush of the North Woods. It nests in mature mixed or coniferous forests. **Swainson's thrush,** *C. ustulatus,* breeds mostly to the north of our area, but these birds do nest in northern Michigan, far northern Wisconsin, and northern Minnesota.

The most northerly thrush is the **gray-cheeked thrush,** *C. minimus,* whose breeding range extends as far north as the treeline. It breeds in the United States only in the mountains of northern New England.

The fifth thrush is the **veery,** *C. fuscescens,* which has much the same breeding range as the hermit thrush. It is most common in swamp forests.

Wood thrushes usually nest in the lower limbs of trees. Swainson's thrushes may nest in the lower branches of spruce or fir or they may nest on the ground, like hermit thrushes and veerys. Raising a brood typically takes about 25 days, about equally divided between incubating eggs and feeding the young.

Like the robins, these birds feed largely on insects and other small invertebrates on the forest floor. In season, they eat wild fruits. Their hunting method is to hop or run over the forest floor turning over leaves with their bills.

All the thrushes are highly migratory. Only the hermit thrush spends its winters in the United States. This species is the first of the family to return north, reaching parts of our area late in April.

Robin, *Turdus migratorius.* Robins have made a very thorough adjustment to the presence of people, but the tame bird pulling up earthworms on the front lawn is a bit different from the woodland bird. Wild robins are often very skittish and difficult to approach.

The major items of animal food for woodland birds are beetles, caterpillars, flies, and grasshoppers. Earthworms, spiders, millipedes, and snails are eaten less often. Robins are also very fond of fruit. In the woods, they favor mountain ash, hawthorn, dogwood, viburnum, raspberry, wild cherry, sumac, and blueberry, among many others.

While robins typically hunt on the ground, they build their nests in trees on horizontal limbs or in crotches. They usually raise two to three broods a season. Unmated males roost together, and as the season progresses, they are joined by the newly independent young birds and eventually by the mated males and females. Roosts of thousands of birds are sometimes formed; often these birds will later migrate together.

Brown thrasher, *Toxostoma rufum.* This spectacular singer—it is a relative of the mockingbird—is a ground feeder that lives mainly on insects, although it takes seeds and fruit as well. Its name probably comes from its habit of tossing aside dead leaves with its beak as it hunts. The action apparently suggested a hay cutter tossing hay with a pitchfork.

Brown thrashers are birds of edges and young forests. They are somewhat domesticated and often feed on lawns. The closely related catbird favors similar habitat, but it eats far more fruit and fewer insects.

Woodcock, *Philohela minor.* An upland species of shorebird that favors shrubby areas—like alder thickets—or young forests. Woodcocks nest and feed on the ground. They have very long bills, over 2.5 inches (6.4 centimeters) in most birds. They feed by probing the ground for earthworms and similar subterranean fare. The tips of their bills are very sensitive. When they encounter a worm, the prehensile upper beak opens near the tip and snatches it up. A woodcock's eyes are at the back of its head, which allows the bird to sink its beak full length into the ground while still keeping watch for predators above. Woodcocks need soil that is moist enough to allow them to feed. Rows of bore holes in wet earth are a good sign of their presence.

Reptiles and Amphibians

Herptiles, the collective name for these two classes of animals, are a rather inconspicuous part of the fauna of the North Woods. Only two snakes occur throughout the region, and both are quite small. The common **garter snake,** *Thamnophis sirtalis,* is the more frequently seen. It occupies a variety of habitats and eats insects, frogs, toads, and some mice. The even smaller **red-bellied snake,** *Storeria occipitomaculata,* averages only 8 to 10 inches (20 to 25 centimeters) in length. The record specimen was 16 inches (40 centimeters) long. You may see it around bogs. It feeds on soil animals such as insects, earthworms, and slugs.

Some other snakes are found in parts of the North Woods. Among these are the **fox snake,** *Elaphe vulpina,* in the western Upper Peninsula and Wisconsin, except the northwest corner; the **smooth green snake,** *Opheodrys vernalis,* (rare or absent in Minnesota); and the **eastern hognose snake,** *Heterodon platyrhinos,* found in Lower Michigan and the southern two-thirds of Wisconsin.

The only poisonous snake found anywhere in the North Woods in the **massasauga rattler,** *Sistrurus catenatus.* It may be encountered in Lower Michigan. Its range in Wisconsin and Minnesota is south of our area. The massasauga is a shy, unaggressive snake of modest size. The record specimen was just over 3 feet (1 meter) long. Its preferred habitat is swamps and bogs, but drainage of such places, combined with direct persecution, have made it very rare. It is on the endangered species list in Wisconsin.

The common amphibian of the woodlands is the **American toad**, *Bufo americanus*. Toads need shallow water to breed in, but outside of mating season they may be found a considerable distance from water in almost any place that offers a good supply of insects and a damp spot for shelter. The **wood frog**, *Rana sylvatica*, and the **northern leopard frog**, *Rana pipiens*, may sometimes be encountered in woods away from water. Tree frogs such as the **spring peeper**, *Hyla crucifer*, may also stray from water. These tiny frogs seldom climb very high, generally preferring low brushy thickets. They are difficult to see, but their high piping call is a common sound in the spring.

The Larger Carnivores

We include in this group all the animals big enough to catch a mouse. One is big enough to catch a moose. The wolf is undisputedly the top carnivore of the North Woods. Where wolves are absent, their niche remains vacant, except insofar as humans fill the office.

THE RAPTORS: EAGLES, HAWKS, OWLS

All the raptors have sharply hooked beaks adapted for tearing meat. Their feet are powerful talons for gripping— and killing—the animals they catch. These traits are general in both hawks and owls, but individual families and genera show specific traits that reflect the way they hunt and the kind of prey they prefer.

EAGLES (SUBFAMILY BUTEONINAE) The eagles are very large raptors with long, broad wings and broad tails. They are adapted for soaring, and can ride updrafts for hours with very little effort. **Golden eagles**, *Aquila chrysaetos*, migrate through the North Woods, but only the **bald eagle**, *Haliaeetus leucocephalus*, breeds here. Our national bird underwent a nearly catastrophic decline in population after the introduction of DDT in the late 1940s. The pesticide interfered with egg production, causing the females to lay eggs with shells so thin they seldom survived incubation. Reproductive failure in a long-lived species like the bald eagle does not show up immediately, but by the early 1960s, populations were dangerously low.

DDT was finally banned nationally in 1973. Wisconsin anticipated the national ban by three years. Since then the eagles, and other predatory birds, have begun to come back. They are not out of danger yet, but the situation is certainly better than it was. Today bald eagles are more abundant and breeding more successfully in the North Woods than in any part of the United States outside of Alaska.

Eagles feed in and around the water, so you are most likely to see one on the larger lakes and streams. They nest in the tops of tall trees. They take both fish and aquatic birds from the water and various animals from the shore. They frequently eat carrion, and they are famous for robbing ospreys of their meals. Eagles will harass an osprey flying with a fish in its talons until the fish hawk drops its meal.

Bald eagles need open water to find their food, so they migrate south of the North Woods in winter.

Osprey, *Pandion haliaetus.* These fish hawks sometimes dive completely under the water to catch their food. Their talons are ribbed, a trait that makes it easier for them to grip their slippery dinners.

SOARING HAWKS (SUBFAMILY BUTEONINAE) Smaller than eagles, the soaring hawks have the same general outline: long broad wings and wide tails, adaptations for soaring. Three species breed in the North Woods:

Red-Tailed Hawk, *Buteo jamaicensis.* Nests in the trees but hunts over open ground. Look for it soaring over cut-over ground or where farms are interspersed with forests. Red-tails feed on small mammals: rabbits, chipmunks, and mice.

Red-Shouldered Hawk, *Buteo lineatus.* Look for it around water, where it searches for frogs, crayfish, small snakes, and other small animals that live along the water's edge.

Broad-Winged Hawk, *Buteo platypterus.* The most common hawk in the woodlands. Broadwings hunt by perching on tree limbs and scanning the ground below. When they spot something, they drop to the ground and

130. Immature red-tailed hawk, *Buteo jamaicensis*. *National Park Service, Jim Bull.*

snatch it up in their talons. They eat all sorts of woodland creatures, from rabbits and weasels down to beetles. Mice and chipmunks are common prey. Most of the birds taken are ground feeders: thrushes, ovenbird, various sparrows. These are highly migratory birds, and in spring and fall flights of thousands can sometimes be seen riding the up-drafts as they drift south.

ACCIPITERS (SUBFAMILY ACCIPITRINAE) These are woodland hawks that feed primarily on birds. They usually hunt by sitting on a perch until a bird gets close enough,

Animals of the Forests 335

then make a short rapid flight to snatch their meal. Their wings are short and broad, a configuration that gives them an explosive start. Their tails are long and slender. Birds' tails are primarily rudders, and a hawk that lives by chasing birds in the confines of a woodland needs a long tail to make quick turns. All the accipiters are very aggressive hunters, and will finish a chase on foot if their prey takes refuge under dense brush. Three species of accipiters live in the North Woods:

Sharp-Shinned Hawk, *Accipiter striatus.* The smallest of the three. Not much larger than a robin, it nonetheless takes prey as large as the domestic pigeon. Most of its food consists of birds its own size or smaller, including wood-peckers, flycatchers, orioles, blackbirds, jays, warblers, and chickadees.

Cooper's Hawk, *Accipiter cooperii.* A larger version of the sharp-shin, this scarce hawk takes prey as large as grouse and the smaller ducks. Both sharp-shins and Cooper's hawks migrate out of our area in winter.

Goshawk, *Accipiter gentilis.* The largest of the accipiters, it is nearly the size of a pheasant. Its breeding range is mostly north of our area, so most sightings here are in winter, though this bird is always and everywhere uncommon. It takes ducks and grouse.

FALCONS (SUBFAMILY FALCONINAE) Their long pointed wings make them very fast fliers, and their long slender tails give them maneuverability. **Peregrine falcons,** *Falco peregrinus,* used to breed on cliffs around the Great Lakes before DDT wiped them out. Now they are seen only on migration. The one common falcon in the North Woods is the robin-size **kestrel** or **sparrow hawk,** *Falco sparverius.* This is a bird of woodland edges and open ground. It feeds on small birds and mice, although the bulk of its food in summer is probably insects. It has a habit of hovering in one place while scanning the ground below for likely prey. A third falcon, the **merlin,** *Falco columbarius,* breeds in spruce–fir woods.

HARRIERS (SUBFAMILY CIRCINAE) The only representative in our region is the **marsh hawk,** or **northern harrier,** *Circus cyaneus,* a bird with long, slender, blunt-tipped wings and a long tail. It hunts chiefly over wet open ground. Flying low, it covers the ground systematically looking for mice, frogs, and other small animals.

OWLS (ORDER STRIGIFORMES)   Owls take over from the hawks as night is falling. They hunt over the same ground with some of the same methods, and in many places they take the same prey. Owls are preeminent mousers, since more mice are active at night.

Most owls hunt by perching silently on a tree limb and waiting for something to show itself. A short, silent flight, and a mouse is in the talons. Owls have very good eyesight day or night, and their ears are so acute that they can find and catch a mouse in total darkness.

Owls of different sizes and habits favor different kinds of habitat. Five owls nest throughout the North Woods:

The **great horned,** *Bubo virginianus,* is the biggest nesting owl. It is a fierce predator that takes many skunks, minks, and weasels. Great horned owls have been known to kill and eat house cats and they have killed birds as large as Canada geese. More usual food is mice, rabbits, birds from grouse-size down, and a miscellany of cold-blooded animals. Great horned owls nest and hunt in mature deciduous woods, though they favor conifers for roosting. They can get along in woods mixed with fields. They begin to nest in late winter, February or March, and this is when they hoot most often.

Long-eared owls, *Asio otus,* are slightly smaller inhabitants of mature woods. Mice comprise about three-fourths of their diet. These birds are very nocturnal. They spend days roosting quietly in conifers.

Barred owls, *Strix varia,* are the most common owls in the North Woods. They favor mature wet woods and swamps. Their nest sites and eating habits are quite similar to those of the red-shouldered hawk. Barred owls take over old nests of these hawks. Both birds eat frogs and crayfish as well as mice, and neither have talons strong enough to take bigger prey.

Short-eared owls, *Asio flammeus,* hunt day and night. They search the same terrain as the marsh hawk in much the same way, quartering over the marshes and fields in low flights.

The **saw-whet,** *Aegolius acadicus,* is a tiny owl, only 7 inches (18 centimeters) long. It favors conifers and catches mice, insects, and small birds.

In addition to these owls found throughout the North Woods, the **screech owl**, *Otus asio*, is resident in the southern half of our area. Four northern owls also penetrate parts of the North Woods: the **great gray owl**, *Strix nebulosa*, the **boreal owl**, *Aegolius funereus*, the **hawk owl**, *Surnia ulula*, and **snowy owl**, *Nyctea scandiaca*. The great gray may occasionally nest in northern Minnesota, but the others are here only in winter. Owls are among the northern animals whose populations irrupt periodically. When they outbreed their food supply, they will flee their home ground and head south. Irruptions occur at intervals of up to 20 years. Some have taken snowies all the way to Tennessee; others have made boreal owls locally common in northern Wisconsin. These northern owls tend to be very tame and approachable.

THE MUSTELIDS

This group includes weasels, fisher, pine marten, mink, otter, and skunk. Eight species of these small sinuous hunters divide the North Woods. Three hunt for mice and chipmunk on the ground in the uplands; two do most of their hunting in the trees; and the remaining two get their food in or along the water. All hunt mainly at night and all except the skunk are elusive and rarely seen.

We have three weasels, the **short-tailed** or **ermine**, *Mustela erminea*, the somewhat larger **long-tailed**, *Mustela frenata*, and the tiny **least**, *Mustela rixosa*. The least is very rare, almost never seen. It is the smallest member of the order Carnivora. Only the largest males top 2 ounces (57 grams). The long-tailed and short-tailed weasels are similar species whose ranges meet in the North Woods. The long-tailed is the more southern form and is not found in northeastern Minnesota. The more northern range of the short-tailed extends south only to southern Wisconsin.

Weasels hunt on the ground or just below it. Their long slim bodies and short legs are ideal for creeping into chipmunk burrows. They eat mice and insects and ground-nesting birds. All three species turn white in the winter and shades of brown in summer.

The **fisher**, *Martes pennati*, and the **pine marten**, *Martes americana*, are the two arboreal mustelids. They hunt on

131. Fisher, *Martes pennati. Wisconsin Department of Natural Resources.*

the ground, too, but their major prey, squirrels, birds, and—for fishers—porcupines, are mainly found in trees.

Both of these animals died out over much of the North Woods after logging destroyed their habitat. Heavy trapping hurt them, too. Today, breeding populations of pine marten exist only in northeastern Minnesota. There have been attempts to reintroduce them to parts of their former range, so far unsuccessful. A new attempt was started in 1979 in the Nicolet National Forest in northeastern Wisconsin.

Martens are seldom seen outside mature forests, especially those with a good mixture of conifers. Red squirrels, whose prime habitat is conifer woods, are regarded as one of their favorite foods.

Fishers are larger than martens and can take bigger prey. They seem to have developed ways to kill porcupines without being injured by the quills. This makes them very desirable, from the forester's point of view, since high porcupine populations mean trees destroyed by girdling.

Like the marten, the fisher was driven into northeastern Minnesota by logging, but in the late 1950s the Wisconsin Department of Natural Resources began releasing fishers in the northern part of the state. Where the woods had come

Animals of the Forests

back enough to support porcupines in abundance, the fisher reestablished itself. Today more than 2,000 of the animals live all across the Wisconsin North Woods. This is a healthy population for animals that maintain a home range of 10 square miles (25 square kilometers). Fishers are less exclusively nocturnal than martens and weasels.

Minks, *Mustela vison,* hunt the shorelines, although they can swim well enough to catch trout occasionally. A more common diet is frogs, crayfish, mice, and young ducks and duck eggs.

The long slender bodies and short legs of the mustelids adapt well to water. The **otter,** *Lutra canadensis,* largest of the North Woods mustelids, is also the most aquatic and the only one with webbed feet. Some otters are over 5 feet (150 centimeters) long and weigh 30 pounds (14 kilograms), but the usual weight is under 20 pounds (9 kilograms). They dig dens along lakes and streams and hunt for fish, crayfish, and frogs. They do seem playful, and they do make slides in mud or snow that they can ride into the water. They are the most social of the mustelids and usually live in groups.

All the mustelids have musk glands, but only the **striped skunk,** *Mephitis mephitis,* has turned them into defensive weapons. Skunks can throw scent up to 15 feet (5 meters), but concentrations are greater at closer range. The odor hangs on, and the fluid is irritating if it gets in the eyes. This defense is usually effective, but not always. Birds in general have very poor senses of smell, and great horned owls in particular seem completely oblivious to foul odors. They regularly eat skunks. Mammals, too, especially coyotes, will eat skunk if they are hungry enough.

The skunks's diet puts it with the omnivores: insects, birds' eggs, fruits, and carrion. Skunks are easily tamed. In some campgrounds they are practically pets. Skunks are also a common carrier of rabies.

In addition to these resident species, the occasional **wolverine,** *Gulo luscus,* largest of the mustelids and once a resident of the North Woods, may wander from Ontario into Minnesota.

THE CATS

Puma, *Felis concolor.* Pumas used to live here, but the last sightings were around the turn of the century. There have been probable tracks around Duluth, so a sighting in northern Minnesota is remotely possible.

Bobcat, *Lynx rufus.* These small cats used to range over the whole United States. The northern boundary of their range is just north of our region in Ontario. Bobcats are nocturnal. They feed on rabbits and hares, other small mammals, and ground-nesting birds. In hard winters, they take weakened deer around yards.

Bobcats can adapt to the fragmenting of the woods better than their close relative, the lynx. The lynx is a more northern cat and will retreat into unbroken wilderness, but the bobcat will remain and hunt where woods and fields are interspersed. They may hunt over several square miles. They are loosely territorial, marking boundaries with scratches on trees or by spraying scent posts with urine.

Bobcats are louder than domestic cats, but their range of vocal performance is about the same. During mating season in late winter, they may scream much of the night. A male bobcat may stand 2 feet (60 centimeters) high at the shoulder and weigh from 15 to 30 pounds (7 to 14 kilograms).

Lynx, *Lynx canadensis.* More often seen northward, but not common anywhere. Snowshoe hare is its major food. It is less exclusively nocturnal than the bobcat, but chances of seeing a lynx are very small. In winter you may see a track: its feet are huge, heavily furred and almost round. Like the hind feet of the snowshoe hare, this is an adaptation for running in deep snow.

THE CANINES

Coyote, *Canis latrans.* Like the smaller red fox, the coyote eats small mammals, birds, carrion, and a good deal of fruit. Coyotes were very scarce east of the plains until settlement opened up the woods. They have since spread through the east as far as Maine. They are now common over most of the North Woods.

Coyotes are less social than wolves. They hunt alone most of the time, although two animals may team up to bring down larger prey. Deer would be the largest animals they could catch, and they would be unlikely to even try a healthy adult animal. Even when coyotes were the largest predators on Isle Royale, there is no indication that they killed any moose. After wolves came to the island, the coyotes disappeared, apparently killed by the wolves simply for food and perhaps to wipe out a competitive species. The decline in wolf populations throughout the east has certainly helped coyotes colonize the woods.

Red Fox, *Vulpes fulva.* Red foxes are small animals, weighing up to 12 pounds (5.5 kilograms) and standing about 15 inches (38 centimeters) high at the shoulder. They are most common at forest edges or in younger woodlands, although they range widely. They fit their diet to the season. In spring and early summer, during the nesting season, they search for eggs and young birds; in July, when the young red squirrels leave the nest, they hunt squirrels; in late summer and early fall, they mostly eat fruit: wild sarsaparilla berries, strawberries, blueberries, thimbleberries, mountain ash berries, and red oak acorns. The snowshoe hare is a major food of the red fox in winter, although squirrels and muskrats are taken, too. The foxes also take carrion, visiting wolf kills or just discovering dead animals.

Timber Wolf, *Canis lupus.* Wolves were the top carnivores in the North Woods before Europeans inhabited the region. At the apex of the food chain, they preyed on the largest plant eaters—deer, moose, and woodland caribou—and nothing preyed on them. With settlement came loss of habitat and hunting by humans that exterminated wolves over most of their range.

The pack is a wolf society. It is headed by a breeding pair made up of the pack's dominant male and dominant female. Sometimes a subordinate male will associate with the leading pair. Packs may number 15 animals, but most are probably half that size. Pack members are likely to be related, all of them children or siblings of the dominant pair. None of the subordinate animals breed.

Wolves form nonbreeding groups, too, and sometimes lone animals will trail a pack and scavenge on its kills. Maturing young are often driven away from the home pack to look for a suitable territory of their own. If they find one, they will mark its boundaries with urine. Where a breeding pair sets up a new pack, both sexes mark the borders. In northeastern Minnesota, territories are rather stable and range in size from 48 to 120 square miles (124 to 310 square kilometers).

Wolves' hunting methods take advantage of their num-

THE CONSUMERS

bers. They are known to split up, with part of the pack herding the prey toward the others. Because the pack hunts together, 110-pound (50-kilogram) wolves can kill a 1000-pound (450-kilogram) moose. The wolves surround the moose and make quick, slashing attacks on its hind legs and the anal area. This may eventually bring the moose down, or will disable it enough to prevent it from running. Then the pack will move off, leaving one or two wolves to keep a vigil until fatigue, blood loss, and the lack of food and water finish the moose.

On Isle Royale, moose are the major item in the wolves' diet. Studies of relations between the two species have been going on since the late 1950s. In the early years of the study, moose populations were building up, wolf populations were small, but good browse was getting scarce. During this time, nearly all moose killed were calves or old animals; animals from about one year old to eight years old were rarely attacked. Then in 1969, a period of heavy snow began. The snow made tough going for the moose, and the large population began to concentrate on low ground under conifers. They did not yard up as deer do, but eight or ten of the usually solitary animals might be seen in the same cedar swamp. Wolf kills became concentrated in the lowlands, and their numbers went up. The moose were short of food and the snow made it hard to look for more. Meanwhile, this concentration on low ground was letting a year's worth of browse come back in the uplands.

The snowy winters continued. Again the moose headed for the lowland, which the previous year's overbrowsing had made even less productive. There were fewer young born during this time, and they were smaller, weaker, and matured more slowly. Their prey no longer confined to the old and the very young, wolf numbers began to build. They began to take individuals in their prime, and went from a kill every three days to one a day. Instead of picking the carcass clean, they ate the choice viscera and left most of the rest.

We don't know where this process will lead, but it does suggest the sort of cyclical fluctuations that go on between predator and prey. If moose numbers keep going down, they will eventually reach a level that the environment will support. The moose that remain when this point is reached will again be well-fed healthy moose, and few will be forced into marginal habitats in search of food. The years of sparse moose populations will have helped the forest come back enough to provide the food needed. It will be harder for wolves to make a kill, and their population will come down, too, partly as a result of strong social constraints on breeding that help keep their numbers appropriate to the food supply. As the moose population begins to grow, the cycle will begin again.

Wolves today are confined largely to the Superior National Forest and adjacent areas in northern Minnesota and nearby Isle Royale in Lake Superior. Three packs are known to be operating in Wisconsin: two in Douglas County in the northwest corner of the state, and one in Lincoln County along the Wisconsin River. Sightings of lone wolves in Vilas County at the northern edge of the state suggest that a pack may be operating in nearby northern Michigan and sending its young south.

Wolves are never going to dominate the whole North Woods, but it is heartening to know that they have hung on in the region in the face of grim persecution. With a change in public attitudes, their small, scattered numbers may survive.

Omnivores

All of the animals in this group eat insects and dozens of plant foods, and they may take some small mammals, too. With the likely exception of the blue jay, they are all carrion eaters. Ravens specialize in this role, particularly in winter. Soaring over the frozen woods, they perform the same task that turkey vultures undertake farther south. Carrion eaters are part of the process that breaks into simple substances the dead bodies of animals and releases the materials in them to be used again.

Birds

THE FAMILY CORVIDAE

Members of this family—which includes the crows, ravens, and jays—are usually regarded as the most intelligent of birds. They are very adaptable. Omnivores, they feed on whatever is available. We have four species of the family in the North Woods, two jays, the common crow, and the raven.

Blue jays, *Cyanocitta cristata,* are common throughout the eastern United States, especially in oak and pine woods. They are not generally migratory, but they do withdraw from the northern end of their range in winter, which means they are much less common in the North Woods during the colder months. They feed from the ground to the treetops on insects, spiders, snails, tree frogs, small fish, eggs, young birds, acorns, beechnuts, hazelnuts, and berries of all kinds. They cache food when supplies are abundant. Their habit of burying acorns is credited with helping maintain oak forests.

Blue jays are noisy birds whose alarm calls are responded to by many other birds and mammals. They have a special mobbing call which they sound when they spot a predator, especially a hawk or owl. When one bird sounds the call, all the jays in the vicinity pick it up and head for the bird that started it. A hawk or owl surrounded by screaming blue jays has little chance of sneaking up on anything.

The **gray jay** or **Canada jay,** *Perisoreus canadensis,* is a boreal forest bird with a number of nicknames, among them, whisky jack, which is a corruption of the Ojibwa name for the bird, and camp robber, which is a good description of the bird's behavior. Gray jays are much more common in northern Minnesota and on Isle Royale than they are farther south. They favor conifer stands, especially swamps, for breeding, and they survive the harsh winters in part by eating almost anything. They do rob camps. In fact, they will snatch food right off your plate. Trappers hate them for stealing their bait; if the trap has caught anything they will steal that, too.

Crows, *Corvus brachyrhynchos,* are famous for their sagacity. Farmers have sought for centuries to hunt them to extinction, but they are more abundant than ever. They are among the creatures who have thrived as the continent became settled, since they favor trees for nesting and open fields to feed in. Since crows can be serious pests in farmer's fields, there has long been an effort to find out what they eat. So far, the list includes 650 different items, including insects and spiders, carrion, eggs, (including a particular favorite, waterfowl eggs), small birds, and mammals. This variety of animal food accounts for a little over a quarter of their total diet. The rest is plants.

Crows are very cautious and difficult to approach, and flocks generally have a lookout to sound the alarm if anything suspicious gets too close. Like jays, they will mob predators, particularly owls, sometimes following them for hours.

Crows flock together in winter, and most of them migrate out of the North Woods.

Ravens, *Corvus corax,* are the largest birds in the family. They are soaring birds and frequent eaters of carrion. However, ravens also take live prey, sometimes ganging up on creatures as large as young deer. They need large areas of big trees to live and are common only in near wilderness conditions. They are seldom seen south of northernmost Wisconsin and upper Michigan.

Mammals

Black Bear, *Ursus americanus.* The black bear is the largest carnivore in the North Woods, and next to the moose, the largest animal of any kind. A Wisconsin hunter once shot a black bear that weighed over 800 pounds (360 kilograms), but the usual full-grown bear is less than half that big.

Bears seem superbly equipped as predators. They are big, powerful, able to sprint at high speeds; they can climb trees and swim, and they have huge teeth and powerful claws that can tear open a deer with one swipe. In spite of all this weaponry, bears are mainly vegetarian. They prefer fruit and nuts, but they will eat grass and leaves and buds as well. The powerful claws and teeth rip open ant hills and rotting logs to get at the eggs and grubs inside. Most of the meat they do eat is carrion, and their live prey is generally limited to snakes, mice, and nestling birds.

A bear in the North Woods faces three months of inactivity during the winter. This is not true hibernation. The bear's temperature and pulse rate drop slightly but not to

THE CONSUMERS

the low levels attained by true hibernators. Bears bed down in hollow logs, rock overhangs, or just in piles of leaves in sheltered spots. They may awaken occasionally and move about groggily, but they do not feed or defecate throughout the winter.

To prepare for its fast, the bear has to put on a 4-inch (10-centimeter) layer of fat during the spring, summer, and fall, so it eats almost everything in reach. In good habitat a male bear might occupy 5 square miles (13 square kilometers) of feeding territory. Bears are solitary. Male and female may remain together for as long as a month in the June–July breeding season, then they separate. Cubs are born in midwinter while the sow is denned. The cubs stay with their mothers through their first winter and are driven off when she prepares to breed again the following year.

Bears wear regular paths traveling to and from feeding areas, and their cylindrical droppings and their flat-footed prints may show up there. They pull bark off trees in sheets to get at the cambium layer, the inner bark. Perhaps the most common sight of bear presence is a log turned over or clawed apart in the search for insect eggs and larvae in the rotting wood.

Bears need space, so you are most likely to find them where the woods are large and human presence is small. Where they have the room, black bears exploit every type and age of forest. They eat blueberries on newly burned pine land and beechnuts in an old-growth mixed-hardwood forest. They feed in uplands and along lakeshores. They grub for roots and climb trees after fruit. Broken branches on a Juneberry or mountain ash may come from bears grabbing for their meal. Bears may be active at any time, but unless human pressure is heavy they are more often out in daylight than at night.

Life in the Soil

In Part II, The Producers, we pointed out that the canopy is the center of food production in the forest and the soil is the center of consumption. In fact, some production goes on in the soil: Near the surface, where light can penetrate, microscopic algae carry on photosynthesis and provide food for single-celled protozoans. For the most part, however, the activities on and within the soil are those of consumption. Nearly all the remains of dead animals and plants eventually come to rest on the soil, and there the complex organic substances that make up their bodies, leaves, stems, and roots are reduced to their constituent elements and made available for new generations of plants and animals.

Most of the life of the soil consists of bacteria, fungi, and tiny invertebrate animals dependent on this constant rain of dead plants and animals. Some of these animals are found as much as 2 feet (60 centimeters) below the surface, but the great majority are in the upper 6 to 12 inches (15 to 30 centimeters), in the humus and the A layer of the soil. Bacteria are present in staggering numbers, sometimes millions to the gram (0.035 ounce) of soil. They are highly specialized creatures. Some derive their energy from oxidizing nitrogen compounds, with one genus breaking down ammonia into nitrites and a second genus breaking down the nitrites into nitrates, which can then be absorbed by other plants. There is evidence that bacteria are more abundant in soils with mull humus than in those with mor humus. Mull humus is a mixture of decaying plant material and mineral soil characteristic of hardwood forests. Hardwood leaves are rich in mineral bases. Mor humus, characteristic of coniferous forests, is a thin mat of only slightly decayed needles, high in acids, lying over a sharply separated mineral soil. In soil with mor humus, fungi are likely to be more abundant and more important agents of decay than bacteria. Most of the fungi operating in a forest are microscopic, but the fungi also include the mushrooms so common on the forest floor, particularly in late summer.

Macroscopic Fauna

Several phyla of invertebrate animals are important parts of the soil fauna. Doubtless, the most familiar are the earthworms (Annelida). Earthworms eat dead leaves and other decaying plant material. Their burrowing helps aerate the soil, and their droppings improve its fertility in other ways, too. Earthworm casts (as the droppings are called) contain nitrogen, in the form of ammonia, and various mineral bases liberated from the leaves. They make excellent fertilizer. Earthworms show a strong preference for finely textured alkaline soils. Tests of their food preferences show a leaning toward big-toothed aspen, white ash, and basswood. They also eat red and sugar maple, but they will not eat red oak. Millipedes (class Diplopoda) are another saprophage (eater of dead plant materials) found in soils with mull humus.

While earthworms are common in alkaline soils, they are very scarce in mor humus. In these soils, the most abundant saprophagous creatures are arachnids of the order Acari, collectively called mites. A count of these creatures in a podzolized soil under balsam fir showed 15,000 in a square foot between the surface and a depth of two inches, and another 3800 between two and six inches deep. Many mites are highly specialized. One species lays its eggs inside fallen balsam fir needles. When the larvae hatch, they feed on the needle until they are ready to emerge as adults.

Springtails, insects of the order Collembola, are another group of saprophages that are more numerous in mor humus than in mull. Other insects of the soil include the larvae and adults of various beetles and the larvae of some flies. Sow bugs (members of the class Crustacea), molluscs in the form of snails and slugs, and nematodes are other important feeders on dead plant remains.

All of these saprophages are fed on by predators, particularly spiders and centipedes. They also provide meals, of course, for vertebrates of many kinds. Shrews, frogs and toads, snakes, birds, and many others eat members of the soil fauna.

The small mammals that feed on these creatures also have some effect on the soil. Moles search for insects, earthworms, and other soil fauna below the surface. There is one species of mole in the North Woods, the **star-nosed mole,** *Condylura cristata*. Other small animals that dig burrows move material from the subsoil to the surface, promote aeration of the subsoil, and enrich the soil with their droppings. Shrews, moles, mice, and chipmunks may reach cumulative population levels of 100 an acre in some particularly rich woods, and their total effect on the soil is considerable.

Forest Habitats

Vegetation determines the distribution of animals—directly in the case of herbivores, indirectly for carnivores—but the consumers don't always follow the same divisions we outlined in our chapters on plant communities. Age, size, and density of trees is generally as important as the species mix of vegetation in determining what animals live in the forest.

Herbivores look for the plants they eat. Carnivores look for their favorite prey. Many large carnivores will not live around people or in the broken landscape of woods and fields that people create. Lynx and timber wolf will not live in settled land even where prey is plentiful.

Animal succession in a woodland is as regular as plant succession. Certain species invade newly cut or burned ground. They remain for a time as the young trees begin to grow. Other species join them as the habitat changes, and eventually the pioneers become scarce or absent.

We have chosen five vegetation types with distinctive animal populations to show the changes that occur and the common species at each stage. The types are:

1. Recently disturbed ground with young trees, forest edges, and shrub stands such as alder thickets
2. Pole-size deciduous forest, trees 15 to 30 feet (5-10 meters) high
3. Pole-size coniferous forest
4. Mature deciduous forest
5. Mature coniferous forest

The distinction between coniferous and deciduous forests is in practice rather arbitrary, since so much of our forest is a mixture. Expect an animal continuum with species from both habitats showing up more or less in proportion to the relative presence of broad-leaved and coniferous trees.

These five types are cross-referenced to plant communities. We list the major animal species, with some remarks on their distribution and habits. An (N) following the name of a species means that it is more common in the north, and (S) means it is more common south.

1. Recently disturbed ground and other shrubby areas. Animals found in young tree growth, seedlings and saplings less than about 15 feet (5 meters) high, may be found in alder thickets as well. Species in coniferous and deciduous trees are quite similar at this stage of growth. Most of these animals are also common along forest edges where the understory gets enough sun to support a narrow band of shrubbery. Birds that need low dense vegetation concentrate along edges.

HERBIVORES

Cedar Waxwing

Insect eaters on ground
Flicker
Brown thrasher
Robin

Insect eaters in brush
Chestnut-Sided Warbler
Mourning Warbler
Yellowthroat

Insect eaters in air
Kingbird
Tree Swallow

Insect eaters on standing dead trees
Red-Headed Woodpecker (S)

CARNIVORES

Red-Tailed Hawk
Kestrel
Red Fox

OMNIVORES

Skunk
Common Crow

Tree swallows, kestrels, and red-headed woodpeckers are most common where standing dead trees provide nesting holes.

2. Pole-size deciduous forests. Trees 15-30 feet (5-10 m) high, 5-9 in. (13-23 cm) in diameter. Could be second-growth or a fairly dry swamp forest with black ash or red maple. Could be a pine forest now dominated by red oak, red maple, and paper birch. Could also be a young mixed-hardwood forest.

HERBIVORES

Seed eaters on ground
    White-Throated Sparrow

Seed eaters in trees
    Rose-Breasted Grosbeak

Browsers
    White-Tailed Deer
    Snowshoe Hare
    Moose
    Porcupine
    Ruffed Grouse

CARNIVORES

Insect eaters on ground
    Veery (especially on wet ground)
    Ovenbird

Insect eaters in trees
    Mourning Warbler
    Chestnut-Sided Warbler
    Redstart
    Black-Capped Chickadee
    Red-Eyed Vireo
    Downy Woodpecker
    Least Flycatcher (where a deciduous understory has developed)

Larger carnivores
    Fisher
    Weasel
    Timber Wolf

OMNIVORES

Blue Jay
Red Fox

Note the mixture of species remaining from younger woods (chestnut-sided warbler) and late arrivals (red-eyed vireo). The early species should be less common as trees get larger; the late species reverse this trend.

This is prime habitat for browsers, providing young trees and a rich understory. Porcupines and ruffed grouse are particularly partial to aspen stands of this size. The presence of the browsers will bring the predators that feed on them, too, if other conditions, such as absence of human influence, are right.

3. Pole-size conifers. This could be pine, boreal, swamp, or bog forest. There is little difference between this and the deciduous trees of the same size except that magnolia warblers (N) become common here. Deer and moose use young conifers for both food and cover.

4. Mature deciduous forests. Could be mixed-hardwood, older second-growth stands, swamp forest of red maple and black ash, or pine forest of red maple and oak.

HERBIVORES

Seed eaters on ground

Chipmunks
Various Mice and Voles
Towhee

Seed eaters in trees

Rose-Breasted Grosbeak
Gray Squirrel

A maturing forest becomes progressively poorer habitat for deer and other browsers as the shrubs are shaded out.

CARNIVORES

Insect eaters on ground

Wood Thrush (S)
Veery
Hermit Thrush

Insect eaters in trees

Downy Woodpecker
Hairy Woodpecker
Pileated Woodpecker
Yellow-Bellied Sapsucker
Great Crested Flycatcher
Wood Pewee
Least Flycatcher (where understory is rich enough)
Black-Capped Chickadee
White-Breasted Nuthatch
Red-Eyed Vireo
Redstart
Black-and-White Warbler
Black-Throated Blue Warbler (feeds in low shrubbery, especially in yew)
Scarlet Tanager

Larger carnivores

Broad-Winged Hawk
Cooper's Hawk
Great Horned Owl (uplands)
Barred Owl (in wetter forests or near water)

OMNIVORES

Black Bear

5. Mature coniferous forests. Boreal, pine, swamp, bog forest, and hemlock stands in mixed-hardwood forest.

HERBIVORES

Seed eaters on ground

Chipmunks
Chipping Sparrow (especially in pine forest)

Seed eaters in trees

Red Squirrel
Crossbills
Pine Siskin
Evening Grosbeak

Browsers

Spruce Grouse (N)

CARNIVORES

Insect eaters on ground

Swainson's Thrush (N)
Hermit Thrush

Insect eaters in trees

Three-Toed Black-Backed Woodpecker (N)
Three-Toed Northern Woodpecker (N)
Boreal Chickadee (N)
Brown Creeper (N)
Ruby-Crowned Kinglet (N)
Golden-Crowned Kinglet (N)
Black-and-White Warbler
Black-Throated Green Warbler
Parula Warbler
Yellow-Rumped Warbler (N)
Blackburnian Warbler (N)
Cape May Warbler (N)

Large predators

Goshawk (N)
Broad-Winged Hawk
Long-Eared Owl
Pine Marten (N)
Lynx (N)

OMNIVORES

Gray Jay (N)
Raven (N)
Black Bear

CHAPTER SEVENTEEN

Life in Northern Waters

Lakes are the typical form of surface water in the North Woods. Ranging in size from world's largest to tiny ponds that dry up in August, they are scattered throughout the region, clustering where the glaciers left them. Many of them are almost closed systems with very little interchange with their surroundings.

Life in the water is affected by light, temperature, and most of all by the distribution of the gases and minerals essential to living things. Of these essentials, none is more important than oxygen. Water can pick up oxygen and other gases directly from the atmosphere or from photosynthesis by aquatic plants. Moving water picks up more oxygen than still water. In streams, rapids and riffles are oxygen sources. In lakes, the wind moves surface waters and they take in oxygen. However, in many lakes the water somewhat below the surface where algae concentrate and carry on photosynthesis is the most thoroughly aerated part of the lake.

Oxygen dissolves in water, but at best it is present in much smaller quantities than it is in the atmosphere. In lakes this scarcity is compounded by typically slow circulation. Parts of a lake may have enough oxygen to support rich, diverse populations of livings things, while other parts of the same lake, lacking oxygen, are completely stagnant. The processes that affect the distribution of oxygen, and hence the distribution of life, are quite complex. What follows is a very simplified version.

Lake Ecology

Seasonal Cycles

All solids and liquids contract as they cool, but when water reaches a temperature of 39.1° F (4° C), it suddenly reverses this trend and begins expanding, becoming less dense. It continues to expand slowly until it reaches the freezing point, when it undergoes a drastic expansion, jumping almost 10 percent in volume. This characteristic of water is responsible for circulation patterns that bring oxygen to the deep waters of lakes.

In spring when the ice begins to melt, the deep waters in northern lakes are about 40° F (4° C) and therefore quite dense. The surface waters—and ice—are below this critical temperature and therefore lighter. Once the ice is gone, the sun heats the surface layers until the whole lake becomes roughly uniform in temperature and density.

At the same time, the prevailing winds create currents in the surface layers, moving water toward windward shores. Gravity requires some sort of compensating back flow, and most of this occurs below the surface. Thus the whole lake is revolving, with water blowing one way across the surface and then sinking and returning. This circulation, called the spring turnover or spring circulation, moves some oxygen down to the deeper waters.

Through the summer, the surface layers continue to get warmer while the deeper waters remain cold and dense. The return circulation cannot displace this dense water, so it rides up over it. The whole circulation produced by wind then occurs in a warm and oxygen-rich upper layer that is called the *epilimnion* or upper lake. Below the epilimnion is a transition zone, the *thermocline*, where temperatures fall off rapidly. Typically the thermocline is 15 to 30 feet below the surface. Under the thermocline is a cold dense layer, the *hypolimnion*, that is isolated from oxygen after the spring circulation; yet it receives a constant rain of organic matter in the form of corpses and wastes from the plants and animals above. Since deep water fish and the bacteria reducing this organic matter require oxygen, the oxygen level in the hypolimnion continues to decline throughout the summer. In some lakes, oxygen may be completely absent in the hypolimnion by late summer, a condition called *summer stagnation.*

Summer stagnation ends with the fall turnover. With the approach of winter, the surface waters cool until they are denser than the waters of the hypolimnion. At that point, the surface waters begin to sink and the deep waters rise. The oxygen-rich water from the surface flows into the depths and the depleted water comes to the top.

The annual shot of oxygen in the fall turnover is sufficient to supply the entire needs of deepwater creatures in many lakes.

Winter stagnation sometimes develops in small lakes. Almost no oxygen can penetrate the ice, and photosynthesis is kept to a minimum by low temperature and lack of light. Although metabolic activity is low in winter, oxygen depletion can become serious enough to kill fish.

Types of Lakes

Lakes can be classified according to how much life they support and what kind of balance exists between production, consumption, and decomposition. *Oligotrophic* lakes are low in minerals and low in living things. Populations are sparse and species few. Oligotrophic lakes typically have large hypolimnions, and with life sparse, these retain oxygen through the summer. *Eutrophic* lakes are rich in life, so rich that decomposition cannot keep pace. Sediments, both runoff and incompletely decomposed organic matter, build up on the bottom, removing minerals from the cycle of life. As the lake fills, the hypolimnion becomes steadily smaller, while oxygen demand remains high. Deep waters in eutrophic lakes become stagnant in summer. A third type of lake is called *dystrophic.* Here production and decomposition are so far out of balance that the lake is disappearing under a rain of plants and animals. Bog lakes are dystrophic.

The factors that go into determining which of these classes a lake belongs to are numerous and complex. Temperature plays a role. Lakes in the North Woods are frozen part of the year and generally quite cool through the summer, and this supplies a limiting factor on life. The amount and type of runoff the lake receives from the surrounding land is also important. Runoff carries the minerals needed by living things. Lakes on the Canadian Shield have a greater tendency toward oligotrophy since the resistant rocks around and under them supply fewer minerals than the sedimentary rocks under lakes in the eastern half of our area. The Great Lakes are all oligotrophic, but runoff, particularly of phosphorus and other minerals essential to life, may be changing that status. The shape and depth of a lake basin are also important. U-shape basins are typical of oligotrophic lakes. Saucer-shape basins are common under eutrophic lakes.

Lake Habitats and Food Chains

For living things, there are at least four well-defined kinds of habitat in lakes. Nearest the shore is the *littoral zone* where enough sunlight penetrates to the bottom to allow plant growth. In the shallowest water the plants are emergent types—cattails and bulrushes. In slightly deeper water, plants with floating leaves such as pondweed and water lilies are found. Farthest from shore but still within the littoral zone is a zone of submerged vegetation. Plants here may form a dense carpet on the bottom, but they do not reach the surface.

Just beyond the littoral zone is a small *intermediate zone* that is prime habitat for shellfish. The water is too deep to allow rooted plants to grow, but it is well oxygenated by plants nearby. Mussels, snails, and clams thrive.

The upper waters of the middle of the lake are called the *limnetic zone.* Light penetrates here and plant life is rich, but it is made up almost entirely of microscopic, floating forms. The plants support a diverse animal life—including most of the fish—which we will describe below. The littoral and limnetic zones are parts of the epilimnion.

Below the limnetic zone and beyond the reach of the sun is the *profundal zone,* which corresponds to the hypolimnion in summer. Here the only food sources are organic remains from above; animals depend on bacteria and other saprophytic plants. Small shallow lakes may lack a profundal zone, and many ponds and marshes are entirely littoral, since the sun reaches the bottom everywhere.

The conditions in these zones create different kinds of niches. Many of the animals of the littoral are called *benthons* (from *benthos*, meaning 'bottom'). They walk or creep over the bottom or on plant stems, logs or rocks. Snails, crayfish, mussels, and many insect larvae are in this category. Some benthons are permanently attached to one spot.

Neustonic animals are the tiny creatures that live on or under the surface film. Water striders and whirligig beetles are the most familiar of these. They, too, prefer the littoral zone.

The limnetic zone is the home of most of the plankton, the most abundant life in the lake. Plankton are drifters with little or no capacity for independent movement. They include the algae, diatoms, and dinoflagellates—as well as the tiny animals that feed on them—whose photosynthetic activity provides most of the production in the lake.

The *nekton*, or swimming animals, depend directly or indirectly on the plankton for food. In freshwater lakes the nekton are virtually all fish, although turtles and water snakes may sometimes act like benthic animals and sometimes like nekton.

A huge and diverse population of invertebrates, many of them microscopic, depends on the plants of the lake, both rooted and floating. Single-celled protozoans, along with hydra, flatworms, roundworms, rotifers, annelids, and molluscs live on the bottom or float in the water.

The arthropods, the phylum that includes insects, spiders, and crustaceans, are very important in lakes. Tiny crustaceans, copepods and freshwater shrimp, eat algae and protozoa by straining them out of the water. They are typically present in huge numbers, and they provide food for small fish.

Most of the insects spend their larval stage in the water and take to the air as adults. Dragonflies, caddis flies, mosquitoes, and horseflies are good examples. All the biting insects of the North Woods spend their youth in water. Larvae of the infamous black fly need streams of wilderness purity.

The food webs in lakes are very complex. An animal may

be food for another species at one point in its life cycle and prey on the same species at a later stage. Dragonfly larvae feed on the newly hatched fry of many fish. When the fish get big enough, they eat the dragonfly larvae. A fish may start out life eating tiny crustaceans, then progress to larvae and smaller insects, then to tadpoles and crayfish, frogs, and finally to small fish and then bigger fish.

Acid Rain

In recent years, rainfall containing unusual amounts of sulfuric and nitric acid has been discovered to be a major pollutant in inland lakes. These acids originate as sulfur dioxides in smoke from coal-fired boilers and as nitrous oxides from automobile exhausts and other kinds of oil burning. Once in the air, these oxides undergo chemical changes into acids.

Normal rainfall is already slightly acidic. We described in Chapter 6, Soils of the North Woods, how rain combines with carbon dioxide to produce a mild carbonic acid solution that plays an important part in weathering bedrock. But contemporary acid rain may be 40 times as acid as normal rainfall, and an increase this large produces drastic effects. Intense "weathering" by acid rain releases metals from rock, including such highly toxic elements as mercury, lead, and nickel. These metals may be taken up by aquatic animals, including fish. More directly, the increased acidity can kill fish. A number of lakes in New York's Adirondack Mountains have received large amounts of acid rain and are now entirely devoid of fish. A study in Norway showed that seven out of ten lakes with a pH of 4.5—about ten times as acid as the normal rainfall reading of 5.7—were devoid of fish.

Acid rain falling on the already acid surface of northern bogs has the paradoxical effect of stimulating a series of chemical reactions that actually make the bog more alkaline. This change could favor the invasion of plants such as speckled alder or white cedar at the expense of bog shrubs and herbs.

The severity of the effects of acid rain depend in part on the size of a lake and in part on the composition of the bedrock. The Great Lakes are in no immediate danger because of their great size, but smaller lakes can acidify quite rapidly. Lakes on bedrock such as limestone that contains large amounts of calcium are also relatively safe. The calcium neutralizes the acid. However, crystalline igneous and metamorphic rocks such as those on the Canadian Shield contain little calcium. The lakes here are typically soft water—that is they contain few dissolved minerals—so the effects of the acid precipitation are much more pronounced. The Adirondack lakes that have been so severely affected are over bedrock similar to that of the Canadian Shield.

Acid rain is a more serious problem in the northeast than in the Midwest largely because the prevailing westerly winds contain more acids there. Winds reach northern New York after passing over the heavily industrialized areas of Ohio, Michigan, Illinois, Indiana, and Ontario. Westerly winds reach the northern Great Lakes from the plains where there are far fewer sources of pollution. However, acid rain has been discovered falling on Isle Royale. The likeliest source is the paper mills of Thunder Bay, Ontario, just a few miles to the northwest. Some streams on the Canadian side of Lake Huron have become so acid that fish will not enter them to spawn. A coal-fired power plant planned for Atikokan, Ontario, just across the border from the Boundary Waters Canoe Area, could threaten the soft-water lakes of that wilderness.

While the effects of acid rain are most drastic in water, it may affect soils as well. We noted in Chapter 16 that large populations of earthworms and bacteria were typical of more alkaline soils, while fungi were the major decomposers in acid soils with a mor humus layer. It has not yet been demonstrated that acid rain can produce an acid soil with fewer earthworms, less bacteria, and less fertility, but the possibility does exist.

Life in the Depths: The Fish

Many of the small fish that feed on the insects and crustaceans in northern lakes belong to the family Cyprinidae, the minnows, a name that is often applied indiscriminately—and incorrectly—to almost any small fish, though it properly belongs to this family alone. The next link in the food chain is occupied by fish of moderate size that anglers usually lump together as pan fish. **Yellow perch,** *Perca flavescens,* which grows to a maximum weight of one pound (about a half kilogram) is a common pan fish in North Woods lakes. At the top of the food chain are the large predators, the game fish sought after by fishermen. The most ferocious and elusive of these is the **muskellunge** (muskie for short), *Esox masquinongy,* a pike that may grow to 50 pounds, (23 kilograms) or more. The closely related **northern pike,** *Esox lucius,* lives everywhere from warm, shallow, weedy waters to deep cold bays.

Lake trout, *Salvelinus namaycush,* are lovers of cold water that are confined to the Great Lakes and the deeper inland lakes. In summer, when surface waters warm up, lake trout move into the cold waters of the hypolimnion. In Lake Superior, anglers troll for them 200 feet (60 meters) down; in warmer Lake Michigan waters, lake trout have been netted at 800 feet (240 meters). Obviously lake trout cannot live in lakes that undergo summer stagnation in deep waters. The **walleye,** *Strizostedion vitreum,* is another cold-water fish that seeks deep water in summer.

The **northern smallmouth bass,** *Micropterus dolomieu,* which is not native to northeastern Minnesota, prefers moderate-size lakes with clear water and gravel bottoms. The **largemouth bass,** *Huro salmoides,* is more a fish of the littoral zone, preferring shallow weedy waters where it feeds on both minnows and frogs.

Another large group of fish are omnivorous bottom feeders that live on insects, crustaceans, mollusks, and vegetation. In addition to the introduced **carp,** *Cyprinus carpio,* there are the catfish and bullheads of the family Ameiuridae and the suckers of the family Catostomidae.

Food chains in lakes feature the pyramid of decreasing numbers from bottom to top that is also typical of terrestrial ecosystems. Billions of algae feed millions of copepods which support tens of thousands of minnows, and so on. At the top of the pyramid are a small number of very large, and therefore very old, game fish; just below them are greater numbers of smaller fish of the same species who will move into the top spots when the old fish die. The largest fish can be removed with little effect on the ecosystem, but if fishing pressure becomes too heavy and the smaller game fish are removed, an apparently irreversible change takes place in the lake's population. With no larger predators to limit their numbers, pan fish such as yellow perch or **bluegills,** *Lepomis macrochirus,* undergo a population explosion. Their numbers increase dramatically, but their food supply does not. The lake becomes home to a very large number of very small fish.

The natural populations of many North Woods lakes have been considerably altered by overfishing of particular species combined with extensive programs of stocking and introduction carried on in all three states in the region. Tourism is important to the economies of many parts of the North Woods, and anglers are the most numerous group of tourists, so a considerable effort is made to see that they have something to catch. Accidental introduction of non-native species, as we shall see, has also brought changes to lake ecologies.

A History of Great Lakes Game Fish

Because the Great Lakes are relatively young and their ecology thus relatively simple, there were few predators at the top of the food chain even before settlement. **Lake trout,** various species of **chub,** and another, lesser known fish called the **burbot,** *Lota lota,* were abundant in deep waters; **whitefish,** *Coregonus clupeaformis,* **lake herring,** *Leucichthys artedi,* and **sturgeon,** *Acipenser fulvescens,* occupied shallower zones; yellow perch were among a handful of species which made their home in sheltered bays. Indians of the region, who fished with bone hooks, fiber nets, and spears, had little impact on this ecology; and the earliest European explorers were more interested in the animals, like beaver and mink, that frequented only the edges of the lakes, than those which lived in the lake itself.

IMPACT OF SETTLEMENT

The War of 1812 and the American settlement which followed changed the situation drastically. Fishing villages had sprung up around all three upper Great Lakes—Huron, Michigan, and, to a lesser extent, Superior—by the 1830s; populations of all the inshore species declined seriously within a few decades, especially in Michigan and Huron. (Lake Superior, most remote of the three, was least affected. This pattern has continued through most of the human changes brought to the lakes.)

Whitefish and lake herring suffered from the great demand for their delicate meat. Sturgeon were at first considered valueless. They were ugly, to start with, or so local fishermen thought—huge, primitive creatures with bony scales, long pointed snouts, and thick lips which could be extended for picking up food. Weighing 25 to 400 pounds (9 to 180 kilograms), they became tangled and took up space in the nets meant for other, more valuable, species. They were further resented for eating the eggs of the other fish. Sturgeon caught in those days were hauled ashore, stacked high in piles, doused with kerosene, and burned.

Later it was discovered that gelatin obtained from sturgeon swim bladders made excellent isinglass, used in carriage windows. A profitable market also developed for caviar made from sturgeon roe. In 1880, more than 4 million

132. Sharp-nosed, blunt-nosed, and shovel-nosed sturgeons, *Acipenser fulvescens.*

pounds (1.8 million kilograms) of them were caught in Lake Michigan; by 1900 the catch had declined to a mere 140,000 pounds (63,400 kilograms).

Attempts to restock sturgeon failed, mainly because it is a very slow-growing fish. Sturgeon take even longer to mature than humans—22 to 25 years—and after they are mature they spawn only about once every five years. The egg-laying process takes several months, with only a few eggs laid in any one place at any one time.

Although fossil records indicate sturgeon have been around at least 50 million years, only a few stragglers survive in the Great Lakes today. They are among endangered species listed by the U.S. Department of the Interior.

EARLY EFFECTS OF TECHNOLOGY

Whitefish and lake herring did not disappear quite so quickly and irrevocably, mainly because biologists were able to restock them successfully after this first and several subsequent crises. Among those later crises was the destruction of spawning streams by deposition of sediment over gravel beds.

Industrial pollution started earlier than many people realize. The region's first major industry was lumbering, and the Milwaukee River in Wisconsin was already so saturated by sawmill wastes in 1885 that fish seeking spawning grounds were unable even to enter it.

Improvements in fishing technology just before and in the first decades after the turn of the century had more immediately measurable effects, however, not just on the nearshore species but on the lakes' main deepwater predators, the lake trout and chub.

The earliest developments were gill nets, pound nets, and steam-powered tugs, all in use by the 1880s; deep-water traps were introduced in the late 1920s and early 1930s. Gasoline engines and the use of nylon rather than cotton or linen nets added to the impact in more recent years.

Lake trout populations declined steadily and the weight of individual fish caught grew gradually smaller through the first four decades of this century; the final blow to their existence would be struck in the 1940s through an indirect effect of technology—the introduction of the sea lamprey from Lake Ontario by way of the Welland Canal.

Introduction of Exotic Species

The introduction of exotic species—whether plants or animals—has often had disastrous effects on native ecosystems. In the Great Lakes, such introductions so far have had mixed results.

Carp and **smelt**, *Osmerus mordax*, were among the first non-native fish to thrive in Great Lakes waters. Neither, apparently, had any drastic effects on predator–prey balance. Nineteenth-century European immigrants brought with them the custom of raising carp for food in farm ponds, and most of the fish of that species in the Great Lakes today are the descendants of escapees from those ponds. Carp are apparently more abundant in Lake Michigan than in the other two upper Great Lakes, probably because there is more farmland along its shores and on tributary streams. Carp are able, even prefer, to spawn in mud, so agriculture- and industry-deposited sediment in spawning streams— devastating to species like the whitefish which require clear, gravelly stream beds—has daunted the carp not at all.

Smelt were native to Lake Ontario but first appeared in Lake Michigan in 1923. They apparently escaped from a salmon-raising project on Crystal Lake adjacent to Lake Michigan where they had been introduced as forage.

Until the 1940s, changes in the lakes had affected individual species but had altered the lakes' overall stability only slightly.

ARRIVAL OF THE SEA LAMPREY

The Welland Canal was built between Lakes Ontario and Erie in 1825 to allow ships to bypass Niagara Falls. Among ocean species of fish which have taken the same route, the one which has had the greatest effect on Great Lakes ecology is the **sea lamprey**, *Petromyzon marinus* (Linnaeus). In 1921 it appeared in Lake Erie. By 1937 it was in Lake Huron. It was first seen in Lake Michigan in 1943 and in Lake Superior in 1954.

Sea lampreys spawn in clear, cool, gravelly streams, and then the adults die. The eggs hatch in a week or two, and the larval lampreys are wafted by stream currents into quiet waters where they burrow into soft mud and feed on microscopic organisms and debris for the next five years. In the fifth year they develop eyes, a sucking mouth with horny teeth, and the enlarged fins of adults. In the spring of that fifth year they emerge from the mud and drift downstream to the deep waters of the lake where they become parasites, feeding on the blood of larger fish.

Commercial catches of lake trout in Lake Michigan fell from a 75-year average of four to six million pounds to less than a few hundred thousand pounds and then to nothing within eight years of the sea lamprey's arrival. The effects in other lakes were similar. Presumably, the lamprey also fed on burbot. Because it has never been a popular game fish, careful records have not been kept.

A chain reaction thus begun soon affected many other fish. Populations of chub, the lake trout's former prey, exploded briefly, but the sea lamprey soon included them in its diet, too. There were once seven chub species in the Great Lakes; only the **bloater chub**, *Leucichthys hoyi*, smallest and slowest-growing of the seven, remains today.

Decline of the chubs favored another new species, the alewife, *Alosa pseudoharengus*. The first alewife made its way through the Welland Canal into Lake Erie in 1931; 18 months later one was captured in northern Lake Huron. Alewives crossed the Straits of Mackinac to Lake Michigan in 1949; they were first documented in Lake Superior in 1954. This small fish, a relative of ocean herring, never became abundant in Lake Erie; the deep water alewives favor in winter is limited in that lake; Erie has also always had a large population of predators. Lake Huron, too, had a large population of lake trout and burbot that would have preyed on the alewife when it entered that lake in the 1930s. Lake Superior is too cold to be prime alewife habitat, so this newcomer's most devastating effect has been on Lake Michigan. Timing was an important reason. Alewives reached Lake Michigan just after that lake's main predator, the lake trout, had been depleted almost to extinction by the sea lamprey. By 1966, 70 percent of the commercial catch in Lake Michigan was alewife, with carp and other foragers making up the remainder. A population explosion and subsequent dieoff of this species occurred the next year, but reproduction soon brought the numbers back up.

THE CONSUMERS

SOME GOOD NEWS

The Great Lakes in general, and Lake Michigan in particular, reached a peak of instability in 1967. The lakes have since, at least temporarily, become more stable. A chemical larvicide for sea lamprey was developed in 1958, and by 1966 all tributary spawning grounds had been treated with the larvicide at least once. Sea lamprey populations have now dropped dramatically, although there is some slight evidence that the lamprey may be adapting to the chemical.

The introduction of several oceangoing fish—steelhead trout, coho and chinook salmon—has since provided a new predator population; whitefish in Lake Superior and northern Lake Michigan have begun reproducing naturally (rather than merely in hatcheries) in greater numbers each year; lake trout have begun reproducing naturally in a few protected spots.

Yellow perch, long a favorite of shore fishermen, had moved farther out into the lakes when the alewife at its peak was crowding inshore areas. The perch, too, are now showing up again within reach of sport anglers' lines.

THE TOXINS

Newer and more subtle menaces, however, still threaten the Great Lakes and other lakes and streams of the North Woods. They are chemical toxins, byproducts of industry and agriculture.

Rachel Carson made everyone aware of the dangers of DDT when she wrote *Silent Spring* in 1960. It took another decade for commercial manufacture of the deadly pesticide to be banned, and DDT only began in 1980 to drop to low levels in the food chain that includes Great Lakes fish and the consumers of those fish. The chemical still resides in lake bottom sediments.

Polychlorinated biphenyls, better known as PCBs, were used in carbonless carbon paper and also as insulating fluid in the electrical industry before they were made illegal several years ago. They were first recognized as a threat to human health in Japan in 1968. In addition to causing headaches, eyelid swelling, temporary loss of vision, and other immediate effects, PCBs in very high concentrations were also found to be carcinogenic in laboratory animals.

PCB levels are still dangerously high throughout the Great Lakes. Pregnant and nursing women are cautioned not to eat lake fish.

Among other modern threats to life in the lakes are thermal and radioactive pollution. Water used to cool industrial machinery and power-generating equipment is often flushed into the lakes at temperatures several degrees above normal levels. Small rises in temperature can trigger hatching of fish eggs before their food supply has developed.

Radioactive pollution can result from leakage at nuclear power plants or, in the extreme, from a "meltdown" of such a plant, the phenomenon which came within a few hours of happening at the Three Mile Island nuclear facility in Pennsylvania.

Phosphorus, a common nonmetallic element in the environment, also endangered the lakes in recent years when excessive use of it in agricultural fertilizer and detergents speeded up the natural process of eutrophication and deprived lake animals of needed oxygen. Phosphorus levels have recently declined in the lakes, partly because of local bans on phosphate detergents and partly because of improvements in city water systems. Scientists also learned that phosphorus flushed out of the lakes more quickly than they had anticipated.

A potential new threat to the food chain is a rising concentration of chloride which is already producing red algae, a salt-water species, in some nearshore areas of Lake Michigan. Chloride is a waste product of steel production.

Life on the Edge: Birds and Mammals

Life in the lake is all cold-blooded, but on the surface and around the edges birds and mammals live in abundance. In the limnetic zone, loons and mergansers dive for fish; ospreys and bald eagles snatch them from just under the surface. Otters hunt in streams or in lakes close to shore.

In the littoral zone, dabbling ducks, beavers, and muskrats feed mainly on rooted vegetation, while diving ducks go after small invertebrates on the bottom as far out as the shellfish zone. Kingfishers hunt near lake and stream shores. Gulls feed on carrion, both in the water and along shore. The great blue heron, mink, red-shouldered hawk, and short-eared owl all hunt in shallow water or along the shore, searching for fish, crayfish, frogs, turtles, and small mammals. Raccoons and black bears often come down to the water to feed on similar fare or on carrion. Red-winged blackbirds nest in cattails or shrubs along the shore and feed on seeds and insects. Their close relatives, the grackles, feed along the shore or in shallow water on an omnivorous diet.

The remainder of this chapter is devoted to information about these animals, beginning with deepwater carnivores and continuing with herbivores, carnivores, and omnivores of the littoral zone. Ducks, whose various species fall into several categories, will be treated together.

Deepwater Carnivores

Common Loon, *Gavia immer.* Loons breed on large lakes, particularly those that are remote from civilization. They are big birds with a wingspan close to 5 feet (150 centimeters). An adult may weigh 15 pounds (7 kilograms). Their legs are placed at the rear of their streamlined bodies, where they are most effective as paddles, but of very little use on land. Loons have been taken in nets set 180 feet (55 meters) below the surface. They have been clocked in dives lasting 15 minutes, although a minute or less is more usual.

Loons come ashore only to nest, and most of the time they build their nest in the water amid cattails or rushes or right on the shoreline in alders or willows. Ideally, the birds will be able to swim directly to the nest. Traveling on land is a slow and difficult business for them. They lurch and stagger and shove themselves along on their bellies.

In the water, they swim with much of their bodies underwater. They can dive in an instant, and once below the surface move fast enough to catch trout and other game fish. Loons prefer fish in the 4- to 6-inch (10- to 15-centimeter) range. They spear the prey with their long beaks and then surface, flip the fish off, and swallow it whole, usually head first. Loons can fish in the deepest parts of lakes, and they are big enough that nothing can eat the adults.

Loons begin arriving in the North Woods as soon as the ice is off the lakes. They are powerful, fast fliers, but their small wings make it hard for them to land and take off. They slam hard into the water coming in. Taking off, they run over the surface, wings flapping furiously for as much as 100 yards before they can get airborne. Their problems with flight may be what confines them to larger lakes.

Loons are wilderness birds. Development along northern lakes has cost them much of their old range. There are signs now that remaining loons are not reproducing well, perhaps because of human disturbance. Loons may live 25 years, so the lack of offspring may not show up for a time. If you see loons, be content to admire them from a distance. Don't try to chase them in a canoe, and don't clomp through likely nesting sites along the shore.

Loons call through spring and summer, often at night. The call is eerie and maniacal, a demented laughter. The birds are very territorial. Only the largest lakes can support two breeding pairs. Loons often visit other lakes to feed.

Other open-water carnivores are osprey, bald eagle and otter, all of which are described along with other members of their families in the preceding chapter. Other open-water predators are mergansers, ducks specialized for catching fish. Their habits are described below with the other ducks.

Divers and Dabblers

Ducks of the North Woods (family Anatidae) can be divided into three groups: dabblers (subfamily Anatinae), diving ducks (subfamily Aythyinae), and mergansers (subfamily Merginae). The dabblers are primarily vegetarian and feed by tipping up in the water with their hind quarters in the air. They can reach the bottom only in very shallow water. Divers eat animal food and are heavy-bodied ducks that can swim under water and feed at depths of 20 feet (6 meters) or more. Mergansers are divers who specialize in eating fish. They have long, slender bills with serrated edges that help hold onto slippery prey.

Mallards, *Anas platyrhynchos,* **black ducks,** *A. rubripes,* and **green-winged** and **blue-winged teal**, *A. crecca* and *A. discors*, are all dabblers that breed in the North Woods (although the green-winged teal breeds only in northern Minnesota). Mallards can reach bottom in water 12 to 16 inches (30 to 40 centimeters) deep. Teals are much smaller than mallards and black ducks and feed in even shallower water.

All the dabblers eat seeds of sedges, pondweeds, and other aquatic plants. They also eat leaves, stems, and tubers of rooted plants in the shallows. Animal food includes snails, shrimp, insects, and other tiny creatures. All the dabblers can take flight instantly, leaping into the air in a single bound.

Wood ducks, *Aix sponsa,* perhaps the most beautiful North American birds, are dabblers who nest in holes in trees, often as high as 50 feet (15 meters) up. Their nests may be some distance from water. They feed on the usual aquatic seeds but sometimes leave the water to feed on acorns and beechnuts in upland forests.

Diving ducks swim under water to search for food. The **goldeneye,** *Bucephala clangula,* a diver that nests and winters in the North Woods, can feed on the bottom under 20 feet (6 meters) of water, although most of its dives are much shallower. Its food is chiefly crustaceans, molluscs, and other small invertebrates. The heavy diving ducks must run along the water to get airborne.

The goldeneye winters on the Great Lakes and inland where it can find open water. We once flushed a flock of goldeneyes from a small patch of open water just below Pipestone Falls in the Boundary Waters Canoe Area Wilderness. It was the last week in February. They were in what was probably the only open water in miles.

Three species of merganser breed in the North Woods. The smallest—the **hooded merganser,** *Lophodytes cucullatus*—nests on small ponds or along woodland streams. It is the only one of the three mergansers that can spring into flight in a leap. The other two have to run along the water.

Both the **American merganser,** *Mergus merganser,* and the **red-breasted merganser,** *M. serrator,* hunt on larger lakes. The red-breasted is the most social of the three. They sometimes form long ranks that move forward together to

133. Female American merganser, *Mergus merganser*—a diver. *National Park Service.*

drive fish into shallow water. The mergansers are the only birds that might rival loons as predators in deeper water.

Herbivores of the Littoral Zone

Beaver, *Castor canadensis.* Beavers rank second only to humans in their ability to deliberately alter their environment. Beaver dams turn swift-flowing streams into ponds. As water behind the dam rises over the former stream bank, trees are killed. "Forests" of standing dead timber mark many recent dams. In time this timber will fall, leaving open water or marsh vegetation. If the dam breaks, water levels will go back down, and a low meadow, primarily of sedges will grow where once there was a forest. Silt deposits leave former pond bottoms level and very fertile. These beaver meadows are common throughout the North Woods.

The beaver is the largest rodent in the North Woods. Adults weigh 60 pounds (27 kilograms), and a few individuals reach 90 pounds (40 kilograms). They live in colonies, typically consisting of two breeding adults, kits born during the year, and yearling youngsters. An average colony's territory includes 6 to 10 acres of water and surrounding land up to 400 yards from the water's edge.

Beavers are monogamous, and they may mate for life. Breeding occurs in winter; the young are born in early spring. They remain with their parents until the spring of their second year, when they have to strike out on their own.

Beavers are entirely vegetarian. Their summer diet is varied: seeds, stems, roots of sedges and water grasses, water lilies, and other aquatic plants. They also eat bark, leaves, and twigs. In winter they eat the inner bark of tree branches they have stored during the summer. The food is stored under water, and the food supply is the reason beavers need dams. In cold winters, very shallow streams can freeze to the bottom. If this happens, the underwater food cache becomes inaccessible, and the beavers starve. On larger streams or in lakes where there is always open water under the ice, the animals do not try to build dams.

Beavers get their food by felling trees with their teeth. Once the tree is down, the beavers gnaw it into sections. The larger branches are used for dam building and house construction. The smaller go into the food supply. Beavers seldom travel more than a few hundred yards on land looking for food. They may even dig small canals from the main pond to take them to good things to eat and make it easier to get the timber back to their cache. Their most favored food is aspen, but others that are frequently used include alder, willow, mountain maple, white birch, pin cherry, ash, and hazel. An acre of aspen trees will feed a colony of seven for a year.

Beavers build dams by laying down sticks and packing them with stones and mud dredged up from the bottom of the stream. This dredging helps to further deepen the pond. Some of these dams reach immense size. One measured 12 feet (3 meters) high and 650 feet (200 meters) long. A single colony of beavers may build a series of dams along a stream, perhaps for additional safety. If any damage occurs to any dam, the beavers hurry to repair it immediately.

Beaver lodges are also built of sticks. The lodge is placed out in the pond away from shore. The entrance is always under water and below the depth of winter ice. A large beaver lodge may be 5 to 6 feet (150 to 180 centimeters) high and 15 to 20 feet (4.5 to 6 meters) across at the water level. The walls of a large lodge may be 4 feet (1 meter) thick, which means it is nearly impossible for predators to break through. Inside, the lodge is one room up to 3 feet (90 centimeters) high and 5 feet (150 centimeters) wide. As many as 10 beavers may occupy a single lodge. On large lakes and rivers, beavers live in burrows in the banks rather than in lodges. The burrows also have underwater entrances.

Beavers are largely nocturnal. They stay in the lodge by day and come out at night to work on their dams and to feed. Beavers are unaggressive and very slow on land—a person walking fast can overtake one—so they seldom go far from water.

When ice covers the water, the beavers remain in the lodge. They swim out under the ice only to take food from their underwater cache. A beaver's nose and ear valves shut as it submerges. Transparent membranes protect the eyes. Their lips close behind their teeth, so they can carry—or gnaw through—sticks while underwater. They can remain underwater for 20 minutes, time enough to gnaw through a 6-inch (15-centimeter) tree.

134. Beaver, *Castor canadensis. National Park Service.*

THE CONSUMERS

135. Tree gnawed by beaver. *Glenda Daniel.*

Beavers leave abundant signs of their presence: dams, lodges, trees gnawed through, canals, and scent mounds. A scent mound, apparently a territory marker, is a small pile of mud, grass, and sticks shoved together and marked with castoreum, a bitter, orange–brown musk oil produced by glands under the tail.

Beavers use their broad flat tails chiefly as rudders when they are swimming. A slap of the tail on water also serves as a warning of danger. If you hear the slap as you approach a

Life in Northern Waters

377

pond in the woods, you can be sure that beavers are there; you can be just as sure that they will be out of sight by the time you reach the shore.

Beavers were the chief quarry of the international fur trade in North America, which began to move into the North Woods in the late 17th century. Their dense inner fur could be felted and turned into hats, and the demand for it was large and constant. The trade in the early days was dominated by French–Canadians who came in 30-foot (9-meter) canoes called Montreals and set up trading posts around the shores of the Great Lakes and later inland on rivers. Indians did the actual trapping, taking their furs to the posts to barter for iron pots, steel knives, needles, muskets, wool blankets, and other useful goods.

In time, beaver populations around the Great Lakes became so depleted that the trappers had to go far to the north and west to get good skins. The chaos and habitat loss that followed logging combined with the trapping to reduce beaver populations to dangerously low levels. By 1900, estimates are that there were fewer than 500 beavers in the state of Wisconsin. Trapping seasons were closed and restocking efforts begun. At the same time, the forests began to come back, including millions of acres of aspen, the beaver's favorite food. Today, trappers in Minnesota alone take 20,000 to 30,000 animals a year, and populations are still large and probably growing. In some places, beavers have become a nuisance species. Their dams may flood pastures and plowed fields.

Muskrat, *Ondatra zibethica.* Small, hugely prolific rodents that live in and along shallow lakes, marshes and streams. Largely vegetarian, they eat cattail tubers and young shoots and various other aquatic plants. They also eat clams and dead fish in smaller amounts.

Like beavers, they build dome-shape houses in the water, though the muskrat houses are much smaller and less substantial. They build chiefly with grasses, cattails, and rushes, using few sticks. Like beavers, they also burrow in banks. Entrances to both kinds of dens are under water.

Muskrats typically produce two to three litters of 5 to 11 young every year. Over a million hides are taken yearly by trappers in the North Woods. Muskrats are also taken by hawks, owls, foxes, and mink.

378

Carnivores of the Littoral Zone

FROGS

The common frogs of North Woods lakes include the **green frog**, *Rana clamitans*, and the **mink frog**, *Rana septentrionalis*. The green frog is nearing the northern edge of its range here, while the mink frog is a northern form whose range extends only as far south as central Wisconsin. The **bullfrog**, *Rana catesbeiana*, does not occur naturally in western Upper Michigan and in northern Minnesota but has been introduced in various places in hope of stimulating a commercial frogging industry. Both green frogs and bullfrogs require two years for the transformation from tadpole to adult in the short summers of our region.

Frogs are all mainly insect eaters along the shores of lakes, ponds, and streams. The best way to find and identify them is through their songs. A recording of frog songs is listed in the Bibliography.

TURTLES

Snapping Turtle, *Chelydra serpentina*, is the largest local turtle. Wild specimens weighing up to 35 pounds (16

136. Green frog, *Rana clamitans. National Park Service.*

Life in Northern Waters 379

kilograms) have been found, and captives fattened for the table may weigh much more. Snappers can be quite aggressive on land, but in water they typically lie half buried in mud and wait for something edible to happen by. They could be categorized as omnivores or carnivores, since they eat aquatic vegetation, insects, crayfish, fish, reptiles, aquatic mammals and birds (including young ducks), and carrion.

Painted Turtle, *Chrysemys picta.* The most visible North Woods turtle, since it often basks on logs and rocks. Painted turtles live in shallow weedy places, and like the snapper their food habits are varied. They tend to be mainly carnivorous when young, becoming increasingly vegetarian as they mature.

SNAKES

Northern Water Snake, *Natrix sipedon.* The only water snake in the North Woods. It is quite common within its range, Wisconsin and Lower Michigan, but it is not found in northern Minnesota or the Upper Peninsula. Water snakes may be found in all kinds of wet situations: swamps, marshes, bogs, streams, ponds, and lake borders. Their main food is frogs, toads, and small fish.

BIRDS

Pied-Billed Grebe, *Podilymbus podiceps.* Grebes are diving birds like loons, but they are very much smaller. The largest species to breed in any part of the North Woods is only 13 inches (33 centimeters) long, and its wingspan is less than 3 feet (90 centimeters), but the most common grebe, the pied-billed, is much smaller than that, only 9 inches (23 centimeters) long.

Pied-billed grebes are birds of quiet shallow waters. They nest in ponds, in shallow protected arms of big lakes, and in marshes. They do not hunt in the open water as loons do. They eat small fish, but also various crustaceans, frogs, aquatic worms, leeches, and insects. They eat some plant seeds. Look for them where reeds and cattails are invading the water. They build floating nests anchored to such plants.

The young often ride on their mother's back until they are old enough to dive for themselves. Grebes usually dive

137. Immature great blue heron, *Ardea herodicus*. *Wisconsin Department of Natural Resources.*

headfirst, but they can control their buoyancy well enough to just sink out of sight or swim along with only the tops of their heads showing.

Great Blue Heron, *Ardea herodicus.* In the North Woods, the most conspicuous heron is the great blue. Its wingspan of nearly 6 feet (180 centimeters) is exceeded only by the eagles in this part of the world. Standing along a lakeshore, it is nearly 4 feet (120 centimeters) high. Herons fly with slow, steady wingbeats, legs stretched out behind them, necks bent into a tight U.

They arrive early in spring and feed mainly in the shallow waters near the shores of lakes, ponds, and rivers. They have been seen floating in deep water as they fished, but most of their work is done in water less than 2 feet (60 centimeters) deep. They may stand absolutely still and wait for something to swim by. Their patience apparently cannot be exhausted. They may stalk their food, stepping slowly and cautiously through the shallows and peering around for something likely. While most of their diet is fish, they take appreciable numbers of frogs, tadpoles, crayfish, and various small reptiles. They eat an occasional marsh bird and some mice. They sometimes feed in uplands in open fields, especially when good insect crops attract them. They are at the top of any food chain in which they are found, since the adults are too big and formidable to be likely prey. Eggs and young are taken by various large birds of prey: red-tailed and red-shouldered hawks and great horned owls, as well as crows and ravens.

Great blue herons nest in colonies that sometimes number hundreds of birds, though North Woods colonies are likely to be much smaller than that. They build their nests near the tops of tall trees, sometimes in swamps, sometimes in the uplands. Loss of suitable nest sites to heavy logging has hurt their population, and human disturbance is hurting more. If you come across an active heron rookery in the woods, look at it quickly from a distance and move on.

Kingfisher, *Megaceryle alcyon.* Kingfishers are a familiar sight along the shores of lakes and streams. They live mainly on fish with a supplement of crayfish, shellfish, insects, and some mice. They hunt from perches in trees and shrubs along the shore. They often hover over likely spots in the water before diving in to snatch a fish. They nest in burrows in banks steep enough to be largely free of vegetation.

SWALLOWS, (FAMILY HIRUNDINIDAE) Six species of this family of aerial insect eaters live in the North Woods. They all feed by capturing insects on the wing, and they spend most of the day in flight. All tend to nest in colonies near water. The **purple martin,** *Progne subis,* and the **barn swallow,** *Hirundo rustica,* are the most domesticated, frequently nesting near people. **Cliff swallows,** *Petrochelidon pyrrhonota,* build mud nests on rock faces, while **bank swallows,** *Riparia riparia,* and **rough-winged swallows,** *Stelgidopteryx ruficollis,* dig burrows in earthen banks. **Tree swallows,** *Iridoprocne bicolor,* favor holes in standing dead trees.

Other carnivores on or near shore include mink, red-shouldered hawk, marsh hawk, short-eared owl. (See Chapter 16.)

Omnivores

The **red-winged blackbird,** *Agelaius phoeniceus,* and the **grackle,** *Quiscalus quiscula,* are the most common omnivorous birds of the shores. Both belong to the ground-feeding branches of the family that also includes the tree-feeding orioles. Both are very adaptable birds whose populations have exploded since European settlement changed the continent. Redwings are primarily birds of wetlands, both marshes and shrub stands, but they have learned to feed in plowed fields as well. Grackles now nest almost everywhere that people live. They feed on lawns, golf courses, plowed fields, and pastures.

Both these birds like open ground, so you will not find them living under trees, though nearly every cattail marsh, open bog, alder thicket, willow clump, or bog birch stand is likely to have redwings nesting in it. Redwings are polygamous. A single male may defend a territory that shelters two or three nesting females. They tend toward colonial nesting in choice locations.

Redwings are omnivorous feeders. They are mainly insect eaters in spring and early summer. They eat more seeds and fruit late in the season. Most redwings and grackles winter in the mid-South: Arkansas, Tennessee, Virginia, and the Carolinas. They are among the earliest spring arrivals, moving into the southern end of the region by early March. In early August the redwings begin to flock, and they are gone from many areas by the middle of the month.

Grackles live wherever there is any civilization; in the wilderness they are rarely seen away from the shores of lakes and streams. They feed along beaches, scavenging carrion, eating insects. They also wade into the water to capture live crayfish and minnows. And they will fly down and touch the water to pick up floating food. There are some reports of them swimming. Grackles can be fierce predators on land, too. They eat eggs and nestlings of other birds and sometimes take adults as large as robins. They have been seen killing mice.

Grackles often nest in colonies. Their nests are always off the ground, sometimes 50 or 60 feet (15 to 18 meters) up. They sometimes nest over water where rising levels have killed trees and left the dead trunks standing.

APPENDIX A

A Guide to Public Lands

THE NORTH WOODS contains more than 12 million acres of public land—in national parks and forests, state forests, state parks, and county forest property. Most of it is accessible by road; more can be seen on trails or by canoe.

Michigan

Michigan contains 3 national parks, 3 national forests, 33 state forests, and 80 state parks and recreation areas. Together they make up more than 5.2 million acres. Places of special interest to naturalists include:

Isle Royale National Park. An island 45 miles (72 kilometers) long and 9 miles (14 kilometers) wide in Lake Superior, about 50 miles (80 kilometers) from Michigan's Upper Peninsula and 15 miles (24 kilometers) from the Minnesota shore. Accessible by ferry. Attractions include basaltic ridges of Middle Keweenawan age; sea caves, arches and beach ridges formed when lake levels were up to 200 feet (60 meters) higher than at present; boreal forest; moose and timber wolves. Write Isle Royale National Park, 87 N. Ripley St., Houghton, MI 49931.

Pictured Rocks National Lakeshore. On Lake Superior's south shore between Munising and Grand Marais. Wave-cut cliffs, arches, and caves cut in sandstone along the lakeshore date from Cambrian times. Two waterfalls, Munising Falls and Miner's Falls, also expose rock of Ordovician age. Spectacular dunes formed over glacial deposits at the park's eastern end rise 360 feet (110 meters) above the lake. Write Pictured Rocks National Lakeshore, P.O. Box 40, Munising, MI 49862.

Sleeping Bear Dunes National Lakeshore. On the Lake Michigan shore west of Traverse City. Includes two islands,

North Manitou and South Manitou. The dunes, perched on glacial moraine 450 feet (140 meters) above modern-day Lake Michigan, formed when glacial Lake Nipissing occupied the lake basin. Write Superintendent, Sleeping Bear Dunes National Lakeshore, 400½ Main St., Frankfort, MI 49635.

Ottawa National Forest. On Canadian Shield land in the western Upper Peninsula, this forest contains many Precambrian rock exposures, waterfalls. Especially notable is a virgin forest of hemlock, sugar maple, and yellow birch in the 21,000-acre Sylvania Tract on the Michigan–Wisconsin border near Watersmeet. The tract, maintained as a roadless recreation area, also contains 36 wilderness lakes. Write Forest Supervisor, Ottawa National Forest, Ironwood, MI 49938.

Hiawatha National Forest. Located in the eastern Upper Peninsula, this forest lies mostly on glacial terrain, includes numerous bogs. Paleozoic rock, part of the Niagara escarpment, is exposed at the southern tip of the forest on the peninsula which ends at the Straits of Mackinac. Write Forest Supervisor, Hiawatha National Forest, Post Office Building, Escanaba, MI 49829.

Huron–Manistee National Forest. The westernmost of this forest's two units lies in western Lower Michigan, between Cadillac and Manistee on the north and Muskegon on the south. It contains a mixture of pine forests and hardwood forests, numerous small streams. The eastern unit, which stretches east from Grayling to Lake Huron, contains numerous large pine stands on sandy glacial outwash plains. The endangered Kirtland's warbler breeds in an area of this forest near the town of Mio. Write Forest Supervisor, Huron–Manistee National Forest, 421 S. Mitchell St., Cadillac, MI 49601.

Michigan's 33 state forests occupy 3.8 million acres, mostly in the Upper Peninsula and northern Lower Michigan. Backcountry camping is allowed throughout the system; primitive camping in designated sites is available for a nominal fee.

Write Michigan Department of Natural Resources, Forest Management Division, Box 30028, Lansing, MI 48909.

The 80 state parks and recreation areas in Michigan occupy 207,000 acres. Three are of particular interest for naturalists.

Porcupine Mountains Wilderness State Park. This 50,000-acre park, much of it roadless, is in the western Upper Peninsula. It contains large tracts of virgin hemlock/yellow birch/sugar maple forest, and numerous rock outcrops of Keweenawan age. Write Park Supervisor, Porcupine Mountains Wilderness State Park, Star Route, Box 314, Ontonagon, MI 49953.

Hartwick Pines State Park. This park, near Grayling in Northern Lower Michigan contains a 49-acre forest which is the last virgin white pine stand in the Lower Peninsula. Write Hartwick Pines State Park, Grayling, MI 49738.

Tahquamenon Falls State Park. Located in the eastern Upper Peninsula near the towns of Paradise, Newberry, and Eckerman, this park contains virgin pine, hemlock, beech, sugar maple, and yellow birch forests. The twin falls for which the park is named are on the Tahquamenon River. The upper falls is the second largest east of the Mississippi. Both cut through Cambrian sandstone of the same Munising formation visible on lakeshore cliffs at Pictured Rocks National Lakeshore. Write Tahquamenon Falls State Park, Paradise, Mich. 49768.

For general information about public lands in Michigan, write Michigan Department of Natural Resources, Stevens T. Mason Building, Lansing, MI 48926.

Wisconsin

Wisconsin contains three national parks, two national forests, eight state forests, 50 state parks, and 2.3 million acres of county forest lands administered by the state in 28 northern counties. The state also manages its own wild rivers system. Together, the lands consist of about 3.3 million acres. Of special interest are:

Apostle Islands National Lakeshore. Twenty uninhabited islands off the south shore of Lake Superior and a narrow strip of mainland along the shore west of Bayfield make up this park. Some of the islands contain small stands of virgin forest; the wave-cut cliffs, caves, and arches are Cambrian sandstone. Write Superintendent, Apostle Islands National Lakeshore, P.O. Box 729, Old Courthouse Building, Bayfield, WI 54814.

St. Croix National Scenic Riverway. The deep gorge on the St. Croix River in this park was carved in Middle Keweenawan lavas by meltwater from the glacier that formed Lake Duluth in the Superior basin. Write St. Croix National Scenic Riverway, Grantsburg, WI 54840.

The Ice Age National Scientific Reserve. Strictly speaking, the nine separate units of this reserve are a national park; they are managed, however, by the Bureau of Parks, Wisconsin Department of Natural Resources. Each unit contains characteristic formations of the terminal moraine of the Woodfordian glacier. Write Wisconsin Bureau of Parks, 4610 University Ave., Box 450, Madison, WI 53701.

Chequamegon National Forest. The southern unit of this forest, near Medford, lies partly on the terminal moraine of the Woodfordian ice advance. The northern unit, near Iron River, contains traces of the Valders terminal moraine and remnants of the Penokee–Gogebic mountain range. The northern unit contains numerous kettle-hole lakes and is characterized for the most part by northern hardwood forest. An exception is the Moquah Pine Barrens, which is designated a state scientific area. Write Chequamegon National Forest, Park Falls, WI 54552.

Nicolet National Forest. This forest in north-central and northeastern Wisconsin is on the edge of the Canadian Shield and contains the headwaters of numerous rivers. Write Nicolet National Forest, Federal Building, Rhinelander, WI 54501.

Northern Highland State Forest. Also on the edge of the Canadian Shield, this forest contains numerous lakes, bogs, and swamp forests. Write Northern Highland State Forest, Trout Lake Forestry Headquarters, Rt. 1, Box 45, Boulder Junction, WI 54512.

Kettle Moraine State Forest. The two units of this southeastern Wisconsin forest, which are also part of the Ice Age National Scientific Reserve, contain numerous drumlins, eskers, kames, kettle-hole lakes, and other features of the Woodfordian glacier's terminal moraine. Write Kettle Moraine State Forest, Northern Unit, P.O. Box 426,

Campbellsport, WI 53010; or Kettle Moraine State Forest, Southern Unit, Box 87, Eagle, WI 53119.

Amnicon Falls State Park. This park, near Duluth–Superior, is notable for the boreal forest within its boundaries and for the falls, which is located on the Douglas fault.

Peninsula State Park. This park on the Door County Peninsula contains rock outcrops of the Niagara escarpment and a great variety of forest types.

For general information about public lands in Wisconsin, write Wisconsin Department of Natural Resources, P. O. Box 7921, Madison, WI 53707.

Minnesota

Minnesota public lands include two national parks. One of them, Grand Portage, is historical; the other, Voyageurs, is a wilderness park. The state also contains 2 national forests, 55 state forests, 66 state parks and recreation areas, and 812 wildlife management areas that total more than a million acres.

Voyageurs National Park along the Canadian border contains numerous Precambrian rock outcrops; its forest is boreal in character. Write Voyageurs National Park, International Falls, MN 56649.

Superior National Forest. Located in northeastern Minnesota, its million-acre Boundary Waters Canoe Area is the largest roadless area in the eastern United States. Includes numerous Precambrian rock outcrops, boreal forest. Wildlife includes moose and wolves. Write Superior National Forest, P.O. Box 338, Duluth, MN 55801.

Chippewa National Forest. This forest in north-central Minnesota contains numerous large shallow glacial lakes through which the Mississippi flows near its headwaters. Write Forest Supervisor, Chippewa National Forest, Cass Lake, MN 56633.

Duluth City Forest. A 10,000-acre forest within the city limits contains numerous fast-rushing streams which cut through Precambrian rock on their way to Lake Superior. Wildlife includes moose, bear, and wolves. Write Department of Forestry, City of Duluth, Duluth, MN 55801.

A series of state parks strung out along the north shore of Lake Superior also contain numerous Precambrian rock outcrops. Among these parks are Gooseberry Falls, Split Rock Lighthouse, Baptism River, Caribou Falls, Temperance River, Cascade River, and the Judge C. R. Magney State Park.

Itasca State Park, in the northwestern part of the state, contains the headwaters of the Mississippi. It is also located on an ecotone between boreal forest, northern hardwood forest, and prairie, so its vegetation contains unusual variety. Write Region 1, Minnesota State Parks, Rt. 5, Box 41A, Bemidji, MN 56601.

For general information about public lands in Minnesota, write Minnesota Department of Natural Resources, Centennial Office Building, St. Paul, MN 55155.

APPENDIX B

Further Reading

Part I

INTRODUCTORY GEOLOGY TEXTS

Flint, R. F., and Brian Skinner. *Physical Geology*, New York: Wiley and Sons, 2nd ed., 1977. Clearly written, lavishly illustrated. Incorporates latest information on plate tectonics and continental drift. Foster, Robert J. *Geology*, Columbus, Ohio: Charles E. Merrill, 3d ed., 1976. Brief introduction to basic concepts.

REGIONAL GEOLOGY TEXTS WRITTEN FOR LAYMEN

Dorr, John A., and Donald F. Eschmann. *Geology of Michigan*, Ann Arbor: University of Michigan Press, 1971. Contains chapters that detail geological history of the state, including places to see rocks and landforms dating from each period; has chapters that describe and locate good spots for finding typical rocks and minerals; has ample information on fossil hunting and fossil identification in Michigan.

Paull, Rachel Krebs and Richard A. *Geology of Wisconsin and Upper Michigan*. Dubuque, Iowa: Kendall/Hunt, 1977. Written in a style accessible to readers with no previous knowledge of geology or physical geography. Summarizes regional geological history and offers geological "tours" to different areas of the state.

Schwartz, George M., and George A. Thiel. *Minnesota's Rocks and Waters*, rev. ed., Minneapolis: University of Minnesota Press, 1978. This book has gone through numerous editions since it was first published in 1954, but recent editions do not seem to incorporate much new research. Has detailed directions to specific locations where various geological features can be seen.

MORE TECHNICAL GEOLOGY

Sims, P. K., and G. B. Morey, ed. *Geology of Minnesota*, St. Paul: Minnesota Geological Survey, 1970. A thorough and up-to-date treatment of the subject. Written for geologists, it uses many technical terms that may not be familiar to laymen.

SOILS

Hunt, Charles B. *Geology of Soils*, San Francisco: W. H. Freeman, 1972. Clearly written introduction to the subject.

FIELD GUIDES

Chesterman, Charles W. *The Audubon Society Field Guide to North American Rocks and Minerals*, New York: Alfred A. Knopf, 1978.

Pough, F. H. *A Field Guide to Rocks and Minerals*, Boston: Houghton-Mifflin, 1953.

Poindexter, O. Floyd. *Rocks and Minerals of Michigan*, 3rd ed., Lansing: Michigan Geological Survey, Pub. 42, 1951.

THE PLEISTOCENE AND POST-PLEISTOCENE

Wright, H. E., Jr., and David G. Frey, ed. *The Quaternary of the United States*, Princeton, N. J.: Princeton University Press, 1965.

GREAT LAKES FORMATION

The following provide differing theories on dates and causes of various stages:

Bretz, J. H. "Correlation of glacial lake stages in the Huron–Erie and Michigan Basins," Journal of Geology, 72 (1964): 618–27.

Hough, J. L. *Geology of the Great Lakes*, Urbana: University of Illinois Press, 1958.

Part II

FIELD GUIDES

Brockman, C. Frank. *Trees of North America*, New York: Golden Press, 1968. Excellent color illustrations. Follows the Golden Field Guide format, putting illustrations, printed information, and range maps on facing pages. Disadvantages are that it includes no shrubs and that it has no key to help narrow down the possibilities when you are trying to identify a strange specimen. Covers the whole United States, but includes only 594 of the 865 species that are known to grow here.

Petrides, George A. *A Field Guide to Trees and Shrubs*, New York: Houghton Mifflin Co., 2d ed., 1972. Includes every species of tree, shrub, and woody vine known to grow wild in the northeastern quarter of the United States and therefore thoroughly covers the North Woods. Has an elaborate key system which we have found difficult to use at times. Plant descriptions are excellent. but drawings are so simplified and diagrammatic that they are often difficult to apply to real plants, especially for beginners.

Preston, R. J., Jr. *North American Trees*, Cambridge: MIT Press, 3d ed., 1976. Includes all the trees growing in North America outside of Mexico and southern Florida. Has a key system. Puts black-and-white drawings, range maps, and descriptions on facing pages. Descriptions are very complete and include environmental information on where the tree grows and its common associates.

Little, Albert L., Jr. *The Audubon Society Field Guide to North American Trees* (Eastern Region), New York: Alfred A. Knopf, 1980. Features full color photographs.

Newcomb, L. *Newcomb's Wildflower Guide*, Boston: Little, Brown and Co., 1977. We have found this excellent. It is quite comprehensive, showing many flowering shrubs as well as herbs. The simple key is based on flower parts and the shape and arrangement of leaves. It can lead you astray on species whose flower parts vary in number, but it almost always takes you to the right place without requiring a lot of botanical knowledge along the way. The illustrations—line drawings—are good, but not up to the excellence of the rest of the book.

Peterson, Roger T., and Margaret McKenny. *A Field Guide to Wildflowers*, Boston: Houghton Mifflin Co., 1968. Another Peterson field guide, this one illustrated by the master himself. The pictures are excellent and the descriptions are just as good. The latter emphasize the diagnostic characters of each species. Ranges are written out. Flowers are organized by color, a system that is slow and, with the variations in color in some species, sometimes confusing.

Niering, William A., and Nancy C. Olmstead. *The Audubon Society Field Guide to North American Wildflowers*, (Eastern Region) New York: Alfred A. Knopf, 1979. This book uses color photographs, 658 of them, to illustrate most of the flowers and flowering shrubs that grow east of the Rockies. Descriptions are thorough and include information on habitat, associates, and human use of each species. Ranges described in text. Organization is by color with sub-categories like "simple shaped flowers" and "odd-shaped flowers," ill-defined groups whose borders are hard to draw. Inevitably, the quality of the photographs varies, and many show only the flowers and not the leaves. At the publication price of $9.95, it is a tremendous bargain, but probably more as a reference book than a field guide.

Cobb, Boughton. *A Field Guide to the Ferns*, Boston: Houghton Mifflin Co., 1963. Another in the Peterson series, this guide is well organized and well illustrated, with pictures and descriptions on facing pages. Ranges described in text. The area covered is south of 47° north latitude and east of 88° west longitude, so western Wisconsin, the Keweenaw Peninsula in Upper Michigan, Isle Royale, and northeastern Minnesota are officially outside the guide's area. However, the common species in these areas are all included in the guide.

MORE TECHNICAL REFERENCES

Beyond the field guides, there are two standard reference works for the plants of the northeastern United States and eastern Canada. They are: Fernald, M. L., *Gray's Manual of Botany*, 8th edition, New York: D. Van Nostrand Co., 1958, Corrected Printing, 1970; and Gleason, H. A., *The New Britton and Brown Illustrated Flora of the Northeastern States and Adjacent Canada*, New York: Hafner, 3rd printing, slightly revised, 1963. Both of these include all the plants known to grow in the region, and their decisions on classification and naming represent the current standard. Fernald's book is probably more widely used, although both works are highly respected.

The descriptions in these books are terse and highly

technical, employing a specialized descriptive terminology that takes some getting used to. Both have glossaries. and you can expect to consult them often until you learn the meanings of the more common terms. Gleason's descriptions are clearer and easier to follow. Fernald is published in one volume. The somewhat expensive three-volume Gleason set has the advantage of offering line drawings of every species described.

Gleason collaborated with Arthur Cronquist on a *Manual of the Vascular Plants of Northeastern United States and Adjacent Canada*, New York: Van Nostrand Reinhold Co., 1963. This one-volume work is very similar to the New Britton and Brown, minus the illustrations.

The old Britton and Brown, *An Illustrated Flora of the Northern United States and Canada*, by Nathaniel Lord Britton and Hon. Addison Brown, published in 1913, is available in a Dover paperback reprint in three volumes. The pictures are smaller than those in the new edition and many taxonomic groups have been changed in the nearly 70 years since this was published.

REGIONAL GUIDES

A number of good regional floras are available for the North Woods. All are confined to specific areas within the region, and some are further confined to specific groups of plants. Among the good works are:

Voss, E. G. *Michigan Flora*, Bloomfield Hills, Mich.: Cranbrook Inst. of Science, 1972. This is the first volume of a projected two-volume work. It covers the ferns and other spore producers, conifers, and the monocots among the flowering plants. Monocots include grasses, sedges, orchids, and lilies.

Billington, C. *Shrubs of Michigan*, Bloomfield Hills, Mich.: Cranbrook Inst. of Science, 1949.

Clements, F. E., C. Otto Rosendahl, and Frederic K. Butters. *Minnesota Trees and Shrubs*, Minneapolis: University of Minnesota Press, 1912.

Lakela, O. *A Flora of Northeastern Minnesota*, Minneapolis: University of Minnesota Press, 1965. This is a very helpful book, since its area of coverage is almost identical to the North Woods in Minnesota.

Morley, T. *Spring Flora of Minnesota*, Minneapolis: University of Minnesota Press, 1969. Covers plants that flower before the end of June.

Fassett, N. C. *Spring Flora of Wisconsin*, Madison: University of Wisconsin Press, 4th ed., 1976.

Seymour, F. C. *Flora of Lincoln County, Wisconsin*, Taunton, Mass.: P. F. Nolan, 1960. Interesting local flora from a county that lies just north of the tension zone.

SPECIAL REFERENCES

Curtis, John T. *Vegetation of Wisconsin*, Madison: University of Wisconsin Press, 1959, 3rd printing, 1974. A thorough description in easily readable English of vegetation types, with species listed, in the North Woods and that part of Wisconsin just south of our region.

Braun, E. Lucy. *Deciduous Forests of Eastern North America*, New York: Hafner Press, 1967. Reprint of the 1950 edition. A readable account that places the North Woods in a broader regional context. Generally follows the scheme of regional climax vegetation types developed by F. E. Clements.

Part III

MAMMAL FIELD GUIDES

Burt, William H. and Richard P. Grossenheider. *A Field Guide to the Mammals*, Boston: Houghton Mifflin Co., 2d ed., 1964. Spend a couple of evenings with this guide and you should be able to name all the larger mammals of the North Woods.

Murie, Olaus. *A Field Guide to Animal Tracks*, Boston: Houghton Mifflin Co., 2d ed., 1975. Could more accurately be titled animal signs, for in addition to drawings of typical mammal, bird, reptile, amphibian, and insect tracks, it also contains information on scat, roosts, dens, or burrows, habits and other evidences of animals' presence. Territory includes North America, Mexico, Central America.

Whitaker, John O. Jr. *The Audubon Society Field Guide to North American Mammals*, New York: Alfred A. Knopf, 1980. Probably the best of the new Audubon field guide series. Includes color photographs of 227 species, plus range maps, range charts, and detailed descriptions—including habitats and some tracks.

BIRD FIELD GUIDES

Peterson, Roger T. *A Field Guide to the Birds East of the Rockies*, Boston: Houghton Mifflin Co., 4th ed., 1980. Great new edition of a classic. Pictures larger, clearer than in old edition. Descriptions on facing pages. Range maps. Retains Peterson system for easy field identification.

Robbins, Chandler S., Bertel Bruun, and Herbert S. Zim. *Birds of North America*, New York: Golden Press, 1966. Covers all of North America. Descriptions, excellent paintings on facing pages along with range maps.

REPTILE AND AMPHIBIAN FIELD GUIDES

Conant, Roger. *A Field Guide to Reptiles and Amphibians of the United States and Canada East of the 100th Meridian*, Boston: Houghton Mifflin Co., 1958. The classic identification guide for these species. From the well-known Peterson Field Guide series.

Behler, John L. *The Audubon Society Field Guide to North American Reptiles and Amphibians*, New York: Alfred A. Knopf, 1979. Contains 657 color photographs; text includes range maps.

RECORDINGS

A Field Guide to Bird Songs of Eastern and Central North America, Boston: Houghton Mifflin Co., 1959, revised 1971. Recorded by the Cornell University Laboratory of Ornithology. Arranged to accompany Peterson's Field Guide.

Voices of the Night, Boston: Houghton Mifflin Co. Recordings of the calls of 34 species of frogs and toads of the U.S. and Canada.

INDEX

Numbers in boldface refer to pages on which plants and animals are described; numbers in italic refer to pages with illustrations, including maps.

334, 335, 351; sharp-shinned, 336; soaring, 334–35
Hazel, 177; American, 178–80; beaked, 178, 179
Heaths, 277
Heinselman, Myron, 302
Hemlock, 228, 294; eastern, 152, 159, 159, 160 (range map)
Herptiles, 332–33
Heron, great blue, 381, 381–82
Herring, lake, 364, 365, 366
Hesperiphona vespertina, 310
Heterodon platyrhinos, 332
Hewitt phase, 72
Hiawatha National Forest, 386
Highland moraine, 73
Hinckley sandstone, 45
Hinge lines, 96, 97
Hirondo rustica, 382
Hirundinidae, 382
Holly, northern, 290, 291, 295
Honeysuckle: American fly, 249, 251–52; bush, 210, 212–13, 212; swamp fly, 295, 297
Hornbeam, hop, 233, 234, 235
Horst, 42
Human history, 5–6, 364–65
Humus, 111; mor, 225, 348; mull, 225, 348
Hunting, 318
Huronian time, 26–28
Huron–Manistee National Forest, 386
Huro salmoides, 363
Hyla crucifer, 333
Hylochichla genus, 330–31; *mustelina*, 330
Hypolimnion, 357–58

Ice Age, 59–84
Ice Age National Scientific Reserve, 388
Icterus galbula, 327
Ilex verticillata, 291
Indicators, 129
Insect eaters, 322–32
Insects, 248, 349
Interstadials, 62
Intracratonic basins, 51
Iridoprocne bicolor, 382
Iris versicolor, 267, 268
Iron formations, 22–23; Huronian, 28–33
Ironwood, 211, 234, 235
Isle Royale, 48, 341, 343, 344
Isle Royale National Park, 385
Itasca moraine, 70, 71
Itasca State Park, 390

Jack pine forest, 194–97, 195; associates of, 196–97. *See also* Pine, jack
Jacobsville sandstone, 44–45, 48
Jays: blue, 345, 353; gray or Canada, 345, 355
Joe Pye weed, 271, 274–75
Joints in rock, defined, 73
Junco hyemalis, 312
Juneberry, 177, 180, 181
Jurassic period, 58

Kalmia polifolia, 282, 282
Kames, 76
Kankakee arch, 51
Keewatin time, 19, 21–23
Kestrel, 351
Kettle Moraine State Forest, 388–89
Kettle holes, 66, 67
Kettles, 66
Keweenawan copper, 38–40
Keweenawan diabase, 72–73
Keweenawan intrusive bodies, 40–42
Keweenawan period, 36–42
Keweenaw fault, 47
Keweenaw Peninsula, 36, 37, 39, 83
Kingbird, 329, 351
Kingfisher, 382
Kinglet: golden-crowned, 323, 355; ruby-crowned, 323, 355
Knife Lake period, 23–24

Labrador tea, 290, 291, 291, 301
Lady's slipper, 211, 219
Lake Agassiz, 94, 299–302
Lake Algonquin, 91, 92, 93, 94
Lake Chicago, 88, 89, 90
Lake Chippewa, 95, 96
Lake Duluth, 93–94, 93
Lake-effect snows, 104–105
Lake Erie, 88
Lake Houghton, 95, 96
Lake Huron, 85
Lake Maumee, 88, 90
Lake Michigan, 61, 85
Lake Minong, 95
Lake Nipissing, 96–98
Lake of the Clouds escarpment, 39
Lake Ontario, 88
Lake Owen fault, 48
Lake Stanley, 95, 96
Lake Superior, 37–38, 38, 42, 48, 85; ancestor of, 91
Lake Wadena, 71–72
Lake Wisconsin, 77–78, 78
Lakes, 4, 265–70, 356–84; acid rain and, 361–62; and birds, 370–74; changing

402

levels of, 89; dystrophic, 358; ecology of, 357–62; eutrophic, 358, 359; exotic species in, 367–68; habitats and food chains of, 359–61; in Huron and Erie basins, 90–91; intermediate zone of, 359; key to common plants of, 266–70; limnetic zone of, 359; littoral zone of, 359; and mammals, 370–71, 374–78; oligotrophic, 358–59; profundal zone of, 359–60; proglacial, 88–89, 92; seasonal cycles of, 357–58; southward drainage of, 98; and technology, 366–67; toxins in, 366, 369–70; types of, 358–59

Lamprey, sea, 366, 367–69
Larix laricina, 157–58, *158*
Laurel, pale, 281, **282**, *282*
Laurentian Orogeny, 20, 23
Lava, 16
Leatherleaf, 281, **282**, *282*
Leaves, 140–45, *140–44*
Ledum groenlandicum, 292, *292*
Lepomis macrochirus, **364**
Lepus americanus, 316–17, *316*
Leucichthys spp.: *artedi*, 364; *hoyin*, 368
Lichens, 245–46
Life forms, first records of, 48–50
Linnaea borealis, 183, *183*
Lithologic types, 45n
Lithosphere, 15
Littoral zone, 379–83
Livingston, Burton, 207
Loess, 60, 110
Logging, 5; and animal habitat, 317, 320, 339, 342; in boreal forest, 243; in mixed-hardwood forest, 222, 231–33; in pine forests, 192, 198, 204–10; in second-growth forest, 255, 260
Lonicera spp.: *canadensis*, 251–52; *oblongifolia*, **297**
Loons, 374; common, **371–72**
Lophodytes cucullatus, **373**
Lost Interval, the, 58
Lota lota, **364**
Loxia spp.: *curvirostra*, 311; *leucoptera*, 311
Lutra canadensis, **340**
Lycopodium spp.: *annotinum*, 238–39; *clavatum*, 254; *complanatum*, 221; *lucidulum*, 239–40; *obscurum*, 221, *221*
Lynx, 316, 317, **341**, 355
Lynx spp.: *canadensis*, **341**; *rufus*, **341**

Macroclimate, 107–108

Macroscopic fauna, 348–49
Magma, defined, 16
Maianthemum canadense, **185**, *186*
Mallards, **372–73**
Maples, 153, 163–66, 225; mountain, **166**; red, **164**, *164*, 294; sugar, **163–64**, *163*, 277; striped, **165**
Maquoketa shale, 55
Marigold, marsh, 296, **297–98**, *298*
Marquette Range, 28
Marshes, 264, 265–70
Marten, pine, **338–40**, 355
Martin, purple, **382**
Martes spp.: *americana*, **338–40**; *pennati*, **338–40**
Mayflower, Canada, 177, **185**, *186*
Meadowsweet, 271, *272*
Measurements used in this book, 11
Megaceryle alcyon, **382**
Melampyrum lineae, **216**, *216*
Melanerpes erythrocephalus, **328**
Melospiza spp.: *georgiana*, **312**; *lincolnii*, 312; *melodia*, 312
Menominee Range, 28
Mephitis mephitis, **340**
Mergansers, 372–74; American, **373–74**, *374*; hooded, **373–74**; red-breasted, **373–74**
Mergus spp.: *merganser*, 373, *374*; *serrator*, **374**
Merginae, 372
Mesabi Range, 28–29, 58
Mesic forest, characteristics of a, 223–36. *See also* Mixed-hardwood forest
Mesozoic era, 58
Metamorphism, 17, 26
Mice, 353
Michigan: basin, 51, *53* (map), *55*; bedrock of Upper, *34*; in Ice Age, 66, 79–82, *79*, 80 (table); public lands in, 385–87; Valders in, 83–84
Microclimate, 107–108
Micropterus dolomieu, **363**
Mid-Continent Gravity High, 36
Millipedes, 349
Miner's Castle, 46, *46*
Mining, 5, 28, 34–35, 38–40, 99
Minks, **340**
Minnesota: bedrock of, *30–31*, *32*; glaciation in, *74*; Hewitt phase in, 63–64, *64*; in Ice Age, 69–75, 70 (table), *71*, *74*; public lands in, 389–90; Valders in, 82–83, 83 (table)
Mitchella repens, **236**
Mitella nuda, **298**
Mites, 349

Phoebe, 329
Phosphorus, 370
Picea spp.: *glauca*, **160–61**, *160*; *mariana*, **160–61**, *161*
Picidae, 328–39
Pickerel weed, 267, **268**
Picoides spp.: *arcticus*, **329**; *pubescens*, **328–39**; *tridactylus*, **329**; *villosus*, **328–29**
Pictured Rocks National Lakeshore, 45–46, *46*, 385
Pike, northern, **363**
Pillow structures, 22
Pine, 192–210, 289; blister rust, 204, 209–10; Jack, 131–32, 152, **156–57**, *156*, 193–197; red, 152, **157**, *157*, 197; white, 152, **154–56**, *156*, 198
Pine barrens, 194–96
Pine forest, 192–221; communities, 193–98; future of, 208–209; human history of, 204–10; plants of, 199–200, 210; red, 197; succession in, 200–204; white, 198
Pinicola enucleator, **310**
Pinus spp.: *banksiana*, **156–57**, *156*; *resinosa*, **157**, *157*; *strobus*, **154–56**, *156*
Pipilo erythrophthalmus, **311**
Pipissewa, 211, **217–18**, *218*
Piranga olivacea, **327**
Pitcher plant, 281, **285**, *285*
Plant: communities, 125–35; identification, 136–50; life, 123–302
Plants: behavior of, 138; of boreal forest, 249–54; carnivorous, 278–79; characteristics of, 137–49; growth form of, 138–40; keys to, 177–78, 210–11, 233–34, 249, 266–67, 271, 280–81, 290–91, 295–96; of boreal forest, 249–54; of mixed-hardwood forest, 233–40; of pine forests, 199–200, 210–21; range limits of, *3*; ubiquitous, 176–91. *See also individual species*
Pleistocene epoch, 18, 59–84
Pneumostrongylus tenuis, **321**
Podilymbus podiceps, **380–31**
Podzol, 111, 112, 113–14
Poison ivy, 211, **213–14**
Poison sumac, 290, **291**
Pokegama Quartzite, 29
Polychlorinated biphenyls (PCBs), 369–70
Polygonatum pubescens, **238**
Polygonum sagittatum, **274**
Pondweed, 267, **269–70**
Pontederia cordata, **268**

Poplar, balsam, 153, **168–69**, *169*, 259
Popple, 255
Populus spp.: *balsamifera*, **168–69**, *169*; *grandidenta*, **169**, *170*; *tremuloides*, **171–72**, *172*
Porcupine Mountains Wilderness State Park, 387
Porcupine, 313, **321–22**, *321*, 329, 340, 352
Porphyritic rock, 41
Port Huron advance, 79–81
Potamogeton gramineus, **269–70**
Precambrian period, 14, 17, 21 (table); early, 19–26, *21*; late, 35–42, 36 (table); middle, 26–35, 27 (table)
Precipitation, 101
Producers, the, 8–9, 123–302
Proglacial lakes, 72, 88–98
Progne subis, **382**
Prunus spp.: *pensylvanica*, *174*, **175**; *serotina*, **175**
Pteridium aquilinum, **220**, *200*
Public lands, 385–90
Puma, **340–41**
Pussy willow, 271, **273**, *273*
Pyrola, one-sided, 249, **254**
Pyrola secunda, **254**
Pyrus americana, **251**

Quaking aspen, *see* Aspen, quaking
Quartzite, 27
Quercus spp.: *borealis* or *rubra*, **166**, *166*; *ellipsoidalis*, **167**
Quiscalus quiscula, **383**

Radioactivity, 370
Rain, acid, 361–62
Rainy lobe, 69, 71
Rana spp.: *catesbeiana*, **379**; *clamitans*, **379**, *379*; *pipiens*, **333**; *septetentrionalis*, **379**; *sylvatica*, **333**
Raspberry: dwarf, 295, **297**; red, 211, 213
Rattler, massasauga, **332–33**
Ravens, 346, 355
Red beds, 58
Red pine forest, 197–98. *See also* Pine, red
Red River, 62, 63–64, 69, 73–74
Redstart, 352, 354
Redwings, **383**
Ream, Robert R., 208
Reed, Bur, *see* Bur reed
Regolith, 110
Regulus spp.: *calendula*, **323**; *satrapa*, **323**
Reptiles, **332–33**